The Duchess of Dino

Addington

The Black Death

King William IV

Omdurman

Melbourne

Crown and People

Diana Cooper

Diana Cooper

A BIOGRAPHY BY

PHILIP ZIEGLER

ALFRED A. KNOPF

New York 1982

This Is a Borzoi Book
Published by Alfred A. Knopf, Inc.
First American Edition
Copyright © 1981 by Philip Ziegler
All rights reserved under International and
Pan-American Copyright Conventions. Published in the
United States by Alfred A. Knopf, Inc., New York.
Distributed by Random House, Inc., New York.
Originally published in Great Britain by Hamish
Hamilton Ltd., London.
Library of Congress Cataloging in Publication Data
Ziegler, Philip.   Diana Cooper.
Originally published: London: Hamish Hamilton, 1981.
Includes index.
1. Cooper, Diana, Lady, 1892-
2. Actors—Great Britain—Biography. I. Title.
PN2598.C783Z98 1982
791.43'028'0924 [B] 81-48129
ISBN 0-394-50026-1   AACR2

Manufactured in the United States of America

Contents

Illustrations

Foreword

This book is a labour of love, in the sense that I do not believe anybody could have got to know Diana Cooper as well as I have without feeling for her affection strong enough to deserve so extravagant a description. It is not hagiography. When I began work I warned Diana that the many generations of middle-class respectability which lay behind me would make me out of sympathy with her attitude towards, for instance, privilege and money. She was delighted, holding that only a touch of sharp criticism could redeem what she felt must otherwise prove a humdrum enterprise.

People have frequently asked whether it was difficult to write about somebody who was still alive. The only honest answer is – yes. I have sought to meet my problem by pretending that it did not exist. I have constantly appealed to Diana for help in working out who was so-and-so in 1911, why she did such-and-such in 1920. I have talked to her for many hours. When it came to writing, however, I have never asked myself what she would think when she eventually read my book. Except for two short passages at the end where she breaks triumphantly into the present, I have written of her entirely in the past. She for her part has been generous in the correction of errors of fact but has made no attempt to change what must sometimes have seemed to her my perverse interpretation of events and motives.

Whether the book should be published in her lifetime I left to her. She had no doubt that it must be; was indeed amazed that any other idea should have occurred to me. Whatever people might say of the book or her, the result was bound to be interesting and might well be amusing. To reject such a chance of fun would have been contrary to her every instinct and the pattern of her life.

Acknowledgments

First acknowledgment must obviously go to Lady Diana Cooper herself, without whom, for a variety of reasons, each more conclusive than the last, this book would never have been written.

Next to her son, John Julius Norwich, who with my publisher, Mr Hamish Hamilton, conceived the idea of this book and talked me into writing it. He and his wife, Anne, have been miraculously helpful and have made what could have been an embarrassing experience into an enormously enjoyable enterprise.

I must also make special mention of Sir Rupert and Lady Hart-Davis. As custodian of Duff Cooper's diary as well as an editor of incomparable skill, Sir Rupert has made an enormously important contribution to my work.

The list of those who have contributed in some way is alarmingly long and would be longer if a page of my notes had not mysteriously vanished. To any not mentioned for that reason I offer my apologies. All those mentioned below have helped in some way or another, and to all I am grateful. Of each one I can say that, but for their help, something in this book would be different.

Miss Barley Alison; Mr Joseph Alsop; Mrs Susan Mary Alsop; Mr Mark Amory; the Marquess and Marchioness of Anglesey; Lady Helen Asquith; the late Hon. Michael Astor. Sir John Balfour, Mr Nicolas Barker; the Marquess and Marchioness of Bath; the late Sir Cecil Beaton; Sir Isaiah Berlin; the Hon. Mrs Richard Benyon; Sir Lennox and Lady Berkeley; Mrs Deirdre Bland; the Hon. Mark Bonham-Carter; Dr Michael Brock; Mr Kevin Brownlow; Mrs David Bruce; Miss Felicity Bryan; Miss Elaine Burrows. Lord Caccia; Lord David Cecil; Lord and Lady Charteris; Mr Paul Chipchase; Sybil, Marchioness of Cholmondeley; the late Mrs June Churchill; the late H.S.H. Prince Clary und Aldringen; Mr Peter Coats; the Hon. Artemis Cooper; the Hon. Jason Cooper; Miss Virginia Cowles; Mr Aidan Crawley.

Helen, Lady Dashwood; The Earl of Drogheda. Pamela, Lady Egremont. The Hon. Mrs Daphne Fielding; the Hon. Mrs Ian Fleming; Mr Alastair Forbes; Mr Simon Fraser. Viscount and

Viscountess Gage; Miss Martha Gellhorn; Mr Milton Gendel; Mr Martin Gilbert; Mrs Barbara Ghika; Lord and Lady Gladwyn; Mr John Gore; Mr John Grigg; Mr John Gross; Mr Peter Grosvenor. The Dowager Lady Harlech; the Hon. Mrs Averell Harriman; Mr Walter D'Arcy Hart; Lady Hartwell; the Hon. John Harvey; Sir William Hayter; Mrs Edna Healey; Sir Nicholas Henderson; the late Hon. Mrs Antony Henley; Lady Hesketh; Mr Derek Hill; Miss Patricia Hodge; the late Lady Elizabeth von Hofmannsthal; Lady Home of the Hirsel; Lord and Lady Hutchinson.

Mrs Carol Brown Janeway; Sir Charles Johnston; the Hon. John Jolliffe. Miss Philippa Kay; Sir William and Lady Keswick. Sir Alan Lascelles; Mr Patrick Leigh Fermor; the Earl and Countess of Longford. Mr Robin McDouall; the late Sir Robin and Lady McEwen; Mr Gordon Mackenzie; Sir Fitzroy and Lady Maclean; Mr Michael McLuhan; Mr Harold Macmillan; Sir Lees Mayall; Mr Ivan Moffat; Mr Malcolm Muggeridge. The Earl of Oxford and Asquith. M. Gaston Palewski; Mr Philip Palmer; Mr Stanley Prior; Mr Alan Pryce-Jones. Mr Peter Quennell. Mr Charles Ritchie; Mr Kenneth Rose; Lord Rothschild; Sir Steven Runciman; Mrs Gilbert Russell; Mr Martin Russell; the Duke and Duchess of Rutland; the Dowager Duchess of Rutland; Mr Nigel Ryan. Mr Jeremy Smith; Mr Stephen Spender; Dame Freya Stark; Sir Michael Stewart; Mrs Virginia Surtees; the Countess of Sutherland; Mr Sweeny. Mrs Marietta Tree; Mr Michael Tree, Mr Hugo Vickers. Mrs Daphne Wakefield; Mr Moray Watson; Mr Auberon Waugh; Mr Sam White; the late Mrs Violet Wyndham.

Mrs Wilber devoted far more of her spare time than I like to think in typing and re-typing parts of my manuscript. Her help throughout has been invaluable.

Finally, my wife and family have endured four years' preoccupation with Diana Cooper and all her doings. It is a tribute to everyone concerned that they are still ready to take an interest in her today.

Diana Cooper

ONE

Childhood

In the eyes of its inhabitants at least, Great Britain in the last decade of the nineteenth century was unequivocally the leading country of the world. With the benefit of hindsight it is possible to see that already the economic base of Britain's prosperity was being eroded, the will to dominate was failing; yet no such doubts assailed the island people. Confident that their empire was of unparalleled extent, that their navy was the size of any two others put together, that a third of the world's trade travelled in British boats and was financed with British money, that Britons never would be slaves, they surveyed the future with the arrogant complacency of a master race. The world was their oyster and they would devour it as they chose.

For many Britons, it was a question not of oysters, but of bread and water. The country was edging towards democracy but all its wealth and almost all its political muscle were still the perquisite of the middle and upper classes – at a generous estimate the top quarter of the population. The time was not far distant when the working classes would learn how to use their power but to the late Victorian it seemed that the rich man would live permanently in his castle, the poor man at his gate.

The landed gentry and aristocracy had lost the exclusive power which once they had enjoyed but their share of the nation's resources was still extravagantly large. Ninety-nine percent of the land in private hands was held in substantial units, and of this a huge preponderance had been passed on within the same family for two or more generations. In the countryside the rule of the squire was still one of vast authority. The *nouveaux riches* flexed their muscles and increasingly asserted their grasp on the machinery of government but the traditional upper class remained blandly confident that it was the true, the destined ruling cadre.

Within this already exclusive group some fifty or sixty great families preserved a status glorious out of all comparison with lesser mortals. Russells and Cavendishes, Cecils and Howards, Pelhams and Bentincks, they had ruled the country for centuries and could not wholly disabuse themselves of the conviction that it was still their fief.

Their palaces, their possessions, their vast estates were the envy of the world. They were not parasites; many were conscientious landlords, if remote from the preoccupations of their tenants, and they made a substantial contribution to the running of the country. Nor were they wholly caste-ridden; even marriage out of their order was tolerated provided the financial incentive was sufficiently attractive. Some of them were cultivated; most of them were tolerably polite, even to members of the lower and middle classes. Their pride, however, was overweening; their self-confidence astonishing; their inbred sense of superiority daunting to all who did not share their advantages. The world, by and large, took them at their own valuation.

It was into the heart of this innermost elite – the cream of the cream of the cream – that Lady Diana Manners was born.

Her mother was a Lindsay, grand-daughter of the 24th Earl of Crawford. The Lindsays were a swashbuckling crew of considerable wealth and great antiquity. Diana's grandfather, Colonel Charles, swashbuckled as lustily as any of them. A 'fine, bearded, swarthy Crimean colonel', as Diana's sister Marjorie described him, he was a favourite with Queen Victoria; Master of Horse at the vice-regal court in Dublin and an intimate friend of Louis Napoleon. He married above his intellectual station Emilia Browne, daughter of the Dean of Lismore: a blue-stocking beauty with orange-tawny hair and 'a perfect oval face with cream and apricot colouring'. They were not rich by the standards of their friends but they lived in considerable style in a country house near Wantage, where Diana's mother, Violet, was born.

From her early childhood it became clear to everyone, including Violet, that the Lindsays had produced something of a prodigy. 'The most beautiful thing I ever saw,' Mrs Patrick Campbell described her; tall, slender and moving with a dreamy elegance that complemented her pre-Raphaelite features and ivory complexion. But her looks were not her only advantage. Encouraged by her mother, she developed considerable talents as a sculptress and draughtsman: Rodin was to compare her sculpture to that of Donatello; Watts her drawing to Holbein's. Neither authority could be called entirely objective, but she still deserved to be taken seriously as an artist. She played the piano competently and sang *Lieder* and romantic ballads with skill and feeling. Without being an intellectual herself, or even widely read, she commanded the respect of intellectuals and instilled a vague unease in the more philistine sections of the upper classes. She attended the original dinner party at which Lord Charles Beresford is supposed to have turned on Arthur Balfour and complained: 'You all sit talking about each other's souls. I shall call you "the Souls"'; and though the innermost membership of this amorphous body remained predominantly male, she was a camp-follower of the Souls so long as they existed.

An artistic temperament, pre-Raphaelite appearance and taste for high Bohemia did not preclude prudent pawkiness. She fought ferociously and without scruple for her own interests or the interests of those she loved, and never allowed her romantic urges to interfere with the serious business of life. As a girl she cherished an unrequited love for a neighbourhood hero forty years older than herself, Lord Wantage V.C. When Lord Wantage married an heiress she repined briefly, then addressed herself to the task of making the most suitable match in Britain. She found her mate in Henry Manners, great-nephew and heir-presumptive to the sixth Duke of Rutland.

Cecils might be more clever, Pagets might make more row, but there was something awe-inspiring about a Victorian duke. They enjoyed a status second only to that of royalty, superior in some ways in that royalty remained mysteriously remote while dukes were divinity incarnate. Their grandeur, though not dependent on, was invariably linked with great material possessions, and the Manners were among the wealthiest. They owned 30,000 acres of land in Leicestershire, 27,000 in Derbyshire, 6600 in Cambridgeshire, 1100 in Notts, 760 in Rutland. Their rent roll was £97,000 a year; their income from coal mines substantial and growing rapidly; their principal seat, Belvoir (pronounced Beaver) Castle, among the most massive, if not antique, of ducal palaces. Their achievements were less conspicuous. As a family the Manners had never done very much. The seventh Duke, Henry's father, had admittedly turned down the chance to be Viceroy of India and Governor General of Canada but this, though not unimpressive, may reasonably be felt negative as an exploit. He had, however, risen to be Minister of Works and a member of the Cabinet, a status never attained nor indeed aspired to by his son.

Henry Manners was better than a dull dumb duke, but only just. He had his qualities. He was an exceptionally handsome man with charm and graceful manners. Though subject to furious tantrums – he once dashed an entire breakfast service to the ground when told that Princess Beatrice of Battenberg was coming to lunch – he was generally kindly and tolerant. He was, however, almost entirely without ambition; when he married he was private secretary to Lord Salisbury and this was the zenith of his public life. His principal interests were dry-fly fishing and fornication; pursuits requiring much dexterity but not intellectually demanding. Beaverbrook spoke of him as 'a man of considerable stupidity' and most references to him by his contemporaries are couched in terms of more-or-less affectionate contempt. There is no reason to doubt that Violet Lindsay was in love when she married him, but it seems unlikely that her love would have been bestowed in this quarter if he had not been a future Duke of Rutland.

Marital fidelity was not a virtue highly esteemed among the British aristocracy. Many husbands kept women on the side; once the wife had produced an heir she often felt that her work was done and she could now relax. The only requirement was that one should not be caught out; in Mrs Patrick Campbell's no doubt apocryphal phrase, 'It doesn't matter what you do in the bedroom as long as you don't do it in the street and frighten the horses.'

Violet Manners dutifully settled down to bear her husband's children. A girl, Marjorie, came first; then followed a son and heir, Robert, in 1885; another boy, John, next year and Violet in 1888. By this time the marriage had seen its best days. Whatever sexual delights it had once offered had faded and no sense of companionship had replaced them. Instead they organised their lives in a pattern that made the marriage tolerable to both of them. Lord Granby, as Henry Manners became after the death of the 6th Duke in 1888, developed a keen interest in the stage, concentrating his attention on the most attractive actresses. At one point he was strongly drawn to Gladys Cooper, sending her flowers with affectionate notes: 'Dear and Beautiful One. I am venturing to send you some half-dozen "Daffys".' His most lasting liaison, however, was with Violet Vanbrugh, a performer whose acting skills were limited but whose physical charms were outstanding. He had a child by her, left her £200 in his will, and for several years devoted to her much of the affection that might more properly have been granted to his wife.

Lady Granby did not repine. After some tentative forays she took herself a lover, Montagu Corry, later Lord Rowton, a dashing young man-about-town who was alleged to have won his place as Disraeli's private secretary by his aptitude for singing comic songs while simultaneously performing a strenuous dance. More importantly, he was hard-working, tactful and devotedly loyal to his master. He was loyal to his mistress, too; long after their liaison was over his house provided an asylum to which surplus Manners children could be despatched when need arose.

Corry, however, was no more than a sighting shot for what was to be Violet Granby's most passionate and lasting love. Harry Cust was an altogether more striking object of her affection. He was a nephew of Lord Brownlow and a man of charm, intelligence and outstanding beauty. At Eton a master who taught all three reckoned that he was more likely to become prime minister than either Rosebery or Curzon. He entered parliament and shone there, but his performance was marred by its fatal facility. He found it all too easy, became easily bored and was distracted by the delights of that social life for which he was so admirably fitted. Literature, he decided, was more his forte than politics. He wrote minor verse and, in 1892, was offered the editorship of the *Pall Mall Gazette*. Here too he shone at first, gathering contributors such as Kipling, Balfour, Alice Meynell and H. G. Wells. Wells, in particular, admired him greatly, inscribing *The World Set Free* to 'Harry Cust: Noblest and best of Editors, Inventor of Authors, Friend of Letters'. Yet even Wells was disconcerted when he arrived at the editor's office to find it apparently empty. Then the sound of sobbing disclosed Cust 'prostrate on a sofa indulging in paroxysms of grief'.

For Cust was as self-indulgent in his emotions as he was over drink or women. The last, in particular, dissipated his energies and blighted his career with scandal. He could never resist trying to seduce them and they frequently succumbed. 'He was the Rupert Brooke of our day,' wrote Lady Horner. 'Gold-haired, well-born, a poet. Irresistible.' Unusually, for a professional womanizer, he was well liked by men; a member of the sternly masculine Crabbet Club and a participant in the celebrated nude tennis match in which he and Curzon beat George Wyndham and Scawen Blunt. His charm did not always work, however. Among his juniors in particular there was sometimes a feeling that he was a tiresome poseur; 'an old bore,' Julian Grenfell described him trenchantly, 'with vulgar hair and disgusting habits.'

When Violet Granby grew to know him well in the late 1880s, Cust was already the hero of a celebrated scandal involving Lady de Grey and Lady Londonderry and had had his name linked – fairly or unfairly – with a score of women in London society. Lord Granby can hardly have been pleased at his wife's liaison with this notorious philanderer, but he had his own fish to fry and at least must have felt confident that the couple would stick to the rules and avoid any show of flagrant passion. Lady Granby, indeed, handled the affair with immaculate discretion, concealing her private meetings with Harry Cust under a cloak of tea-parties with her great friend Lady Tree. The relationship throve for several years until Cust grew bored and began to look elsewhere. Nemesis struck in the guise of Miss Nina Welby-Gregory, pretty daughter of a Lincolnshire neighbour whom Cust seduced more or less from force of habit. Miss Welby-Gregory pretended, or possibly believed that she was to have a child by him; Cust married her under protest and at once abandoned her; no child came, and Nina was left adoring but disconsolate. For years she dressed and tried to behave like Violet Granby in the hope she would win back her errant husband. In old age and decrepitude Cust did indeed return to her and she looked after him devotedly till he died.

Diana Manners was born on August 29th, 1892, at the family's London house in Bruton Street. No one can prove that she was Harry Cust's daughter but her parents' contemporaries took it for granted that she was. It is dangerously easy to convince oneself that a likeness exists where one expects it to do so, but Diana does seem to have had the features, build and colouring of Cust far more than of the swart and stockier Manners. From the moment that the possibility was pointed out to her she herself never doubted that it was the truth, writing some time during the First World War: 'I am cheered very much by *Tom Jones* on bastards and like to see myself as a "Living Monument of Incontinence".'

Whatever his private feelings, Lord Granby accepted this new addition to his family with dignity. His youngest daughter was christened with due pomp: Diana after Meredith's *Diana of the Crossways*, Olivia, Winifred after her godmother the Duchess of Portland, Maud after her other godmother Lady Tree. Her godfather was Arthur Balfour, an unsatisfactory choice since he forgot his responsibilities until Diana reminded him of them when she was thirteen and he Prime Minister. 'Oh, fancy that,' said Balfour, and changed the subject. The only curious feature about her birth is that Lord Granby – who, to save endless reiteration, will in future be referred to without qualification as her father – failed to register it. When asked why, he is said to have replied that he didn't think girls counted, an explanation rendered less convincing by the fact that he had previously done all that was necessary in the cases of Diana's elder sisters.

Almost Diana's first memory was that of being held by her mother and looking down at the pale and wasted face of her elder brother. She was only just two when the nine-year-old Haddon died and the event meant little to her. John, the second son, a studious, good-natured, slightly colourless child a year younger than his brother, now took his place as eventual heir to the dukedom, but it was her sisters who meant most to her. Marjorie, the firstborn of the family, was almost eleven when Haddon died, a child of unusual talent who excelled at anything she touched – drawing, painting, singing, acting. She was restless and already unconventional, showing signs of a taste for the rackety and Bohemian. She craved love and admiration, yet resented it, at once tearing up the picture on which she was working if anybody presumed to praise it. Raymond Asquith, five years her senior, was intrigued by her: 'she is so puzzling, illusory, impalpable, whimsical and dissatisfied – a mixture between a monkey and a moonbeam. I doubt if anyone will ever be much in love with her, but she is a capital companion.'

The three elder children – or two after Haddon's death – were in the schoolroom during Diana's infancy; she and her sister Letty composed the nursery. Letty, four years Diana's senior, should in fact have been with the first wave of children, but she was held back to provide a companion for her little sister. Letty was 'a plain baby,' wrote Marjorie, 'who could not compare with us great-eyed, tangle-haired, almost eastern-hued babies, added to which she, so Mother was given to say, was disagreeable, unloving, a cry-baby and worse.' Whether for these reasons or because she was preoccupied with the other children, Violet Granby felt little for Letty and lavished her love on her youngest child. Letty cried so much that the German governess decided that the corners of her mouth were beginning to droop and tied her chin up with a ribbon. Yet underlying her childish misery was an obstinate determination to make the best of things. Loving and trustful by nature, all her geese were swans, all her reverses for the best. Cynthia Asquith noted her 'stern sense of duty about the maintenance of good spirits'; 'Are we down-hearted? No!' was her constant refrain.

For Diana, Letty's companionship was of inestimable importance. She 'was my be-all, my day spring, my accomplice,' Diana, wrote in her memoirs. An imaginative child, Letty was the narrator of endless sagas, pointless and protracted to those grown-ups who casually over-heard them, to Diana the most exquisite romances. She had a fine sense of the macabre. When Aunt Kitty drowned herself in the lake at Belvoir the children were told she had died of a chill but Letty fer-reted out the truth and gleefully passed it on to her sister. Diana was not discomfited; she had not much liked Aunt Kitty and her suicide was an event rather than a tragedy. Always Diana was ready to welcome anything that would stir things up and upset the even tenor of her ways; the drowning of an aunt was better than nothing.

Of the house in Bruton Street where she was born she had only the haziest recollection. A dapple-grey rocking horse in the nursery had a habit of bucking savagely and inflicted wounds on the elder children

but Diana was forced to content herself with watching wide-eyed
from a corner. A nanny with an anachronistic zeal for saving the
washing-up, mashed mutton, cabbage and potatoes into a thick paste
and poured lemonade on top of the resultant mess, but Diana was still
perched in a high chair sucking fingers of bread dipped in milk.

It was Cockayne Hatley that provided her first real home. A large
but unpretentious ivied house near Potton in Bedfordshire, it belonged to Lord Brownlow and had been Harry Cust's holiday home as
a child. Characteristically, neither Lord nor Lady Granby saw anything odd about Lady Granby's lover providing the family with a
roof. 'The celestial light shone most brightly at Cockayne Hatley,'
were the first words of Diana's memoirs, and for all the children this
ugly, friendly, rambling house, rubbing shoulders with its church in a
tiny village on the edge of nowhere, left a bright image of fun and
laughter and unclouded skies. Roaming the fields with a nursemaid
Diana encountered a notice reading: 'No Birds-Nesting'. 'Poor birds,'
she observed. 'What harm do their nests do?' – thus exhibiting for the
first time a lifelong tendency to assume that no sign prohibiting a
course of action could possibly be aimed at her.

By the time Diana was six Hatley was abandoned. Her father had
acquired a London house more than large enough for all the family.
No. 16 Arlington Street was substantial even for an heir to a
dukedom. It had splendid rooms by William Kent and one of the
largest ballrooms in London. It lay at the end of Arlington Street, far
from the hubbub of Piccadilly and sheltered even from the calm of its
cul-de-sac by the eighteenth-century cobbled courtyard and grand
wooden gate. Today it has been subsumed into the Overseas League
and sadly mangled in the process but in 1900, even though the
Granbys only had nine living-in servants and entertained with what
their neighbours felt to be striking informality, it was held to be one
of London's finest residences. The Duke of Portland, an ardent
admirer of Diana's mother, put up the £20,000 needed to buy the free-
hold and was repaid year by year.

In Arlington Street the nurseries were tucked discreetly away in
their own wing up a wooden staircase on the fourth floor. In The
Woodhouse, Rowsley – a name descriptive of surroundings rather
than building materials since the house was basically stone and Jaco-
bean – child and adult lived far more cheek by jowl. It was here that
the family spent every summer and it took over the arcadian role that
formerly had been filled by Hatley: 'We have had a swing put up in
the field, I love it, Letty loves it and Marjorie loves it but yells hard if
she goes high. You can't think how happy we all are.' Diana took over
a dark panelled room, filled it with 'curious bottles, coloured and

crusted with incandescent sediment from elixiral experiments, delicate gold scales, George Meredith's palsied head', and called it the
necromancer's room – a title it still bears today. It was here that she
first became aware of her disinclination for organised or, indeed, orthodox religion. Every Sunday, dressed in a fawn coat with highway-
man's cape and a wide-brimmed felt hat with silver galloon cockade,
she would parade with the rest of the family and bump in a wet and
smelly hired fly down the mile-long drive to Rowsley. There she
endured an hour or more of torment as the Reverend Mr Parmenter
droned through the service: 'I never remember applying myself to
prayer or to listening. I was only wondering, how much longer, O
Lord?'

The Woodhouse was an appendage of the Haddon estate, centred
on Haddon Hall, the immeasurably romantic second seat of the
Manners family. Haddon had long been deserted in favour of Belvoir
Castle some forty miles away. Though Diana only spent occasional
holidays at Belvoir until her father succeeded to the dukedom in 1906,
it always bulked large in her mind. She would have been a singularly
unimpressionable girl if it had not. Rearing grandly on its hill which
dominates the Vale of Belvoir, the castle is the paradigm of all those
stately homes erected to prove that the upper classes still had the
upper hand. It was built by James Wyatt in the early nineteenth
century, a sighting shot for his nephew's subsequent work at Windsor
and supporting the comparison extremely well. Augustus Hare visited
it a few months after Diana's birth:

> 'How I like all the medieval ways – the trumpeters who walk up
> and down the passages and sound the dressing time; the watchman
> who calls the hours through the night; the ballroom, always ready
> in the evening for those who want to dance; the band, in uniform,
> which plays soft music from an adjoining room during dinner.'

Diana described in her memoirs the castle which she remembered as a
child and showed that it had changed little during the intervening
years. The long corridors, so icy in winter that overcoats were worn to
go from one room to another; the Belvoir fire-brigade, under the
leadership of the domestic chaplain; the white-bearded gong-man
whose solitary function was to announce the time of meals; the lamp-
and-candle man; the water-men, 'the biggest people I had ever seen,
much bigger than any of the men of the family . . . they had stubbly
beards and a general Bill Sikes appearance'; the coal-man, Caliban to
the life; fifty indoor servants; sixty horses in the stables; vast Gothic
halls; a dining-room to seat eighty; a staircase up which eight men
could advance abreast: it was the quintessence of grandeur and yet

somehow a stage-set, the whim of an antiquarian aristocrat with limitless funds. The pomp was formal yet fantastic. Julian Grenfell visited the castle in 1914, after many anachronisms had been swept away, and commented: 'Isn't it an absurd thing, really, that there should still be places like Belvoir? It's just like a pantomime scene. And even the owners can't take it quite seriously.' Diana cherished it, yet she never took it quite seriously. All her life she was to love dressing up, surrounding herself by the extravagant, the exotic, the exaggerated. Never was she deterred by the fear that people might say she was going too far. Belvoir went too far. Whether it formed her inclinations or merely fed them, there could hardly have been a more splendid backcloth against which to enact her childish fantasies.

For most of Diana's childhood Belvoir was the home of her grandfather and his second wife. The duke was an exquisite old gentleman, model for Henry Sidney in Disraeli's *Coningsby*, always beautifully dressed, as Marjorie remembered, in 'corded riding breeches, pale-coloured riding gaiters and a lovely gold serpent chain threaded round his slim waist. He had soft, immaculate white collars and shirt-cuffs and impressive coral links and buttons, and his shock of shining white hair, sleekly parted on one side, swept back over his handsome clear-skinned forehead.' Belvoir was crowded with artistic treasures which the duke surveyed with mild curiosity, once producing from a bureau drawer two miniatures by Cosway and one by Hilliard and speculating whether they might have any value. His wife wrote books on temperance and pressed port and brandy on invalids or those in need of cheering up. On Sunday evenings grandchildren and servants were made to sing hymns to her accompaniment on the harmonium: 'It was bad, very; "Son of my Soul" drawled to agonizing pitch.'

For Diana her grandparents were lovable but remote, nor could a late Victorian father be expected to impinge forcibly upon his offspring. Because of his fierce temper the children always approached their father with some circumspection, asking the butler first whether it was a propitious moment to talk to His Lordship. Diana would address him with slightly glutinous sentimentality: 'My darling one ... When do I see you again, my sweet? Goodbye, my sweetheart. Lots and lots of love. Your ever-loving Diana snubnose.' Her father responded affably to such overtures but took little interest in her upbringing. The children were aware that their parents' marriage was not a particularly harmonious one and Diana attributed some part of the sense of insecurity that has always haunted her to her childhood fear that her mother and father were about to divorce and desert their family. She craved protection and the certainty that she would never have to cope for herself. At The Woodhouse she remembered sitting under the piano while her mother played, thinking: 'O, I'm glad I'm a girl. I'm glad I'm a girl. Somebody will always look after me.' Her most private prayer every night was: 'Let me live till eighty and don't let poppa or mother die before me.'

She was considered plain as a child, podgy with a bump on her nose and a bony protuberance in the middle of her forehead, known in the family as 'the unicorn's horn'. 'Diana will never make a beauty', Letty remembers an aunt pronouncing sadly as she surveyed the lumpish six-year-old. 'Plain but decorous,' was the verdict of a contemporary. The only crime she could remember committing as a child was stealing pennies from a pile in the hall intended for the crossing-sweeper. When she broke things she found it hard to own up or apologize but always did so in the end with a flood of no doubt therapeutic tears.

Her education was extensive but individual. She could read and write by the age of four but never learnt to spell – an accomplishment which she considered at the best otiose, at the worst slightly common. Twenty-five years after her husband was ennobled she was still capable of addressing her son as 'The Vicount Norrich'. She had a passable acquaintanceship with the multiplication tables but never grasped the principles of long, or even short division. Fractions, or still worse decimals, were far beyond her ken. Her reading was omnivorous and she was encouraged to learn much poetry by heart – bribed, indeed, since her pocket-money was often made conditional on her performance. Her mother's only criterion was that the poetry should be good. The first poem she prescribed was Marlowe's 'The Passionate Shepherd to his Love':

> 'Come live with me and be my love
> And we will all the pleasures prove.'

The tradition was carried on to the next generation; at the age of six her son was holding a dinner party enthralled with his rendering of 'How Horatius kept the Bridge'. History was a staple of life; the Gods of Greece and Rome as familiar as her own family; 'Latin, the use of the globes, the acquiring of algebra, ancient or modern philosophy – all such branches of learning were undreamed of in our curriculum; so were domestic science, cooking, preserving and the rest.'

Nursery and schoolroom were at first somewhat distant. 'The ladies Violet and Diana Manners,' read a note written shortly after their father became Duke, 'request the honour of the Marquis of Granby at their tea-party on Friday July 9 at 4 o'clock to meet the Hon Maynard Greville, Miss Lois Sturt and Miss Elizabeth Asquith.' An element of self-parody does not conceal what was by modern standards a curiously formal relationship. As John Granby grew older, went to Eton, became enmeshed in a masculine world of guns, rods and horses, he had still less time to spare for his sisters. Instead Marjorie grew closer. In spite of the difference in age the three girls were singularly united. Together they acquired all those accomplishments considered appropriate for daughters of the aristocracy; not 'cooking, preserving and the rest' but singing, drawing, painting, sewing and embroidery. The sewing, in particular, had its practical aspects; the girls were never encouraged to think of themselves as rich and did far more work on their own clothes than most contemporary teenagers would deem within their grasp.

They played together too, all those interminable after-dinner games that had been so beloved by their mother and her circle: literary consequences, clumps, charades, dumb crambo, qualities, analogies. Happy hours were devoted to considering what would have happened if Sir Roger de Coverley had met Madame Bovary in a conservatory, or to enacting in pantomime: 'It's an ill wind that blows nobody any good'. Diana was too young to compete full-bloodedly in these arcane pursuits, but she bobbed along contentedly behind her sisters, sharpened her wits and learned to make the best use of limited resources.

Anything involving dressing up and acting was especially popular. At Belvoir there was a huge chest crammed with good things; 'a cornucopia spilling out skirts and hats, a few yellow plaits for Wagner, helmets, swords, ballet-shoes, deer-stalkers, boas, Ophelia's straws and flowers, jackboots, wimples and wigs.' Diana's first theatrical experience was to be dressed up in a lacy costume and sing a song of the Netherlands Lass. Then she played Prince Arthur in *King John*, pleading vehemently to her sister Letty that she did not want her eyes to be put out.

She went to her first opera when about twelve – *La Bohème* at Covent Garden sung by Melba and Caruso. The two great singers were by now so podgy that they could scarcely kiss standing up, but Diana was overwhelmed. At her insistence Melba was invited to Arlington Street and soon became a close friend of the family. 'She would bring me smiles and trinkets from Australia and fondle me, and for a birthday O! wonder of wonders! from the great Melba came a huge horned gramophone simulating mahogany with all her records.' Both Lady Granby and Marjorie drew the prima donna: she preferred Marjorie's effort because 'it showed sadness', an attribute of which, in her cheerful way, she was inordinately proud.

Diana's mother was concerned in all things theatrical and was abetted in her interest by her closest friend, Lady Tree. The Trees played a great part in Diana's childhood, indeed in her life. Maud

Tree, an actress of minor ability but a formidable wit, was the wife of Herbert Beerbohm Tree, the actor-manager whose baroque productions and still more flamboyant style of acting filled His Majesty's Theatre in the early years of the twentieth century. The Trees were socially no match for the Manners but Violet Granby, though elitist to a fault, demanded talent or money rather than breeding in her friends. Noble blood was estimable, essential certainly when a match was being considered for a daughter, but if its possessor was dull or stupid then he would get short shrift in Arlington Street. The Trees were at the top of the theatrical pyramid and exceptionally good company – that was enough.

Every Christmas the Trees would come to stay at Belvoir. The ritual was unvarying. Sir Herbert, who hated the country and believed any rustic must be either criminal or idiot, would arrive with the family on Christmas Eve. That night a telegram would arrive: crisis at His Majesty's Theatre, he must return at once to London. Contentedly he would set off for his mistress's arms on Putney Hill. No one was deceived, least of all Lady Tree, but the proprieties were satisfied.

There were three Tree daughters, two of whom became so closely integrated with the Manners that they might have been sisters. Viola was almost the same age as Marjorie, but her easy-going nature and Diana's precocity ensured that she became as much a friend of the youngest daughter as of the eldest. 'Wonderfully large, loose, surprised and disordered,' Cynthia Asquith called her, and the vision of a high-spirited and coltishly graceful cart-horse emerges from the many descriptions of her. For Marjorie and Diana she was the ideal companion: adventurous, inventive, endlessly enthusiastic. At a party, or for a single performance on the stage, she could be magnificent but she lacked the discipline to make an actress of stature and her career was to fizzle out in mediocrity.

Iris, her sister, was almost as much Diana's junior as Viola was her senior, but age was never an important consideration for Diana in the selection of her friends. Blonde almost to the point of being albino, bulky and graceless in movement, Iris possessed – said Osbert Sitwell – 'a honey-coloured beauty of hair and skin that I have never observed in anyone else'. Diana Daly said that she could never decide whether Iris was 'wildly attractive or utterly repulsive' and her indecision was not unusual. The one reaction Iris never inspired was indifference: her hunger for new experience, contempt for comfort and convention, reckless questioning of traditional values, made her disapproved by many but loved by her friends. *'Quelle famille de serpents!'* remarked a French governess, as she shook the dust of the Trees' house from her feet. If the judgment be fair, Iris was the worst snake of them all.

The Manners rented a cottage at Aldwick, near Bognor and, from the time Diana was six, the Trees every spring and summer used to take rooms in a house nearby. Marjorie described what was, for the whole family, something close to Arcadia:

'Bathing by moonlight! Walking as far as one dared up the long, narrow path to the moon, the alfresco dinners with a lamp on the table and no moths or insects ever to trouble us. Herbert in grand form, Max [Beerbohm] in sweetpea-purple and mauve smoking-suit – the fun of it. Primroses like a carpet and tamarisk for a wall, and the beat and suck of the tide, and the rooks overhead fussing, and Maud reading aloud, and sometimes Harry Cust with his wit, out-vying Maud and hers, and laughter and youth – Oh God! – and then we sang and drifted to bed ... The first motor too – either Maud or Herbert brought it triumphantly down from London. A Panhard, one mouse-power. The door at the back like a pony cart. Excellent car on the straight, but stopped dead and ran back at the slightest incline.'

Bemused, entranced, half asleep, Diana would linger on the fringes of this enchanted circle, praying that nobody would notice her and send her off to bed. Here she first fell in love; with Claude Lowther, an exquisite dandy forty years her senior who found the Manners style of living so disturbingly homespun that he once sent ahead of him his bed and bedding, saying that it was 'hideous but comfortable and without fleas'. He wrote the eight-year-old Diana a love-letter on Bromo lavatory paper and she thought him the most beautiful and funniest man on earth. Sex was a fact of life for Diana, with no immediate application to her daily activities. Edwardian country-house parties were arranged according to the traditional precept: '*à chacun sa chacune*'. Diana remembered trailing behind her mother while the bedrooms were allotted for a grander-than-usual weekend. 'Lord Kitchener, must have this room and then, of course, Lady Salisbury must be here'; and then, later that evening: 'If you are frightened in the night, Lord Kitchener, dear Lady Salisbury is just next door.' The relationship between her calf-love for Claude Lowther and what dear Lady Salisbury presumably felt for Lord Kitchener seemed obscure to Diana, but the matter would no doubt become clear in time.

When she was ten Diana fell ill. Though diagnosis then was in its infancy, it seems that she suffered a bad attack of a form of paralysis, known as Urb's Disease. At one time her life was despaired of. Letty reported that she had just seen their mother weeping. Diana asked why. 'Because of you. You're going to die young!' For several years she led the life of an invalid; cosseted, carried from place to place, confined to darkened rooms, poked and peered at by a succession of specialists. She was treated to a course of galvanism, 'a big box of plugs and wires and Ons and Offs and wet pads clamped upon me that I might tingle and jerk'. Whether because of or in spite of this remedy, her wasted muscles gradually recovered their strength.

Though she was liberally indulged during her illness, she was never permitted the luxury of self-pity. With a doctor pain was a suitable matter for discussion since it might be an aid to diagnosis; to complain of it otherwise was common. Diana inherited the attitude from her mother and applied it ruthlessly throughout her life to herself and her friends. Ann Fleming, in agony, once tried to escape from a dinner-party at the last moment. Diana was outraged: 'Only housemaids have pains!' Obediently Mrs Fleming attended the dinner and was operated on next day for a dangerously twisted gut. Patrick Leigh Fermor suffered from a raging abcess in the ear. 'There's no such thing as a pain in the ear,' said Diana severely. 'Only a little ache.' At ten, she never lamented the fate that confined her miserably to bed while her friends and sisters were enjoying themselves; she took it for granted, and developed the tastes for reading, talking and brooding that were to mark her life.

Brooding was part of her nature. Diana had a singular propensity to expect the worst. 'When I was six,' she wrote to her mother, 'and you were late, I used to be sure of your murder and lie awake all night . . . Quite as young as that I can remember catching my breath often at the dread of family ruin or Father and you separating.' Her own health inspired equal pessimism. 'Pretty bad,' was her invariable reply when asked how she was, not piteously or even regretfully but with the calm resolve of one who faces facts. Every ache was cancerous, every cough tubercular. 'If I hadn't heard you were safely back at Chantilly, I would be frantic for fear you were dead as a smelt,' wrote Martha Gellhorn many years later. 'Have all the pains and anguishes gone? Was it anything like the year you decided your heart was weak or the year you had cancer? It's awful to enjoy your ailments as much as I do, but they've always been so wonderful, so fatal and so sad that I cannot help liking them.' At ten Diana was convinced she was going to die, accepted it stoically, and speculated only on the degree of pain that would be involved.

Suppressed emotions must some time emerge. It is tempting to find a link between the rigorous self-discipline which Diana learned as a child and the bouts of black melancholia to which she was prone throughout her life. Far too little is known, however, about the causes and nature of depression to allow any such thing to be more than speculation. Equally right might be the close relation who believed that she suffered from being too much the favourite child, weighed down by an impossible burden of loving expectation. Arnold Bennett told Lord Beaverbrook that her melancholy was that of any talented woman who feels herself under-employed. And who could contradict Duff Cooper when he wrote: 'If the osteopath says your melancholy is caused by a lack of blood in the brain, he doesn't seem to me to say anything unreasonable. I think your depression has a physical cause.'? All that is certain is that from the period of her childhood illness, she suffered from bouts of irrational misery, sometimes lasting a few days, sometimes several weeks, in which all was intolerably black, nothing seemed worth while, even to drag herself from bed to bathroom seemed an unbearable, a pointless effort.

Diana believed that she could pinpoint the moment at which the first fit of depression afflicted her. Aged ten or eleven she walked down the stairs at Arlington Street glowing with contentment, all right with the world. A few moments later she was going up again in darkest misery, asking herself, 'Why was I happy when I went down? Why am I so unhappy now?' She never found the answers. But though she feared and resented her disability, she took a modest pride in it, deeming it a distinction which she felt – probably wrongly – was shared by few of her friends. When somebody suggested that her sister Marjorie was also a victim she was indignant: 'Marjorie doesn't suffer from depression. She's just had an unhappy life!' Diana accepted depression as any other ailment, a subject for regret but not self-pity. She soon evolved a technique for preserving a facade of jollity while secretly in darkest gloom. Her mother, who would have claimed to know everything of importance about her, never suspected the truth. If she had, she would have been uncomprehending and unsympathetic. Only housemaids moped.

TWO

Birth of the Queen of Jericho

Though still vested with the reputation of a sickly child Diana was largely recovered from her long illness by the time her father succeeded as Duke of Rutland. Formal schooling would have been almost inconceivable for a ducal daughter but her parents viewed with some dismay the degree to which her education had been allowed to decline or flourish according to her own whim. What was described as 'the putting-back plan' was now set in action. It spelt the end, wrote Diana:

> 'of my happy-go-lucky useless life. The new régime is schoolroom tea, stiff music-lessons from snobbish masters, days at the Berlitz and perhaps even solitary confinement at Belvoir, the which *bijou maisonette* is in my mind the *ultima thule*.'

A few weeks later she reported that she was now '*une petite fille modèle,*' learning Italian and German at the Berlitz, Greek history and singing at Arlington Street.

The year was to widen her horizons in other ways. That summer she spent three weeks with the Trees at Brancaster in North Norfolk. In neighbouring houses a group of Oxford undergraduates were holding a reading party, eager for any diversion that would relieve them of the need to work. Among them were several who were to become Diana's closest friends. In her memoirs she called the chapter that described this period 'Brave New World', and her delighted wonder when confronted by this group of young men could not better be summed up than in Miranda's ecstatic cry: 'Oh brave new world, that has such people in it.'

The generation that perished in the First World War has earned by so doing a peculiar lustre. Whether in fact it contained more than the usual share of genius or even talent can never be proved, but the little group of Eton and Balliol men at Brancaster was certainly brilliant enough to dazzle a susceptible fourteen-year-old. Among them Patrick Shaw-Stewart seemed most certain to succeed, if only because he wanted to so desperately. He was pallid, freckled, red-haired, with a face so long that when Marjorie Manners sketched him her pencil slipped further and further down the page until she grew 'almost frightened'. His academic prowess was glittering – the Ireland, Craven and Hertford Scholarships followed by a First in Greats. This his contemporaries admired, but they were disquieted by his aggressive ambition. His brains and wit were irreproachable, his heart a less certain quantity. Though he had many loyal friends he also had enemies; Julian Grenfell wrote of him: 'Animals always edged away from him, and the more intelligent they were the further they edged. I think there is something rather obscene about him, like the electric eel at the zoo.' 'Not quite long enough in the bottle,' was Raymond Asquith's astringent verdict. In one of those truth games in which that generation so delighted, Diana awarded him ten out of ten for intellect, eloquence, sympathy and humour, nine for cleanliness, eight for loyalty and manners, five for looks and none for sincerity. Shaw-Stewart awarded her eight and a half, his maximum, for assurance about the universe.

No one would have given Edward Horner ten out of ten for intellect. He was six foot four inches tall with muscles and shoulders to match, strikingly handsome and with a good-nature and bonhomie that shone from his face. Though probably the most generally loved of the group he could hardly hold his own in wit or wisdom; when he got a poor result in his Oxford finals Raymond Asquith comforted his sister with the reflection: 'Of course it has been unfortunate for him that owing to his always living with these brilliant young men, and superficially resembling them in habits and catchwords and so forth, he has come to have an impossible standard applied to his own moderate and less disciplined wits.' Only son of Sir John Horner of Mells, he was the despair of his parents for his drunkenness, gambling and sexual escapades. He lured Lady Cunard's beautiful parlourmaid to an upstairs room and seduced her after a luncheon party; his elders felt this in poor taste, but the teenage Diana thought it 'eighteenth-century and *droit de seigneur* and rather nice'.

Charles Lister was altogether more serious, viewing his friends with mingled affection and disapproval. He was the son of that Edwardian magnifico Lord Ribblesdale and looked the part, 'his long white patrician face,' in Laurence Jones's words, 'crowned with a tight-curling lack-lustre mat that would not be smoothed or parted'. Unique among his friends he possessed, indeed flaunted, a social conscience; felt that the working classes were miserably misused and argued vigorously in their interest. His socialism, though genuine, was far from revolutionary. To Alan Lascelles he was shortly to protest that he felt the grievances of Labour as strongly as ever but had lost faith in their favoured remedies. 'If only they could get back to the old sober Trades Unionism and to collective bargaining. But a change of spirit in most of the Trades Unions is required before this is achieved. They are shockingly out of hand.' Even this modest radicalism he bore lightly, his laugh being daemonic and easily provoked.

Finally Alan Parsons, son of a country vicar but an Etonian like the others, added a touch of glamour with his sombre Renaissance good looks. He lacked the ebullience of Horner, the intellectual distinction of Shaw-Stewart, the idealism of Lister, but had a solidity and good sense not always found among the others. A classical scholar of some merit, he cared more about music, painting, the theatre than did his friends and was more sensitive than they were to the doubts and fears of a fourteen-year-old girl thrust into such company. It was to him that Diana wrote shortly after she left for home: 'Brancaster was heavenly, wasn't it? I nearly cried when I left. Do for pity's sake let's all meet again soon. I hate making friends and then passing on, don't you? When one makes friends, I think one ought to go on being friends *hard* and not let it drop.' It was a precept she was to follow all her life.

The young men, for their part, were delighted by this pretty, precocious and impertinent child. She distracted them agreeably from their studies and breached their bachelor solidarity without posing any serious threat. Several of them already knew her elder sisters, now they added Diana to their innermost circle. Within the next year or two, long before she officially came out, she had accumulated a rich haul of love-letters. 'You're more beautiful every time I see you, and more wonderful and more delicious,' wrote Patrick Shaw-Stewart. 'Do love me a little because I love you so much.' 'I am glad I told you I loved you as Tristan loved Isolde,' contributed Charles Lister. 'Thank you, dear, for saying I'm among your first four or so; one must be thankful for small mercies. I am so happy at finding I *can* love anybody and that I *do* love you.'

It would be absurd to attach great significance to such effusions. This was an age of extravagant expression, passion poured forth by men and women whose emotions were often as tepid as their words were ardent. Lister and Shaw-Stewart were probably writing to half a dozen other girls in similar terms. Nor did Diana regard the letters as much more than trophies to be gloated over. Certainly nobody was seriously in love with anyone else. It was, however, still an impressive tally for so young a girl. Diana longed to hasten her advance into the world of maturity. 'I wish I were there,' she wrote wistfully to Patrick Shaw-Stewart at a house-party at Gosford. 'I don't mean by this that I have any desire to be "out", but that if it *had* been within the range of possibilities that a dirty schoolroom lout might ever be invited anywhere, I should like to have been the one.'

In spite of her patent success she constantly questioned her ability to amuse or interest others, shunning tête-à-têtes in which her deficiencies would be uncovered. 'If we could only form a group,' she wrote in anguish, 'so that I need not have the sole responsibility and fear of being discovered to be stupid and dull.' After fifty years of intensive social life this uncertainty still ran rampant. 'I can live happily with you,' she once wrote to Lady Pamela Berry, 'but an isolated meal gives me fears. I've confidence in myself in adventures, active and illicit conditions, forest glades or dark Arab alleys, the darkened cinema, but I have very little in my conversational powers.' In part because of this lack of self-confidence she hungered for flattery, clamoured for compliments to be passed on by all who heard them. Edward Horner was congratulated on 'a really good letter teeming with dew-drops which mean to me what wine does to you, and there never was dry common earth more grateful for a touch of moisture or so good at lapping it up'.

Gradually during these years Diana was evolving her own style. The Manners daughters were known to some as 'The Hothouse'; an allusion to a greenhouse, explained Julian Grenfell, 'they being renowned for their exotic affectations'. Diana gloried in the appellation, fancied herself as being mysterious, volatile, above all different. 'Don't search among metal elements or men for a metaphor to illustrate me,' she advised Edward Horner; 'just see and describe me as Diana whose curse it is to be incomparable to either the great, the base or the commonplace.' She did not mean it as self-eulogy, she went on to assure him; but she did, of course. To be incomparable was her highest ambition. She sought it in her dress – Greek draperies and sandals, chiffon shirts cut like an Eastern djibbah, Rumanian peasant shirts. She sought it in her room at Belvoir, painted black with the bed upholstered in red damask and the walls hung with swags of everlasting flowers. The results veered between the arty-crafty and the exotic, striving for a sophistication she could not yet possess, but they showed imagination and a spirit of adventure, a genuine originality, which ensured that though she would make mistakes they would be her own and not in imitation of the current fashion. Her appearance gave her little satisfaction. 'Christ, I am so fat!' she complained. 'If only I could even feel like Artemis I should reach the zenith of all happiness. Julian [Grenfell] once inspired me with the spirit of her. For the moment I was slim and sure-footed as the chamois. Now, alas, I'm more like Diana of the moon; round, white, slow, lazy and generally like an unappetizing blancmange.'

Her new friends filled Diana with regrets for her inadequate education. Her youth was marked by sudden darts in search of self-improvement, often quickly checked but usually leaving some trace behind. Patrick Shaw-Stewart inspired her with enthusiasm for Homer, and Edward Marsh taught her the Greek alphabet. Next day she wrote him a letter in Greek characters – 'an incredibly apt pupil. A marvellous brain in a ravishing exterior.' For several weeks she persevered, amazed by her own industry: 'No summer moon has set that has not left me crescent shaped over vales as deep as sea-fishing. I swear to you by this time next year I shall be in the surge and thunder of the Odyssey.' But long before next year had come she had abandoned the hunt, convinced of her own inadequacy. Instead she continued to read and memorize great tracts of poetry, Shakespeare, Keats, Browning, Meredith. This last was a friend of the Duchess. Diana wrote to him and won his praise: 'To judge by her letter she can express herself in a way to give a picture as good as the photograph. This is not usual, and would be condemned as eccentric by every spectacled spinster in the Kingdom. The letter is pronouncedly spontaneous. It exhibits the heart in the head of the writer ... the young person should be encouraged to continue flouting the world.'

Little encouragement was needed. Though her unfailing capacity to find herself absurd saved her from any disastrous consequences, she was becoming decidedly swollen-headed. When playing some after-dinner game at Lord Curzon's house she turned on the Prime Minister and chided him smartly, 'Use your brain, Mr Balfour, use your *brain*!' She was more dismayed than anyone else at her impertinence, but the episode still showed a self-confidence, almost arrogance, disconcerting in one so young. George Meredith sent her a copy of his poems inscribed with the strikingly banal couplet:

> Lady Diana Manners: her book.
> *But if she my muse had been*
> *Better verse she would have seen.*

Proudly she passed on the compliment to Alan Parsons, 'So I'm coming on in literary circles.'

In 1910 Diana, aged seventeen and three quarters, formally came out. Soon she was presented at court and began to attend her first balls in the great houses of London. She had for years dressed and behaved as if she were into if not past the debutante stage, had won frequent mention in the social columns and even been awarded a

column to herself in the *New York American* on the eve of her presentation – 'she is admired more by artists than by ordinary young men'.
It was the extraordinary young men whom Diana was seeking and to
her delight she found that they were to be met even in the sedater
London houses. The first ball that she attended, in fact shortly before
she came out, was given by Lady Manners – a Hampshire family only
tenuously connected with the Rutland Manners. At supper she sat
next to Maurice Baring, who entertained her by throwing rolls in the
air and stabbing them with a sharp knife with his eyes shut. Then he
put matches to his scant hair and let it frizzle. Next day he bombarded
her with telegrams: 'I loved you long ago in Thessaly', *'O, toi, mon
clair soleil.'* Diana was enchanted, startled and a little alarmed. It was
not at all what she had expected.

> 'Society is now one polish'd horde
> Formed of two mighty tribes – the *Bores* and *Bored*'

Diana was determined she did not belong to the former tribe and
resolved to avoid the second if she could. She had some obstacles to
overcome. It was assumed that the unmarried girl was ignorant of the
facts of life and most other things as well. One need not believe in the
Edwardian hostess who, wanting to show a young girl the library,
threw open the door to discover a couple making love in front of the
fire and murmured warmly: 'Mending the carpet, *so* kind,' but most
debutantes of the period would have accepted the explanation without
demur. It was the preoccupation of the older woman to keep her
junior in this ignorance and to make sure that she was never exposed
to any situation which might compromise her virtue. Things had been
relaxed somewhat since before the Boer War, at which time no girl of
gentle birth could walk down St James's Street, even with an escort,
in case the clubmen leered offensively at her from the windows of
White's or Brooks's, but the rules of chaperonage were still strict.
Diana had always to be seen home from a party by a married woman,
could enter no hotel except the Ritz. Even in 1914 she was bemoaning
to Duff Cooper that 'it seems to be a brazen law that you and I may
never crack our eggs, masticate our marrows, coax down our caviare,
without the two-edged sword of a married couple between us. It
seems over-hard but insurmountable.'
Diana did not defy the system but she pushed against it to the limits
of discretion. Youth has always derided the shibboleths of society,
and Diana and her friends were no more rebellious than any other
generation. On all significant issues, indeed, they were anxious to
conform. Nevertheless they felt themselves delightfully wicked.

Diana strove to outdo them all. It was she who went to a grand reception at the Duke of Westminster's wearing her Coronation medal, an eighteenth-century silver St Esprit and two medals for swimming won at the Bath Club. The Crown Prince of Germany goggled at this apparition, accosted her and later sent her a postcard of himself with *Vergiss mich nicht* written across the corner.

Her most celebrated exploit came at a charity ball in the Albert Hall. Lady Sheffield was organizing a procession of 'dancing princesses', masquerading as swans and all dressed in virginal white; they were to be matched by a dozen 'dancing princes', one of them A.A. Milne, who wore silver smocks with very tight tights and a golden wig. At a party the previous night Milne heard Diana asking everyone; 'Have you heard the scandalous story that I'm going to the ball in black? Not a word of truth in it!' It came as no surprise to him, therefore, when a black swan arrived at the Hall, very late and only slightly abashed. Lady Sheffield surveyed her stonily: 'Well, you look very interesting, Diana, but you can't be in the procession.' Diana, who had looked forward to a sensational entry, was in the end allowed to remain with the others. It was felt on the whole that Lady Sheffield had behaved well and Diana gone too far. The Duchess told everyone that 'poor little Diana' had had to go in dull black so as not to outshine the others in the procession.

Such follies may seem innocent enough but Diana won a reputation among her generation for being daring to the point of outrage, exotic, almost corrupt. Raymond Asquith described her presence in a house-party at Lord Manners's home, Avon Tyrrell, as being like 'an orchid among cowslips, a black tulip in a garden of cucumbers, nightshade in the day nursery'. He was far too intelligent himself to believe such nonsense but she played up to her image whole-heartedly, rejoiced when it was accepted by others, almost at times concurred in it herself.

It was all part of the legend which was forming around her. It is always hard to define the quality which makes one person stand out among a multitude. Diana was recognised as a very considerable beauty. Winston Churchill and Eddie Marsh, standing together at London balls, played a game based on Marlowe's line: 'Was this the face that launched a thousand ships?' How many ships would Miss X have launched? Or Lady Y? Only two faces earned the full thousand – Diana Manners and Clementine Hozier, Churchill's future wife. Yet to have great beauty is one thing, to be acknowledged Queen of Beauty for a quarter of a century is something different. One could quote a hundred tributes to her 'love-in-the-mist eyes, samite-wonderful complexion', her 'hair, pale gold and with the delicate texture of ancient Chinese silk', without getting anywhere near the secret of her success. Perhaps nearest to it came Violet Trefusis with her account of Diana's lighting up the room with her 'flawless, awe-inspiring beauty. So must the angel have looked who turned Adam and Eve out of the Garden of Eden. With a face like that she should, I thought, carry a sword or trumpet.' And then there was Enid Bagnold who saw her for the first time at this period, coming down the stairs like a muslin swan. 'Her blind, blue stare swept over me. I was shocked – in the sense of electricity. Born to the city I wanted to storm, the Queen of Jericho swept past me.'

Awe-inspiring, shocking, like an avenging angel, there was nothing cosy or seductive about Diana's beauty. The 'blind, blue stare' owed more to bad eyesight than a challenging disposition, but it was intimidating to those who did not know her. Yet within the classical and chilly carapace there burnt a light that could transform a gathering by its brilliance. Even at the age of eighteen, she could not enter a room without being noticed or leave it without causing a sense of loss. Without this radiance her features would still have been remarkable but she could never have caused the impression that she did.

Not everyone conceded her beauty. Margot Asquith dismissed her brusquely as 'what I most dislike in appearance – German-Greek'. Veronica Maclean, told as a child that she was about to see the most beautiful woman in the world, complained, 'But mummy, she looks like a sheep!' The same was felt by Rachel Ferguson, who admired Diana's perfect heart-shaped face, 'but the whole effect struck me as static and sheeplike'. One of the more unusual things about Diana was that she would have agreed with her critics rather than her admirers. She loved to be told that she was beautiful but never really understood what all the fuss was about. She would peer myopically into the glass, hoping that the blurred outline in front of her was indeed of transcendent splendour but suspecting that it was still the 'unappetizing blancmange' she had found there years before. Constantly she took action to put the matter right. 'I'm preparing my seven bodily sins against your return –' she wrote to an absent friend, 'thinning by banting, oiling my hair, fading my skin. I hope it will all show.' Always she doubted whether it would, always she assumed herself to be in the worst of looks. She would have liked Cecil Beaton's reference to her 'glorious goatish profile' better than Lady Maclean's sheepish analogy, but that was merely because she preferred to identify herself with the restless, intransigent goat rather than the docile sheep. From the point of view of looks she would not have quarrelled with either description.

The public did not take her at her own valuation. The beautiful, daring, delightfully wicked Lady Diana Manners was the rôle in which they cast her, and all she did was news. She was natural fodder for those society magazines that catered for people who might actually meet her or liked to think they might, but she was also taken up by the new popular press, aimed at those millions who would not otherwise have known of her existence. Whether Lady Diana did or did not attend a party, the colour and material of her dress, her *bons mots* about the band, were believed to be just the sort of information for which the working classes were craving. She enjoyed the *réclame* which today would be reserved for the athlete or the pop-star. By contemporary standards the gossip purveyed was always most innocuous, innuendo was kept to a discreet minimum. Nevertheless to the straitlaced such publicity seemed deplorable; Lady Diana might be very pretty, clever too it was said, but she was not quite the thing.

For Diana, not to be the thing was all she hoped for. She delighted in her publicity and did nothing to discourage it. Whether she actually courted it is another matter. She herself always denied it. Certainly she would not have altered her behaviour a whit if there had not been a journalist to record it. No one, however, who contrived to be so consistently in the right place at the right time doing the right thing to ensure the maximum of attention can be acquitted of working to achieve that end. Diana would never have warned a journalist that some exploit was in the offing, but she could feel reasonably confident that somebody else would do so and would feel rather disappointed if in the end the event went unrecorded. Many of the best things that happened to her came because of the publicity that surrounded her, and she was never so hypocritical as to pretend that it displeased her.

A by-product of this publicity was that all her life she was the recipient of letters which were either anonymous or which came from people totally unknown to her. Many of these were touchingly ingenuous; the work of elderly pensioners or illiterate teenagers whose days had been brightened by Diana's doings. Others were from would-be lovers: some proposing marriage; others less honourable behaviour – one such from Jesus of Nazareth of Chorley Wood, Herts. A small but significant number were rich in malice, accusing her of unmentionable vices, which were then not merely mentioned but described in detail. Even seventy years later it is disturbing to read these products of envy and impotent hatred; Diana's *sang froid* was formidable but she can hardly have failed to feel some disquiet and to wonder from time to time whether dull obscurity might not be a happier lot.

In February, 1911, Diana's sister Letty married. She had never been happy at home and, though she was sad to leave Diana, it was in every other way a merciful escape. Her husband was Ego Charteris, son of the Earl of Wemyss. In her memoirs Diana wrote that 'of all men Ego was the nearest to a knight of chivalry,' but at the time she was apt to mock at his thoughtful diffidence – 'Gentle Ego, meek and mild,' she called him. She wanted something a lot more exciting for herself.

Until this moment Diana had shared Letty's bedroom; now she transferred to Marjorie and the two sisters grew still closer together. For some years Marjorie had been in love with Charlie Paget. Her mother disapproved – a 'penniless charity-boy' whom Marjorie cared for only because he was so patently unsuitable. Then Charlie Paget's thirty-year-old cousin died and he unexpectedly became the enormously rich Marquess of Anglesey. All obstacles vanished but the Marquess now grew hesitant and vanished on his yacht with a married woman. In revenge, Marjorie took up with the glamorous Prince Felix Youssupoff. Alarmed, Lord Anglesey hurried back and proposed, Marjorie despatched her Russian prince, and the couple were married in August, 1912. Prince Youssupoff returned home, where in due course he won fame as one of the assassins of Rasputin. 'So Felix is a murderer,' wrote Marjorie coolly. 'Well, well, there it is. I have a feeling for the criminal classes and there it is and is and is. Dirty work all round, it sounds. Does one write and congratulate or condole?'

Diana's family circle had disintegrated. About this time it was dealt another blow. At dinner one night Edward Horner remarked casually that he had seen her father earlier that day. Diana said that he couldn't have, the Duke was at Belvoir. 'Oh, no,' said Edward, 'I mean your real father, Harry Cust.' Then, seeing her expression, he added in consternation, 'Do you mean to say you didn't know?' Diana denied that this revelation disturbed her, she was interested rather than upset, did not even mention the matter to her mother and in no way changed her manner to Harry Cust. Although she was fond of the Duke she found her new father a far more romantic figure. Her standing as the daughter of a Duke – something of great importance to her – was in no way impaired by the fact that London society gossiped about her parentage. Yet her reaction can hardly have been as clear-cut as that. The life of a child is based upon a complex of cherished certainties, of which the solidity of the parents' union is one of the most important. Diana was no longer a child, but she still nurtured childish fears and doubts. However insouciant she may have seemed to others, however little concern she may in later years have convinced herself that she had experienced, it is hard to believe that at the time her confidence was not shaken, that she did not feel distressed and disconcerted. No one would have guessed it if she did, however. It is not possible to detect any change in her character or in her attitude towards her parents, and any psychiatrist seeking evidence of a traumatic wound would be hard put to find it.

By now Diana was gripped by an addiction to foreign travel which was to possess her all her life and provide some of her keenest pleasures. From the age of fifteen no peacetime year passed without her going abroad at least once, and usually several times. Her first expedition was with her mother and sisters to Florence. Whether, as Diana believes, because her father gave his wife only £100 to cover all expenses, or whether the Duchess's delight in parsimony got the better of her, the party seemed perpetually undernourished and lodged sometimes in the grubbiest hotels, sometimes in luxurious but borrowed villas. Diana was not in the least discomfited; new sensations were all-important, comfort insignificant; 'It's character we want, not revolving doors,' was her slogan through life. Anyway, though Belvoir might be grander, it was very little if at all more comfortable. The high spot of the trip was neither a church nor a gallery but:

> 'gala day when we left Milan for Certosa and had an audience of twenty or thirty undergraduates laughing, jeering, sympathizing at our outré lunch and ticket arguments. We were nothing if not prudish for a bit, but melted when eight of them sprang out at Certosa and followed us round the monastery, pressing lilies and wild flowers on us. Calamity at last knit us together, we missed a train back to Milan, so we all took a bank-holiday wagonette to Pavia, singing glees and Neapolitan songs all the way. They were too charming and we finally exchanged cards and sighed to think that we would never see them again.'

Italy was followed next year by The Hague and Paris, then Italy again. In 1911 it was Normandy, an expedition for some reason 'hidden by a web of lies from Father'. Diana enjoyed everything but begrudged the time she was separated from her swelling horde of admirers: 'I shall love stone cathedrals with their hundred straight pillars – man's excellent improvement on tree-trunks – but how much more would I appreciate it if Edward was there to understand, unexplained, the humours and beauty of things.' Then in October 1912

came the first intoxicating visit to Venice, the foreign city that over
the years was to mean more to her even than Paris. The Marchesa
Casati dominated the scene. Diana first saw her 'drifting down the
Grand Canal under a parasol of peacock's feathers' and soon became a
regular attender at Casati's parties, which were exotic, extravagant,
vulgar perhaps but never dull. Once the Piazza San Marco was taken
over as the Casati's ball-room, filled with guests dressed as characters
from pictures by Longhi and Guardi. The hostess herself wore 'the
trousered Bakst-designed dress of an animal-tamer. On her shoulder
was a macaw, on her arm an ape. She was followed closely by an atten-
dant keeper leading a restive leopard, or puma it may have been.' Unfortunately the public were also there in force and greeted the Casati's
party with jeers and abuse. A near-riot followed. Diana revelled in the
scandal, and still more in the fact that, though she could hardly match
the *bizarre* splendour of the Casati, her golden-haired, blue-eyed
beauty won her an army of admirers among the Venetians. 'Every
night a three-hundred-man crowd followed us on the Piazza till finally
I had a duel fought over me by two unknown swashbucklers,' she
proudly told Edward Horner. 'But an Italian success for a fair-hair is a
bloody poor one – though very intoxicating.'

Though she loved to be abroad she had her reservations about the
natives. After a rapturous few days in Rome she wrote fiercely:
'There's nothing like Italy, but gosh, the people! They do run away
with the macaroon. There's not one passable one. All the men should
be crushed beneath the heel.' Next year it was Paris: 'A thought from
an Englishman is worth ten years' devotion from these squalid, mis-
shapen, Jewish, vulgar, loud-tongued, insult-asking Frenchmen'.
Never did she wholly escape from a generalized distrust of foreigners;
before 1914, when her feelings were fortified by the arrogance of the
master-race, they ran rampant. Her prejudices rarely survived long
once she got to know strangers as individuals, but collectively she
viewed them with distaste.

'Jewish' was one of the epithets she flung at the French. It is hard to
know how seriously to take the anti-semitism of the English upper
classes. Rothschilds, Cassels, Sassoons were fêted and flattered,
honoured at court and accepted in the houses of the aristocracy, yet
those same aristocrats abused them freely behind their backs and
sometimes to their faces. 'Filthy Jew' was part of the common cur-
rency of schoolboy invective and the propensity of the English upper
classes to behave like schoolboys has always been remarkable. Billy
and Julian Grenfell, two of Diana's closest friends, were particularly
virulent. At Balliol Julian would watch for Philip Sassoon to come
into the college and then, with a cry of 'Pheeleep, Pheeleep, I see

you!' chase him from the quadrangle with an Australian stock-whip cracking within inches of his head. Even Duff Cooper, ardent champion of Zionism and enemy of every kind of persecution, a man who was in time to dedicate his book *David* to 'The Jewish People', snarled 'These bloody Jews are all the same' when not allowed to borrow Philip Sassoon's Rolls-Royce one rainy night.

Many of the greatest pleasures in Diana's life came to her through Jews whose affection she cherished and to whom she was utterly loyal. Many years later, when her son was describing the virtues of his latest friend, he was rash enough to qualify the catalogue with '. . . though he's a Jew'. He can still remember the stinging box on the ears which his mother administered: 'And what, pray, is there wrong with that?' Yet she grew up with the instinctive anti-semitism of her class and race. When George V acceded she wrote to Patrick Shaw-Stewart that 'he represents to me all that I most heartily dislike . . . except that I thank God that he hates the Jews'. Philip Sassoon was notorious for snapping up secretaryships to important people. One Easter Day Diana sent him a telegram – 'Christ has risen and will shortly be needing a secretary.' Such jibes never meant much to her and she would live to be heartily ashamed of them. In youth, however, she was as intolerant as the majority of her friends. Acquaintances were condemned for their accents, their clothes, their stupidity, their hairstyle. Jewishness was just another to be added to the catalogue of vices; venial, certainly, but a blemish all the same.

Violet, Duchess of Rutland, had less truck than most with such follies. She was as unconventional in her choice of friends as in everything else. Edward VII was so put out by her goings-on that he took the trouble to call at Arlington Street to remonstrate; a woman in her positon 'ought to drop cards and drive in a barouche round and round Hyde Park, and not go to supper-parties and draw and do amusing things'. He was settled in an imposing arm-chair which turned out to be worm-eaten, and collapsed halfway through his harangue, pitching the monarch to the floor. A few years later Queen Alexandra similarly ended up on the floor at Arlington Street when the leg of a sofa snapped beneath her.

In one thing, however, the Duchess was wholly conventional: the selection of husbands for her daughters. Here the most rigid tests of wealth and breeding were applied. Letty had married the heir to a rich earl; Marjorie a very rich marquess; Diana, the favourite, must do at least as well as either. The Duchess was said to keep a list of eli-

gible suitors, putting a skull and crossbones against any that were
inconsiderate enough to marry elsewhere. Foreigners had to be very
grand to be included. The Crown Prince of Germany figured fleet-
ingly. Prince Paul of Yugoslavia was one of Diana's first suitors.
'I despised him as a shiny little black thing.' Diana sat next to the
widower ex-King Manuel at dinner. 'I like kings or commoners,' she
told her sister, 'far better than those chronic eligibles with coronets on
their fingers and coronets on their toes.'

It was enough for a young man to be deemed eligible for Diana to
distrust if not dislike him. Lord Rocksavage, rich and beautiful, was
'an eligible eldest son after Mother's own heart'. Most women considered him attractive but Diana found his conversation 'unluckily
reduced to three words, adaptable to any remark: "Oh", "Really?"
"Right-ho!". Monotonous but a simplification of life.' Some of the
eligibles were later to be among her dearest friends, but at that time
her mother's approval was proof that they were undesirable: Lord
Dudley was slothful and somnolent, 'that bugger Bobbety Cranborne'
wholly unacceptable with his 'loose gaping mouth and lean, mean
shanks' ('bugger', it should be stressed, being an epithet to which
Diana was attached at the time and used with cavalier indifference to
its usual meaning).

Most eligible of eligibles was the Prince of Wales. The future
Edward VIII was three years younger than Diana, which meant that
the war had started before his name began seriously to be linked with
those of women, but it was still permissible to dream. The Duchess
had no doubt that her daughter was eminently well qualified to be
Queen and that this should be her ambition. For Diana the dream was
nightmare; she thought the Prince a snivelling cub and viewed with
horror the prospect of internment in the court. She was far from
being republican, but in her set it was unfashionable to admit to any
enthusiasm for the royal family. When Edward VII died, the bell at
Belvoir tolled all day and the flag was at half-mast. Nixon, the butler,
'gave his views eloquently the whole damned day, always the same: "I
tell you what *I* think, Milady. *I* think it's very serious, not so much for
the royal circle, but for the country!" I longed to say it was a hundred
times worse for Mrs Keppel than all put together.' Her main concern
was clothes: 'Every soul in the nation has a trim black outfit with the
exception of us three, who look the fulfilment of makeshift in black
chiffon wound round in every direction to conceal parrot-colours.' As
it turned out, the Prince of Wales was equally unenthusiastic about
the prospect of an alliance with the Manners family. Whether, if he
had liked the idea, Diana would have been able to resist the pressure
from society and the glamour of the throne, must be doubtful. When

the Duke of Connaught said that she was the only woman who would keep the Prince on the throne she professed dismay, but the flattery was intoxicating.

Her first proposal came from smaller fry. Claud Russell was a grandson of the Duke of Bedford and adequately rich, but he did not rank high on the Duchess's list. He had been in love with Diana since he first saw her at the age of fifteen, tobogganing in the snow with folded arms and eyes shut, 'like a heroine of fairy tale going on a last enchanted voyage'. He waited till she was eighteen, then presented her with a diamond-and-ruby pendant and proposed. Diana accepted the pendant and refused the marriage; 'He seemed a frightfully old man, almost like a cripple.' She continued to keep him as a suitor, though. She always hated to let any man pass out of her life. When Edward Horner threatened desertion she wrote in dismay: 'Do you imagine that I don't want you, someone who will talk and listen to me and perhaps love me? Let me know, and I'll settle whether to console myself with winter sports, or let green, slimy river-bubbles burst above me.' And yet, though she wanted Edward Horner to love her, she was by no means sure that she wanted to love him in return. Love, she told Patrick Shaw-Stewart, 'brings pain and sighs in its train and endless rue, whereas I would bring nothing but fun, gladness'. Flattery, courtship, flirtation, a mutual pursuit of pleasure, this was all very well, but anything more serious was a threat to be countered by hostility or indifference. 'I love you desperately,' wrote Shaw-Stewart, 'but it's no use saying so, as the statement is always a signal for an outburst of brutality.' 'Your *remote* look in that taxi,' complained Edward Horner, 'seemed like an instrument of torture.'

Diana knew that in some way she was failing to give them what they wanted; not physically, which the social climate of the age would anyhow have precluded, but in any kind of whole-hearted commitment. She regretted it, was even slightly alarmed by it, but did not feel it within her to offer more. Patrick Shaw-Stewart wrote reproachfully after a weekend at The Woodhouse in which he felt she had neglected him. Diana replied in terms that showed contrition yet little hope of amendment:

'What can I say, except that I was fairly unconscious of being anything different from my heartless 'umble self and that I've got one of those new marble hearts, and that I like you as well as (not an atom more than) anybody – and surely now you must realize that I'm not so good a woman, and please you mustn't love me, because I'm only one of those Children of Illusion. It's damned nice and unselfish of me to ask you this, so realize it.'

It is to be doubted whether the recipient took much pleasure from this muted apology.

By 1912 or 1913 Diana's circle had widened far beyond the original Brancaster group. Its inner nucleus, however, remained tight-knit and exclusive. 'The Corrupt Coterie,' as it was called affectionately by its members and disparagingly by those not admitted to membership, consisted largely of the children of members of the Souls – Asquiths, Listers, Horners, Trees, Grenfells. But where the Souls prided themselves on their spirituality, the Coterie flattered itself that it was 'unafraid of words, unshocked by drink, and unashamed of "decadence" and gambling – Unlike Other People, I'm afraid'. Its debaucheries were innocuous – at least until the war liberated London society to sin more spiritedly – but its pretensions to wickedness were many and vociferous.

The Asquiths were at the heart of the Coterie and immeasurably important to Diana. Katharine Asquith was Edward Horner's sister – 'a lovely, tall creature,' Laurence Jones described her, 'large-eyed, long-lashed, with a magnolia complexion.' She was far more intelligent than her brother, a perturbed spirit endlessly questing perfection and causing herself much tribulation in the search, capable when young of a reckless gaiety which at times seemed to border on hysteria. Her friends loved her but found her withdrawn, even mysterious. 'All girls – like all men – long to know you well because you are so beautiful,' said Blanche Stanley, 'but are puzzled how to do it because you are so uncommon and remote.'

In 1907 Katharine Horner married Raymond Asquith, eldest son of the Chancellor of the Exchequer who the following year was to become Prime Minister. Raymond was a scholar of Winchester and Balliol, winner of the Ireland, Craven and Derby Scholarships, a First in Greats and a Fellowship at All Souls. With these towering academic achievements went indifference to worldly success; he had chosen the Bar as a career and would undoubtedly have excelled at it, perhaps too done well in politics, but he could not be bothered to fight hard, preferring to cultivate his friendships and his intellectual pleasures. John Buchan described him as a demi-god: 'a scholar of the ripe Elizabethan type, a brilliant wit, an accomplished poet, a sound lawyer – these things were borne lightly, for his greatness was not in his attainments but in himself ... Most noble in presence and with

every grace of voice and manner, he moved among men like a being
from another world, scornfully detached from the common struggle.'
Demi-gods are by definition inhuman; Raymond Asquith could
appear so to his acquaintances but to his friends he was warm, sympathetic, an exhilaratingly good companion. Posterity may fairly doubt
the qualities of many members of the lost generation but about him
there can be little dispute.

He was fourteen years older than Diana, ten years older than
Horner, Shaw-Stewart, Lister, the Grenfells, or others of the group.
One cannot be sure why he chose to make so many of his closest
friends in a younger generation; perhaps in part because he loved to
lead, probably still more because he found this particular group more
amusing. Certainly he achieved leadership. 'He was the king,' said
Diana. 'He was the one we liked best and he liked us better than his
own people. He was wonderful.' His influence on her was far greater
than that of any other of her friends; she read books to please him,
echoed his opinions, feared his criticism. She loved him with a
fervour that only first love can inspire.

It is more difficult to be unequivocally enthusiastic about the Grenfells. Julian and Billy Grenfell were the two elder sons of Lady Desborough, a fashionable hostess whose wealth, ambition, toughness and
hunger for applause ensured her pre-eminence in a crowded field.
'Ettie is an ox, she will be made into Bovril when she dies,' said
Margot Asquith, Raymond's step-mother. Lady Desborough craved
the exclusive love of her sons and resented the affection they felt for
Diana. Billy, the second son, was undeterred. 'You get 100 out of 100
for companionship, beauty, wit, intelligence *and* intellect, 77 for ath-
leticism and 7½ for lawn tennis,' he wrote to Diana, and then again a
few months later, 'You have given me wonderful and amazing love; I
dare not think how much.' In fact, though Diana was fond of both the
brothers, she felt no love for either. There was a brutal heartiness, an
insensitivity about them which accorded ill with the decadence that
was her favoured affectation; she did not actively disapprove of their
anti-semitism, their crude consciousness of caste, their worship of the
traditional manly qualities, but there was a stridency, a vulgarity
about them that she deplored. Few of the people she loved were conspicuously full-blooded and she found a little of the Grenfell boys
went a long way.

Denis Anson had some of the same attributes, though he did not
elevate them to the level of a philosophy. A rich, sporting baronet, he
could never resist a challenge and passed from one wild excess to
another. Billy Grenfell recalled 'a glorious dinner' in his rooms, after
which 'fifty rabbits were lowered out of Trinity in wicker baskets –

whereupon one hundred excited humans and one mangy bull-dog ran after them, and the Dons ran after us, and afterwards collected the defunct rabbits into large piles and buried them.' An unattractive scene; but Denny Anson was as likely to risk his own life as that of a rabbit, and his charm and genuine kindness redeemed what otherwise might have seemed boorish or even brutal.

Lord Vernon was another who was more loving than loved. George Vernon was short, stout, spoiled and very rich; endearingly hopeless and inducing in almost every woman a wish to mother him and put him right. He was extravagantly generous, and though it was not his readiness to foot the bills which won him a place in the Coterie, he was undoubtedly valued for his bank-balance as well as for his gentleness and sweetness. Edward Horner once accused Diana of being engaged to Vernon. Diana dismissed the charge as absurd, but it was not for want of soliciting that she was not. 'If you could imagine a millionth fraction of the amount I worship you, you would be obliged to forgive me,' wrote Vernon. 'Oh Dibbins, I implore you to say you'll marry me. You sit in every chair and I see you in every step and I can think and imagine nothing else but you.'

Tommy Bouch also suffered from unrequited love. He was a rich fox-hunting squire, Master of the Belvoir and a man of greatness in that hunting world; but the Coterie saw nothing great in such a role and found him elderly and something of a bore. He adored Diana and wrote her countless poems, some of which were mediocre, most worse. Diana, who considered the typical Belvoir house-party to consist of 'a collection of senile, decayed relations and a second-childhood aunt,' welcomed him as a county neighbour and a generous friend, but found he could be a trial in London, especially when his jealousy led him to call three or four times a day and bombard her with letters in the intervals.

And then there was Duff Cooper. His ancestry was interesting. His mother, Lady Agnes, was sister to the Duke of Fife. After two elopements and a divorce she found herself ostracized by polite society and sought solace in nursing. There she met and married Alfred Cooper, a surgeon of considerable ability who specialized in the more embarrassing complaints. His carriage was well known in Mayfair and the fact that 'Cooper's clap-trap' had been seen outside a noble house was the subject of ribald speculation in the clubs. Mr Cooper would have enjoyed the ribaldry, he is supposed to have remarked that he and his wife between them had inspected the private parts of half the peers in London. In old age he grew eccentric, wore white kid gloves to shoot and refused to play bridge until the looking glasses had been draped in cloth so as to remove the chance of cheating.

Duff himself was far from eligible. A young man working for the Foreign Office examination and living on a small allowance from his mother would not anyway have seemed an enticing prospect to the Duchess of Rutland, but Duff had more against him than that. 'Writing in my sixty-fourth year,' he claimed in his autobiography, 'I can truthfully say that since I reached the age of discretion I have consistently drunk more than most people would say was good for me.' He might have said the same thing about eating. He was notoriously unsafe with women, viewing almost anyone between the age of sixteen and sixty as his rightful prey. His temper was ferocious; his indolence, except when something particularly interested him, was formidable. He was one of the least tolerant of men; when asked why he had been so rude to a fashionable designer he snarled: 'I don't like men who live, by choice, out of their own country. I don't like interior decorators. I don't like Germans. I don't like buggers and I don't like Christian Scientists.'

What to the Duchess seemed irresponsibility was to Diana deliciously dashing. Duff's vices were balanced by a crop of virtues. He was courageous, loyal and generous to a fault. He was exceptionally funny and mocked himself with more vigour than he did anybody else. He wrote and talked with exquisite facility and did anything he set his hand to with competence always and usually with distinction. His love of life was fierce; his failings, indeed, arose generally from his determination to enjoy it to the full. He was perennially optimistic and there were few occasions when his presence did not enhance the pleasure of the participants.

For a long time Duff was no more than one of the many young men in Diana's life. 'Our letters cross as quick as knitting needles,' wrote Duff in March, 1913, but he was in love with at least two other women at the time and the correspondence was more for their mutual entertainment than to fuel the fires of passion. He wrote ruefully to report that he had been crossed in love. 'Christ I have reason to believe is crazy about me so I shall probably marry the church ... I think you are well out of it really. You did not know till now that my feet are ever so slightly web, also I am a somnambulist when crossed, also very decadent and theatrical, inclined to look fast.' His relationships with women were for Duff an enthralling game; his friendships with other men lacked the savour of flirtation but seemed to him at that time immeasurably more important. He was almost as reluctant to commit himself as Diana, though in his case the reasons were less complex, being little more than a reluctance to sacrifice the delights of bachelor independence. With Diana, too, he feared rebuff, not only from her parents but from her. He was more sincere than was his wont when he wrote to her: '. . . as for loving you best in the world, I think that might happen all too easily. I am really rather frightened that it will, for I feel that you would be terrible then and have no pity.'

Usually his love-letters were romantic, ecstatic, delicately ironic; a little too well-honed to stem from the heart. After seeing her portrait painted by Sir John Lavery he erupted:

'If I were a painter then you would be properly painted. Not once but a thousand times, in every dress you have ever honoured, in every setting you have ever shone in. And if I were a millionaire I would found a picture gallery in which only pictures of you might be exhibited. The gallery would be open only to the nobility and clergy, the entrance fee would be £1,000 and visitors would have to take off their shoes on entering. And if I were an architect I would design that gallery to look something like a church but more like a heathen temple. And the best of your pictures should hang above the high altar where the pale-faced high priest of Dianolatry would worship every hour. And if I were a musician I would make music so passionate that when it poured out of the temple organ it would reach the souls of your thousand idolaters and make them drunk like wine. And if I were a poet I would write psalms and prayers so beautiful and so unhappy that your picture, half intoxicated with the incense streaming up from the censers, would stretch out its hands in pity to the worshippers below. And if I were God I should let all those unfortunates die in the ecstasy of their devotion – all except one who should live for ever after in a palace of pearl and purple with you sitting on a throne of chrysoprase by his side. But unfortunately I am neither artist, millionaire, architect, poet, musician or even God, but only a rather sentimental, shy young man with ambitions beyond my energy and dreams beyond my income. So shall I send you a small box of chocolates, or would you rather have a postal order?'

It was irresistible nonsense, but no less nonsensical for being irresistible. Diana relished it but did not take it seriously. The Duchess too would have appreciated it, indeed she appreciated Duff and most of her daughter's other friends, enjoyed their attentions, only jibbed when it seemed possible that they might present themselves as putative sons-in-law. Some years later Diana summarised her mother's opinion of the young men in her life at this period: 'Edward, drunk and dangerous; Patrick, the same and hideous; Vernon, mad; Charles, just a gasp of horror; Alan, gesture of sickness; Claud, never heard him speak or met his eye; Raymond, missed my character.' The description was a caricature; but the least suspicion that her daughter was becoming too fond of one of these ineligibles was enough to set the Duchess fuming. Diana's friends recognised the obsession and delighted in feeding it. Raymond Asquith wrote to his sister: 'I wish I might live to see the Duchess of Rutland's face on the simultaneous announcement of engagement between Marjorie and Oc [Arthur Asquith] and Diana and Cis [Cyril Asquith] respectively. As I don't belong to an Empire-building family, I take a certain pride in belonging to a mother-wrecking one.' The Duchess had confidence in Diana's prudence; yet as she surveyed the career of her headstrong daughter she must have asked herself from time to time whether her confidence might not prove misplaced.

The last years before the First World War were the most carefree of Diana's life. The family – an extended family with a plethora of aunts and cousins – would spend Christmas and see in the New Year at Belvoir. 'That ass Diana doesn't like country or tree-tops or chapel practice or anything,' complained Marjorie. 'It is a waste, by Jove!' Diana did indeed feel cut off in this remote fastness: at other times of the year a retinue of male admirers would usually follow her to Belvoir, but Christmas was sacred to the clan, with only the Trees thrown in as a sop to the children and the Duchess.

This was the season of the servants' ball, 'that most appalling of all orgies'. Whatever members of the family were at Belvoir had to attend for at least six dances. Nervous giggling outside the door was followed by dances with the butler, the chauffeur, the head groom. The waltz was an animated affair in which Diana's partner, after four rounds of vigorous pat-a-cake with her knees and feet, enquired, 'Shall we do a little gliding, milady?' Someone presumably must have enjoyed the affair, but not the daughters of the house. 'I adore children of the soil and what Viola calls peasants, and prize-fighters, and all plebeians practically, but I abhor genteel servants,' wrote Diana splenetically. 'They're despicable for their trade alone. I'd sooner be a cod-fish than a bower.'

Diana's affection for peasants and prize-fighters illustrated the romantic illusion of the British upper classes that they understood the workers and could establish a good relationship with them if only the middle classes would go away. She knew nothing of the problems of the proletariat, let alone of that still unborn concept 'The Third World'. If poverty or misery was thrust under her nose she was as distressed as any other teenage girl, but it would not have occurred to her to seek them out; she would indeed actively have avoided them. Socialists were either like Charles Lister, well-intentioned but misguided idealists, or dangerous revolutionaries jealous of the good fortune of their superiors. Diana and most of her friends were unthinking conservatives. At Bakewell, not far from Rowsley, she canvassed for Lord Kerry, the Unionist candidate, against the moderately radical Mr Himners. She found the electorate divided 'between fools and eloquent wise men'; enjoyed the former but was perpetually confounded by the latter.

'Weel, I've always voted Cavendish and hope to till I die,' said one old lady. Diana pointed out that Mr Victor Cavendish had been Duke of Devonshire for eighteen months and Lord Kerry was member in his place.

'I don't fancy Kerry. He's a wee bloody mouse.'

'Well, anyway, he's preferable to Himmer, my pretty.'

'Who's Himmer?'

'Why, his opponent!'

'Do you mean Himners?'

'Oh, blast you, of course I do!'

'Then why did you say Himmer? I believe you're a suffragette!'

The 'wee bloody mouse Kerry' won by over a thousand votes. Diana's interest in politics was largely confined to the knockabout fun of elections. Certainly she was no suffragette and would have considered any such activity common and pointless. She had no wish to vote, being confident that she could get what she wanted from life without recourse to so arcane a method. No divine discontent stirred within her. When a clairvoyante predicted that she could accomplish whatever she wanted she wrote to Patrick Shaw-Stewart: 'Sometimes I long to be a man and hear the mad claps of an appreciative multitude, but alas the longing doesn't last long. There is no joy so lazy and delicious as to find one is a woman who *depends*.'

When the family returned to London towards the middle of January it was to an endless sequence of concerts, operas, charity matinées, ballets and, above all, parties. London in the last years before the war was gripped by an almost frenetic gaiety, when, in Osbert Sitwell's phrase, 'the great, soft, headless amorphous mob of rich people of indeterminate origin produced by the business activities of the previous century was bent on pleasure'. The easiest way to obscure the difference between *nouveaux riches* and aristocrats was for the former to lure the latter to their houses with lavish entertainments. The presence of Lady Diana Manners was considered one of the ultimate accolades; proof to the hostess at least that she had made it to the inner circle.

These years saw the birth of ragtime. New night-clubs burgeoned every week in which negro bands moaned platitudes about the Mason-Dixon line or stirred the hearts of their listeners with the syncopated rhythm of 'Who paid the Rent for Mrs Rip Van Winkle?' Even in the magnificent halls of Stafford or Bridgewater House the fox-trot and the tango disturbed the aristocratic calm, though the more traditional Baron Ochs's plaintive waltz from *Der Rosenkavalier* above all haunted those last London summers. Diana was considered somewhat raffish by the staider hostesses. The Cecils, who lived only one house away in Arlington Street, rarely visited their neighbours. Lord and Lady Salisbury felt that, though the Duchess of Rutland had amusing people to the house, 'foreign actresses and people like that', it was not quite the sort of place to which you sent your children; so the young Cecils were left somewhat wistfully outside. Sylvia Henley escorted Diana to a ball. At 2.30 a.m. she decided it was time for bed, but could see no sign of her charge. Diana finally reappeared from a night club at 4.15. Such an excess might seem modest today but was dashing indeed in the climate of 1912 and 1913.

The Edwardians adored dressing up. Diana's first public appearance was aged fourteen as a Knight of the Round Table; since when, reported the *Aberdeen Journal*, 'no fancy dress ball has been complete without her'. She was constantly being called on to make spectacular entries as the Queen of Sheba borne by sweating slaves or to play the central role in some *tableau vivant* depicting Titania surrounded by her fairies or 'Venus and Child' by an unknown Tuscan artist. She responded to such calls with alacrity, loving to be the centre of the picture and also finding in such extravagances a release from the constraints of everyday life. To dress up was a visual expression of her craving for new experience and her wish to be all things to all men. 'Your game,' wrote Duff Cooper perceptively, 'is to play all games. Catherine of Russia one day, Mimi of Bohemia the next, David Copperfield's child wife alternately with the Emperor Claudius's only too grown-up one. Cleopatra sometimes, sometimes Desdemona, occasionally Juliet, still more occasionally Portia, but never, never Cordelia.' Apotheosis of this fantasy world took place at Earl's Court, where a replica of the courtyard at Warwick Castle provided the scene for a revival of the Eglinton Tournament. Lady Curzon was Queen of Beauty, but Diana stole the show in a black velvet Holbein dress designed by herself and wholly out of period, mounted on the horse that played Richard II's Roan Barbary. By her side rode Prince Youssupoff on a snow-white Arab 'foaming and flecking and pawing'.

Diana was as stage-struck as any of her family and would have relished a chance to play Titania in the theatre rather than simpering in a

tableau vivant. Herbert Tree would allow her a walk-on part in some
of his productions, mingling with the crowd and muttering 'Yes,
Antony, we'll lend you our ears' at appropriate moments. Sometimes
too she believed that she might have been a concert pianist and prac-
tised the *Liebestod* assiduously in the ballroom at Arlington Street.
She told Alan Parsons that she could play it faultlessly 'with the technique of the platform player. The face of nature is changed when one
feels Richter fathoms beneath one.'

Spiritualism was much in vogue in London society. Lady Wemyss
told of a seance conducted by a Mrs Herbine, during which Harold
Large addressed the gathering on the curious case of a man whose
brain exuded a scent of sandalwood whenever he thought hard.
Diana, seated on the floor, 'rocked with ill-suppressed laughter at the
grave absurdity with which H L told the tale'. Robust scepticism was
Diana's usual attitude; she visited palmists and clairvoyants for the
fun of it, but with little expectation of enlightenment. When Letty,
on the verge of her engagement to Ego Charteris, was assured with a
plethora of convincing details that she was about to marry the man she
loved, Diana assumed that the Duchess had done an efficient job of
briefing the clairvoyant in advance. Yet her cynicism was not impregnable. When an aviator friend vanished in mid-Channel, she wrote to
Marie Mathieu, a celebrated medium, to ask if he was really dead –
hardly the behaviour of a sceptic. Her attitude, in fact, reflected the
same eagerness to believe in *something*, yet reluctance to accept anything in particular, which marked her religious life. She inclined
towards a vague and optimistic pantheism. When Patrick Shaw-
Stewart's mother died Diana wrote to him: 'People here say, no one
since the year dot has been as Godless as me, but it's not true, is it?
There is nobody in the world who had more trust in God, who is me
and you, the stars, the dead, all. Of course it matters very little what
one believes, so long as one believes in something. I, thank God! am
brainless enough to believe absolutely.'

From March or April the season of weekend house-parties was
under way. Every Friday evening or more usually Saturday morning
the upper classes would pour out of London to congregate twenty,
thirty or forty strong in the country houses within a railway-journey's
distance of the capital, to shoot, fish, hunt; play golf, tennis and after-
dinner games, of which adultery was the most popular; or to conduct
the business of the country in dignified seclusion. Belvoir was a great
centre for such gatherings and Diana found herself reluctantly on
duty, showing guests the terraced gardens or walking with them to the
elegant eighteenth-century kennels some half a mile from the house.
Some weekends were more imposing than others, as one in which:

'the passages were lined with great men, ambassadors hung on banisters – glorious men who like Atlas carry empires on their very incapable-looking shoulders. Conceited schoolboys like F. E. Smith and others like Rosebery bristling with independence, Alfred Lyttelton brisk as a brush. One and all with great brows oppressive with their minds.' To alleviate the mass of solemn statesmen was 'a marvellous girl called Vita Sackville-West, rollingly rich, who writes French poetry with more ease than I lie on a sofa'.

When Diana's presence was not needed at Belvoir, a score of other country houses were eager to receive her. There was Avon Tyrrell with Lord and Lady Manners; 'Diana was looking radiant,' reported Billy Grenfell, 'and was exquisitely witty and full of *joie de vivre*'. She and Angie Manners dressed up as suffragettes and pelted the company with biscuit boxes thrown from the top of a gazebo. There was Stanway with Lord and Lady Wemyss, a beautiful house but short on comfort, 'lukewarm water, blankets that are no prison to one's wayward toes, and every horizontal object wears a coat of dust, like a chinchilla. It's a wonder that the inmates look as clean as they do.' Welbeck with the Duke and Duchess of Portland; Beaudesert with the Angleseys; Hatton with Alfred de Rothschild, his private detective, lawyer and doctor permanently on the premises; Blenheim; Hatfield; Sutton Courtenay; Hackwood with the Curzons: it is tempting to portray a group of bored and blasé *fainéants* endlessly touring the countryside in search of diversion, but in fact Diana and her friends enjoyed themselves hugely and were just as likely to spend an afternoon reading poetry aloud or acting scenes from Shakespeare as in the more traditional diversions of the English upper classes.

For a month or so of the summer the family migrated to Rowsley, where entertaining continued but guests were fewer and the style less formal. Billy Grenfell recorded a week in August when the downpour was continuous but 'the wit and pleasant drawing and cheerful reading of our hostess, as well as the beauty of Haddon Hall in slashing rain, have made life a pleasaunce. Tennis, fencing and battledore fill up the intervals.' In 1913 H. G. Wells's game 'Little Wars', played with toy mechanical guns and tin soldiers, was all the rage. Diana, Ego Charteris, George Vernon, John Granby and the Austrian Alfy Clary spent all day on their stomachs in a courtyard at Rowsley, shifting the pieces from one place to another. War was still a game but premonitions that it might become something more serious were beginning to be felt. Diana was summoned to the German Embassy where the Ambassadress, a buxom lesbian, was embarrassingly eager to photograph her in the nude. In the interests of international goodwill Diana obliged, but even as she posed she wondered nervously what use might be made of her photograph in case of war.

Travel was now a regular feature of the programme. In the years before the war Diana went several times to Paris; to Rouen; to The Hague to stay with Violet Keppel – 'all the brilliant doomed young men the war was to annihilate, George Vernon, Patrick Shaw-Stewart, Raymond Asquith, Bim Tennant, flocked to Holland,' wrote her hostess. 'Diana Manners, dazzling, disconcerting, came with her mother'; to Florence; to Genoa to visit Viola Tree who was rehearsing for an opera; above all to Venice. It was Venice that provided the apotheosis of these festive years. Diana was staying with Lady Cunard in a party that included the Prime Minister and his wife Margot, Harry Cust and Ronald Storrs. Not far away George Vernon had taken a palazzo and filled it with Diana's dearest friends: Raymond and Katharine Asquith; Billy Grenfell; Duff Cooper; Denny Anson; Charles Lister, now at the Embassy in Rome; Edward Horner. Hand in hand with the Prime Minister Diana marvelled at the sights of Venice and then in the evening the Coterie would fête and cosset him: 'On his birthday we dressed him up as a Doge and hung the *sala* with Mantegna swags of fruit and green leaves and loaded him with presents, tenderness and admiration. I think he was ecstatically happy that day.'

But it was with her own friends that Diana was happiest. 'There was dancing and extravagance and lashings of wine, and charades and moonlit balconies and kisses.' Denny Anson tried to liven up the Piazza San Marco by throwing a series of epileptic fits, was towed off to jail by indignant police and had to be rescued next day by Charles Lister and the influence of the Embassy. There was amateur prize-fighting and a girls' sparring match. Denny Anson and Duff raced each other across the canal: 'I can see Duff now, jacket flung to me, miraculously climbing up one of the great posts that moor the gondolas at the entrance steps – posts quite fifteen feet high and in part slimy with sea-water.' Duff won, and it was all for love of Diana, or so the men said, though any other object would probably have done as well.

The life of the young and rich in pre-1914 England was an easy one. The idle were in no way disapproved of; even those who worked followed a schedule that today seems hardly taxing. Their self-confidence, even complacency, was daunting. 'I've been to Rowsley,' recorded Viola Tree, 'where I've had God's own time. I swear that all of you are without doubt the "Superior People" of history. It is almost too exciting; you are all quite unlike ordinary people – you are like the heroines of Greece and the popular novels. England can never sink while we've got a king like good King E and while it is inhabited by a few such as us.' Viewed from the lofty heights of late twentieth-century rectitude it is easy to condemn the 'Superior People' as frivolous and futile, fiddling while the fires were laid for Europe's holocaust. Whether the modern moralist would have used his time and money any better is an open question, but even the sternest critic can hardly avoid compassion at the contrast between this carefree gaiety and the carnage that was to come. The Coterie left Venice intoxicated by the delightfulness of its existence and vowing to repeat the triumph annually. But 'this was the *Carne Vale* of 1913. Only Duff and I ever did return.'

In July, 1914, a presage of the catastrophe to come brought the first touch of tragedy into Diana's adult life. Constantine Benckendorff and Edward Horner had arranged a party in a boat on the Thames. Several members of the Coterie were there: Claud Russell, Raymond and Katharine Asquith, Duff Cooper and his sister Sybil, Iris Tree and Denny Anson. The band was drawn from Thomas Beecham's orchestra at Covent Garden and at 11.30 p.m. the party set sail from Westminster Pier. By 3 a.m. they were opposite Battersea Park on the return journey. Earlier there had been some talk of bathing and now Raymond Asquith offered Diana £10 if she could get Denny Anson to go in. What happened then is unclear. Claud Russell was sure Diana made no response but she herself thinks she may have said something like: 'Oh, the whole idea was we should bathe and nobody's done it.' Whether or not he was egged on to jump, certainly nobody tried to stop Anson when he took off his coat, handed his watch to Diana and dived in. Within a few seconds he realized the force of the current and, as he was swept away, called out 'Quickly, quickly!' Benckendorff and one of the bandsmen followed to his rescue; Duff had his coat half off when Sybil and Diana seized his arms and held him back as he cursed and struggled to get free. Benckendorff, an exceptionally strong swimmer, was pulled back on board, totally exhausted, a few minutes later. Anson and the bandsman were drowned.

When the inquest was held a few days later the coroner was startled to find himself confronted by the fine flower of the London bar defending the interests of the various participants: F. E. Smith K. C., later Lord Chancellor; Ernest Pollock K. C., J. P., later Master of the Rolls; William Jowitt, another Lord Chancellor to be; and Hugh Fraser, a future Judge of the High Court. Raymond Asquith conveniently had another case on hand and was excused attendance; no mention was made of his role in encouraging Anson to dive. As a result of the intervention of the Duchess, Diana too was not called as a witness. The verdict was predictably 'Death by misadventure', with a few platitudes about the wildness of youth and no particular blame attached to anyone. The press had been having a field-day over the affair and some sort of demonstration was expected outside the court, but the imposing spectacle of Herbert Tree, with a beautiful daughter on either arm, soon stilled the murmurs.

Diana was given more attention by the press than any other protagonist. After Sir Denis Anson's funeral the evening papers carried the placard 'Diana's Love'. 'Nothing can exceed the blackguardism of the press,' commented the Prime Minister, 'but by misfortune or design some people are always in the limelight.' London society was no kinder. It was said that she had been heard singing the morning after the tragedy; that she went to the Bath Club and gave an imitation of Anson drowning; that she visited the opera the following night and caused such indignation among the orchestra that they refused to continue with the performance until 'that woman' left the theatre. None of this was true, though the Covent Garden orchestra did feel that their colleague had been unfairly sacrificed and Thomas Beecham had to work hard to stop them passing on their indignation to the press. A more justified complaint was that Diana did not personally return Anson's watch to his family but instead sent it round by Edward Horner. Perhaps correctly, she had felt that she would be unwelcome at the Ansons' house, but her conduct fed the rumours of her chill indifference. Diana always shrank from painful confrontations, and left it to others to pass on bad news. Thus she earned a reputation for being unfeeling, when at the worst she was guilty of a kind of cowardice. The wreath she sent to Denis Anson's funeral 'With Diana's love' was the target of an anonymous letter which urged her, when next in Venice, to persuade some man to jump from the top of the Campanile to the roof of St Mark's – making sure first there was a good crowd to admire the exploit and its instigator.

The pain caused her by this miserable folly can not be doubted. Two years later she told Raymond Asquith: 'I have an hour ago been thrown entirely off my balance by seeing Denny in the corner – not dripping slime or festering in a shroud, but he always looked at best like "a shrieking mandrake torn out of the earth" so it was as bad as if he had worn the symbols of my murder.' In less dramatic form the tragedy haunted her all her life; when she wrote her memoirs fifty years later she was still asking herself whether she was to blame and what she could have done to stop it. Shortly after the incident Diana found herself abruptly dropped from the list for the Guards Ball, one of the events of the season which few of her group would expect to miss. No explanation was offered and none was asked for. Indignant, the Duchess organized a rival party at Arlington Street and brought considerable pressure on the faithful and not-so-faithful to attend. Duff was one of those who rallied and he was rumoured too to have knocked down a man whom he heard disparaging Diana in his club. Nothing would at that time have made the Duchess think of him as other than a drunkard and a spendthrift, inconceivable as a son-in-law and dangerous as a friend, but even she was touched by such evidence of loyalty.

The lesser tragedy was soon submerged by the greater. 'Goodbye, my darling,' wrote Duff late in June, 1914. 'I hope that everyone whom you like better than me will die very soon.' It seemed an idle joke but it was not long to remain so. On August 4, 1914, less than a month after the disaster on the Thames, war broke out. Diana's untroubled youth was over.

THREE

The Great War

'It must be wonderful to be in England now. I suppose the excitement is beyond all words . . . It reinforces one's failing belief in the Old Flag and the Mother Country and the Heavy Brigade and the Thin Red Line and the Imperial Idea which gets rather shadowy in peacetime, don't you think?'

Julian Grenfell's awful exultation at the coming of war found its echo among others of Diana's acquaintance. Herbert ('Beb') Asquith, Raymond's younger brother, was another who found the moment provided a new purpose for him and welcomed it whole-heartedly. Among her closest friends, however, there is no evidence of that eagerness for war which Nicholas Mosley, in his biography of Grenfell, detected among the British upper classes. For Raymond Asquith at the Bar, Patrick Shaw-Stewart in Baring's Bank, Charles Lister in the Diplomatic Service, all that was involved was an interruption to a successful career. Duff, as a clerk in the Foreign Office, was not allowed to join the army, but he would have been as unenthusiastic as any of his friends. None of them believed that the interruption could last more than a few months; nor were they, outwardly at least, preoccupied by the danger involved; but they all regretted the necessity. Men like Edward Horner and George Vernon were less dedicated to their careers, but they were still getting too much fun out of their peacetime lives to relish this distraction.

Nobody in Diana's circle seems to have asked whether the war could have been avoided, still less whether it was just. For Diana it was enough that Britain was involved – 'there it is and what do I do?' She did however feel that she should make a positive effort to end the fighting before it was too late. On August 7, 1914, she wrote to Edward Horner:

'I think it's up to the Coterie to stop this war. What a justification! My scheme is simple enough to be carried out by you at once. It consists of getting a neutral country, either America or Spain or Italy or any other you can think of, to ask each fighting country to pledge their word – on condition that *each one's* word is

given – to cease hostilities, or rather suspend them totally until a
treaty or conference is made. That they should then meet, agree not
to dissolve until a decision of Peace is come to ... It seems to me
an admirable suggestion. For God's sake see to it, backed by
Patrick and the P.M. How splendid it would be! "Who stopped the
war?" "Oh, haven't you heard, Edward and Diana, members of that
Corrupt Coterie!" You mightn't believe it, but this is written more
seriously than I've ever written. *Do* see to it! God, if I were only
Judith or Jael or Salammbô or Corday or Monna Vanna – or at
worst the crazy Kaiser's mistress.'

As Diana herself remarked when she quoted the letter in her
memoirs, it might have been written by Daisy Ashford. But it would
be wrong to ridicule the generous impulse. Behind the naiveté, the
touching belief in the powers of her circle of friends, there was an appreciation of the need to avoid disaster which was signally lacking in
those in authority. If more people had felt the need to act, rather than
to wring their hands and deplore the passage of events, the lives of
millions might have been spared.

Edward Horner had no illusions about his capacity to head off
Armageddon. Within a few days of war being declared, he was off
with the North Somersets, taking with him his mother's two best
hunters, a valet and a cook. Soon, stripped of all such agreeable
appurtenances, he would be in France. Julian and Billy Grenfell and
Tommy Bouch followed him there. Patrick Shaw-Stewart, Charles
Lister and George Vernon were destined for Gallipoli. Ego Charteris
joined the Gloucestershire Yeomanry and also set off for the Middle
East. Raymond Asquith enlisted in a shadowy body called the
London Volunteer Defence Force which, since it did not exist and
would probably never be allowed to exist by the War Office, guaranteed its members the certainty of staying alive at least until after
Goodwood, 1915. In fact, in spite of his vigorous efforts to the contrary, he did not go to France until October of that year. 'Isn't it
awful,' said Diana to John Simon when she met him, 'looking very
juiceless,' in the street. 'Raymond is going out next Wednesday.' 'No,
I think it's quite right,' replied Sir John, with all the confidence of a
desk-bound cabinet minister. 'The time has come now when one can
only feel sorry for those who are unable to go.'

The Coterie had disintegrated; all that was left was Duff and Alan
Parsons in Whitehall and the women bemoaning the disappearance of
their admirers. Diana wished to do more than keep the home fires
burning. 'How can I best serve my country in this crisis?' she asked
Duff. 'How but by writing hourly to me?' Duff replied, but this was

not good enough. Yet, service with the army and navy was almost impossible; other varieties of employment, such as work in an armaments factory, inconceivable both to her and to her mother. There
remained nursing, a vocation both useful and compatible with gentle
birth. But nursing did not mean the same thing to everyone. For the
Duchess it conjured up visions of some sequestered grange, an
ethereal being in white gliding through the wards, a smile here, a kind
word there, perhaps a laying-on of hands. Emptying bed-pans and
dressing wounds would be left to some resident Caliban. Diana would
accept no such nonsense. If she was going to nurse then she would do
it properly.

Her first intention was to go to France, where various field hospi-
tals were being set up behind the lines and where, incidentally, she
would be near some of her dearest friends. Her mother was outraged
and called in Lady Dudley, who explained that for an attractive girl to
mingle with the libidinous soldiery so far from home could lead only
to Rape. Diana was unconvinced but reluctant to defy her mother
altogether. Similarly short shrift was given to a project to join Maxine
Elliott, Lady Sarah Wilson and Lady Drogheda in their barge on the
river Yser where, reported the Prime Minister, they conducted 'some
unnamed mission of philanthropy. What a Trinity! I am told that
Diana Manners feels tempted to join the gentle bargees.'

A compromise was reached. Diana would not go to France but she
would leave home and do a serious job of nursing in a London hospital. On October 3 she applied to be admitted to Guy's and end her 'life
of grim monotony'. 'I shouldn't think they'd have me,' she wrote
gloomily to Raymond Asquith, 'even if I get out of the castle with
their Graces love-crown still on my brow.' Asquith was disturbed by
her resolve and sceptical about her motives. 'I can't help thinking that
it is not a thing like the Slade School to be lightly undertaken as a
mere essay in parent-dodging. The contract is lengthy, the drudgery
unbearable and the uniform disfiguring ... A hospital has all the
material discomforts of a nunnery without the spiritual glamour of
chastity.'

Guy's Hospital is at Southwark, south of the Thames; a stark Victorian barracks with eighteenth-century trimmings, probably warmer
than Belvoir Castle but in every other way making the ducal seat seem
a paradise of comfort. Diana expected to be 'lonely and sick in the
extreme'. Although she was now twenty-two she had led a sheltered
life, never sleeping from home except in carefully selected house-
parties, chaperoned everywhere, cosseted and indulged in one way,
stiflingly repressed in another. She was used to a world of deferential
servants, admirers assuring her that she was the centre of the uni-

verse, parents guarding her from any tremor of impurity. Now she found herself transported to a world where she was nobody; subjected to strict discipline; expected to speak only when spoken to; dressed in a stark and unbecoming uniform; called at six, lights out at ten-fifteen; entrusted only with the most menial tasks; kept on her feet for nine hours with only brief breaks for meals; most taxing of all, confronted constantly with pain and misery.

The hospital viewed with some suspicion this gorgeous apparition. Nurses were not expected to feature in the newspapers or to have a retinue of elegant young men waiting regularly outside the gates for their emergence. The Prime Minister was not supposed to enquire about their welfare. After her first visit to her family in Arlington Street she was summoned to the Matron's office and given a severe rebuke for gossiping about hospital matters. If she was thought to be picking at her food or in any other way showing herself superior to her surroundings, she was at once slapped down and reminded of the sacred nature of a nurse's vocation; she was nothing, the task was all. She would not be accepted until she proved that she could do as good a job as any other nurse, and keep on doing it after the novelty had worn off.

Diana *did* prove herself and she *was* accepted. She never became the selfless sister-of-mercy of the visionary's dream. 'They put me in a men's ward of unsurpassed horror and filth,' she complained in November 1914, 'and then kept me at work till 10 o'clock, which brings it out at ten hours at a stretch in one stinking bolting-hutch of beastliness. What I bear from these thirty whining Calibans!' But Diana became a hard-working, conscientious and thoroughly competent nurse. Her conduct-sheet was immaculate. She had enough curiosity and interest in others to make her a sympathetic bedside presence, yet was sufficiently detached not to be harrowed by their sufferings. She was physically strong and had an inner toughness that was even more important. She remarked after a few months that she had 'lost the instinct to turn away from repulsive things'. She took the whining Calibans for granted, never convinced herself that they were Ferdinands in disguise, but grew fond of them and did a professional job of tending to their needs.

As a V.A.D. – member of the Voluntary Aid Detachment – Diana had in fact no right to claim professional status. To her pleasure, however, she found that she was soon treated as a not particularly expert but still capable member of the nursing staff. She recorded proudly that she was allowed to give injections, intravenous and saline, to prepare for operations, cut abscesses and even once say prayers in Sister's absence. Time spent in the kitchen at Arlington

Street watching the disembowelling of a hare proved well spent when
she attended her first operation and survived without coming anywhere near to fainting. It was hard work, but she was doing it well,
more than holding her own where her friends had forecast disaster.
Her role was extravagantly publicized:

> 'I'll eat a banana
> With Lady Diana,
>   Aristocracy working at Guy's'

was one of the boasts of that hero of the music hall, Gilbert the
Filbert, the Colonel of the Knuts. For once Diana genuinely depreca-
ted her notoriety; she had no wish to ruffle feelings at the hospital or
earn the disapproval of the terrible Matron. The publicity seems to
have done her no harm; she was well liked by her contemporaries and
one at least of those who worked with her remembers her as friendly,
unassuming and cheerful in the most gruesome circumstances.

Satisfied though she was with her life at Guy's, she could not resist
temptation when the chance again offered to work in France. This
time it was her mother who championed the idea. The Duchess had
decided it would be appropriate for somebody in her station to open
her own hospital. She raised a substantial sum of money, employing
Diana as fund-raiser, and acquired a suitable château near Boulogne.
The necessary refurbishment was almost complete when the Red
Cross changed their minds and refused to sanction the hospital's
opening. The château was turned into an Army School, but two years
later, when Patrick Shaw-Stewart was posted there, it still boasted a
'Marquess of Granby Ward', a 'Marjorie Ward' and a 'Diana Ward'.
'Incidentally, some humorist has inserted an N before the T in
"Violet Ward",' reported Shaw-Stewart.

Frustrated, the Duchess decided that Arlington Street should be
turned into a hospital for officers. Diana was enthusiastic about the
project. She would have been ready to return to Guy's, but a few
months back at home had shown her the advantages of a looser
regimen. Her friends were all-important to her, their appearances in
London were short and unpredictable; if she were cooped up in
Southwark and only allowed out every two or three nights for a couple
of hours she might well miss them altogether. At Arlington Street
with a Sister and two trained nurses on the staff, Diana could do
useful work as a V.A.D. yet enjoy relative freedom. With her sister
Letty and one of her closest friends, Phyllis Boyd, also on the staff,
she could be sure of congenial society and, incidentally, feel
pleasantly superior to it because of her more thorough training. Her
own bedroom was needed for the hospital so she moved upstairs to

what had formerly been a servant's room. Her exile delighted her. Her new quarters might be humble but they boasted a separate telephone on which the Duchess was no longer able to listen to her daughter's calls.

At Guy's Diana's social life had been snatched in odd hours rescued from the rigorous routine. At Arlington Street her two lives constantly flowed over into each other. Friends would drop in at all hours, Alan and Duff would pay regular visits on the way back from their offices, the ebullient 'Scatters' Wilson would arrive from Rumpelmeyer's with packets of cream cakes and bottles of sherry. One Friday in August Diana recorded that she had had to stay in because an officer had 'suddenly had to have a rib cut out of his side, the which was flung into a sewer instead of being fashioned into a woman, and from his side came a cataract, two basins full of flowing poison, and now he's gasping restlessly, poor man.' The job done, she left for dinner at Wimborne House and a ball given by the Duchess of Sutherland. Another evening she left a dinner at the Cheshire Cheese so as to help in an emergency operation, then rejoined the party two or three hours later at Alan Parsons' house in Mulberry Walk. She did not find it too difficult to put the horrors of hospital life behind her and throw herself into a different world. She might have been a less competent nurse if she had failed to do so.

When things were slack at Arlington Street she would occupy herself elsewhere. With Katharine Asquith she would go down to the East End to provide an evening meal for workers in munitions factories. She appeared regularly in the *tableaux vivants* and displays of mime which so enraptured Londoners in the first decades of the twentieth century and which raised large sums for charities. Except for brief periods when the hospital was crowded in the wake of some bloody battle, her life was not physically a taxing one. In his novel *The Pretty Lady* Arnold Bennett portrayed Diana as Lady Queenie Paulle: beautiful, aristocratic, highly-strung, expensive, ruthless. Queenie did 'practically everything that a patriotic girl could do for the war'; she sat on a dozen committees where she seemed far more at ease than the elderly men who surrounded her, 'her thin, rather high voice, which somehow matched her complexion and carriage, had its customary tone of amiable insolence.' She was a busybody who, with discipline and application, might have done great things, but who through flattery and self-indulgence had been transformed into a neurotic sensation-seeker, dangerous to others but ultimately still more dangerous to herself.

Bennett had never met Diana when he wrote his novel. His portrait caused great indignation to her friends. 'Monstrous and abominable,'

Tommy Bouch described it, 'not even witty . . . If I wanted to I am sure I could draw you better than that, with a cruelty which would be far more hurtful, but not so crude and mistaken and heavy-handed.' Diana did not condemn it so forthrightly. She could see the resemblance between herself and Queenie, and found the tricks of speech, the attitudes of mind, even some incidents of which Bennett could not possibly have known, disturbingly familiar. What she felt unfair was the portrayal of her wartime activities as centering round a group of committees on which she was supposed to play a leading role. Diana hated committees, rarely contributed if she had to attend one and kept such occasions to a minimum. She did a worthwhile job which Queenie Paulle would have considered dull and degrading and, incidentally, felt that she got a lot more fun of life than her *alter ego*. Queenie Paulle died in the end, cavorting on a London roof-top in an air-raid. Diana might have cavorted too, but she would have taken cover fast enough when the shrapnel began to fall. Life offered far too much to risk it with foolish bravado.

For life, even though England was at war, was filled with pleasures. Some of them, indeed, she owed to the war. Guy's, servitude in one way, had meant freedom in another. What she did with her spare time, whether she *had* any spare time, the Duchess could not know. In fact she did nothing very dramatic; sometimes she dined alone with a man in a restaurant, but she had neither energy nor inclination for anything more daring. Her freedom, however, seemed all-important. With her return to Arlington Street, the Bovril Duchess, as Cynthia Asquith called her, began to reassert her maternal rights. Diana reacted with hostility. By the time she and her mother went to France to investigate the setting up of the hospital, tempers were already frayed. Once Diana complained angrily because the Duchess made a noise turning over the pages of *Le Matin*:

'She said tonight sadly "Does everything I do make you uncomfortable?" By Jove, it does, every bloody thing: squabbling with the Base Commander over the rent of the château; forcing useless and unwelcome objects – calendars, napkin-rings etc – on the officers; standing always in Princess Louise's way in hopes of a word; "*Vous savez, Monsieur, je suis très importante*" to all barrier-keepers; worst of all that staring at and questioning of the wounded. That eternal asking them *where* they are wounded, and the answer is always "Buttocks, lady", or "Just here" with an ominous pointing index, or else a crimson face and a trembling lip from a sensitive man who wants no one to know he has lost both legs and a hand.'

Once back in London both sides settled down to a war of attrition. The Duchess never shut her bedroom door and insisted that Diana should always look in before she went up to her room, however late it was. Whatever state she was in, Diana always forced herself to sober up before returning. And then the lies would begin: 'The Wimbornes' ball is only just over, Lady Drogheda drove me home', when in fact for the last hour she had been in a taxicab driving round and round Regent's Park with a man. By day Irene Lawley provided the most regular alibi when Diana did not want her mother to know that she was seeing Duff or some other friend. Both sides hated the sordid ritual. Diana felt cheap and ashamed while the Duchess deemed herself betrayed. She sickened of the fight but could not bring herself to let go, while Diana never braced herself to the point of brazen defiance. In the end the Duchess was bound to lose. As the hospital became better established, so she lost interest in its running and spent more and more time at Belvoir, now a convalescent home. Standards were not what they had been. Provided Diana did not marry any of the young men with whom she was no doubt misbehaving, then the Duchess would leave her in peace. What else could she do except retreat from the field and keep her armies intact to fight the final, all-important battle?

In December 1914 Billy Grenfell described 'a bust' in London, 'mostly with the remnants of our little clique'. Raymond and Katharine Asquith, Patrick Shaw-Stewart, Duff and Diana were there, 'the latter looking very handsome'. 'There is a sort of "Lights-Out" and "Eyes Right" air about London which makes merry-making incongruous. Though why should one not cull the fruit of the days that may yet remain?' The circumstances could hardly have been more ripe for unbridled culling of any fruit in sight. The men, conscious that this might be their last chance, were out to make the most of it; the women, oppressed by a sense of debt to those who were going out to die for them, felt guilt in denying them any pleasures. The sharp division between military and civilian, the immunity of London to attack in the early phases of the war, meant that the soldier on leave from the front enjoyed a far more privileged position than his equivalent in the Second World War. The miracle is that so many of the taboos of polite society survived more or less inviolate.

Not that much remained inviolate at 'Fitz', No. 8 Fitzroy St, the studio in which Nancy Cunard, Iris Tree, Phyllis Boyd and a few more of Diana's friends held court. Often the inhabitants would urge her, 'Come to Fitz, Diana'. Always she refused, a little jealous of the freedom the others enjoyed, the excesses they no doubt perpetrated, yet too frightened to accept the invitation and anyway doubtful whether it was quite her sort of thing. Once she went round to help clear up after a party. Champagne bottles broken at the neck to save the trouble of drawing the cork, pools of blood and vomit, frowsty unmade beds, a black velvet divan thick with dust: the squalor disgusted her and she never visited the studio again. Yet she could not escape a feeling of regret that, in sexual matters at least, her friends had stolen a march on her.

In every other way her conduct was far from prudish. At Arlington Street she had easy access to drugs and every chemist was ready to sell on the flimsiest excuse goods that now would have to be ordered on prescription. Chloroform was the easiest to obtain. Aubrey Herbert was reported to be 'in a state of frenzied resentment and irritation against Diana, who rasps his war nerves.' After a dinner in which she had been particularly vociferous she suddenly announced: 'I *must* be unconscious tonight.' A taxi was sent off to a nearby chemist and soon returned with a packet. 'Jolly old chlorers,' Diana exclaimed, at which point Aubrey Herbert removed his wife before the orgy started.

Another time, when Diana was dining with Edwin and Venetia Montagu, a message was sent to Savory and Moore in St James's requesting a supply of chloroform. Lady Diana Manners, the chemist was told, was having trouble with her eye. The conscientious Mr Savory, or perhaps Mr Moore, decided the Duchess should be informed of her daughter's plight and within half an hour Diana's mother was ringing at the door of the Montagus' house in Queen Anne's Gate. She was relieved to find Diana's eye was safe. 'But then comes the tangle. What for were we wanting the stuff? I felt Edwin crimson through his black, myself an unclouded sunset, and heard a muddled muck of unorganised loud-lying tongues.' The dog was in great pain, Venetia had neuralgia, finally everyone agreed that Edwin Montagu's hay-fever had been causing him trouble. The Duchess can hardly have been deceived, but politeness forbade any protest. She must have found it more difficult to restrain herself if she realised that Diana sometimes indulged her taste alone at home. Duff and Raymond Asquith arrived at Arlington Street late one night in August, 1915, and demanded to see Diana. After some expostulation they got in, to find Diana, in Duff's words, 'slightly under the influence of chloroform which she's been taking to cheer herself up'.

Morphia was another favoured refuge if the pains of the war became too great. Katharine Asquith was a staunch champion of this drug. In December, 1915, Diana told Raymond Asquith that the only moments of pleasure she had found in the last month had arisen when she and Katharine had lain 'in ecstatic stillness through too short a night, drugged in very deed by my hand with morphia. O, the grave difficulty of the actual injection, the sterilizing in the dark and silence and the conflict of my hand and wish when it came to piercing our flesh. It was a grand night, and strange to feel so utterly self-sufficient – more like a Chinaman, or God before he made the world or his son and was content with, or callous to, the chaos.'

The habit was never regular enough for it to become addictive, but it was dangerous for all that. Three weeks later she had another orgy with Katharine Asquith and spent the next day in bed with an alarmingly violent hangover. 'I hope she won't become a *morphineuse*,' commented Duff. 'It would spoil her looks.'

Alcohol proved equally seductive. Champagne was the stock drink, consumed in such quantities and so much associated with the hysteria of war that for all her life thereafter Diana viewed it with distaste. Vodka and absinthe were other possibilities, usually resorted to in the early hours of the morning. Whisky and gin were almost inconceivable drinks for a woman: to reduce oneself to a stupor with morphia was risky, perhaps immoral, but to drink a whisky and soda would have been common – a far worse offence.

Outside the houses of their friends, the Cavendish Hotel was the favoured resort of the group. Diana was forbidden by her mother to enter Rosa Lewis's notorious establishment, which made it far more enjoyable, and two or three evenings a week would start in the Elinor Glyn room, with the impressively ample purple couch, or end up swirling tipsily around the corridors in search of diversion. Upstairs an old gentleman called Lord Kingston was taking an unconscionable time a-dying. 'Come and cheer up Lord Kingston,' Mrs Lewis would say, and off they would traipse to stand round the bedside of this unfortunate dotard and try to think of things to say. Then it was: 'Let's have a bottle of Lord Kingston's champagne.' Lord Kingston was too weak to protest and every so often a monumental bill was prepared and sent to everybody whom Rosa Lewis could remember having seen in her hotel. Usually somebody paid. Lord Ribblesdale and Sir William Eden were among the regular residents who got drawn into the revels. The former, in youth a most dashing figure, was one of the many elderly gentlemen who found Diana's charms irresistible. Once she was rash enough to dine with him *à deux* in a private room at the Cavendish and reported: 'a very severe rough and tumble with him at the goodnights. It was an uglyish scene, but I won, and ruffled him a good deal ... O, the audacity of senility! It is the children's menace. How they mousle them, touzle them; they are so fond of children.'

Brushes with the police occurred from time to time. At the Cavendish there were few problems. The guests would take refuge in the garden at the back while Mrs Lewis, with a firm 'Leave it to me. I'll cope with that,' would settle the intruders with a mixture of bribes, blandishments and muttered references to friends in high places. Elsewhere England's licensing laws could cause more serious trouble. At 10.30 one December night Diana, Alan Parsons, Viola Tree who was soon to marry Alan, Duff Cooper and Edward Horner were dining at Kettner's restaurant in Soho. Three glasses of brandy were on the table when the police burst in. They took the names of the men and, having seen Diana try to hide one of the glasses, asked her name as well. Diana lost her head and, after some hesitation, answered 'Miss Viola Tree'. The police were suspicious but noted down the information. 'It was all rather unpleasant,' Duff recorded in his diary, 'and Diana was very frightened of what the consequences might be.' Predictably there were none. Next day Alan Parsons spoke to Sir Edward Henry, Permanent Under Secretary at the Home Office, and was assured that the matter would be overlooked.

In part at least Diana's somewhat raffish life-style was designed to shock – her mother in particular but also the bourgeoisie or, for that matter, the staider sections of the aristocracy. The latter did not always prove easily shockable. At dinner with the Horners the conversation at one end of the table turned to sodomy and somebody told the story of the officer who had buggered his batman in a shell hole between the British and German lines. Old and deaf Sir John Horner called down the table to ask what was causing the laughter. His son Edward tried to turn the conversation but Diana insisted on repeating the anecdote. Sir John thought for a moment. 'He must have been an uncommonly handy feller,' he grunted.

Duff saw Diana at a party in the Grafton Galleries, where all the other women seemed to be the lowest kind of actresses and chorus girls. 'She was probably the only virgin there.' Afterwards he took her to task. 'She said she wanted to prove she could do these unconvenal things without losing caste. She quoted Lady Ripon as having done the same. I said that Lady Ripon married first, to which Diana answered that she must surpass Lady Ripon by doing what she pleased *before* she married. One must not imitate the best but improve on it.' Her consuming wish to be different, to excel if possible but at all costs to stand out from the ruck, marked her no less at twenty-two or twenty-three than it had done five years before. There

might be many reasons for regret or shame, but the ultimate failure
was to be inconspicuous.

Some people felt she tried too hard. 'I am not up to her *glare*',
wrote Cynthia Asquith after a weekend with the Howard de Waldens
at Chirk. 'I prefer more of a mental twilight – her exuberance is too
much of the electric-light.' Yet to most people her presence was a
guarantee of exhilaration. No party was dull if Diana was there; she
might go too far, but at least she was going somewhere and those who
went along with her were sure of being well entertained. 'Dear Diana,
what a snag you are in our lives,' wrote Tommy Bouch. 'Why
shouldn't we have a happy party without you? Why does everything
fall flat as soon as you slip away?' An electric light can indeed be
embarrassingly bright, even garish, but the dark when it is turned off
is not necessarily preferable. Cynthia Asquith was an intelligent and
attractive woman but she knew her own light burnt low compared
with Diana's and the knowledge vexed her.

Some of Diana's friends shone with equal effulgence. Nancy
Cunard was one. She was the daughter of Maud Cunard, a celebrated
hostess who in 1926 was to surprise her friends by announcing that
Maud was a dull name and that she wished in future to be known as
Emerald. Nancy's father, Sir Bache, was a shipping millionaire who
devoted most of his energies to hammering silver and carving coconuts preparatory to mounting them in ornate cups. He spent several
months manufacturing a collection of pony-sized horse-shoes which
he then mounted on the gate so as to read 'Come into the garden,
Maud' – a touching gesture which signally failed to charm his wife.
Lady Cunard was an intellectual snob, a Mrs Leo Hunter whose
knowledge of literature and music was genuinely profound but who
collected celebrities with the eagerness of a greedy child in a sweet-
shop. Except as a provider of worldly goods she had no use for the
amiable, affectionate, slow-witted Sir Bache; for very different
reasons she was beginning to look with equal distaste on her daughter
Nancy.

Nancy Cunard had been destined to rebellion almost since the
moment of her birth. Rich, elegant, dazzlingly blonde, she defied the
world in which she belonged. No one was more quick to perceive in-
justice and fight to remedy it; sometimes it seemed that if no cause for
battle existed she would set out to invent one. More intellectual than
Diana, and more sluttish, she inspired in her friend a vague unease,
compounded of admiration and disapproval. 'Well, Maud,' Margot
Asquith is supposed to have rasped a few years later, 'What's Nancy
up to now? Is it dope, drink or niggers?' In 1915 or 1916 'niggers' were
in the future, but dope, drink and promiscuous sex all bulked promin-

ently in her life. Duff and Diana called on her one morning at eleven. 'We found Nancy not yet dressed, looking squalid, having been very drunk the night before. Diana was disgusted. Nancy's *dégringolade* is so complete that I find it rather romantic.'

Nancy Cunard, Diana and Iris Tree, wrote Janet Flanner, 'formed an inseparable trio of beauties – a kind of Mayfair troika of friendship, elegance, intelligence and daring'. Diana was never as close to Nancy Cunard as that would suggest, but Iris Tree she loved dearly. In the casual relish with which she took to sex and in her intellectual turbulence, Iris was closer to Nancy but she possessed a warmth, a naiveté almost, that was lacking in her friend and which Diana found wholly endearing. For most of her life Diana seemed to be protecting Iris, smoothing her path, rescuing her from the results of her wilder follies; and there was no surer way to Diana's heart than to require her help. They enjoyed each other's company with rich enthusiasm; when they met after a separation it was with an explosion of laughter and gossip and catching-up so extravagant that it seemed they could never bear to part again.

Venetia Stanley was another star in Diana's firmament. Tall, strongly built, formidably intelligent, she was lacking in seductive charm. She had the reputation of rendering even the most virile man impotent. She was handsome in her way; Laurence Jones wrote that she 'rode like an Amazon and walked the high garden walls of Alderley with the casual stride of a boy. She was a splendid, virginal, comradely creature.' Herbert Asquith, the Prime Minister, found her splendid and comradely at least. He was devoted to her, made her his confidante and wrote her letters of startling indiscretion in which personal revelation and official secrets were nicely blended.

In July 1915 Venetia Stanley married Edwin Montagu. Montagu was Jewish and immensely rich, a member of Asquith's Government and a man of power. His long, bony features were so pock-marked that Katharine Asquith, playing tennis on a particularly dilapidated asphalt court, remarked that it reminded her of Edwin's face. His eyes were sombre and unhappy; his mood oscillated between gentle melancholy and despair; 'My fires give no heat,' he would mournfully remark. Diana and her friends appreciated his humour, relished his wealth and generosity, and accepted him as one of themselves. He was little older than Raymond Asquith, yet seemed of a different generation; he yawned like a hyena after dinner; in Katharine Asquith's phrase 'he had no thread to his personality'.

The Montagus' marriage and the couple's installation in Queen Anne's Gate were of great value to the Coterie since they provided a base where they could meet free from intrusive chaperones, more comfortably than in the Cavendish Hotel. Three or four nights a week Diana would dine there, Duff would also often be there, as would Alan and Viola Parsons, Katharine Asquith and whatever other members of the group might be in London. Edwin Montagu appeared genuinely pleased to see them, possibly finding that an influx of talkative friends eased what quickly proved to be a difficult marital relationship. Diana believed that Venetia had married Edwin 'for her days rather than her nights,' and quickly found that the latter were more troublesome than she had expected. Being resourceful as well as ruthless, the burden did not prove intolerable to her, but it was evident to anyone who knew the couple well that the marriage gave little pleasure to either party. Nor did their friends feel that there was anything to be done about it. 'It is no use our trying to put the Montagus right,' wrote Katharine Asquith, 'as they don't exist at all.'

Venetia's defection had left the Prime Minister distraught. Since Diana had first got to know him well in Venice, she had become very attached to Mr Asquith. She enjoyed the schoolmaster in him; the solemnity with which she was made to recite the first line of Baedeker's guide to Northern Italy, 'Over all the movements of the traveller the weather exercises its despotic sway'; the endless questioning on who wrote what and in which play did so-and-so appear. At one point before the war the Duke so disapproved of the policy of the Liberal Government that Diana was forced to visit Downing Street without his knowledge, yet she continued to go, mainly to see the children but also for the pleasure she gained from her meetings with their father. Once war was declared party differences were largely forgotten. The Prime Minister described the Duchess of Rutland and Maud Cunard descending on him in the Cabinet room 'like an Atlantic tornado. The Duke wants to have the vacant Garter – which he doesn't in the least deserve and which I certainly shan't give him.' He was sure, he told Venetia Montagu, that this plot had nothing to do with an invitation to lunch which he had recently received from Diana. Probably he was right, Diana had as little as possible to do with her mother's scheming. He sat next to her at dinner a fortnight later. 'She is a gifted creature,' he noted, 'oddly enough, according to her own account, rather lacking in real *joie de vivre* and much handicapped by her family and some of her surroundings. I think she rather likes me, but I am not sure.'

Two weeks later they were side by side at dinner again. The Duchess was a champion of the campaign for enforced teetotalism in wartime; a crusade which had with some reluctance been espoused in Buckingham Palace. Somewhat dubiously Diana raised the question. 'How do you feel about putting down champagne?' she asked. 'Let's

put it straight down!' answered the Prime Minister, and drained a
deep glass. 'The King is pretty guarded about his pledge,' Diana told
her brother John. 'I don't think it will come to much with all the
cabinet sots and swiggers – but God help England if it does! It is the
cornerstone of their brains.'

Then came Venetia Stanley's engagement to Edwin Montagu. Mr
Asquith visited Diana in bed where she was recovering from an accident. He made evident both his distress at Venetia's desertion and his
affection for Diana. Next day a letter arrived; prominently marked
'Personal' and with the instruction that any reply should be similarly
labelled. Somewhat daunted by the letter's contents, Diana that
evening consulted Duff:

> 'Diana is quite certain that Venetia was his mistress, which rather
> surprises me. This letter, which was rather obscurely expressed,
> seemed practically to be an offer to Diana to fill the vacated situ-
> ation. She was in great difficulty as to how she was to answer it,
> partly from being uncertain as to its meaning and partly from the
> nature of the proposal it seemed to contain. She was anxious not to
> lose him but did not aspire to the position of his Egeria, which she
> felt sure would entail physical duties that she couldn't or wouldn't
> fulfil. I advised her to concoct an answer which would be as
> obscure as his proposal and leave him puzzled.'

Duff never liked Mr Asquith; partly because of his designs on Diana;
perhaps still more because the Prime Minister did not have much time
for him: 'He is oblivious of young men and lecherous of young
women.' Diana, however, though she managed to avoid any close
entanglement, grew fonder and fonder of him as he grew more
drunken and pathetic and power slipped away from him. At the end
of 1916 she was reporting to Katharine, his daughter-in-law, 'The
feeling today seems to be that the old boy cannot eat dirt by remaining
lopped of his war powers. His form on the other hand is perfect,
detached and bobbish, but I fear lately too conspicuously buffed.
Poor darling, I know what he feels.' One of the things he felt was that
it was high time Diana married, but when he broached with her the
possibility of finding a suitable mate she replied that he would have
first to produce another son like Raymond – a riposte that surprised
and slightly shocked him.

Margot Asquith was another matter. She professed great affection
for Diana and abused her liberally as proof of it, 'What a pity that
Diana, so pretty and decorative, should let her brain rot!' 'Diana's
main faults are that she takes money from men and spends her day
powdering her face till she looks like a bled pig'; such comments were

duly passed on and caused, if not distress, then at least irritation. 'As bridge twelve hours in the twenty-four cannot really make the brain active, she should keep her comments in her pocket,' she retorted crossly to Patrick Shaw-Stewart. One weekend Mrs Asquith put Diana off at the last minute, which, since Duff and Alan Parsons were to be in the party and Diana had already thrown over another hostess in Margot's favour, was by no means well received. Viola Tree, already staying with the Asquiths, rose in Diana's defence.

'It's really a dreadful thing to have done. Diana isn't accustomed to being treated like that.'

'I thought she wasn't accustomed to being received at all,' retorted Margot.

'Well, I expect Duff and Alan will both chuck. There's nothing for them to come for now.'

'Chuck! Surely they won't be as middle-class as that?'

To which Viola retorted that Margot was both middle-class and a chucker. To make matters worse for Diana, Duff and Alan did not chuck; but she had the satisfaction of telephoning the Asquiths at 3.15 a.m. to report that fourteen Zeppelins were overhead and she was in imminent danger of her life.

There were many weekends when nothing arose to keep Diana away. At Walmer Castle the rooms were numbered. 'I have been asked my number by the Prime Minister, his secretary, Hugh and Patsy. I keep my powder on through the awesome nights.' Margot stamped around the castle with skins of bears and filthy hearthrugs 'which she threw over the shoulders of her guests, muttering that she had nursed five sisters and three nephews through consumption and she knew what was needed'. At Bognor the Asquiths wolfed their lunch so as to get to the bridge-table and played all through a blazing summer weekend, boxed up in a den overlooking the pantry. Diana was in disgrace for bathing after dinner in a near hurricane; 'at which they had an unequalled blue, more fuss made at the risk than we made when Denny drowned'. At the Wharf, the Asquiths' country house, Lady Ottoline Morrell called one afternoon when Diana was there. 'All these people seem curiously apart from real life,' she commented, 'As if they had no comprehension of what goes on except in their own little "Set".'

Though Diana was not prepared to help her mother in a campaign to secure a Garter for the Duke, there were times when she felt bound to cooperate in her plots. John Granby, Diana's brother, was 'the last male issue of our noble house and the trenches were certain death'. The Duchess was determined to get him into a staff job where he would be in relatively little danger. Sir John French, the

Commander-in-Chief, was a friend who could have fixed the matter with a stroke of the pen, but a more oblique approach seemed desirable. French's closest friend and confidant was a sinister American adventurer called George Gordon Moore – George Gordon Ghastly as Duff and Diana called him. Moore showed every sign of being in love with Diana, Moore's influence with French was unlimited, Moore said that Diana was the only living soul of whom French was jealous because he feared she might over-stimulate his friend. If Diana would offer Moore even modest encouragement, then Lord Granby's future would be secure. So she did 'and the results were excellent. John got on the staff, wore a red-and-gold band on his hat and was a bit despised.' Hearing of this, Edward Horner at once asked Diana to intercede for him, too. The difference was that he wanted to be detached from the staff and sent to the front line. This too was done.

The trouble was that Diana loathed Moore. She was sickened by his physique, which was that of a squat and podgy Red Indian. She could hardly understand a word he said. She despised his vulgarity and ignorance of all she had been taught to find civilized. She was terrified by his obsessive love. He was said to be divorcing his wife in America so as to marry her. Diana had an awful feeling that he might succeed. 'I was very young and couldn't cope at all.' To Raymond Asquith she described his passion as 'that vile torrent of gravy and steaming, putrefying blood' compared to the 'rainbowed ornamental fountain' of Duff's affection.

Once, in a side room of Moore's house, he got her to himself, pinned her arms to her sides in a bear hug and kissed her greedily. Fearing rape she wrenched her arms loose and tried to strangle him. But Moore had been a pugilist in his time, 'the windpipe clutch which I did not relax for an easy three minutes proved useless and his throat muscles pulsed to the, to his mind, stimulating caress'. In the end he released her and she stormed from the house: 'O Raymond, it was so sullying, almost mutilating and scarring. I can still fancy I see the traces on my features.' Duff took her home and she protested, with a nice sense of melodrama, that her lips were not worthy of him any more. Duff took out his handkerchief, gave her lips a perfunctory wipe and said he thought that would do nicely.

By her standards, she was making unusually heavy weather of what was neither a particularly violent nor an unprecedented assault upon her virtue. There was indeed an element of self-mockery in her protests, but she was genuinely frightened by Moore and had found the experience a disagreeable one. There were compensations, however, in Moore's friendship, beside the doing of good turns for friends and relatives. He lavished presents on her: an ermine coat, a monkey with a diamond belt, a set of Maupassant bound in morocco, a cream poodle with pompoms on each buttock and shaved shanks and shins, a gigantic sapphire said to have belonged to Catherine the Great. 'All this had to be accepted,' she wrote drily to her son many years later. 'Not difficult to accept, you'll say, but I really did hate him.' The Duchess, who believed in spoiling the Egyptians as well as making use of their talents, urged her to take anything that was offered, and Diana never needed much urging to accept a present.

It was in Diana's honour that Moore gave a series of parties nick-named 'the Dances of Death', because no one knew which man would be alive when the next dance was held. Negro jazz and Hawaiian bands were summoned from afar; decors created from Bakst or Beardsley for the evening, vanishing at dawn like an insubstantial pageant; rivers of champagne, mountains of red and white camellias. At the heart of the revels, dazzlingly white and fair, Diana ruled. Her presence, wrote Iris Tree, 'always brought to such feasts something of myth and legendary revival, glory Greece, grandeur Rome plus the clowning escapading of Villon. After one of these revels we came home on a horse-drawn hay-cart – how? – from where? – the dance-tunes singing through our limbs as we mounted into country sun-light.'

Pleasant though it was to be the centre of attention, Diana could have done with less of these evenings. For one thing, Moore would turn down the lights and dismiss the band the instant she left, thus forcing her to linger on or cut short the pleasure of the other guests. For another, her friends were not disposed to pay more than scant attention to their host, and he for his part wanted only to dance with her. She had to sit next to him at dinner and let him 'murmur love or Chich-techicher-chich-chich hotly in my ear as we shuffled and bunny-hugged around'.

When she escaped from Moore it was as often as not into the arms of Basil Hallam. Hallam was that rarity, a music hall performer who even by the exacting standards of 1915 could pass muster as a gentle-man. He was slim, elegant, lacking in conversation but with a dreamy charm. His hammer-toe prevented him marching to war but did not impair the magnificence of his dancing. He was distinctive, romantic, pleasantly absurd. Diana adored him in a quiet way and called him 'her little stick of barley-sugar' – though more to annoy George Moore than because she thought the metaphor appropriate. Night after night he would linger to the end of the party and then take Diana home at 4 or 5 a.m. with two or three circuits of Regent's Park to allow time for professions of love. He was jeered at by some who did not know why

he had not joined the army and was given his quota of white feathers
at the stage door. Diana too came in for a share of the abuse. 'Is it you
or your sister who is most responsible for keeping shirkers and
cowards like Basil Hallam from fighting for his country?' asked an
indignant Dubliner. 'You are no better than a traitress!'

'Life is much as you remembered it,' Raymond Asquith told
Edward Horner in April, 1915. 'There is desultory speculation in
the Coterie as to whether Dotty is in love with Hallam. Hopes are
entertained by some; doubts by others – but not I think by Hallam.
On the whole my own impression is that her beauty is increasing
and her humanity dwindling – a double portent which you may
find it hard to picture. I am training myself to admire her as a
natural object – the Alpine sunset, the Pink Terrace in New
Zealand – instead of the damned unnatural and extremely provocative one she really is.'

Asquith's accusation of inhumanity was echoed by many of her
friends. 'You, the Soul of Souls, yourself have no soul,' wrote
Tommy Bouch accusingly. 'You told me I ought never to have taken
you seriously and now I know you were right.' Those who loved her
and wanted her exclusive love in return were maddened by her determination to remain detached; her eagerness to offer friendship; her
refusal, perhaps inability, to do more. 'I *can't* understand your form
of loving people,' wrote an agonized Edward Horner. 'I can't constitu-
tionally believe in your loving me and a couple more.' George Vernon
was maddened by the vision of Diana surrounded by George Moore,
'Duff hazarding his all. Edward buying licences. Michael
[Herbert] and his oiliness. Raymond and his insinuations. Claud and
his persistence, and you apparently distributing your favours to all
with impartiality mixed with a curious caprice.'

Diana, now aged twenty-three, would in many ways have liked to
commit herself, even though she might live to regret it, but when it
came to the point she found herself unable. To George Vernon she
wrote:

'Nellie Hozier is off the hooks to a man with a head injury but
I'm still on them – and likely to be till I wither and grow sour and
unpalatable. Felicity [Tree] too is "off" with Cory-Wright, while
Iris quenches a dozen blue-flies' thirst, and God knows her face
betrays her. Nancy too is in the same boat of so-called iniquity,
with better show yet a smuttier name. God help them both! They
have more courage than me – and can seize an opportunity and hug
and crush it against their palates irrespective of the taste and they
are very happy while I go starved, and hesitating and checking my

every impulse for fear of losing my pedestal of ice which was never of any worth to those who saw it and considered fabulous by strangers.'

One can find several reasons for her reluctance to quit her chilly pedestal. The marriage of her sister Marjorie Anglesey was going through a disastrous passage while the other marriage which she observed most closely, that of Venetia and Edwin Montagu, was hardly an advertisement for matrimony. In an age when any man you loved today might be dead tomorrow, restraint seemed the minimum required by prudence. Though flirtation could be delightful, the pleasure did not seem to increase with physical intimacy. But perhaps the most important single factor, one which she hardly admitted even to herself, was that she compared all other men to Raymond Asquith and found them wanting.

For a woman who fears commitments and who likes to share responsibilities, a relationship with a securely married man has obvious advantages. At several points of her life Diana was part of a well-ordered triangle. The Asquiths hardly provided this, yet her deep and lasting friendship with Katharine and her love for Raymond provided a tangle of loyalties and affection which seems curious to the outsider and must at times have perplexed even the protagonists. When Raymond was away she wrote to him two or three times a week and he responded with lyrical enthusiasm: 'I swear that you are easily the Queen of Corpse-Revivers. A dozen syllables of your electric illiteracy would suffice to raise Lazarus'; 'There is life in every word you write, Dilly; I can see the sap pulsing in the syllables, the vowels sing together like the morning stars, and the i's toss their heads to heaven like daffodils in March.' Diana shared a special place with his wife: 'You and my beloved Katharine are the only women my vocabulary can't more than cope with.' When Raymond realised that he had no photograph of his wife to carry into battle he wrote to protest. 'I have got a dinky little photo of Dilly and if that is found on my corpse instead of a picture of you, I know you will give me a wigging in the next world.'

Everyone, it seems, was satisfied. Yet one wonders if Katharine can really have had the self-effacement not to resent the precious hours of leave which her husband devoted to their friend; whether Diana did not sometimes wish that she could have the prior claim. Sometimes Katharine seems to have betrayed at least a flicker of jealousy. It must have been in response to some such protest that Raymond Asquith wrote to his wife in April, 1915:

'I felt quite guilty when my writing to Dottie made you

whimper. I hardly ever do write to her, I hardly ever see her except in public, and it is not she but Fawnia [his nickname for his wife] whom I love. At the same time she flashes and dazzles and provokes "animated adoration" and transient moods of guilty passion and licentious rhetoric which "blaze high and quickly die". I think you make insufficient allowance for moods and for the imperative necessity of indulging them and – in the dingy times in which we live – of artificially stimulating, fostering, and cherishing the faintest spark of abnormal excitation. Whatever you may think of Dottie as an ideal, as a fact she is a very remarkable creature and it would be a gross abuse of opportunity not (as A. Bennett would say) to "savour her with every fibre of one's palate". But enough of Dilly. I don't think of her much except when I see her, whereas I consistently feed my mind upon the perfections of the Fawn.'

The tone of this letter is somewhat defensive, yet it is probably a fair representation of his priorities at the time. The following months saw a growth in the frequency and intensity of his correspondence with Diana. She meant far more to him than ever before. That Raymond Asquith never betrayed his wife in any legal sense of the word is certain. Whether she might ever have felt herself betrayed, whether their marriage might have been one day in peril, must always be a matter for speculation. The children of that marriage believe firmly that it would not, that the honesty between their parents was total and the relationship so strong as to be unshakeable. Certainly to have shaken it would have caused Diana deep distress. Yet her love for Raymond was so passionate that it could only with the greatest difficulty have been contained. She was to have many years of deeply happy married life, yet she was never to feel again an emotion so intense or so impetuous.

In Febrary 1916 Raymond Asquith was sent briefly on a course to Folkestone. Diana went down there for the night and next day he wrote in ecstatic vein: 'Even into this foul and dingy inn the recollected glory of your beauty flings its unquenchable beam – and your darling, darling charity of last night – a sponge of bitter wine held upon a broken reed to the lips of a crucified fool . . . For four hours – or whatever the day's ration may be – I never wittingly remove my eyes from you, and yet at the end it is only as if a shooting star had flashed like a ribbon across a Stygian night'. A gap in the correspondence follows but Diana wrote a few weeks later: 'My darling, darling Raymond. I have loved so utterly your last two beseeching letters. I was longing for you to claim me again, and now you have done it fully, leaving no crumbs for another, thank God!'

Compared with this, all her other relationships seem to some extent artificial. Yet to the other men involved they were real enough. Patrick Shaw-Stewart was constantly battering at her to marry him or, failing that, at least to go to bed with him. 'You, you see, always want to keep (1) me (2) your old virginity. Whereas I always want to get (1) your heart and soul (2) your worshipful body.' On one occasion she evidently let him go a little further than usual. He woke up next morning feeling like a cock ready to crow vaingloriously, though only if 'you divided the cock's harem – which probably runs to a score – by twenty, left him with one infinitely desirable hen who happened to be a bit of a freak, and compelled the poor old bird to read "yearly" for "hourly"'. Even his modified triumph only endured a short time: three weeks later he was leaving a house-party rebuffed, 'a perfect specimen of the draggled male ... Anyone might have cried to see me: amazing, isn't it, how women have the heart to inflict such terrible damage?'

Duff, who respected Shaw-Stewart's pertinacity, was always nervous lest his rival should wear Diana down and triumph by sheer will-power. Back from Salonika on his last leave, Patrick Shaw-Stewart hastened to Belvoir to have another try. 'Pray God with me for courage to face this great ordeal and to let me triumph,' Diana telegraphed to Duff. But could God be relied on in so delicate a matter? Duff waited in agony for twenty-four hours, but one glance at his friend's face when they dined together on Shaw-Stewart's return from the country was enough to reassure him.

Probably he had more to fear from Edward Horner, for Diana could always be melted by a man's frailties, and of these Horner had many. 'I want only to remember how I love you, which is difficult when I think of your limpness,' Diana wrote sternly, but in fact Edward's limpness was his strongest card. Like all her would-be lovers he was hot for certainty. 'When you say you love me, what do you mean?' he demanded. Did she want to lie beside him, and more, most nights? Would she like to be with him whenever she felt expansive and whenever she felt sad? If not, she did not love him. Inevitably the answer was a dusty one, but there was an irresistible sweetness about his fecklessness. Duff loved him, but was inclined to dismiss him as a serious threat. Raymond Asquith was more perceptive. When Edward was on the point of departure for the Middle East, Raymond wrote:

'The plain fact is *I do not like* your doting so much more fondly on old E than on me and being so much more wretched at his going than you ever are on mine. I grudge those two days on the hearth-

rug – the sobbings and the huggings and the vowings that he was
the only man you cared a fig for . . . I fear, I very much fear, that
you are Wendy to the rest of us and "wonder wife" to old E. I don't
say it's surprising, still less culpable: on the contrary it's almost too
dreadfully natural to be worthy of a woman of your calibre. I only
say it's surprising, still less culpable: on the contrary it's almost too
Edward but only against God and the world for not making me
younger, richer, wittier or more beautiful.'

It would be tedious to list the full roll-call of those who at least professed their love for Diana. Sometimes it almost seems as if she was so
well known to be inaccessible that men tried out on her endearments
that would have been dangerous on a more susceptible target. To be
in love with Diana was to be member of a club, not particularly exclusive, perhaps, but boasting many distinguished members. Tommy
Bouch wrote from France: 'Here is one more victim for you, and be
honest – you like making victims.' George Vernon called her 'unique,
blood-maddening, love itself incarnate, and you will yet drive me to
my grave. My eyes grow hot when I think of you.' Claud Russell continued to propose to her at monthly intervals. To all of them she was
evasive; not repelling bluntly but offering little hope. She felt bound,
she told Major Bouch, to share her favours: 'To make the many
happy, what alternative is there?'

There was no such play-acting about her relationship with Duff.
Viewed in retrospect there seems to have been an inevitability about
their wooing, in spite of its many vicissitudes and the rival claims on
their affections. As early as April 1914, after a late supper at the
Cavendish in which Diana had been absorbed with Basil Hallam and
Duff making noisy love to Marjorie Trefusis, 'Diana said to me in the
hall that though we both had our stage favourites, we really loved each
other best, and kissed me divinely'. There were many moments in the
next five years when each one doubted whether marriage with the
other was desirable or even feasible, yet they both found it curiously
difficult to imagine being married to anyone else.

Duff had the great advantage over his friends of being permanently
in London. Though he did not feel any shame at being held to his job
in the Foreign Office while most of his friends went off to the war, it
was not a wholly enviable position. It was difficult not to feel at a dis-
advantage when the other men at a party might be dead a week later
fighting for the cause of one's country; difficult not to concede that
they had the right to attentions which one felt would normally be
bestowed elsewhere. Duff was furiously resentful when Diana let
Patrick Shaw-Stewart take her home after a party, but it was the last

night of Patrick's leave. He protested, but felt a cad as he did so. Nevertheless, the fact that he was there, permanently available in times of grief or stress, the one dependable point in a shifting world, meant that his position in Diana's life became gradually more secure until in the end it seemed inconceivable that he should ever be removed.

His behaviour in the early years of the war was not likely to render him more eligible in the Duchess's eyes. He gambled heavily. At a typical evening of chemin-de-fer in Duff's rooms, Alexander Thynne lost £198, Sybil Hart-Davis and Sidney Herbert £472, Diana £30 while Edward Horner won £598, Jack Pixley £76 and Duff £51. Sybil and Sidney couldn't pay, so Duff's winnings disappeared. There was no such dispensation two nights later when he lost £242.

He drank as much as ever and behaved when drunk with the irresponsibility of a teenage undergraduate. One night he deposited Diana and Katharine Asquith at Arlington Street. 'A great wave of buffiness came over Duff as we left.' He decided that he must at all costs rejoin the women. Laboriously he clambered over the high spiked railings that then divided Green Park from Piccadilly, and tottered down the garden walls that flanked the park, trying to count off the houses between the Ritz Hotel and the Duke of Rutland's London seat. 'With a soaked besotted brain' he finally put all to the hazard, scaled a wall and found himself in a strange and silent garden. He crossed the paling into the next garden and again into the next, leaving behind him a trail of battered flowers and betraying footprints. Finally he arrived at the palatial splendours of Spencer House, realised he had gone too far and began a precarious retreat: 'Poor Love, not remembering that at best he would have found his vain, weak nails baffled by Mother's pane. It was "love's light wings" all right – but he paid for them with a new coat shredded and good trousers tattered.'

When drunk his natural pugnacity was redoubled. Dining one evening at Verrey's with him and the Raymond Asquiths, Diana complained that a man at the next table was staring at her. Duff turned and hurled insults at the back of the offender's head: 'You cannot mean that miserable, ugly, little man has dared to look at you?' A few minutes later Diana said he was looking her way again. Once more Duff wheeled in rage, to find himself face to face with Sir William Tyrrell, until a few weeks before Permanent Under Secretary at the Foreign Office. 'Lucky for me that he is a fallen man and he was dining, I think, with a prostitute.'

The Duchess was horrified and outraged by such exploits; Diana horrified and delighted. Duff might be aggressive, bad-tempered, inordinately demanding, yet he was never dull. His style of love-making inclined rather too far towards the hyperbolic to suit contemporary taste. 'My dazzling, many-coloured angel,' he wrote, 'I am wasted with desire for you. I am utterly undone. Oh wonderful cold red heart so pitilessly entrenched behind the miraculous shield of warm white flesh, you give me no peace, you possess me to the very entrails. Your heart is harder than a tiger's claws, but your skin is softer than the Virgin's heart.' And then again: 'You beautiful, blond, white-breasted bitch. How desperately people adore you. Oh dear, devilish Dilly, I never saw so many swine cast before one pearl.' Such *fin-de-siècle* extravagance did not ring as false in 1915 as it would today, but Diana found that a little of it went a long way. On the whole she preferred him in cool Augustan mood:

> 'The word "love" means little to most people, but to me – nothing. I have read that it should interfere with a man's sleep or even trespass upon his enjoyment of his meals, which, for my own part, nothing but thoughts of my figure have done. But I find that I miss you most inconveniently and the thought of not seeing you at champagne-time is as exasperating as it would be for the moth to miss his candle of an evening.'

A lover who could leap from Dowson to Henry Higgins in the course of a few days might not inspire confidence but at least he was never the same for long enough to grow stale.

The unpredictability was not all on one side. Diana was as versatile as Duff and in her infinite variety lay much of her attraction. One evening they went to a concert of Spanish music at the Aldwych Theatre, Diana wearing Spanish hat and shawl. Afterwards they returned to Duff's flat where Diana stripped to the waist, danced and sang arias from *Carmen*. Then they contentedly ate biscuits and drank white wine before the fire. A fortnight later they took a picnic to the Sussex downs. Duff sat on a little knoll, while Diana, feeling the need for exercise, ran round and round him. 'She looked strange and romantic in her smart London clothes, transplanted to this lonely rural scene. I laid my head in her lap and she read to me "Atalanta in Calydon".' They went on to spend the weekend with the Asquiths, where Diana insisted on going prawning, went into the sea up to her waist, caught nothing and adored it. They matched each other in their capacity for getting fun out of life; Diana more adventurous, more indifferent to discomfort or the risk of being thought a fool; Duff more reasoned, more cultivated in his appreciation.

The simplest pleasures became sublime when they were together. After a typical Coterie dinner one night in October, 1915, Duff and

Diana walked back to 10 Downing Street with the Raymond Asquiths:

'We all loved each other so much. It was very beautiful. We dropped Raymond and Katharine, then Diana and I sat down, or rather lay on the steps that led down from Downing Street into Horseguards Parade. There we remained under the shadow of the damned old Foreign Office, under the very window where I worked by day, locked in each other's arms for quite a time. It was odd and romantic and delightful. Then we walked on very slowly and with many delicious pauses. We embraced under the lamp in the middle of the Parade, and under the dark trees of the Mall, and in St James's Street. Finally we sat again on the steps of Lord Zetland's house in Arlington Street and exchanged the most wonderful kisses of all. A memorable night.'

The stern rules of pre-war chaperonage had indeed been forgotten. Diana held obstinately to her refusal to let any man deprive her of her virginity before her marriage, but this still left much scope for mutual satisfaction. Again and again Duff recorded that they had gone further than ever before, 'and with such art and distinction'. 'She is the only woman with whom excessive intimacy never breeds the slightest shadow of contempt or disgust. This is, I think, not only because we never proceed to extremes. With most women the further one goes, the more one is disillusioned; with her exactly the opposite happens. She assures me that she has never abandoned herself with anybody else in this fashion and I am inclined to believe it. How I adored her. I don't suppose there is any more beautiful thing in the world than she naked to the waist.' Once, when the Duchess was away, they derived particular pleasure from invading her sitting-room, lighting the fire and making love in front of it: 'Diana almost naked with her hair down is a memory to warm and thrill me when I have one foot in the grave.'

The relationship was far from wholly straightforward. Diana had no intention of committing herself irrevocably: yes, she loved Duff; yes, perhaps, she loved him more than anyone else; but she was not really sure, it was all very difficult, how could anyone think straight in the middle of a war? Duff, for his part, suffered from the common masculine complaint of doubting whether it is possible to be in love with anybody who is in love with oneself. When Diana retreated he was in hot pursuit, if she advanced towards him he nervously recoiled. 'I don't know whether I'm in love with her or not,' he wrote only a few weeks after the lyrical episodes just described. 'I fancy not, but I have far more fun with her than anyone.' He could easily contrive to

be in love with three or four women at the same time – and go through
the appropriate motions with half a dozen more; sometimes indeed it
seemed that making overtures to a woman was an automatic reflex, as
another man might reach for his gun when he saw a pheasant, or his
glass when he saw a bottle of wine. 'I think my heart is made of
paper,' he wrote ruefully. 'It catches fire easily, flames beautifully,
but it is all over in a minute and another firmer, harder, slightly
smaller one is born in the ashes.'

Even when the course of true love ran at all, it was afflicted by periodic tempests. One evening in the Cavendish Duff so enraged Diana
that she struck him in the face and made his lip bleed. In return he
gave her what he described as 'the gentlest tap on the cheek', whereupon she stormed out of the hotel. Duff luxuriated in the expiation of
his sin. 'I left you last night with the mark of your fingers on my face,
which I need hardly say I enjoyed and [which]tingled deliciously for
hours ... Bless you, my sweet, and bless your strong cruel hand.'
Not long afterwards Duff detected in Diana doubts about his love for
her and wantonly fed her fears. That evening on the way to the
theatre he rashly admitted that he had been playing with her. Indignantly she slapped his face, jumped from the cab and ran home.
Usually such rows were followed by equally fiery reconciliations
which both enjoyed, but Diana had less stamina than Duff and could
not always endure the quarrels which seemed to him a natural part of
any love-affair. 'Duff dear,' she wrote towards the end of 1916:

> 'I can't bear it at all. You will no longer help me with my moods
> or be patient with my tired ways. You will not even let me lie
> quietly without raging at the little I sometimes needs must deny
> you. There is so rarely a night spent together that we do not make
> hideous with our complaints of one another. Tonight was a climax.
> I kept calm long enough to remind you not to berate me. I did not
> check your ill-temper, but augmented it. You ridiculed me till my
> heart shrank from myself, then you stopped it beating by trying to
> step out of a fast taxi, and then you ground it to atoms by telling me
> I caused you all possible pain. So we will rest from each other for a
> little and if possible return together restored to peacefulness.'

This time it took two days of abject apology before reconciliation was
achieved.

Duff demanded from Diana a fidelity that he had no intention of
offering her himself. When he felt she was paying undue attention to
Michael Herbert – once again a soldier about to return to the war – he
abused her roundly, calling her vile and treacherous and, worst of all,
common. Diana knew the violence of his temper and was usually

ready to let the storm die out, but on this occasion she was stung to protest. 'You have no more love in you than a penny-in-the-slot machine,' she scribbled furiously on the back of an envelope. 'I am tired, tired of your incessant rending of me ... It is not for you to borrow my epithet "common" to use against me, you who behave more like a street dog, with your conspicuous sensuality and loud fighting snarls.'

Duff was inclined to take it for granted that Diana would marry him if only certain financial and familial problems could be regulated. As early as 1914 he had told her that she was the most remarkable woman of her generation. Sir Richard Steele had said of somebody that 'to love her was a liberal education'. Duff sought to improve on this by saying that to love Diana was to love one's own age in its highest manifestation. He had found the mate God meant for him: 'But God's schemes never quite come off and it seems highly improbable that I shall ever marry you.'

The main difficulty was money. Duff believed that if enough of this was available, the Rutlands' other objections could quickly be overcome. But British aristocrats expected their daughters to be maintained in the style to which they had been accustomed, and Duff could hardly support a dustman's daughter, let alone a duke's; could hardly provide her with a bungalow, let alone a Belvoir. From the Bachelors' Club, on the wings of burgundy, Duff put forward a scheme by which he would realise all his capital – perhaps £10,000. On this they would live for a year in great style while Duff gambled heavily. If he won, they would live happily ever after. If he lost, he would kill himself by subtle means and Diana could live on his life insurance: 'What is there wrong with my plan?' Diana thought there was a lot wrong with it. She was not yet finally convinced that she wanted to marry Duff, certainly she did not feel inclined to defy her parents. Elopement, even for a woman of twenty-three, was a drastic step and Diana valued her comfort and her connections too highly to risk them except as a last resort.

Meanwhile things got more rather than less difficult at home. Someone, probably a servant but perhaps one of Duff's disaffected mistresses, had begun writing to the Duchess, reporting that Diana went alone to Duff's flat. The Duchess said nothing of this to Diana but spoke to Claud Russell, who passed on the news. Duff found Diana wretched with worry and reluctant to visit him again. He dined alone. 'If only', he wrote disconsolately in his diary, 'we had some money and could marry.'

Early in July, 1915, Duff and Diana with the Raymond Asquiths and the shortly-to-be-married Montagus, went for a weekend to Brighton. After dinner Duff and Diana decided to ramble romantically on the moonlit beach. They were not extravagantly drunk but far enough gone to make the navigation of a flight of steps a hazardous undertaking. Down they tumbled and Diana broke her leg. She was carried to the hotel and, two days later, by ambulance to London. The Duchess was told that she had unluckily slipped getting out of Edwin Montagu's motor-car, no mention was made of Duff's presence at the weekend party, but somehow he and Nancy Cunard were allowed to make up an incongruous trio with the Duchess in the ambulance escorting Diana to the nursing-home. Sir Arbuthnot Lane, one of London's most eminent surgeons, was summoned to operate. Duff was disturbed by the choice: 'I have always understood that his speciality was not legs. I had heard that he was one of those ambitious people who look higher. I can only hope that he will keep his ambition under control during the course of the operation.' In fact Lane did a workmanlike job, but the fracture was a complicated one and it was nearly two months before Diana left the nursing-home in Manchester Street.

It was one of the happiest periods of her life. Her leg caused her some pain but morphia dulled the agony and, taken in company, helped to create a festive atmosphere. Her friends rallied to visit her and life was a perpetual party. Sir Arbuthnot, looking in at 10 p.m. on his late rounds, found Edwin and Venetia Montagu, Raymond and Katharine Asquith, Duff and several others eating lobster and cold grouse and drinking champagne. When Cynthia Asquith called at a more conventional time she found Lilian Boyd, Jacqueline de Portalès, Katharine Asquith and Felicity Tree in attendance. Diana 'was lying really looking exquisitely gleaming in a lovely primrose crêpe-de-chine nightdress on a very successful theatrical bed, surrounded by flowers and air balloons. Ice-coffee, strawberries, chocolates and nectarines were strewn all around her. The chief topic was the desirability of mothers, and the best methods of circumventing them.' The Prime Minister, Augustine Birrell, Osbert and Sacheverell Sitwell, Maurice Baring – well over two hundred different friends and acquaintances flowed past the sick-bed.

To be cosseted, loved, flattered, made the centre of attention, above all to be wholly free from responsibilities, was close to heaven for Diana. She might not have been content for long with such inactivity – there were too many things to do, people to see, places to visit – but at that time a return to the womb was what she wanted most. She feared the moment when she would have to plunge back into real

life, and as the moment of departure neared, so her apprehension
heightened. 'It's bloody autumn in this room – fewer flowers and
more faded, decreasing balloons, blasé nurses and in my heart the
panic of recovery and all it entails.' She had created an artifical world
inside the nursing-home – bright, cosy, secure – and she did not wish
to venture forth.

For outside her world was disintegrating. As one by one those
whom she loved most dearly were killed in battle, so she grew to fear
that all would go, that the war would never end, that nothing would
survive. To those emerging from the carnage of the trenches, the lot
of the civilian left behind in London must have seemed truly enviable. To Diana, resolutely smiling so as to make more enjoyable the
last leaves of her friends, waiting with sick apprehension for the telegram that would tell her there was no need for further fear, it sometimes seemed as if her fate was the unhappier one.

First of her friends to die was Julian Grenfell. Diana had never
been particularly fond of him, nor was she one of those who thought
'Into Battle' the finest flower of English poesy. She had too much
commonsense not to suspect that while he who would not fight might
indeed be dead, he who *would* fight was likely to be dead a great deal
quicker. She did not doubt the necessity for young men to die for
their country, but she could not share Grenfell's heroics or glorify
death in the way of her far dearer friend Maurice Baring: 'I am sorry
for us but not for him. For him it is a privilege and a prize before anything he can have dreamed before the war.' Julian Grenfell's death
seemed to her a pitiful waste, and the waste became tragic when his
brother Billy was killed two months later. She had written to Billy
Grenfell from the nursing-home only a few days before – 'Misfortune
has empire over me and is relentless, first with measles and then with
a double fracture of the tibia and fibula . . . complaints have lost their
value when all complains.' Her moans read pitifully thin when the
letter was returned to her unopened. 'There was nothing more glorious ever born than Julian and Billy,' she wrote to Lady Desborough.
'As their mother I should have been mad with pride; *that* you will still
be.'

Even before Julian Grenfell had died, however, war had obtruded
into the heart of the Coterie. In May, 1915, Edward Horner was
severely wounded and moved to a hospital near Boulogne where his
life was said to be in danger. Diana appealed for help to George
Moore and within forty-eight hours she, Sir John and Lady Horner,
Edward's sister Katharine Asquith, the Duchess of Rutland, Sir Arbuthnot Lane and a special nurse were on the way to France. At the
time Diana gave no thought to the abuse of privilege which her

journey represented and was indifferent to the criticism. It was not even a case of one law for the rich and one for the poor, grumbled many whose sons and husbands were left to die alone, it was one law for Diana Manners and another for the rest of mankind. 'One cannot but sympathise with their deprecation,' she wrote many years later, 'but which of those many would not have grasped at the same chance?' For her the exercise was fully justified when Edward, being carried into the hospital on a stretcher, opened his eyes to find all those he loved best around him and murmured 'O darling, this is heaven!'

Edward Horner did not die, but Charles Lister did, from wounds received at Gallipoli. Patrick Shaw-Stewart wrote in despair when he knew his friend was dying. 'If Edward, George, Raymond, Ego and I are left, we can yet reconstruct a makeshift universe. But I suppose at least one more of us is bound to be killed.' Within two years not one but every one was dead.

George Vernon was the next to go – 'Poor darling little George, always spoilt and pampered, with more frailties than any of us.' On October 26, 1915, Diana wrote to him: 'George, my pretty, please contrive to get a dash of dysentery and be posted home for two months.' By a bitter stroke of irony he had already taken the first part of her advice and was in hospital in Malta. On November 10 he lost consciousness, briefly revived and asked the nurse to write down what he knew would be a last message. Hardly able to raise his voice above a whisper he dictated: 'Darling Dottie: Goodbye, darling. Love. Love. Love. Goodbye sweetest, God bless you.' Then he took the pen and tried to write his name. He got as far as G, gave up and began to scrawl 'Love'. Halfway through the word his strength was exhausted, the pen wavered and straggled to the bottom of the page, his head fell back on the pillow and he died.

When Diana heard the news she summoned Duff and they lunched together at the Hanover Restaurant, trying with mulled claret to dull the edge of pain. Later that night she scrawled a note to him: 'My darling. It's 11 and for two hours I can't stop crying. If only you were by me, I would. O Christ, the misery, and the morphia not working. O Duff, save yourself. If you die where shall I be? My poor George. If only I could stop crying.' It was the worst blow that had so far struck her and she was herself surprised by the intensity of her reaction.

'I didn't realise quite what George's death would mean to you,' wrote Letty from Egypt where she had followed her husband Ego Charteris. Her moment of agony was soon to follow. Ego was missing, reported a prisoner, then discovered to have been dead all the time. Letty was prostrated. She lacked the resources to deal with such a tragedy. 'I don't believe I've got any brains – only a heart, oh, such a heart. No philosophy, no religion. Ego was my religion!' Diana was called back from a country visit to succour her sister. She wrote next day to Edward Horner:

'What the despair is like you cannot think. 10,000 times would I sooner bear it, or see you or any of us (except Katharine) in such torture than poor darling Letty. She lies still all day and night moaning gently and with the prettiest babble – 'Sweet, sweet Ego. How can I face the long years? What shall I do with all his clothes? What does one do?' – till I feel more desperate than her and would love her to die. I know in her mind she is dreading herself, dreading never knowing love again, never having more children – but perhaps my eyes are out of proportion for tears.'

It was about this time that Basil Hallam wearied of the white feathers and sneers and joined the Balloon Corps. His balloon was shot down by a German fighter and he fell 6000 feet. Raymond Asquith watched his death and wrote with chilling nonchalance: 'He came to earth in a village half a mile from where I stood, shockingly foreshortened, but recognisable by his cigarette case.' For Diana it was just one more blow but a cruel one. She was dancing to Alex and his all-black band when the news was whispered to her. For once she broke down in public and fled the room.

Her spirits now seemed permanently low and the battle to keep up a good appearance became increasingly exhausting. To Edward Horner she complained that her will had become a mere cypher, it could hardly impel her to open her eyes in the morning, let alone to go out in search of pleasure. To read, to think, even to talk seemed gargantuan tasks. 'My mood is maudlin. I cry so often, even at parties, and have to go home, and at night for loneliness.' Yet she never allowed her grief totally to conquer her; when she felt that it was her duty to appear in public and put on a good face, she could still do so. Duff recorded one evening at Belvoir when she broke down just before dinner and doped herself with brandy and sal volatile. 'She is strange and wonderful in the way she takes her sorrow, treating it like an illness which must be got over as soon as possible, doing all she can to be cheerful, laughing and talking till tears come like a sudden seizure and she has to give way. She tells me that when she cannot stop crying she reminds herself that in a comparatively few days she will cease to wish to. I think this is a new way of treating grief and perhaps the best.'

The severest test was still to come. On September 19, 1916, came the news of Raymond Asquith's death. After his last leave he had written to her from France:

'Your beauty and the deep despair of parting from it made me spin like a whipped top. The chance that I might never see you again seemed, like all chances, negligible, but the certainty that I should not see you again for several months, like all certainties, was – and is – as black as hell and as heavy as the hand of God. In those blessed ten days I had moments so dazzling that an eternity of torment could not square the reckoning. I had almost persuaded myself of impossible things and then suddenly I felt I was dragging you patiently but painfully through a valedictory routine staled for you by heaven knows how many reluctant repetitions ... I know that I have pitched my claims immoderately high, that I have been exacting and rapacious beyond decency or wisdom, but before your beauty I am utterly helpless and can do no otherwise.'

For Diana, Raymond's claims could never have been pitched too high; she might not concede all he wanted but in her heart she felt that he had a right to it. His last letter was posted only two days before he died: 'In an hour or two I leave the particularly odious place where I now am for one infinitely more odious. I fear it is a case of a peerage or Westminster Abbey.' From a man who habitually belittled the dangers to which he was subjected, such a prophecy, however flippantly worded, inspired terror in the recipient. She did not often pray, but she spent much of the next two days on her knees, once in church before a lighted candle. Her state was so desperate that it came almost as a relief when the news arrived. The pain, she said, was physical: 'a sensation never before felt ... my brain is revolving so fast, screaming "Raymond killed, my divine Raymond killed" over and over again.' She was experiencing a despair far more absolute than anything she had endured before. 'I have lost with him my energy and hope and all that blinds one to life's horror. I loved him a little better than any living soul and the near future seems unfaceable.'

Almost her first impulse was to rush to the aid of Katharine; Katharine who loved her husband so totally, whose moon revolved perpetually around his sun, who had no Duff, no Patrick, no Edward in her life to offer consolation. She travelled to Mells where she discovered her friend crouched in a dark room over the fire, 'too dead a thing to seek death, only craving to die from numbness'. She found some relief in trying to rescue Katharine from the blackest pit of misery, but her own grief grew no less sharp and she could not escape a nagging irritation that in the eyes of thè world the widow was the one with the greatest right to mourn.

'Raymond adored you,' wrote Patrick Shaw-Stewart. 'I hesitate

how much I may say so when I think of Katharine'. So far as
Katharine was concerned, no such caution was necessary. 'I love you
and bless you always,' Katharine wrote. 'How could I have minded
you loving Raymond and his loving you so much? It was in the fitness
of things.' Diana for her part comforted herself with the thought that
she had not wholly lost Raymond; her feeling for him lived on in her
love for his wife. 'You are more Raymond than anything else, than his
writings or his letters or his expressed thoughts remembered, and so
you are more loved by me than anything or anybody.' The two
women did not always see a great deal of each other; their different
patterns of life inevitably put a barrier between them; but each was
always to regard the other as her dearest and closest friend.

Diana was a fighter, not one to lie down under the blows of fate.
She knew what it was to live with depression, but recognised that in
time it would pass. She fought the pain of Raymond's death, fought it
with all the resolution of one who knew life must go on and was determined to live it to the full. A month later she wrote to Patrick Shaw-
Stewart:

'The emotion of misery seems to me so squalid, low, devitalizing
into stagnation and dregs, not purifying and spiritual as the last
generation determined to think ... Strange that grief should be so
infinitely the biggest emotion. In no ecstasy that we know of can
there not be found a thousand touches of chance that will reverse
our state: physical pain, however slight; sudden uncertainty of
pleasure and its never forgotten wings. Whereas in sorrow nothing
can lighten one's darkness, appearing as it does certain and unend-
ing. It is only energy of life and love that will drag us through ...
My darling Katharine has not got it; I *have*, thank God!'

Her energy of life and love was never to burn so low again until Duff
died thirty-seven years later, but on both occasions it dragged her
through.

FOUR

'That Awful Duff'

By the beginning of 1917 it seemed as if the war had been going on for a lifetime and would never end. Among those of Diana's closest friends who had gone to the war, Edward Horner and Patrick Shaw-Stewart were still alive, but though she would never have articulated the thought, Diana had written them off in her mind as already dead. A protection of a kind against being badly hurt is to anticipate the worst and discount it in advance. Diana did this all her life. No one she loved could take an aeroplane without her spelling out to herself the horrors of crash, conflagration, violent death, funeral; no friend could blow a nose without influenza, pneumonia, protracted and fatal illness flashing through her mind. Edward and Patrick were doomed; it was only a question of when the telegram would arrive. Till that time came she would lavish her affection on them, devote to them every spare moment while they were on leave; but that each meeting would be the last she never doubted.

There remained Duff. There were those who said that, if he really wanted to, he could have escaped from the Foreign Office and joined the army. One of the de Crespigny brothers – either 'Creepy' or 'Crawly' de Crespigny, history has forgotten which – swore that he would shoot Duff if he had not joined up by the day the war ended. Neither physically nor morally was Duff's courage ever in doubt – the discomfort of military life alarmed him more than the danger – but he accepted the embargo on his leaving the Foreign Office with the same equanimity as he later did his conscription. He was never one to waste his energies on shame and Diana worried far more than he did about his reputation.

Meanwhile he made hay while the sun shone. He still could not bring himself to concentrate exclusively on Diana. Cynthia Asquith recorded with satisfaction an evening when Duff 'hovered around with would-be fondling hands'; shortly afterwards he tried to get her to himself when, to his ill-concealed annoyance, 'Diana, Letty and Alan Parsons hooked on to us'. More serious was his fleeting passion for Lady Rosemary Leveson-Gower. He tore himself away from a house-party at Panshanger where he had been fluttering lustfully around her to dine with the Parsons. 'I am not in love with D and I am tired of Viola and Alan,' he recorded in his diary. 'This is a terrible thing and is probably only a phase but there it is.' It *was* only a phase but it almost proved disastrous. Duff and Diana had a ferocious row, and the usual reconciliation did not take place next day. Piqued by jealousy as well as outraged by his harshness towards her, Diana was 'bright and cold and diamond-hard'. Duff was dismayed. 'Fool and brute that I am! This is terrible. All my love for her has come back and I could not bear to lose her.' It took nearly three weeks of persistent courtship before his apologies were accepted. 'I don't believe we shall quarrel again,' wrote Duff, 'and I loathe myself for my temporary infidelity and vileness.'

Infidelities recurred and they did quarrel again, but never with the same savagery. They settled down into a happy almost conjugal pattern: lunching at small unfashionable Soho restaurants where none of their friends was likely to go, or privately in Duff's rooms in St James's Street, where they would eat slimming meals of lean meat or, still more austerely, Brand's Essence and mineral waters; meeting at Arlington Street or in Duff's rooms when he left the Foreign Office; dining frequently in the same parties or with the Montagus in Queen Anne's Gate; moving on to the same balls; ending up in the same group at the Cavendish; at weekends often staying in the same country house where Duff would seek out Diana's bedroom and lie with her in chaste if compromising intimacy. Their relationship, with all its strengths and limitations, was defined in a conversation which they held after a ball at the very end of 1916; Duff unusually sober, Diana rather drunk.

> 'She told me that she had always loved Raymond more than me . . . That last night at Brighton he had lain with her though he had not been there when I went to her room in the early morning and couldn't get in. I was much moved and amazed and it curiously made me like Raymond more than ever, though were he still alive I don't know how I should feel. She assured me that she loved me best of the living, particularly lately, but I reminded her that she had often said as much while Raymond was alive. Why should I believe her? It was a thrilling revelation.'

The Duchess by no means considered him best of the living; indeed her disapproval of Duff became more emphatic as her daughter's partiality for him grew more pronounced. She could still do much to disrupt the even tenor of their wooing. Duff telephoned Arlington Street to be greeted by 'some bitch who was neither your maid nor your mother,' who announced that Lady Diana was out. The bitch was Diana herself, unwilling to talk with her mother in the room. Archibald Sinclair had been causing trouble by reviving the theory that Diana was destined to be Princess of Wales, the Duchess seized on the idea and for weeks would talk of nothing else. When the Prince failed to dance with Diana at Irene Lawley's ball the Duchess was furious, not with the Prince but, somewhat unfairly, with her daughter. Even when dreams of the throne faded, she was no better disposed towards Duff. She had allies in her campaign. Winston Churchill lectured Diana on the merits of Patrick Shaw-Stewart. Diana pleaded that Patrick was physically repulsive to her and that she preferred Duff. Churchill agreed that Duff was better looking, 'and physical desire he thinks the only basis to marry on,' but felt that 'the animal can be selected by one's brain and not one's attraction' and that Shaw-Stewart would be in every way a worthier mate.

In March 1917 the Foreign Office decided to let some of its regular staff join the armed forces; 'the scrimshankers were combed out' in the phrase of a spiteful acquaintance. Duff's reaction was exhilaration, though, he wrote in his diary; 'I don't own to it as people would believe it was bluff, and I dare say too that I shall soon heartily wish myself back.' He felt as if everybody else had been taking part in an adventure from which he had been excluded; it would be uncomfortable and dangerous but it was not something to miss. 'I am not afraid of death, though I love life and should hate to lose it.' The main drawback to his joining the army was the pain it would cause his mother; 'I think Diana too would mind.'

Diana did mind, with an intensity that both delighted and dismayed Duff. He tried to explain to her something of what he felt as they lay side by side early one morning. 'She was so white and darling and pathetic.' She understood what he was trying to say but could feel nothing herself beyond fear and a vast sense of loss. 'I am reconciled to the advisability of Duff, the straw, breaking the back of the Central Powers,' she wrote wistfully to Patrick Shaw-Stewart, 'but none the less loth to part from that straw to which I cling.' He was to join the Grenadiers, the Colonel saying resignedly that, since they had already had the Sitwells, things could hardly get worse. 'I hope he won't be their mascot,' Diana went on, 'for we know what happens to those the Guards love.'

Duff's record of his first days in the army was hardly soldierly. He was dismayed by the discovery that he would have to sleep with seven other people, mostly risen from the ranks, who appeared to him 'common and inhuman. It seems unthinkable that I should have to share a room with them. There are really moments when I could have cried. The strangeness, roughness and degradation of it all appalled me. I wrote to Diana and told her how unhappy I was.' Diana passed on the news of Duff's misery in vivid detail to the Duchess, who spat out vengefully: 'Do him a lot of good to rough it a bit!' While Diana meditated some violent riposte, her brother John came to the rescue and assailed the Duchess with a catalogue of Duff's qualities: his courage, his fitness, his skill at tennis. Diana wrote Duff a letter of comfort mixed with sage advice: 'Fears surge that you will take neither trouble nor interest in it all, or the others, therefore they will not adore you. You will think this doesn't matter, being temporary, but of course it does matter. To be thought to be keen, non-grumbling, generally jolly and loyal, is of the vastest importance.'

Duff went for his basic training to Chelsea Barracks and then, as an officer cadet, to Bushey, only a few miles from central London. He was never far out of Diana's life, but she had grown to depend on him to occupy her days and his departure left a painful void. There was no shortage of people anxious to fill it. Among the most prominent was Ivor Wimborne. Ivor Guest, Lord Wimborne, was an Edwardian grandee of immense wealth, who considered that his money entitled him to anything which the *droit de seigneur* would not anyway secure him. It was of him that Belloc wrote:

> 'Grant, O Lord, eternal rest
> To thy servant, Ivor Guest.
> Never mind the where or how,
> Only grant it to him now.'

The various high offices of state that had been conferred on him – culminating in that of Viceroy of Ireland – had signally failed to curb his greed and lechery. His redeeming feature was his generosity; as Diana said, he would rip the shirt off any girl's back but give the coat off his own to the first person who asked for it.

He took a fancy to Diana and pursued her hungrily, lavishing on her presents and expensive meals. Diana always relished wealth and power and loved to be indulged; besides, Wimborne was good company. One night he took her to dinner at Oddenino's – £4 for two with two bottles of good claret, which seemed indecently extravagant; paid the taxi-driver £1 for a four shillings fare on the ground Diana was the passenger; bribed the porter with £1 to let him take somebody else's taxi; 'I guess his evening out cost him near a tenner'. He got little return for his investment. When he assaulted Diana in the taxi on the way home she repelled him vigorously. He sulked, and asked why she had to be different from every other girl, to which Diana replied that he had always told her she was unique, so she was trying to live up to her reputation. Undismayed, Lord Wimborne continued to pursue her, lasciviously muttering: 'Baby, baby, I want you baby. I want to *have* you – not only in the vulgar sense, but I want to *work* with you and be your help and your foil, baby!'

His siege came to a climax when they were both staying with Diana's old admirer, Claude Lowther, at Herstmonceux. Winston Churchill had been dining there, 'poor love, frankly down and wretched, speechless, morbid, grim,' but good claret and grouse had cheered the party and Diana went contentedly to bed at 1 a.m. At 2 a.m. the Viceroy stood expectant at the door. Diana quailed but prepared for battle. 'For half an hour I fought with amazing valour in darkness and utter silence. At 3, not getting a pea of his greens, he retired.' Diana lay gloating over her triumph, half asleep. Then Lord Wimborne was back, this time in repentance. 'Visualize the lecherous aristocrat kneeling at the bed-post, kissing and being silly with my blanketed feet, with, 'O, baby, I've tossed for so long, I shall never sleep till I know I am forgiven. O, *ma Diane*, pity me. I will treat you as something so unique, baby, not like other women.' Diana rashly laughed at him, which Lord Wimborne interpreted as encouragement. He flung himself back into the attack. Diana feigned submission, then leapt for the door, 'but in one goat's leap he was beside me, and me off my feet and held high.' Rape seemed imminent, so Diana fell back on her last, least dignified line of defence and called to Phyllis Boyd who was in the next room. Her friend was already awake, speculating with interest on the tempestuous events next door; she rushed to the rescue 'and cleansed and garnished the room in two ticks'.

Diana gleefully recounted her saga to her friends. Duff was outraged, not so much by the behaviour of the Viceroy as by the fact that Diana took it so lightly, telling him that she found it delightfully *dixhuitième* (always high praise in her vocabulary) and that she had no objection 'to a few pictorial and featherlight adventures'. Next time she went to Herstmonceux Duff made sure that he was in attendance. ance. He successfully protected Diana, but not her white poodle Fido. Claude Lowther alleged this animal would damage his trees, so it was shut in an upstairs room from which, piqued, it jumped twenty feet to the ground. Miraculously the dog survived, though Diana's feelings suffered severely.

Of one thing Diana felt confident; the Viceroy's eyes were open; never again would he attempt violation. Her mother was less sanguine and when Diana went to spend a weekend at Blenheim – notoriously a palace of ill fame – the Duchess issued her daughter with a service revolver that Patrick Shaw-Stewart had for some reason abandoned at Belvoir, and instructed her to announce loudly at tea-time that her maid always slept in the same room as her. The Duchess's caution was more than justified; the Viceroy struck again. Luckily he was carrying a candle, which shed its first faint gleam on the barrel of the revolver. Lord Wimborne blenched and settled nervously at the end of Diana's bed, alleging that he had merely looked in for an early morning chat.

With these experiences fresh in her mind it was bold of Diana to visit Lord Wimborne in his viceregal splendour in Dublin. She reasoned that, with Lady Wimborne on the premises and A.D.C.s and footmen in every cranny, she would be reasonably secure, but she reckoned without her host's determination. On her arrival she was taken directly to the Viceroy's study. She found him 'all dithery and tossing down endless vermouths, babbling of how this visit was a dawn and going to be so strategically carried out that it would form a basis of an easy and unsuspected relationship'. Diana, who had no such relationship in mind, pointed out that a prolonged tête-à-tête was hardly the way to disarm suspicion. She was delighted by the pomp and gold plate, the footmen boasting pink calves and per-ruques, but was disconcerted when Lady Wimborne drew her confi-dentially to one side. She thought a word of counsel about the Viceroy was coming but instead heard: 'I must warn you, dearest Diana, that in curtseying after dinner to H.E., we don't use the gavotte or Court curtsey but rather the modern Spanish.' Diana choked back the reply 'You'll get what bob you can from me, plus hiccups if it's after dinner.'

Later came another interview with the Viceroy, with petitions to 'come and say goodnight' when the others were asleep. Diana thought that she had finally cowed him, but two hours later there he was again, crashing around her bedroom in the dark, cursing as he stubbed his toes against the furniture. He retreated after only a mod-erate tussle and Diana's threat to leave Viceregal Lodge at dawn if she were molested any further. 'God knows what in my demeanour has changed,' she mused wistfully, 'or why in a strange house I can never curl my hair or grease my face in security.'

Farce threatened to take on a more serious aspect when it was rumoured Ivor Wimborne was to divorce his long-suffering wife:

> 'I have never seen Her Grace in such torment,' Diana wrote to Duff. 'In five minutes she saw in me the only co-respondent, spoke of servants bribed by Alice Wimborne to spy, elaborate and inform against me, till really she roused me to a fear of my own and I remembered the emerald in the drawer behind her [a present from Lord Wimborne] and letters of mine which could be read in court and reading incriminatingly.'

Wimborne denied having any such intention, but when he drove Diana home a few nights later he hinted that this need not always be the case: 'I am prepared to make sacrifices and take risks, baby.' Diana was prepared to make sacrifices too, in this case to sacrifice her old friend Phyllis Boyd. Miss Boyd was delighted to divert the Viceroy's ardour; she was paraded before him in Diana's 'indecently scanty bathing-dress' and scored an immediate success. But Lord Wimborne had sufficient energy for a wife and a multitude of paramours; his death-bed was to be the only resting place in which he did not hope Diana could be induced to join him.

Duff disapproved of Lord Wimborne, but of Sir Matthew Wilson he was frankly jealous. 'Scatters' Wilson was a prototype of the Edwardian rake; 'a fussy ebullient bounder,' Cynthia Asquith described him, 'with his blue eyes and hoarse whisper.' His tastes were as traditionally rakish as his appearance; he prided himself on being responsible for more divorces than any other man in London and liked playing poker for high stakes with rich but innocent young men. Early in 1917 he set out to add Diana to his list of conquests. Diana promised Duff that Scatters did not attract her in the least, but her actions seemed to belie her words. At dinner with the Montagus she deliberately lingered so that Wilson could take her home; Duff stumped off in a black rage 'not only of jealousy but also of sorrow that she should sink to such depths as Scatters and should offer herself to him under the eyes of men with the stamp of F. E. Smith'.

Duff's misery came to a head when they were all staying at the Lovat Arms in Beauly, Inverness. Diana went off early to bed, promising she would lock the door of her room to keep Scatters at bay. Scatters disappeared. His suspicions aroused, Duff crept upstairs and listened at Diana's door. 'I heard whispering voices and sounds of the bed shaking. I listened in agony, such emotion as I have seldom known. At last I heard Diana say in a slightly mocking voice, "Goodnight, ducky".' Duff hid round the corner, watched Scatters emerge fully clothed and then stormed in to take his place. Diana was at first on the defensive; Scatters had arrived before she had time to lock the door, she had beaten him off with only a minor tussle. Then Duff admitted he had been listening at the door for ten minutes, and the tables were turned. 'She cried and reproached me bitterly with not trusting and spying on her.' Eventually honour was satisfied and a reconciliation ensued – 'We had a night of the most wild and perfect joy.'

By this time Diana was working an average of five or six hours a day in the hospital at Arlington Street; less when things were peaceful; considerably more in the aftermath of a major battle. This schedule left her with plenty of time and energy for outside activities. Her passion for the theatre had not diminished. Katharine Asquith had told Raymond that Diana was utterly stage-struck. 'Tell me when next you write about the stage and why you like it,' Raymond commanded from the front line, 'It makes me think that you might like Ypres.'

Diana's taste in plays was conservative but by no means narrow. She loved Shakespeare, Marlowe, Restoration comedy, Sheridan. She enjoyed most of Shaw, though her strongly literal mind rejected *Heartbreak House*: 'Is it a real air-raid? If not, what does it symbolize? If it is, why haven't they spoken of the war at all?' Ibsen she found grotesque: 'What an antiquated old corpse *Ghosts* is – such passions to expend passions on, almost as antiquated as Oedipus's panic at incest past.' Almost anything that took place on a stage, however, would engage her attention; she only drew the line at a poetry reading: 'You can imagine how old buggers like Newbolt and Hewlett and Seaman and Yeats – worst of all – lost themselves in the luxury of their drawling.'

Above all, she wanted to perform herself. Lowest form of theatrical life was the *tableau vivant*, and in such Diana often played a leading rôle. Cynthia Asquith remembered one in which she portrayed the Blessed Damozel – 'funny enough!' she commented sourly. It had first been suggested that Diana should be a fallen woman at the knee of Mrs Lavery's Virgin Mary, but she did not take kindly to the idea. Among the other participants was Mrs Harold Nicolson, as Vita Sackville-West had now become – 'Dear old Vita,' Diana remarked, 'all aqua, no vita, was as heavy as frost.'

Charity matinées were a cut up on this. Lady Essex organised a performance at the Gaiety Theatre in which professional actresses, mannequins and fashionable ladies mixed uneasily in a play which would have been bad under any circumstances and under these was appalling. The amateurs complained that the professionals did not know their parts and made no effort, while one of the professionals, Gladys Cooper, said: 'It was a great success but the Society actresses couldn't be heard at all.' In this criticism it seems she was justified. 'I hear that Dottie was "natural" but inaudible,' wrote Raymond Asquith, 'a queer reversal of her normal rôle.' She achieved audibility at least when she played Britannia in a pageant at Leicester. She noted with satisfaction that she liked to hear her own voice on the stage, 'though I have a strange conviction just after each phrase that I said the words completely wrong'. It was suggested that she might play Juliet for charity but the idea came to nothing. 'It couldn't be good,' wrote Diana, 'but it would be terribly exciting and good for me to do something of which I am truly frightened.'

Meanwhile she was herself being satirised in Mr Butt's revue at the Empire. Duff and Diana went there in a party with the Aga Khan – 'damned impudence' considered Duff, and was relieved they arrived too late to see the offending scene. The Duke of Rutland took the same view and for once bestirred himself; the Lord Chamberlain was lobbied, Mr Butt reprimanded, and the scene cut so severely that only veiled allusions to Diana remained. She herself rather regretted it; her personality as purveyed by the Empire Theatre was not wholly flattering, but it was gratifying to be singled out for such treatment and she preferred tarnished fame to public indifference.

Her theatrical bent strayed over into private life. Dinner-parties were frequently enlivened by 'stunts' and Diana's imitations of certain dowagers were celebrated. Clumps, one of the many after-dinner games that involved acting, was much in vogue. On the whole, though, her friends went in for more intellectual pastimes. The parentage game was popular. Eddie Marsh's were deemed to be Tom Tit and Sappho, Patrick Shaw-Stewart's Uriah Heep and Bernard Shaw, while Diana was generously endowed with Voltaire and Venus. Reading aloud was also in favour. At a dinner given by Alan and Viola Parsons for Augustine Birrell, Viola and Birrell read Lady Gregory's 'Workhouse Ward' in a passable brogue, Duff intoned melodiously from Sir Thomas Browne while Diana 'reclined on a couch à la Madame Récamier and was in excellent face and lovely dress'. Musical evenings occurred with regularity; usually highbrow or at least classical though once figuring 'one Novello, who is by way of being a sort of ragtime composer'. Viola Parsons was supposed to be in love with Ivor Novello at the time. Duff disapproved of the liaison; Novello was 'a very pretty, very suspicious-looking little creature, half the size of Viola and not nearly so manly.'

Her friends were not always appreciative of Diana's performances – whether on stage or in private. After a party given by Lady Howard de Walden, Viola Parsons told her that she had looked 'like a degraded peacock, that she had swayed and talked silly, that many had exclaimed in horror'. Diana was offended, especially since the two painters, Ambrose McEvoy and Philip Wilson Steer, reported that she had been the star of the party. Her morale was fully restored when Winston Churchill's remarks were passed on to her: 'The world has dealt very harshly with her, but she's brave and hard-working and very misunderstood, and she's of great worth in this *sad* world. Why the poor soldiers dying in agony breathe her name as they die.

Clemmie, you must have her to lunch.'

The Howard de Waldens were hosts at a house party in September 1917 at Chirk, a vast and dour castle in Wales in which they would put up their friends and a resident orchestra. The peace of the countryside was disturbed at 1 a.m. by a blaze of lights with rockets exploding round the house and the rattle of rifle-fire. Was it a zeppelin raid, an invasion? The guests met anxiously in Diana's bedroom: Hugh Rumbold, in fancy dressing-gown, calling out melodramatically, 'For God's sake keep the women quiet!'; Margot Howard de Walden in hysterics; Wilson Steer maintaining it was a practical joke; Alan Parsons pouring scorn on so ridiculous an idea; Diana herself, 'in glittering demi-toilette, rouged and powdered,' trying to telephone Lord French but getting no further than the village post-office. For three days the mystery was allowed to simmer, then it was admitted that in fact the whole thing *had* been a practical joke organized by some bored officers stationed nearby. A row followed, more explosive than the previous firework display. Viola Parsons, indignant at her husband being made to look a fool, protested that it was no surprise England was losing the war when such cads were running it. Lady Howard de Walden resumed her hysterics. Olga Lynn and Alan Parsons supported Viola and wanted to protest to the War Office. 'Diana was gorgeous,' recorded Cynthia Asquith, 'generously acknowledging the excellence of the joke and redeeming the situation by her energy and address.' If it amused the poor devils of soldiers, she maintained, it must be all right. In the end the subject was dropped and the party turned to table football.

Unpleasant piquancy was added to the joke when a few days later a stray bomb really did fall near Chirk, blowing in the windows of Diana's bedroom. This was a freakish accident, but in London air-raids were relatively common. Diana disliked them greatly but felt it was the duty of the upper classes to set a good example. She was particularly put out when Smuts – 'the biggest funk-stick of all' – cried off dinner at Wimborne House at the last moment. He pleaded malaria but in fact, so Diana alleged, was afraid to venture out. 'I personally have a dull permanent fear of raid-nights,' she wrote to Patrick Shaw-Stewart, 'luckily a little lessened by the appalling noise. The class difference in behaviour is tremendously obvious. Poor Edwin [Montagu] is the only throwback I have seen – he cannot eat or sleep and his hands go cold.'

Guy's Hospital was bombed while she was there. She was just about to fall asleep when 'those fucking maroons started. I darted into my uniform, expecting drill and every man his place; not a bit of it.' After some moments' indecision 'a blowzy half-scared sister' stuck her head in at the door and announced: 'You can do just what you like, stay in bed, get up, anything.' Diana was perplexed: she had no wish to be thought a coward, yet was quite as unwilling to show off by remaining exposed to unnecessary danger. Finally she attached herself to a group of obviously frightened nurses – reckoning they would be likely to behave most sensibly – and allowed herself to be led off to the massively constructed concrete nurses' home. When the bomb fell many of the patients who were too ill to be moved were injured and some killed. Diana nursed the survivors and found them 'proud as punch of their misfortunes, and inlaid all over with patines of brick and beams'.

The war ground inexorably on. In November 1917, Duff was playing cards when his sister Sybil asked him to come out for a moment. Irritated by her mysterious manner he complied, to be told that Edward Horner had been killed and that Diana was outside. He found her standing by the area rails, crying; and together they went off to her room in Arlington Street where they sat by the fire 'talking a little and crying a lot. Edward meant so much in our lives.' It took his death to bring home to Diana how much she had loved him; she told her brother John, 'I used sometimes to long that conditions, even a ca-tastrophe, might force me to marry him against my too sane judg-ment'.

Patrick Shaw-Stewart alone remained of those close friends who had gone off to fight at the outbreak of war. He lasted only another six weeks. On December 18 he wrote to say that he thought he might be sickening for measles, 'but there may be something pleasant coming up for me about the second week in January which I should lose by being sick'. On December 30 he was shot through the head and died instantly. Diana was dismayed above all by her failure to experience the sharp pain that had followed the deaths of other friends:

> 'First in my heart is an unceasing sigh for my blessed Edward,' she told Duff, 'so that although Patrick's death is agonising, I am truly numb to lesser woes. Or is it really that we are beasts and mind the loss of bodies that we loved and beauty that delighted us? How coldly I write – and yet you know that I loved Patrick, and had a greater sense of duty towards him than to anyone. I wish most ter-ribly that you were with me to hold and melt me. I want melting. It is dreadful to feel like a frozen limb, incapable, paralyzed, ugly too, very – and with forebodings of pain at the thaw.'

They were together again two days later, but time was running out for them. Duff knew that within a few months, perhaps even weeks, he would be sent to France. In February, when Viola Parsons was acting in Bournemouth, Duff and Diana followed her there for a week's holiday. Scatters Wilson and Michael Herbert were technically part of the group, but did not intrude; Viola, in theory the chaperone, was at the theatre day and night. Lord Wimborne arrived and announced that he proposed to stay nearby at Canford and spend every day with Diana. He was assured that the Duchess of Rutland was to arrive the following day, Duff's presence was concealed, and the unfortunate Viceroy was sent packing back to London. Duff and Diana spent almost their whole time alone together. 'It was,' wrote Duff in his diary, 'a perfect life of companionship. I don't think we either wearied for a moment of the other's company. I certainly did not, but rather grudged every minute that we were separated, or accompanied by a third.' When they got back to London Duff went to his flat to discover that his old brass bed had disappeared to be replaced by Diana's present of an eighteenth-century wooden bed. 'We felt like a couple returning from our honeymoon.'

At the beginning of April 1918 the departure date was fixed for two weeks ahead. They were driving round St James's Park, ecstatically happy together, when they saw a body of men marching down the Mall. They were Grenadiers, Duff's regiment, and they were on their way to France. 'Immediately she burst into such a passion of tears that I have never heard from her. She cried that she could not bear me to go. I felt so sad and so proud; the moment was so beautiful and so dramatic.' He was due to leave on a Friday, then the draft was postponed till Monday, so they had a final weekend together. The last night Diana drove Duff to Chelsea Barracks. Monty Bertie, who was supposed to march the company to the station, 'was too drunk to lead a horse to the water,' so Duff took his place. 'I was so glad of this,' Diana told Katharine Asquith. 'The crashing band and drums through the deserted streets exhilarated him and made him gloriously happy and excited – but it was deathly to me. I went to the station. I had meant not to, but Duff begged – I think he wanted to be seen marching in – and there it was so terribly real and looked so terribly *invraisemblable* that it was all I could do not to run away. Darling Duff, I do think he is fairly content with his horrible lot, and that's all the comfort I can find. The desolation is going to be dreadful.'

Looking around her she saw little reason to hope that her desolation would be short-lived. Asquith's Government had fallen at the end of 1916 and Diana, who was fiercely loyal to her friends and viewed politics solely in the light of the personalities involved, could believe little good of the man who had replaced him. Asquith had been accustomed to poke fun at Lloyd George; he had told Venetia Montagu that he had once found him searching for Gallipoli on a map of Spain. Lloyd

George was uncouth and common and had seemed singularly imper-
vious to Diana's charms. What could be expected of such a man? Yet
what could be expected now of Asquith? Edwin Montagu had just got
back from India and had painted a vivid picture of 'the Old Bird – a
vision of a great sack, an upright, righteous, patriotic, fine, worshipful sack, but shoved and flung about and goaded by Margot and
McKenna and Runciman and all the Old Gang, and told to strike, be
a man, look up.' In Edwin's opinion his epitaph should be: 'Here lies
the body of H. H. Asquith who married Margot Tennant but was
Prime Minister for ten years.'

Diana was growing restless at Arlington Street. An air-raid briefly
enlivened things – twenty planes overhead; indignant complaints
from the Duchess, 'It's scandalous! Why do they let them get right
over the house?'; men with fractured thighs who had not stirred for
weeks leaping lithely from their beds; servants Diana had never seen
milling around in the basement, 'things from under sinks and stoves
with light, blind eyes' – but the savour soon faded. She bought two
rabbits to keep on the roof but they fought instead of mating; an
unpropitious augury, thought Duff. The Duke read in the newspapers that Diana had bought a pig and assumed resignedly that it
would soon be established in her bedroom, but the alarm proved to be
a false one. The Duchess sought to divert Diana by luring her down
for a prolonged stay at Rowsley, 'where she shall have a real rest, with
no adorers with all their thousand demands and turnings-up'. Diana
found the prospect unappealing.

After overt hostility or, at least, coolness for many months, the
Duchess had suddenly warmed to Duff when he was on the point of
leaving for the front, asking Diana what he would like by way of a
present. Diana was not impressed by what she considered to be no
more than a death-bed repentance – Duff's, in the Duchess's view,
being the death. Relations with her mother had grown steadily worse
over the previous two years. The Duchess had largely abandoned any
attempt to control Diana's daily life, but her passionate interest in her
daughter's doings grated on Diana's nerves. Late in 1917 the Duchess
decided that she had cancer. 'I left her with mixed feelings,' Diana
told Duff. 'Her death would make me straightaway free, brave and
great, and yet now, impartially, I cannot face so much agony for her.'

Diana decided on flight. She would go back to Guy's. The Duchess
was outraged, swore that it would break her heart. Nursing at Guy's
was little better than walking the streets as a prostitute, 'that awful
Duff' was at the bottom of it. Diana flared up and called her mother a
tyrant, Letty intervened and argued that her sister was so over-
wrought that she would undoubtedly commit suicide if she were

thwarted. In the end the Duchess gave way and by May 1918, Diana was back at Guy's. She did not take the step lightly – 'I shall loathe so much, not the hours, discomfort and life, but the dirt, suffering, smells and squalor' – but she had somehow to distance herself from her family. In part, too, she felt that Duff was living in misery and danger and that she should not remain cosseted in luxury while he suffered; an urge to share his pain which would have been incomprehensible to Duff.

She stayed at Guy's only a month, but it was a month that impressed her lastingly. She found herself for a time in a ward full of children of three and four who had been badly burnt. The current treatment was to pour hot melted wax on their wounds. Diana did the pouring or held the child down. 'The pain is excessive and they scream like tortured, not babyish things.' When Diana was not with the children she found herself in a ward of thirty senile incurables. Every morning she would lead one particularly pathetic old lady down to the Light Department for treatment. Once there, she left her with a group of syphilitic old men. 'They are half-naked and more bled than bladders of shining lard. Their noses have apparently sucked all the blood from their bodies and scalps, for these glow like flames in a wax surround. Over them sit four pretty girls directing a blazing light upon them by way of cure. It's enough to unhinge shaky minds.'

While she was at Guy's, her old governess, Mrs Page, lost her beloved only son in battle. For eight weeks Diana braced herself to visit her nurse's home and finally allowed her mother to drag her to the door, 'sick with horror and embarrassment. Six times I shammed trying the bell while Mother watched me from the taxi. I drove home, relieved by the respite, and groused aloud that she should have been out. Isn't it contemptible?' Next day she returned alone and this time passed the door, but it cost her a sleepless night. In Guy's she was forced to confront pain at its starkest. At least there was something practical she could do to relieve it, but her time in hospital fortified her in her belief that, if there were no such obvious contribution to be made, then the best thing to do about human misery was to pretend it was not there.

She left Guy's with some regret. Hospital life, she concluded, was as much a waste of time as anything else, 'but it certainly kids one into thinking one is indispensable, and home life after it is wanton and trivial'. She had been particularly dismayed by an operation for appendicitis performed by a beginner while the surgeon shouted advice. 'No, no, not like that! There, now you've hashed it.' Poor patients who could not afford the surgeon's fees had to submit themselves as training-grounds for the inexperienced. 'Money is fine,' Diana concluded.

'Money is fine,' was one of her rules in life. She had no wish to be extravagantly rich, but she wanted the things that money could buy – comfort, clothes, holidays abroad, security – and she saw no need for over-sensitive scruples in getting what she wanted. If it pleased the rich to give her money or lavish presents, then it certainly pleased her to receive them. She would shamelessly exploit friends with wealth or power. Freedom with her friends' money was linked to parsimony in the use of her own. Staying with Lord Rosebery at Dalmeny she begged the use of his Rolls Royce to drive with a companion early one morning to a railway station some miles away. As they were leaving the house she disappeared for a moment, then reappeared furtively concealing a small package. Only when they were on the train and Diana rejected the railway breakfast did her companion discover what the package contained. Diana had stolen the kipper from the tray deposited briefly by a footman outside Lord Rosebery's bedroom door. She told Duff that, when Thomas Beecham's father, Joseph, was made a baronet, he had to pay £10,000 for the privilege. £4000 went to Lady Cunard, £500 to Diana and the rest to Edward Horner to pay his debts. The feature about this curious story that particularly surprised Duff was that Edward's debts should be so large.

Late in 1916 Lord Wimborne had been dismayed to see Diana getting on to an omnibus and next day sent her £100 in new, crackling notes. Diana longed to accept it but appealed to Duff and Edward Horner for advice. Duff refused to give his opinion; Edward had no such doubts and denounced her so fiercely for tolerating men like George Moore and Ivor Wimborne that he reduced her to tears. His view prevailed and the money was returned. 'It was sorely needed,' Diana wrote sadly, 'but I had to do it, not in fear of him and his brag and his claims and quid pro quos, but for fear of that demon gratitude, that might blossom in my heart when next I am cornered . . . I argued with myself that gold should not carry such weight . . . but its value is tremendous and above all argument.' The offer was repeated eighteen months later. This time Edward was dead and Duff laconically recorded in his diary: 'Ivor gave Diana £100 of which she insisted in giving me £50. I took it.'

Another source of funds was Max Beaverbrook. 'This strange attractive gnome with an odour of genius about him,' as Diana described him in her memoirs, used regularly to hand out cheques for £100 to particularly favoured women – the criterion being only that they appealed to him on grounds of wit, beauty, or position. By the 1930s six women, including Diana and Venetia Montagu, received the press lord's bounty at Christmas and on his birthday. Beaverbook radiated wealth and power; at a whim he would transport his friends across the world in princely luxury, with a telephone call to his docile editors he could ensure that Diana's latest exploit was trumpeted to the world or tactfully forgotten. He demanded from Diana nothing but her companionship, and she, beguiled by his charm and his ability to gratify her most outré wishes, was eager to give him what he wanted. She could sometimes treat him roughly, however. A friend seated behind them at the theatre heard Beaverbrook make some reference to Diana's admirers. 'A humble group,' said Diana deprecatingly. 'Oh don't say that, I count myself as one.' 'I meant humble in *my* opinion, not in theirs.'

It was with Lord Beaverbrook that Diana first met Arnold Bennett, the author who had pilloried her in *Pretty Lady*. 'How I loved my Arnold and how he loved my champagne,' Beaverbrook wrote of him; a sad comment that was also unjustified, since Bennett too was captivated by his host's daemonic charm. Bennett was apprehensive about how he would be received, but all went reasonably well – 'some miscellaneous talk about life and women'. After the other guests had gone Beaverbrook asked Bennett what he thought of Diana. 'I told him I thought she was unhappy, through idleness. He said he liked her greatly.' Diana, though she found Bennett improved on further acquaintance, was at first not impressed by the novelist. Bennett argued that nothing one might notice was too mean to be written down. 'I asked if there wasn't surely a lot of illumination required in good writing – he said no, emphatically. I said anyway repetition of an unimportance might be avoided – he said no. I said you shouldn't go on writing down a woman's eyes as blue every time she walked on the scene, he said a woman's face is not so important as her ankles, the which was exceedingly common, and the whole conversation stupid.'

Diana's hunger for money was not inspired solely by self-indulgence. At the end of 1916 she had finally told Duff that she would marry him if they were rich enough. 'There seems, alas, little prospect of that ever being the case,' wrote Duff gloomily. He had not done much to improve the situation himself. Ten days before he had lost ' a preposterous £1660' at chemin de fer; on the day of the diary-entry he lost another £125. There were winnings too, but on the whole he was an unlucky or unskilful gambler. Diana constantly besought him to give up the pursuit. Each time he would promise to do so, only to succumb to temptation at the next opportunity. When she got news through Venetia Montagu of Duff's second loss Diana cried the whole morning. 'I felt most repentant and humiliated,' wrote Duff sadly.

Several times Duff wrote from France to try to establish the
amount of money she thought they would need before they could
marry. He himself alternated between bouts of depression and more
characteristic optimism. Diana wrote from the Angleseys' house,
Beaudesert, to describe the cloud of opulent misery that hung around
her sister's marriage. 'Because the very rich are often unhappy,' Duff
commented, 'we mustn't make the common mistake of forgetting that
the very poor always are. However, if we were married, we shouldn't
be very poor for long and would soon contrive, I feel sure, to be rich.'
The crux of the matter was the definition of 'very poor'. Duff would
have held acceptable penury to cover a small house in a relatively
unfashionable part of London with no more than two servants,
perhaps only one. Diana would happily have settled for this. To the
Duke and Duchess of Rutland, however, it was inconceivable that
such hardship should be inflicted on their daughter. 'Two old people
with three legs in the grave between them should surely never be
allowed to hinder us,' wrote Duff crossly, but Diana was still not prepared to defy her parents and embark on matrimony with no financial
support beyond what Duff could offer. Somehow the Rutlands must
be persuaded that Duff was acceptable as a son-in-law, and before
there could be any hope of this the war must be over and Duff safely
back in the Foreign Office or some more profitable occupation.

Meanwhile Diana was full of projects for making their fortune.
What she was seeking was ' a dignified money-making plan entailing
the minimum of work'. First idea was for a nursing-home to be
opened under the management of herself and Katharine Asquith –
'No nursing-home fails, at least very few, and it seems to me that we
start with tremendous advantages.' A few weeks later came a still
more ambitious vision, an aviation company for the carriage of passengers. For both these Beaverbrook was to put up the money; but
though he was ready to lend the odd £100 whenever needed, he was
too good a businessman to fling himself into serious enterprises
without some assurance about their management. Diana did not
inspire such confidence. He did, however, encourage her to invest in
sugar futures and at his instigation she wrote to a commodity agent.
The minimum investment required was £3000, and in the end her
courage failed her.

A flavour of desperation pervaded Diana's thinking at this time. All
her eggs were in one frail basket. If Duff were killed, what would be
left to her? If he survived, would he ever make a husband acceptable
in any worldly sense? At dinner at the Montagus, in June 1918, she
found herself sitting between Lords Curzon and Hardinge. Each in

turn asked her what she was going to do with her life.

'My age claims the question, I suppose. It's quite unanswerable. Curzon stuck to it in the obstinate way powerful brains do, blunt to sensitiveness, and cross-questioned me as to ambitious marriage. I renounced all ambitions and saw for the first time it was the truth. Hardinge's breath was asphyxiating, so he had to be kept off the confidential touch. I lit a cigarette after dinner and outfaced Mother. I heard Edwin swearing it was the first time he had seen such a thing. After dinner I had a long, very confidential conversation with Lady Curzon. She was charming. She told me an amazingly characteristic fact about George. On marriage he made her sign a pledge that, in case of his death, she would never remarry.'

But was to marry Duff to renounce ambition? As the letters flowed in from France, Diana became more and more convinced than he was a man of outstanding ability. With Duff in London his intemperance, infidelity, endless gambling, could cause dismay in even the most indulgent heart; when he was hundreds of miles away, in urgent danger, such peccadilloes were forgotten, only his charm, intelligence, high spirits, capacity for love were remembered. There was a didactic element in his letters which Diana, always greedy for knowledge, delighted in. 'I must try to carry on your education even at this distance. In the first place you mustn't put at the top of your letter '12 p.m.' because it signifies nothing. 12 can't be p. or a. because it's m. itself.' A few days later he corrected her spelling of propaganda – 'propreganda' in one paragraph and 'propergander' in the next.

But they were love letters above all, and love letters to satisfy the most demanding. 'Didn't Julian write "Life is Colour and Warmth and Light, And a striving evermore for these"? I always thought them the best lines in a rather over-praised and barbarous poem. And as colour and warmth and light become rarer and the possibility of their complete eclipse more thinkable, so much the more does one hunger and thirst for them and lie down and bask in them when they appear. You, my love, are the embodiment of all those three: the brightest colour, the sweetest warmth and the one dazzling light of my life.' Coming from the bloody mire of Flanders such romantic rhapsodies had a ring of sincerity which might have been lacking in a letter despatched from St James's Street to Arlington Street. Still more did they touch the heart when the words were scrawled in pencil on the way up to the front for what was to be a singularly fierce and almost Duff's last battle:

'. . . to tell you that I love you more today than ever in my life before. That I never see beauty without seeing you or scent happiness without thinking of you. You have fulfilled all my ambitions, realized all my hopes, made all my dreams come true. You have set a crown of roses on my youth and fortified me against the disaster of our days. Your courageous gaiety has inspired me with joy, your tender faithfulness has been a rock of security and comfort. I have felt for you all kinds of love at once. I have asked much of you and you have never failed me. You have intensified all colours, heightened all beauty, deepened all delight. I love you more than life, my beauty, my wonder.'

Duff suggested that one day their letters might be brought together to provide a picture of the age. Alan Parsons perhaps might edit them. 'It is I that must edit them,' replied Diana proudly, 'and if I must be old it is I that shall read them to the envious young, flauntingly, excitingly, and when they hear yours they'll dream well that night, and waking crave for such a mythical, supreme lover.'

Alan Parsons wrote to Duff from Breccles to tell his friend how deeply Diana loved him. He was not sure how far Duff realised the strength of her feelings. 'Sometimes when I have been happiest with her, and when I thought she was happy too, her face would suddenly sadden and she would say "I wish that Duffy was here." I wish you would marry her, Duffy.' Duff told Diana of Alan's letter, how in his reply he had told Parsons how far they were already committed to each other and that, 'on your return, I intended to take you to my sleep and make you my joy, so at least there is one less to guard against, and at least one whom you can hold a candle past with unsecretive step'. Duff and Diana were perpetually amazed at the blindness of their friends to the love they felt for each other. At dinner at the Montagus', Augustine Birrell asked what news there had been of Duff. Venetia said she had had one letter and asked if anybody else had heard. Some of their closest friends were there, yet none seemed to think it obvious that Diana would have been the most likely to hear. 'With what dignity must we have lived before them,' wrote Diana, '. . . with refinement and blatancy unseen.'

From Duff's point of view the drawback to this was that Diana was still considered by others to be open to every kind of proposition. In August he was alarmed to hear that Scatters Wilson was the only unattached man at a house-party at Breccles, matched by Diana as the only spinster. Her letter reporting the party said suspiciously little about overtures, rattling of door-handles, midnight tussles. 'But I suppose I am to believe that Scatters has taken a dislike to you . . .

How hideous is my jealousy. I am ashamed of it.' And so he should be, was Diana's view. 'Childish, old-fashioned, dirty little mind, cease your crudities!' she retorted roundly. There was, could be, no other man in her life.

But all the resentment was not on one side. Stories reached Diana that Duff had been playing cards for high stakes while behind the lines; worse still, the failure of mail to be delivered for several days convinced her that she was forgotten. Her response was a wail of pain:

> 'I am utterly wretched. All my misery has given way before a new agony, the proof that you don't think of me. I fit all my actions to your whims, neither forgetting to date my letters, nor not to eat chocolates in the street. I beckon no new lovers, I take no pains to fetter the old, I even read for you and bone my meat, all this for someone who is as remote as God ... Queen Elizabeth, when she dubbed knights, said 'Be faithful, be brave, be fortunate'. I found it in a book yesterday and thought I would wish it to you tonight. It seems an irony now, when you prove faithless to me. I shall not write for a space.'

She did, of course, the following morning indeed, when a crop of letters arrived. Duff had been in the front line and out on patrol the previous night. He had had to fix the password and had almost settled for 'Diana'. 'Would you like to think of fierce men crawling about no man's land in the darkness and whispering your name to one another?' Once Diana knew that Duff was actually in battle her imagination took flight. One night staying with friends near Beaconsfield she lay awake till 7 a.m., planning for the worst. Duff dead, there could be no future then. Duff seriously wounded. To whom should she first appeal: to A. J. Balfour, Beaverbrook, the Quartermaster General? 'A threat of *suicide* if they opposed, and how it should convincingly be phrased.' What to pack? From whom to borrow money? Max Beaverbrook was the answer. 'My letter to Mother – all the wording of a frank and total confession.' Diana was accustomed to weave tragedy from the thinnest threads of misadventure; with her lover in real peril her fantasies grew fearsomely. 'No one but you among the fighting millions is thought of so continuously or adored more.'

Duff's luck held. He escaped injury, behaved with great gallantry, was singled out for his behaviour and eventually awarded the Distinguished Service Order, a rare achievement for a subaltern in the Guards. Diana thought it should have been a Victoria Cross and regretted only that General French was no longer Commander-in-Chief – 'with me and Ghastly Moore to show him truth, your fame should have excelled'. She was immensely proud of Duff's achievement, yet again quick to take offence when several days went by without a letter being received. She accused him of being so 'puffed up and bewildered with conceit' that all he could do was sit in solitude and think about himself. 'Oh, little Miss Lackfaith,' wrote Duff reproachfully, 'Lady Jealousy, Countess Petulant, Marchioness of Pouts, Duchess of Malice, Queen of my Heart – God bless you, God kiss you since I cannot.'

The war was almost over. It was soon clear that Duff would never go into battle again. Instead he contrived a few days' leave in Paris. For Duff Paris was the earthly paradise, city of infinite and subtle dissipation. He wrote to Diana, asking her how much he could or should tell her of what he did there. Her reply was the last letter he received from her before they were reunited:

> 'Tell me as much or as little as you enjoy to confess. You know that I want your happiness above my own. From your arrival in Paris I absolve you from all letters, sincerity, superficial thoughts. "Rush into the folly," baby, darling, tell me nothing or all, I shall love you the same. If I was forced to voice a whim it would be (a) that you absented yourself from felicity with your own caste; (b) that with the help of every known device you keep your body clean for me; (c) that you do not gamble.'

It was a generous letter, sincere beyond doubt; strange, perhaps, coming from a woman so much in love. It set the pattern for a lifetime.

FIVE

Marriage

The London to which Duff returned was superficially much the same as the city which his friends had left four years before. Many of the faces had vanished, but the dress, the houses, the social rituals survived. Man and master took off their uniforms and settled back with apparent satisfaction into their former rôles. There was no such conspicuous social revolution as followed the Second World War; the Unionists triumphed at the general election and the nation returned a parliament of 'hard-faced men who had done well out of the war'; Labour won only some sixty seats and the day when they might form a Government seemed still remote; the red flag was hoisted on Glasgow Town Hall, but its brief flutter caused only a *frisson* in the complacency of the ruling classes. The rigid protocol of pre-war society was never fully restored but the structure remained intact. To men like the Duke of Rutland, little if anything had changed.

Least of all had anything changed so far as the marriage of his daughter was concerned. Duff came back from the wars on October 31, 1918. As he walked into his flat the telephone rang. It was Diana. Duff passed the time till she arrived pacing up and down the room, wondering if it could all be really happening. 'She came, and all that I had hoped of happiness in the last six months came true.' The following weekend they went to stay with the Montagus at Breccles. Diana went to Duff's room but hardly had she arrived than Alan Parsons walked in. Viola was ill, he had gone to seek help from Diana but had found the room empty. All their good resolutions about flaunting their relationship to the world were at once forgotten. Duff pretended to be half asleep; Diana hid under the bedclothes; as soon as Alan had gone she rushed back to her room by another staircase and was ensconced there by the time he arrived to look for her again.

To go on in this way would have been impossible, yet Duff knew that in the immutable world of the Rutlands he was as unacceptable as ever. His D.S.O. counted as nothing against the fact that he was, in *The World's* amiable phrase, 'a mere lieutenant without fortune, title or position'. Without future either, in the Duke's judgment; a clerk in the Foreign Office in 1918 could achieve respectability but hardly greatness. 'I think by gutter journalism, shady politics and crooked finance we might climb to pinnacles of power and have great fun en route,' wrote Duff cheerfully, but the Duke would not have seen the joke. Duff had £300 a year from the Foreign Office, about the same amount of his own and £600 a year from his mother; no great wealth but enough to maintain a handsome standard of living. To the Duke, however, it was poverty; added to which Duff was what Lady Sackville described as 'a contemptible parvenu' and popularly believed to be a drunkard, a lecher and a gambler.

The situation seemed to be dragging on indefinitely with no one wishing to be the first to speak. Diana longed for one of her friends to take on the task. The Duchess interrogated Katharine Asquith, complaining that she could not sleep at night for fear her daughter might marry 'that awful Duff'. Katharine denied any knowledge of such a plan. 'It's a pity,' commented Diana, 'for the poor old thing needs acclimatizing – but I'm very glad it's worrying her.' In the end it was Viola Parsons who plucked up her courage and broke the news. An appalling scene followed, from her room upstairs Diana could hear her mother screaming and moaning and a night-nurse being summoned to administer sedatives. Yet still nothing was said directly between the people principally concerned.

It was ten days later, at the Victory Ball at the Albert Hall, that Duff finally bearded his future mother-in-law. They retreated to a sofa on one of the upper floors and Duff addressed her, to his own mind at any rate, with 'great eloquence and marvellous command of temper'. The latter was called for. The Duchess was 'insulting, illogical and quite impossible to keep to any point'. She started off on Duff's finances, then when he began to argue his case, said she knew nothing of money and cared less. It was his drunkenness she objected to, his bad character, his dissipated friends. The whole thing was a plot organised by Alan Parsons and Olga Lynn. Anyway, Diana did not even love him; otherwise she would not have gone to parties the previous week when Duff had been ill with flu. She had some reason for misunderstanding her daughter's feelings. Diana always found it hard to talk of love, to her mother she felt it was impossible. She never stated bluntly that she adored Duff and could not live without him; the Duchess, eager to believe the contrary, was convinced Diana was only advancing this ridiculous project out of pique or a wish to escape from parental discipline.

Next morning Diana at last confronted her mother. The Duchess was beside herself. She said she would prefer her son to have been killed in the war or Diana to have cancer to this impossible alliance.

Then she stormed from the house to recruit allies elsewhere. She did not find as many as she had hoped: 'Her Grace is raising tally-whack and tandem all over London,' wrote Ettie Desborough unsympathetically. Diana retired to bed, as was her habit in moments of stress, and by the time her mother returned to the battle some calm had returned. Her great cause for despair, it seemed, was that Diana's love for her was dead. Diana could have withstood her mother's rage more easily than her misery. That night, she told Duff, she dreamt that she and her mother were walking down a long passage at the end of which they saw Duff coming towards them. A meeting was unavoidable; so the Duchess said: 'This is fate, so see how I will make full reparation and greet him lovingly.' Open-armed and smiling she advanced, 'and I just remember seeing you raise your gold-knobbed cane to her when I woke exhausted'.

'Mummy is in an awful state,' the Duke of Rutland wrote to Marjorie Anglesey. 'I really think Diana will kill her.' If the Duchess had not been in an awful state, it is unlikely the Duke would have been particularly put out by these developments. He was a detached and easy-going man and could soon have been cajoled into acceptance of what most people felt to be a reasonable if not particularly meritorious match. The Duchess, however, offered him no opportunity to weaken. When Duff, fortified by a stiff dose of port, called on him at Arlington Street, he was met by a wall of courteous obstinacy. The Duke was affable, 'dear-fellowed' Duff liberally, admitted he had always liked him, but gave no hope of a change of attitude even if Duff reappeared in six months, with £1000 a year. 'This,' wrote Diana indignantly, 'is analogous, though more gentlemany, to kicking him out of the house, and a great insult to the man I have told them with holy resolve that I intend to marry.'

John Granby was now brought into the firing line. He was more temperate than his parents, but argued that a year's delay was desirable to give all parties time to think. He doubted whether Diana really knew her own mind. Diana's reply was firm:

'For many years I have wanted to marry Duff because I know that when I am with him I am perfectly happy, that his mind I adore, that his attitude towards me and love and understanding are only equalled by mine towards him. I am not a giddy baby of eighteen but sensible, calculating for my happiness and in this well tried, for I have spent all my time and thought for two years with and for Duff . . . If I gave you the impression that I was not fond enough of Duff to warrant the disaster I have brought on this unfortunate household, it is because I find tremendous difficulty in baring my heart, much more than my body, and even now it is costing me a lot to confess.'

She had a nightmare Christmas at Belvoir. John, Letty, and her sister-in-law Kakoo took it in turns to reason with her, and when she tried to discuss the matter with her mother, the Duchess turned the conversation to cancer and her own imminent demise. Her uncle Charlie Lindsay was most nearly an ally, but even he spoiled the effect by admitting that he had never seen Duff rise from the table completely sober. He too felt a year's delay reasonable and Diana at last agreed to put this to Duff. 'I could hardly bear it but suppose we must. Suppose we love each other less in a year? God, what a conspiracy of cruelty it is! Strengthen me, Duffy, I feel in despair.'

Early in 1919 the Duke wrote to Duff to say that if he would take no further steps regarding his engagement for twelve months, and the couple still wanted to marry after that period, then no further obstacle would be put in their way. The Duchess had prepared the first draft of this letter and scribbled in a covering note: 'I told D that I found you very obdurate and firm. I said this wishing to get out of her head that I was the only one against it, and that you would do anything I wished.' The Duke proved that occasionally he could ignore his wife's wishes when he crossed out her final sentence, which said that he could never look on the match with any favour, and replaced it by a promise to do all he could to help. He wrote the same day to Diana asking her to read the letter. 'In doing so I would urge you to remember that your mother and I are only anxious for *your* future happiness – their own don't much matter – and you must also remember that it is within the bounds of possibility that they may have a clearer vision as to this than you. Anyway, do not doubt their very deep love for you, which is the reason for their present action – as I assure you they are suffering for and with you, very deeply.'

By now the press was hot on the trail. *Cassell's Saturday Journal* gleefully reported that the couple would have to live on '£300 a year and a ducal curse'. Anything about Diana was grist to their mills; the *Bulletin* even announcing that she had seemed unusually pale at a recent weekend party. 'She explained that she had sat up all night tending a sick lily but that it had died at dawn.' The real explanation, it was archly hinted, was to be found in the failure of a certain father to pay attention to the bidding of his daughter's heart. The Duchess was so enraged by newspaper reports that an engagement already existed that she caused a formal *démenti* to appear in *The Times*: 'We are requested to state that there is no truth in the report that Lady Diana Manners is engaged to be married.'

Neither her father's dulcet tones, nor her mother's intransigence, affected Diana's determination to marry Duff. She was more disconcerted by the attitude of certain of her friends. Claude Lowther besought her to draw back. 'Don't, I pray you, bind yourself for life to some slave you neither adore nor respect – but for whom you may have a profound pity. You possess youth, transcendental beauty, genius and a darling nature. Don't for God's sake be weak and in a moment of despondency marry a man who does not even know how to love.' Tommy Bouch was equally discouraging. He could accept Duff as a fellow-subject 'but as soon as you raise him up to be King, the situation is changed'. He would return to his hunting, Viola to her drama, the magic circle of Diana's vassals would be dispersed. So much might have been expected from the former courtiers who saw themselves displaced; more surprising was the thinly disguised hostility of Edwin Montagu, who urged restraint and showed sudden and unexpected affection for the Duchess.

The rich old men who always rejoiced to serve her saw no reason to take any such line; Lord Wimborne and George Moore were both offering to pay the rent of whatever house Duff and Diana chose to live in: 'Few other couples, I wager,' wrote Diana proudly, 'have men fighting to pay rents, rates, taxes for them.' George Moore did even better and offered to give them £6000 a year from the time of their marriage. They discussed the matter and at first decided to reject it, but, wrote Duff, 'the more I think about it, the more I like it'. In the end Diana wrote to refuse the offer but in the tones of one who hoped to be over-persuaded. She perhaps over-rated her skill as a letter-writer. The £6000 were never forthcoming, though Moore deposited £500 in Diana's bank, guaranteed her overdraft and took a box at Covent Garden in her name. 'I hate the Opera,' wrote Duff gloomily. Meanwhile Beaverbrook paid £200 for four articles in his new Sunday paper which Diana was to sign and Duff to write.

During the period of waiting it was tacitly agreed that Duff would keep away from Arlington Street. Once, when the Duke was at a Garter ceremony, the Duchess away and Diana recovering from flu, she was tempted to smuggle Duff in for a quiet supper. Prudence prevailed: 'the risk of dignity suffering was too great, and besides the old bugger might have caught him in the courtyard and, being armed, would have belaboured him with his sword.' Inevitably they all met in London society. At a party given by Lord Furness, Duff and Diana going up the stairs met the Rutlands coming down. Duff decided it would be best to cut them, Diana thought anxiously of her dream, but the Duke looked benign and gave his daughter a playful tap.

The Duchess tried to distract Diana by taking her to Paris. The

Peace Conference was on and they saw much of Lord Beaverbrook who was with Venetia Montagu 'living in open sin at the Ritz in a tall silk suite with a common bath and unlocked doors between, while poor Ted is sardined into the Majestic, unknown and uncared for'. Beaverbrook enraged the Duchess by telegraphing to the *Daily Express* that Diana and her mother had come to Paris to buy the trousseau. They dined with the Aga Khan, a meal so memorably rich that Diana, who cared little what she ate, took the trouble to record the menu. Emerald-green oysters were followed by fine soup in which floated a marrow-bone boiled to a shining ivory. Then came what Diana described as 'souls in sauce' and with them, served on great flat silver dishes, frizzling soft roes. Chickens' wings resting on inky truffles gave way to foie gras 'pinker than Helen's cheek and cut like cottage loaves – in its wake a dozen fresh green asparagus apiece'. Entremet and Brie concluded the meal. The company was less satisfying, particularly the Frenchman who told her: '*Je suis très keen sur le sport. Tout l'hiver c'est le rugby et puis, l'été, le waterpolo.*' Next day she took a long and no doubt badly needed walk with the Aga Khan. 'I talked to him at length about my life, as I do to all who will listen. He was sympathetic and wound up with an offer to furnish my house – but I am losing faith in these promises.'

On March 25 the Rutlands gave a great ball at Arlington Street; the Queen of Roumania and the Prince of Wales dining there first. Duff went with Diana to Covent Garden in the early morning to help buy the flowers but was pointedly not invited to the ball. The Prince danced twice with Diana and talked to her at length. 'So I take it you are to marry the Prince of Wales after all, and Duff will be appointed Lord High Chamberlain,' wrote Tommy Bouch archly. The Duchess may even have cherished some hope of a last-minute miracle but she was given no satisfaction. The Prince asked Diana whether she was really engaged, congratulated her and said that he knew Duff by reputation and would like to meet him.

Diana had never agreed that the delay should be more than six months, and in April they debated anxiously what they should do when the time ran out. The Rutlands stuck to their insistence on the full year. Duff and Diana meditated defiance, then opted for discretion. Diana wrote a letter to her mother, half loving, half reproachful, in which she accepted the further delay. As in some jujitsu match where feigned submission throws the opponent off balance, the Duchess was disarmed by her daughter's unexpected docility. She told her that if she would approach the Duke she might get a better reception than the time before. Diana did so, to be met by total surrender. 'Don't go upstairs for a little,' the Duke said nervously. 'I don't want your mother to think I gave in at once.' Duff's interview the following day was equally friendly. The only flaw was financial. 'He said he would allow Diana £300 a year. I think he ought to do more than that. She costs him twice as much now.' Duff promised to settle a total of £10,000 on Diana, most of it from a trust fund out of which he could dispose of no more until his mother's death. His annual pay from the Foreign Office had now gone up to £520 and his mother promised to continue his present allowance of £600 a year.

'The engagement is of the romantic order,' announced the *Daily Mirror*, 'and the wedding, which is bound to be picturesque, will be on June 2.' The national press quickly decided that, in a lean season, Diana's wedding was the story that would catch the public imagination. Her presents, in particular, were fine food for vicarious romance as the rich and the grand emptied their cornucopias at her altar. The list occupied eighty-eight pages of a large notebook from the Army and Navy Stores. The King and Queen gave a blue enamel and diamond brooch bearing their own initials; Queen Alexandra a diamond-and-ruby pendant; the French Ambassador a gold ewer for incense-burning; the Princess of Monaco a diamond ring; Lord Wimborne a William and Mary gold dressing-case; King Manuel a gold sugar-sifter; Sir Philip Sassoon a paste basket brooch; Lord Beaverbrook a motor car; Dame Nellie Melba a writing-table; Augustine Birrell a first edition of *Tristram Shandy*; General Freyberg a handsome edition of Froude's *History of England*; Solly Joel a vanity box of gold and diamonds; Mrs Belloc Lowndes a first edition of *Edwin Drood*; cheques came from, among others, Sir Ernest Cassel, the Aga Khan, Lord French and Sir Basil Zaharoff, the last for £250. Sir John Lavery, Mr J. J. Shannon and Mr Ambrose McEvoy all gave portraits of the bride.

A few days before the wedding Duff and Diana went to the Italian consulate to get visas in their passports. Queues were long, bureaucracy stultifying, and Duff soon became bad-tempered. He snarled at Diana. 'Never shall I forget how her face, which had been all smiles and laughter, turned suddenly to tears. It was so beautiful that I could hardly regret it. It taught me how gentle I must be.' It is remarkable to what an extent he remembered this lesson. He never learnt to control his temper and would lash out when provoked with unthinking deadliness, but it was rarely indeed that his wife was the victim of his venom.

'There was more of the Duff than the Manners touch about Lady Diana's on the whole rather dull wedding,' reported the *London Mail* loftily. It is hard to imagine what antics the journalist was expecting. St Margaret's, Westminster, even when decorated with rose-bushes

and orchids from Blenheim, is no place for informality, and the formidable weight of royalty was enough to ensure that the conventions
would be observed. Diana sat forlornly in the sombre morning-room
at Arlington Street until her father came to claim her – 'his temper
was short and his gills were white and his top hat had no jauntiness.'
Once past the great wooden gates she was swept into a maelstrom of
clamour and light and headlong rushing from one point to the next.
There were crowds in St James's to see her go, several thousand more
spectators around the church, a still denser throng to surround the
house for the reception and finally cheer her on her way. 'Diana's
popularity with the mob is only comparable with that of Kitchener,'
wrote Duff in slight dismay. For Diana the day was a kaleidoscope of
half-absorbed impressions; the malign gnome-face of Lord Beaverbrook with tears coursing down his cheeks; the photographers jostling
for position and clambering up trees and lamp-posts; Duff holding
her hand throughout the service; the Tree grandchildren in Greek
robes scattering rose-petals before the bridal couple; the mad admirer
who burst through the crowd and thrust a letter into her hand – 'Read
this, read this before you proceed!'. Diana's mind rushed to the Ides
of March but the message only wished her well.

And so the car forced its way through the rampageous mob and the
couple slipped away on honeymoon. First stop was Philip Sassoon's
house at Lympne, left empty for them for as long as they cared to use
it. Opulent comfort, unobtrusive servants, fountains playing in the
smoothly tailored gardens through which they sauntered after dinner
while Duff read aloud from Donne's *Epithalamions:*

> 'He comes, and passes through sphere after sphere,
> First her sheets, then her arms, then any where.
> Let not this day, then, but this night be thine,
> Thy day was but the eve to this, O Valentine.'

'Our night,' wrote Duff, 'like so many of the main incidents in our
love story, was very old-fashioned and conventional.' The only unto-
ward incident came when he tried to turn out the light and by mistake
summoned Diana's surprised but gratified lady's maid. A day of
letter-writing, love, and reading the interminable reports of their
wedding in the newspapers, and they were ready for Italy and the
honeymoon proper.

They stayed for a few days at Bernard Berenson's villa near Florence, which had been rented by Ivor Wimborne. Duff loved the
library and the champagne, Diana the garden. After dinner their host
tactfully left them; the garden was full of fireflies; 'the scent of the
flowers was intoxicating, the moon was full. We seem to have reached

almost the limit of beauty.' Then it was Rome. Marconi had offered them his house, then gone back on the offer. Instead he booked them into the Grand Hotel. There was anxious speculation whether he intended to pay for them – he didn't, but as the bill was less than £2 a night for bedroom, sittingroom and bathroom his dereliction caused them little concern. Final destination was Lord Grimthorpe's Villa Cimbrone in the hills above Ravello – 'Byzantine cloisters, endless rose-gardens, cypress avenues, statues everywhere.' A thousand feet below lay the sea. After dinner and much white wine they strolled on the terrace. 'Diana's clothes fell from her and she stood by me naked as a statue but whiter and lovelier far. This was perhaps the most beautiful moment of all.'

There is usually cause for relief in the ending of a honeymoon. The pressure-cooker intimacy of enforced isolation, the feeling that it would be a confession of failure to seek other company than one's own, produce tension and a sense of constraint. Diana with her fear of tête-à-têtes, was peculiarly vulnerable to such strain. Yet in the event the honeymoon proved an idyll. On the last night she broke down and cried, Duff recorded, 'because we were going away, and she thought we might never be so happy again. Blissfully happy we have been here and it is sad to go.'

The journey back was beset with disasters. A storm at sea reduced Duff to agonies of sea-sickness. Diana was too frightened to be sick; every voice she heard was an appeal for help with the pumps, every thump the captain taking off his boots. Then they were stranded in Marseilles because of a muddle over tickets: 'I am bad at keeping cheerful when things go wrong,' admitted Duff. 'Diana is wonderful.' But his habitual optimism and her pessimism soon reasserted themselves. When they were almost on the last lap an elderly couple entered the carriage and settled down opposite them. Later Duff and Diana compared their reactions. 'One day we will be like that,' thought Duff with satisfaction; 'One day we will be like that,' thought Diana in despair.

'We are, funnily enough, profoundly different,' Duff had written in 1917; 'without loving me she likes me more than I could like anyone. One of the most remarkable things about her is the strength of her "likes". I am cold-hearted except where I love, her friendships are more passionate than others' loves.' It did not take a honeymoon to show Duff and Diana how sharply they differed in their emotions and their instincts; they had already realised that this was so and decided

that it mattered little. Duff was intensely sensual. Physically he did
not know how to be content with a single woman; even before their
honeymoon was over he was seeking diversions outside their marriage. But such diversions were no more than the gratification of a
nagging appetite. 'My infidelities are entirely of the flesh,' he wrote in
his diary. 'The long habit of promiscuity asserts itself. I feel guilty of
no unfaithfulness, only of filthiness.'

Allied to this craving yet distinct from it was his longing for
romance and adventure. Here it was the quest that counted rather
than the fulfilment. Denied consummation after a protracted hunt, he
congratulated himself on the fact that he was still young enough to
enjoy love-making for its own sake. He felt himself deprived if he was
not engaged in at least one secret and protracted love-affair with all
the fun of the amatory overtures, surreptitious messages, covert assignations, passionate declarations and, with luck, final seduction. He
could never quite believe that Diana did not share his taste. Once, in
Venice, she complained that Duff did not love her enough, or at least
not romantically. He tried to explain that happiness and romance did
not go together. Romance could not survive without the difficulties
and dangers. She was suffering, he concluded, 'from the same thing
as I have been feeling here – these perfect moonlight nights were
incomplete without some love-affair.'

Diana was suffering from nothing of the sort. The physical side of
love meant little to her, and with no wish to see any relationship ripen
into illicit intimacy the whole paraphernalia of romantic seduction
became a tedious irrelevance. Bed was an admirable place to sleep in
and useful for procreation, but she could not imagine why so many
men of her acquaintance were so importunate in their efforts to share
it with her. What she loved was companionship and admiration. She
had a genius for friendship, would work at it, make sacrifices for it,
display furious loyalty in its cause. With her husband this friendship
was transmuted into a devotion and commitment that was awe-
inspiring in its completeness. But if she had been told at the end of
her honeymoon that Duff had tired of sex, she would have received
the news with equanimity, almost relief; regretting only that the
chances of her having a child were thereby reduced.

Some people – most usually men who had not enjoyed the success
with Diana which they had anticipated – assumed that her coolness
towards men proved that she lusted after women. The legend of
Diana the nymphomaniac alternated with a rival version of Diana the
lesbian. The second had as little basis in fact as the first. She loved
beauty and appreciated it in either sex, but that was as far as it went.
'Don't tell me you want to hold me and love me,' she wrote to one

female admirer more than twenty years later. 'It only upsets me and will make me scary. All my life I've been a very normal type: worshipping of Duff; a few lovers; fond of men; and a happy companion of women – but no more, o no, no more.'

'Diana is the kind of wife who will always eat the legs of a chicken and give her husband the wings,' Lady Tree told her daughter Iris. 'Oh for the wings, the wings of a Duff,' replied Iris flippantly, but Lady Tree had identified an essential element in the Coopers' marriage. From the moment that she married Duff, Diana dedicated herself to his interests. Her judgment of new acquaintances was not based on: 'Do I like them?' but 'Would Duff like them or be amused to hear of them?'; half the satisfaction she derived from her adventures lay in the recounting of them afterwards; his success was her success, his happiness hers. Whenever he was out of her sight she worried about his welfare, in their London house she would rush from her bed to the window when he left in the morning to make sure he survived the crossing of the road.

Duff was required to be as much a father as a lover. To Diana at Belvoir he wrote: 'How cold it must be. Poor Baby! She must ask Mr Major [her dog] to keep her warm. Be a good little girl and above all obey Nannie – and obey obediently without whining or asking why.' Diana replied in similar vein – 'Up came poor baby's mummy, who cosseted her and comforted her and gave her a stiff Bromo Selzer, so at last she got to sleep and woke up brave and strong.' 'I'm so happy that Swift wrote baby language and that it interests instead of shocks,' she went on. 'I suppose it doesn't really matter if mine does shock though, for beyond Duffy these letters won't, I fear,* be very widely read.' One of the most capable of women if put to the test, she rejoiced in the myth that she was dependent on Duff to help her with the practical problems of life, and did all she could to propagate the image of herself as the innocent child, unfit to navigate the reefs of a dangerous world.

She recognized that Duff had different needs from her and did not in the least resent them. It was clear from the start of their relationship that Duff was not made for monogamy and Diana was more than content to share with others the burden of a husband's vigorous sexuality. Once at a party he swooped on an attractive girl and made conspicuous advances to her. Lady Cunard suggested to Diana that she might like to take him away. 'Why, he's not bored yet, is he?' asked Diana, who was enjoying herself. 'But don't you mind?' pressed her hostess. 'Mind? I only mind when Duffy has a cold!' On

---

*The biographer, always aware that he is intruding on others' privacy, is relieved that the word was not *hope* but *fear*.

the whole she liked Duff's women, knew that they were unlikely to last long and had a remarkable gift for retaining as friends women whom her husband had discarded as mistresses. When she did not like them – which usually meant that they had not taken the trouble to be nice to her – their reign was short indeed. Diana rarely made scenes but she would laugh at them and make it clear that she found them boring until Duff doubted his judgment and began to look elsewhere. Sometimes she seemed almost to procure for him. At Bognor they had a guest-cottage at the end of the garden. When Ann Charteris, who was staying with them, wanted to go to bed, Duff insisted that he should escort her. Anticipating a pounce in the shrubbery, Miss Charteris looked hopefully at another guest and suggested he should come too. 'Oh, no, don't spoil it!' cried Diana, urging the couple on their way.

But she was not incapable of resentment. One woman whom she particularly disliked was dismissed tartly as 'a silly, giggling, gawky, lecherous bit of dross'. Others inspired as much alarm as scorn. Daisy Fellowes was one of the very few who she felt posed a real threat to her marriage. Malicious, intelligent and formidably elegant, Mrs Fellowes was the daughter of the Duc Decazes and the sewing-machine heiress Isabelle Singer, herself previously married to the Prince de Broglie. Duff first met her at the end of 1919 and immediately took to her, 'Mean, cruel and beautiful,' he described her. 'She is the notorious Princesse de Broglie, the destroyer of many a happy home. I expected to find her attractive and I wasn't disappointed.' The discovery that she thought Flaubert had written *La Chartreuse de Parme* temporarily distressed him, but he rallied bravely. At Deauville in 1921 they met every afternoon for increasingly tempestuous assignations, while Diana resentfully went off for long drives with Lord Wimborne. The climax came when Duff deserted Diana at the Casino and went off to Mrs Fellowes's villa. Diana missed him, searched everywhere, decided Duff had been murdered and, frantic with worry, informed the police. 'I was terribly sorry for her, poor darling,' wrote Duff contritely. 'I fear she will never forgive Daisy.' What Diana found hardest to forgive was that Duff had been so inconsiderate as to disappear without a word and expose her to such cruel fears. Duff's assassination, not his seduction, was the threat she dreaded most.

Where she did feel jealousy she was ashamed of it. Diana Capel was too good a friend to constitute a serious threat, yet Diana could not hide her distress when Duff launched into an unavailing pursuit soon after their marriage. A painful scene followed one party when Diana wished to leave and Duff to stay. 'She blurted out in the middle of her

sobs that it was all due to her jealousy of Diana Capel and she had
hated herself for being jealous, which she had sworn that she would
never be.' Duff wished that she felt less strongly about it but was
flattered by her feelings. 'I do love her infinitely more than the other
Diana. I love also romance and intrigue and cannot live without
them.' He promised to see less of Diana Capel in future, but found it
hard to keep his word, and friends like Scatters Wilson and Ivor
Wimborne gleefully reported every transgression which they
detected. In April 1921 Diana planned a short visit to Paris and was
hurt when Duff encouraged the enterprise with what she felt was
excessive eagerness. Injury turned to indignation when she
discovered that Duff had intended himself to go to Breccles where
Diana Capel would be staying. At once she telegraphed Ivor
Wimborne to meet her in Paris.

If her object was to make Duff jealous, she had chosen the wrong
ally. Duff knew the limits of Diana's enthusiasm for Lord Wimborne
and did not take him seriously as a putative paramour. Chaliapin was
another matter. Greatest operatic bass of his generation, majestic in
stature, barbarously handsome, almost as celebrated a lover as he was
a singer, Chaliapin had dazzled Diana briefly in London before the
war. Now he reappeared to woo her in ardent French – '*Chère, chère
et adorable créature, je t'adore, ma belle Dianotchka.*' Diana was
almost swept off her feet, but her unwavering commonsense told her
that it could be no more than a fleeting fling. She flaunted her
friendship with him and even organised a dinner for Chaliapin to
meet the Prime Minister. Maurice Baring interpreted and Lloyd
George interrogated him on conditions in Russia, a subject on which
the singer did not seem to be conspicuously well-informed. But Duff
remained unmoved; after the dinner: 'Diana wanted to drive home
with Chaliapin, so I drove Diana Capel home – a successful
arrangement for all concerned.' He did at one point express mild
irritation when Diana dined with Chaliapin on two successive nights,
but the protest related more to the fact that he had been left to himself
in a week when White's was closed than to any real jealousy.

Chaliapin was to pursue Diana to Chicago in 1926 when she was
acting in *The Miracle*. He sat in the front row of the stalls and, after
the performance:

'came to my dressing room, red with love and bent on a romp.
Unfortunately, since learning English, he makes love in it instead
of the more veiled Russian tongue. As his choice of erotic words
wasn't too delicate I had a wave of nausea. He said he wanted to
have baby, he said, and I had a struggle with him in which he

pressed baby's white-washed hand on his placey. I tore it away and in so doing left a cloud of white.'

Reluctant to point out this consequence of his antics, yet still less ready to send him out into the world with the mark of shame upon him, Diana cunningly led Chaliapin to the long dressing-room glass and pointed out how nice they looked together. The singer concurred, but fortunately noticed the white stain on his trousers and put the matter right before venturing forth.

Though Chaliapin's fame and charms faded, Diana remained loyal to him and several years later abandoned the delights of a Sussex summer to come up to London and go to an embarrassingly ill-attended recital at the Queen's Hall. 'I loved him greatly in the days of his greatness,' she wrote. 'Now he is older and heavier and has lost his English public, it would be vile to desert him.' After the Second World War she received a letter from Chaliapin's daughter, who had seen her photograph in a Russian newspaper and identified it with the many pictures of Diana that Chaliapin used to hang on his walls. When she had asked her father who the girl in the picture was, he had merely replied that it was a very beautiful English girl whom he had loved deeply many years before.

Such romantic interludes were rare in Diana's life. She was at her happiest with a court of devoted admirers, female as well as male, who would serve her, appreciate her and to whom she was fiercely loyal. In the years after the war, 'The Boys', Alan Parsons and the lawyer St John Hutchinson – 'the arrogant, fearless, mirthful Hutchie' – were in almost constant attendance. Duff was occasionally irritated by their presence – 'Diana never seems to weary of that couple. I do.' – but liked them and was glad that they kept Diana diverted. Certainly he felt no trace of jealousy. Nor did 'The Boys'' respective wives. On the contrary, Viola Parsons and Mary Hutchinson both counted Diana among their dearest friends and seem never to have resented the time which their husbands devoted to her entertainment.

In June 1921 Duff and Diana returned from a dinner-party. It was the anniversary of their wedding. Diana went up to bed and when Duff followed and turned on the light he found her standing in the corner wearing her wedding dress. The romantic gesture enraptured him. Forty years later she could have done the same thing and he have been equally delighted. For all Duff's infidelities and Diana's distractions – perhaps, indeed, because of them – their marriage never staled. Not for an instant did either doubt that the other was by far the most important person in their life. When they were separated they wrote to each other every day. Duff always believed Diana to be the most beautiful, intelligent and delightful of women; there was no sacrifice that Diana would not have made to secure her husband's happiness. They relished the society of others; they were happiest in each other's company. Many would feel that marriage should be more exclusive, that endless amatory adventures are incompatible with a truly happy match. That was not Duff's or Diana's philosophy. They believed that a marriage as strong as theirs could accommodate other relationships, even the most passionate. If others thought differently, that was of little importance: the Coopers knew their marriage was a happy one. It was a curious relationship, but it worked. The success of a marriage can surely best be judged by the feelings of the two parties; by such a test Duff and Diana's marriage was not merely successful, it was triumphant.

Duff and Diana got back to London from their honeymoon on July 6, 1919, and settled temporarily into a house which the Howard de Waldens had lent them in Portland Place. To find their own house was a first preoccupation, but in the meantime Diana was fully occupied trying to master the motor-car which Beaverbrook had given them as a wedding-present. Duff never learnt to drive efficiently, Diana's style was individual and ambitious, immortalised in Evelyn Waugh's Mrs Stitch who, irritated by a traffic jam, took her car down the steps of an underground station and trundled briskly across the ticket hall. On her first day with the new car Diana rammed a milk-cart in Stafford Street and flooded the road. Luckily a dog-shop was nearby. The proprietor rushed out with all his wares on leashes and set them to work lapping up the mess.

All plans were soon disrupted. The Coopers were dining in the house of Norman Holden, a clever and drily witty stockbroker. After dinner they clambered on to the roof to watch a firework display being given in Hyde Park to celebrate the peace. Diana gave a sudden cry and Viola Parsons looked round, to find only her hat marking the spot where she had been. She had taken a step backwards and fallen thirty feet through a skylight, badly fracturing her leg. Guests were despatched in search of doctors and surgeons and Viola went off to tell the Duchess what had happened. She was out, but the Duke, in sombre mood, surveyed Viola balefully and remarked: 'I advise you to have nothing to do with them. They're a bad lot.'

It was to be three months before the extension was removed and Diana could even hobble about her room. She spent most of the time in the Holdens' drawing-room which had been rigged up as a temporary ward. In *Aaron's Rod* D. H. Lawrence described Aaron Sisson's presence in the bedroom of Diana – thinly disguised as Lady Artemis Hooper – as part of a string quartet summoned to entertain the invalid after her 'famous escapade of falling through the window of her taxi-cab'. Lady Artemis 'reclined there in bed in a sort of half-light, well made up, smoking her cigarettes and talking in a rather raucous voice, making her slightly rasping witty comments to the other men in the room... This was the bride of the moment! Curious how raucous her voice sounded out of the cigarette smoke. Yet he liked her – the reckless note of the modern, social freebooter.' Diana never ran to a string quartet but Asquith, who visited her several times, found her surrounded by flowers enough to fill two or three hot-houses and with never less than five or six visitors.

In spite of the rasping witticisms she was in considerable pain. Her leg had been badly set and it was to be nearly a year before she could walk freely again. She had recourse to morphia to help her sleep. Soon she became alarmed at what she feared might become an addiction. A hypnotist was summoned to replace the drug, but he proved wholly ineffective; Diana merely pretending to sleep when he was there and giggling with the nurse over her dose of morphine as soon as he had left. Duff took the threat of addiction more seriously than Diana. He constantly nagged at her to renounce the habit, she as constantly promised to do so and then relapsed. Nearly a year after the accident she spent a night with Katharine Asquith, came back the following morning and went straight to bed. Duff found her there at lunch time. 'I thought she was looking very bad, obviously suffering from a debauch of morphia. She at first denied but at length confessed. I told her how ugly it had made her look. Her fear of ugliness is, I think, the best preventive.'

Whether it was Duff's therapy or Diana's will-power, morphia was never allowed to dominate her life. It seems, however, to have been at this period that Diana developed the acute hypochondria that was so evident in later years. She always ignored discomfort, bore pain stoically, but reacted with extravagant alarm to anything she took to be a symptom of advancing disease. Though rarely afflicted when she was happy or busily employed, depression or boredom were enough to stimulate a plethora of spots, swellings and inexplicable aches. In July 1920 she detected a wholly imaginary hardness on her right breast and at once diagnosed cancer. The doctor pooh-poohed her fears but she persisted and grew almost hysterical. A second doctor was called in and carried slightly more conviction, but Diana's nerves were by now so turbulent that only a stiff dose of morphine would appease them. Fortunately she met the King of Spain at a ball at

Londonderry House. He danced with her several times, tried to put his hand up her dress and asked for an appointment. She told him there was nothing doing but was greatly cheered by the encounter and forgot all about her cancer. A few weeks later, however, it returned. Her morale became so low that Duff had to take a week's holiday to succour her. Sir Arbuthnot Lane was called in and said she ought to have a baby – unhelpful advice, since she had been wishing for nothing better ever since her wedding. In the end a Portuguese quack called Gomez announced that she did not have cancer but intestinal sepsis and a slightly defective thyroid. Diana found this both convincing and comforting, and all thoughts of fatal illness were temporarily dismissed.

When gloomy or afraid, Diana was apt to turn to alcohol. At the height of the cancer scare she wrecked a weekend party by turning tipsily to her neighbour at dinner, Cardie Montagu, Lord Swaythling's son, and reciting Belloc's malicious verses:

> 'Lord Swaythling, whom the people knew
> And loved as Mr Montagu
> Will probably be known in hell
> As Mr Moses Samuel.
> For though they may not sound the same
> The latter was the rogue's real name.'

Cardie Montagu professed amusement, but left early next morning for the races and did not return. This was not a solitary incident. At a ball at Covent Garden Duff found her half seas over with the Duke of Manchester – 'I got her away as quick as I could. She was uncertain in gait and speed.' A few weeks later it was at the Parsons's and the other party was Augustus John, 'who of all men I think the most disgusting,' recorded Duff. 'I took her away and was cross with her. She was most penitent.' She always was most penitent, but drink was too useful an anaesthetic for her to renounce it altogether. She drank partly because she liked it but much more to abate fears and dull nerves, and though she never became wholly dependent on it, it was a valuable prop in times of trouble.

While Diana was convalescing from her broken leg and Duff wheeling her around London in a bathchair, they set up house in a back drawing-room at Arlington Street. This was cheap, convenient and comfortable, but Duff pined to have his books around him and Diana wanted a home of her own. She found it in Gower Street, a pleasant and in those days quiet late-eighteenth-century street in unfashionable Bloomsbury. They took No. 90 on a fifty-year lease for £90 a year, rented the first-floor flat in No. 92 and turned it into bedroom and drawing-room-sized bathroom for Diana. What Chips Channon described as their 'tiny house' was big enough to accommodate a library as well as a drawing-room and five servants. In time they extended still further down the street, taking over the first-floor flat in No. 94 and making a bedroom and sitting-room for Duff.

The move from Arlington Street took place in March, 1920. Housemaid and cook had moved in a few days before but returned to Arlington Street at 3 a.m. in their nightdresses and covered with soot. They had heard strange noises, decided it was either ghosts or burglars, clambered on to the roof and screamed until the police came to rescue them. There was no sign that anybody had been in the house, but the couple refused to return until the Coopers themselves took up residence.

Gower Street was their home for twenty years. Long afterwards Diana described her first years there as being probably the happiest of her life, 'because I loved my husband so dearly and the war was over'. By the standard of most of their friends they were poor enough, but some rich admirers could usually be relied on to provide game, salmon or champagne and they gave lavish parties. Here too friends would help out. Rubinstein came regularly and would volunteer to play. He was endlessly accommodating – 'No, not *that* one, Arthur; we want *this*' – until one day he married, was immediately taken in hand, and never again touched a piano except professionally. At a typical party in July, 1923 the garden was illuminated. First Rubinstein played, then there was supper in the garden. Rose-petals showered on the guests, a Russian orchestra took up station and Chaliapin sang. Maurice Baring and Viola Parsons danced a comic, orgiastic dance. Hilaire Belloc sang *Auprès de ma blonde* and French marching songs. The last guest left at 4 a.m. The drink was furnished by Lord Beaverbrook; the food too was largely provided by others; music and singing were given for love. Immense expenditure in effort, frugality in money, was Diana's rule; and the result gave happiness to everyone, including the donors.

The mainstays of the establishment were Wade and Holbrook. Kate Wade was Diana's maid, who had joined her during the war and remained for more than forty years. Tall, phlegmatic, strong in character and physique, she grumbled her way through a lifetime of faithful service and became so much part of Diana's life that it seemed impossible things could go on without her. Holbrook had been Duff's manservant since 1917 and came back as butler after the war. Diana was perpetually infuriated by the bland satisfaction with which this paragon anticipated all her requests. 'We need some more coal, Holbrook.' 'I took the liberty of ordering it this morning, my lady.' Once she resolved to confound him and announced at the last moment that she wanted two greyhounds to take to the Portrait Painters' Ball, at which she was to appear as Diana the Huntress. 'Would it be prudent to insure them, my lady?' enquired Holbrook calmly. Within two hours they were at the house. 'I hope they won't bite me?' said Diana apprehensively. 'I have ascertained, my lady, that the animals are entirely docile.' Then it turned out that Diana had got the date wrong, the ball was on the following evening. Holbrook was temporarily flummoxed. 'I regret, my lady, that the animals are engaged tomorrow night. They have a prior engagement at the White City Stadium. I will, however, endeavour to secure another pair.' He succeeded, and Diana's greyhounds were the success of the ball. His omniscience, however, faltered when he accompanied Duff shooting, providing a flow of unwanted and often misleading information. As a hare lolloped slowly towards them, he hissed in Duff's ear in a tone of tense excitement: '*Very* large rabbit coming up in front, sir.'

Duff had now been promoted at the Foreign Office, to become secretary to the Under-Secretary of State, Ronald McNeill, but he was restless and dissatisfied with the pay. He had exploratory talks with Barings and Rothschilds but no firm offer transpired. He was consumed by jealousy whenever he visited the House of Commons, yet asked himself: 'Is it worth leaving a decent gentlemanlike job which may lead to an ambassadorship, in order to plunge into the cesspool of politics which can only lead to a few years of precarious power, during which one is the Aunt Sally of the guttersnipes of the earth?' Besides, he felt himself a reactionary who was out of tune with the times. He was both friend and admirer of Winston Churchill. At dinner at Wimborne House Churchill held forth in his most truculent vein. He 'said he was all out now to fight Labour, it was his one object in politics. He was a monarchist and swore we would have all the kings back on their thrones, even the Hohenzollerns.' Duff was delighted with all he said, Diana dismayed. Their feelings were much the same a few weeks later when Churchill rejoiced at the coming of a 'world wide movement of reaction' and said that Gandhi should be bound hand and foot at the gates of Delhi and trampled on by an enormous elephant ridden by the Viceroy. But Churchill was generally downcast, seeing little future for himself in British politics and saying 'if he had the choice between immortality and being blown out like a candle, he would choose the latter'. If his hero saw no chances of success, how could Duff hope to get on in politics?

Money was urgently needed if their life-style was to be maintained, still more if Duff were to abandon diplomacy and take to politics. Many projects were mooted. The *Sunday Evening Telegram* announced that Diana was to become a dress-designer, then that she was to set up as an adviser in house decoration – 'Can't you imagine how the profiteeresses would rush to consult her at ten guineas a time?' Gilbert Miller offered her a share in the management of a theatre at £500 a year, the proposition sounded hopeful but came to nothing. Then she was invited to join the board and subsequently become Chairman of a company manufacturing scent. She was to receive £500 a year for doing nothing, and gleefully accepted. The company crashed, the managing director was arrested, Diana threatened with prosecution for fraud and obtaining money by false pretences. Duff was sympathetic but as ignorant in business matters as his wife. Diana was grilled in court. How much money had she put into the company? None. How did she imagine she could be a director in that case? She didn't know. Had she never been educated? Well, not to speak of. Her patent ignorance of matters financial and her failure to gain a penny from the enterprise saved her from prosecution, but she left the court brow-beaten and abashed.

Journalism seemed more helpful. In 1921 she was appointed editress of the newly-conceived English edition of the French magazine *Femina*. 'A most thankless and wearing job,' Mrs Belloc Lowndes described it, but to Diana it was an agreeable sinecure. 'I said "yes" to everything all my life,' she once commented, and an offer of £750 per annum was irresistible. She made no pretence of knowing how to edit, hardly even went to the office, and did no more than contribute a few articles, mainly written by Duff. In fact she wrote extraordinarily well, with real originality and a vivid turn of phrase, but she had no confidence in her ability and froze into bewildered apathy if required to write 800 words on Augustus John's new exhibition or the latest style in shoes.

One problem was that she was generally required to write on fashion, and fashion bored her. She enjoyed new and beautiful clothes but did not find them a rewarding subject for discussion. Movements in hemlines or frills left her indifferent. No one was less vogueish than Diana. She regarded the *avant garde* with dismayed suspicion: Picasso's drawings were 'a drunk baby's scrawl'; Moore's sculpture 'boring shapeless lumps of polished basalt, as undesigned as unkneaded dough'; Hugnet's surrealist poems 'are of tomorrow, I prefer them of yesterday'. 'I have got to Godfrey Kneller and Watts,' she remarked wistfully to Cecil Beaton, 'but I got stuck at Cézanne.' This hardly equipped her to work on a magazine dedicated to the premise that every new quirk of style was the dawn of a new age. She went abroad shortly after *Femina* opened and returned to find that – transitory as the fashions it celebrated – it had already closed.

There were other papers. Diana contributed regularly to the *Daily Mail* and the *Daily Express*. Duff did most of the work. In February 1922, for instance, she attended Princess Mary's wedding at Westminster Abbey, rushed back to Gower Street, presented the facts to Duff and left it to him to write the piece over luncheon. One difficulty was that Duff found it hard to get on with the press Lords. Lord Rothermere was 'one of the most repulsive men that I have ever met. He looks like a pig and when not speaking snores quietly to himself. He is rude, pompous, extremely stupid, common beyond any other member of his family, utterly devoid of the slightest streak of humour or dash of originality.' Duff suffered fools no more gladly because they were millionaires or press barons, and Lord Rothermere was left in little doubt that Duff despised him. Nor was Lord Beaverbrook a friend. Duff distrusted him more each time he met him. 'He was rude to me and I to him, but I thought I scored,' Duff recorded with satisfaction; hardly a helpful attitude to adopt towards one who was proving a regular source of income. Nor did his habit of calling the *Daily Express* a 'filthy rag', even when its proprietor was present, do much to make for harmonious relations.

Fortunately Diana loved Beaverbrook and he her. At a ball at the Albert Hall in November 1919, while Duff was pursuing Diana Capel, Diana stayed with Beaverbrook in his box. Duff returned to find the maudlin magnate pouring out his heart, saying how devoted he was to Diana and for her sake to her husband. There was nothing in the world he wouldn't do for them; he was the best friend they had. 'He was very drunk,' Duff commented sourly, but the affection was sincere. The Coopers often stayed at Beaverbrook's country house Cherkeley. Once Diana decided to steal some blosssom from one of the more precious shrubs. She broke off several branches and hid them near the gate, meaning to retrieve her loot as she left. When the moment came, however, she found Beaverbrook seated on the grass near the gate in earnest conclave with another guest. He waved benignly as the Coopers drove past, leaving them to speculate whether his presence there was an unlucky accident or the mischievous thwarting of their project.

Diana was distressed by Duff's dislike of Beaverbrook but accepted that she could no nothing to change it; Duff for his part recognised that Beaverbrook's quirkishness, quicksilver mind and fearsome power were qualities bound to appeal to Diana, and made no attempt to interrupt their friendship. Diana took greater pains to reconcile

Beaverbrook with others of their mutual acquaintance. In November 1919 she gave a dinner at which Churchill and Beaverbrook, at that time on the worst of terms, were supposed to make up their differences. The party teetered on the brink of disaster, Beaverbrook was truculent and offensive and Duff, with some glee, anticipated an explosion. Churchill, however, kept his temper and by the end of the evening something close to a rapprochement had been achieved.

As much by his casual benevolence as by the work he put in their way, Beaverbrook came often to the help of the Coopers. It was the cinema, however, which brought the first substantial improvement in their fortunes. Diana had had brushes with this world before. When making his propaganda film *The Hearts of the World* D. W. Griffith had included her among a group of prominent women who had done much for the war effort. (When asked why he had included Diana he replied effusively: 'Because she is the most beloved woman in England.') Just before she married came an offer from Griffith of $75,000 for a three-month filming trip to the United States. The film was to be called *Women and War* and eventually appeared, without Diana, as *The Great Love*. The Duchess of Rutland was horrified at the thought of her daughter posturing in front of the cameras; then was told how much money was involved and became still more disturbed at the thought of her *not* doing so. Diana was greatly tempted and would have succumbed if wedding, honeymoon and finally the accident to her leg had not prevented her acceptance. *Variety* was not satisfied with so simple an explanation. According to that journal, the Duke forbade her to act in America. Diana appealed to the Queen and was told that if she disobeyed her father she would be banished from Court. To quarrel with her parents was one thing; to risk expulsion from the Palace was, *Variety* implied, something altogether too dreadful for Diana to contemplate.

She now fell into the hands of a decidedly inferior artist. J. Stuart Blackton had made a modest reputation as an innovator in Hollywood but his career had not prospered and he came to Britain more as a refugee than as a Messiah. Somehow he raised the capital to float a company and planned two films, in both of which he invited Diana to star. The news of this caused some indignation in the profession. Mr Geames of the Actors Association complained that a lady who took up acting was doing a true actress out of a job: 'Titled folk are, I admit, in a category of their own; but people who have to live by acting resent this sort of competition.' Diana took the remark to heart and put herself out to prove herself a true professional. Blackton's right-hand man, Felix Orman, testified to the success of her efforts. 'Lady Diana was most democratic and serious about her work ... the least troublesome member of the cast.'

Diana's first film was *The Glorious Adventure*, a foolish fandangle based vaguely on Carolean politics and the Great Fire of London. Diana played Lady Beatrice Fair, a stout-hearted simpleton who married Bulfinch, a criminal condemned to death, so as to escape her debts. She was hoist with her own petard when the Fire led to Bulfinch's release and his arrival in his 'wife's' bedroom to claim his conjugal rights. Inevitably all ended well; Bulfinch, it turned out, had a wife already and Lady Beatrice was reunited with her dashing young lover, Hugh Argyle. Bulfinch was played by another debutant, Victor MacLaglen, a former pugilist who went on to make a highly successful career as a film-star.

Diana was particularly incensed by the ineptitude of the history: 'Pepys is made a confidential pimp of Charles II, perpetually digging him in the ribs with a lewd *double-entendre*'; the costumes were out of period; horses in blinkers, something unheard of in the seventeenth century. Mrs Blackton, who fancied herself as a historian, not merely ignored Diana's objections but was so rude to her that Duff felt bound to remonstrate with her husband. The Fire of London took place in a warehouse off the Strand and almost put an end to the production by getting out of hand, destroying much of the scenery and at one point threatening to do the same to the cast. The film being a silent one, Diana mouthed any words that seemed appropriate. 'Don't be such a beast! Oh, please leave me alone. You filthy cad!' not surprisingly failed to repel MacLaglen when bent on rape, while a punch on his craggy jaw merely barked her knuckles.

Only twenty minutes of this film survive and the quality of the print is so poor that it is hard to be certain what it was really like. The epoch-making Prizma Natural Colour which was its pride has faded to a muddy sepia. Diana's beauty transcends the limited range of her expressions, but neither performance nor film can ever have been outstanding. It was on the whole well received. The first night was a properly glamorous affair, Selfridge's gave a window to a wax tableau from the film, the reviews were friendly, even fulsome. The Duchess of Rutland found the film '*lovely*, perfect,' her only criticism was 'Oh, why can't Diana be longer?' For Duff the film was adequate but Diana's performance sublime. 'Her gestures were replete with dignity and breeding, which of course one never sees in film actresses.'

The reaction of some of her more traditional relations and acquaintances shows how the attitude of society had changed since 1914. Before the war the fact that a duke's daughter made money by acting for the cinema would have outraged society, let alone when the performance involved being mauled lasciviously by an erstwhile pugilist.

In 1922 it caused a frisson only among the most diehard. A more common reaction was satisfaction that she had done it well; to have held her own among the professionals was felt to be in some way a victory for her class. Duff was not alone in finding sublime poise in her performance, vulgarity in that of everyone else. It was among the middle classes that indignation was most deeply felt. 'How can you, born in a high Social position, so prostitute your Status for paltry monetary considerations?' asked one anonymous correspondent. 'You THING!'

The only person wholly unenthusiastic was Diana herself. She thought little of the result and still less of the labours necessary to achieve it. Blackton's direction was uninspiring, the rest of the cast second-rate, both professionally and as companions; the heat lobstered her face and arms, the lights made her eyes smart so fiercely that she could not sleep and twice had recourse to a doctor in the middle of the night. She was, however, committed to a second film and would not have contemplated breaking the contract even if she had not had pay outstanding from the first film and feared Blackton would never be able to find the money if his enterprises were disrupted.

For her second and last film Diana moved back a century to play Elizabeth in *The Virgin Queen*. To look the part she shaved off her eyebrows – 'This splendid sacrifice to her sense of art and duty,' proclaimed the *Daily Mail* sonorously, 'is assuredly unique and should alone augur a happy career for the film.' They gave her clothes that seemed to have come off the local scrapheap and a crown 'which I did thrice refuse because it had been made for George Robey and not for Baby'. The result, as Diana complained, was to make her look like Mummy Wart Hog, so grotesque that the donkey belonging to some nearby children shied and refused to pass her on the road. She exaggerated – in her Holbeinesque headgear she looked spectacularly beautiful – but the film had little to commend it. Sir Francis Laking, who played Darnley, was another amateur, amiable, heavy-drinking and wholly undistinguished. Carlyle Blackwell as *jeune premier* featured in endless love-scenes, each more compromising than the last – 'I mind Carlyle's kisses too too terribly.' Inspired by his triumph with the Great Fire of London, Blackton resolved to make a fire the centrepiece of *The Virgin Queen*. Apprehensively Duff telegraphed next day to ask if she had been burnt up like Harriet or was still stamping around. 'A tamer or more wretched performance I never hope to see,' replied Diana. 'I never acted at all because the flames were so minute I could not believe they were filming. A good producer would retake it at any price, but by tomorrow Blackton will have convinced himself that it all went exactly to his hopes.' The film was shot on location at Beaulieu and Diana's separation from Duff was an additional source of woe. They rented a little house, but the servants installed themselves in the best bedrooms and Duff found the charms of a New Forest picnic distinctly limited. For Diana it was a dismal time; her leisure spent largely bemoaning the absence of Duff and the presence of Laking and Blackton.

Diana did not enjoy acting for the cinema. She needed the stimulus of an audience and felt she could never do her best before a camera. Her motives for filming were unabashedly commercial. Mrs Belloc Lowndes brought in an American journalist to see her and begged Diana to make clear that it was the urge for self-expression and not money that drove her on. 'Good God!' exploded Diana. 'It's only for money and distantly imagined fun. Don't let my grimaces to order be called self-expression.' She was well paid for her two films but the need for extra income was still paramount. Duff forwarded a bill for the rates while she was at Beaulieu. 'Can you pay them?' he asked. 'I have just done the Income Tax, the telephone and the gas and can do no more.'

If another suitable film had come up immediately Diana would certainly have undertaken it; *The Glorious Adventure* and *The Virgin Queen* had won her a reputation as a hard-working actress as well as a famous beauty. She considered making another Blackton film, playing Dorothy Vernon in *Haddon Hall*. To overcome her doubts about his grasp of history, Blackton proposed to hire Sir Charles Oman as adviser. Then came the offer to play in *The Miracle* and all thoughts of filming were put aside. While she was acting in America Greta Garbo flounced out of *Anna Karenina* and the part was offered to Diana. She wavered, and by the following morning Garbo was back again and the opportunity gone. Other potential employers were inhibited by the belief that her first commitment would be to film *The Miracle*, an enterprise that somehow never got off the ground. By the time Diana might have felt herself free to look for further film work, Duff was in the Government and she had other fish to fry.

For the moment it was a relieved goodbye to Beaulieu and the film industry and back to London. By now Duff and Diana had settled into a pattern of life which both of them found satisfactory. To some extent they took their separate courses. Duff was far less socially adventurous than Diana. He liked the company of writers and artists provided they were clean and reasonably decorous in their behaviour, but he was just as much at home with politicians. His spiritual home was White's, playing bridge for high stakes, drinking and talking until late into the night. His friends were intelligent, certainly, but they also enjoyed a certain raffish grandeur, a conventionality even in their eccentricities. 'I'm afraid I must confess,' he wrote to Diana, 'that the only milieu I really like is the "smart set". I hate the provincialism of the respectable as much as I hate the Bohemianism of the unrespectable.' Diana liked the smart set too, but they were not enough. She relished the genuine eccentric. Fecklessness, indifference to worldly standards, an inability to cope with the mechanisms of life, were to her endearing, while to Duff they were to be condoned in a friend and despised in others. They shared many friends but recognised that others were better kept apart. After a dinner party at the Maclarens', Duff commented glumly in his diary: 'There was singing and recitations, bad white-wine cup and hosts of Jews culminating in Sir Alfred Mond. I hated and Diana loved it.' Diana would have delighted in the singing and the company and not have noticed the badness of the white-wine cup. Duff liked his dinners well ordered and well cooked; Diana believed in providing good food and drink for her guests, but herself was equally happy picnicking in an attic with bread and cheese. She relished grandeur but did not need it to have fun.

High Bohemia was not Duff's style. He would have disliked the dinner-party that Mary Hutchinson gave for the ten cleverest men in London to meet the ten most beautiful women. After dinner crackers were pulled and Diana collected all the riddles, climbed on to a chair and announced that she was now about to test the wits of the assembled intellectuals. Keynes was best, but his stutter slowed him up so that he could do no more than tie with T. S. Eliot. Aldous Huxley would have done better had not, Clive Bell recorded, 'righteous indignation provoked by the imbecility of the conundrums, in some measure balked the stride of his lofty intellect'.

On the other hand Duff enjoyed himself more than Diana at a grand week-end party given at Belvoir in honour of Prince Henry, later the Duke of Gloucester. After dinner the guests settled down to Prince Henry's favourite game, which was Blind Man's Buff: 'it was played for two hours and the young ladies' dresses were torn and liberties were taken with the King's son – a fine success.' A robin had taken up residence in the castle and followed the party from room to room, perching on the heads of the guests and living on Petit Beurre biscuits. The Rutlands were delighted, but Diana gloomily announced that a bird in the house could only presage death. Prince Henry – 'who, by the way, is not half bad, a great deal better than

Albert,' observed Duff – was inspired by this to tell the story of the dove which entered the mausoleum at Frogmore as the royal family knelt in prayer on the anniversary of Queen Victoria's death.

'Dear Mama's spirit,' they murmured. 'We are sure of it.'

'No, I am sure it is not,' said Princess Louise.

'It must be dear Mama's spirit,' they repeated.

'No,' Princess Louise persisted. 'Dear Mama's spirit would never have ruined Beatrice's hat.'

The theatrical world was another in which both the Coopers liked to mix, though Duff considered that only the grandest stars and the prettiest actresses should be encouraged to venture beyond the footlights. Both Duff and Diana were easily moved at the theatre. By the end of Gladys Cooper's performance in *The Second Mrs Tanqueray* Diana was in such an ecstasy of misery that she had to be removed before the houselights went up. There was a party at the Eiffel Tower afterwards in honour of Gladys Cooper. Duff enjoyed it, but his threshold of tolerance was always low: – 'There was a terrible young man there called Ronald Firbank who writes novels.'

By the standards of most people their life was one of intense social activity. In the last three months of 1920 – a period chosen for no reason except that they were not abroad or in the country for more than two or three days at a time – they went to the theatre fourteen times and the cinema eight. They spent weekends at Mells, The Wharf (Asquiths), Pixton (Aubrey Herbert), Taplow (Desboroughs), Grimsthorpe (Ancasters), Blenheim, Ashby (Wimbornes), and several times at Belvoir. Duff passed, on an average, eight to ten hours a week at White's; time which Diana mainly spent with close friends such as the Parsonses, the Hutchinsons and the Montagus. They spent four days in Paris, during which their life became still more hectic. On only five occasions during these three months did they spend an evening alone at home together. And yet in no sense did they grow apart; on the contrary each was amused by and interested in the other's private life and each prized the other's company more and more highly. At the end of 1923, when they faced a separation of several months, they were rightly felt by their friends to be among the happiest and most complementary of married couples.

SIX

The Miracle

In the summer of 1923 Diana received a letter from Professor Max Reinhardt in Vienna. With the help of the financier Otto Kahn he was planning a revival of *The Miracle* in the United States. Would Lady Diana be interested in acting in it and, if so, would she please arrange to visit him at his home in Austria? Diana knew little about Reinhardt, except that he was popularly reputed to be a genius and probably slightly mad, but she had seen *The Miracle* in London twelve years before and remembered it well. It was a mime play, German in origin, which told, in music, pageantry and dance, the story of a young nun who was lured from her vows by the wiles of a *Spielmann* or Trickster. The nun took with her the image of the Christ Child, which was in the arms of the Madonna before whom she daily prayed. After her flight the Madonna came down from her niche to take on the nun's duties; returning to her place with empty arms when the nun returned, broken and contrite. With the nun came her dead baby, who was miraculously transformed into the Christ Child and restored to its proper place in the Madonna's arms. The Madonna's rôle was one of tranquillity and grace, requiring beauty, dignity and a capacity to stand stock-still for long periods while commanding the attention of the audience. The nun, on the other hand, demanded almost manic energy as she scampered from temptation to temptation, dancing to the tunes played by the *Spielmann*. It was as the Madonna that Diana was invited to play.

Her first reaction was delight; 'it would be such an adventure, and probably great fun'. C. B. Cochran had staged it at Olympia before the war, with music by Humperdinck and the lustrous Maria Carmi – in fact the daughter of a Genoese pastrycook but invested for the occasion with noble Roman ancestors – as the Madonna. For this grandiose production Olympia had been converted into a cathedral with a rose window three times bigger than that of Chartres, two thousand extras, enough incense to scent a hundred farmyards. Success was cut short by the unkind intervention of a motor-show, but before its closure it had been playing to 30,000 spectators a night. Reinhardt promised that the New York production would be equally spectacu-

lar. All seemed set fair; then came a long silence and at last the news
that the project had been abandoned.

Suddenly it was revived. Morris Gest arrived hot foot from conference with the maestro in New York. Gest would have served
admirably as Rumpelstiltskin—dwarfish in size, long-haired, perpetually in a dance of rage or ecstasy, to Duff he was a 'particularly
revolting little Jew'. He claimed that it was he who had selected Diana
in the first place. Walking down Fifth Avenue with Reinhardt he had
suddenly leapt a foot in the air and cried out: 'We shall have Lady
Diana Manners for the Madonna. She does not seem to touch the
ground when she walks. A more aristocratic, a more sympathetic and
beautiful woman for the part we could never find.' This cry proved
instantly persuasive. The financial arrangements for the revival had
proved complicated but were now settled. All that remained was for
Diana to agree. Gest had expected to have to 'pass forty-seven flun-
keys to see her ladyship'; instead, as he delightedly told the *Boston
Sunday Post,* 'with the true democracy of the real aristocrat', she
actually called on him at the Savoy.

Diana would happily have called on him at a boarding house in
Wigan if it had been necessary to secure the job. She saw him in
August 1923. Confronted by this obviously apprehensive woman,
Gest switched from the deference due to the real aristocrat to the contempt reserved for a true democrat, making her hold up her skirts for
inspection and beating her down from $2000 a week to $1500. That
still seemed a fortune to Diana and she was dismayed to discover that
she would have to be approved by Reinhardt before the rôle was
hers.

A week later, en route for Venice, Duff and Diana called on Reinhardt at Salzburg. There they were met by 'the funniest, most fantastical, spherical figure in *Lederhosen* and sky-blue, silver-buttoned
jacket, shirt open on a fat child's neck, round nose, round dark velvet
eyes, thick semi-circular eyebrows and ruthlessly shaved round head'.
This was Rudolph Kommer, Reinhardt's most trusted lackey, friend
and trouble-shooter. Jewish, more Roumanian than anything else;
Lytton Strachey found him 'a ghastly looking dago'; Diana loved him
at sight. He was called 'Kätchen' by everybody since the day Diana
had applied to him the slogan of a famous Viennese café-proprietor
who used regularly to tell his cat: 'Ah, Kätchen, Kätchen, it is
useless for you to park and crowl.' Supremely cosmopolitan, surrounded always by the most beautiful and expensive women, he held
court at the Ritz in London and Paris, the Colony in New York. How
he financed his lavish lifestyle was a mystery; people had thought that
Reinhardt subsidised him until one day the maestro was heard to

muse: 'What *does* Kätchen use for money?' Some said he was a spy; but for and on whom remained obscure.

Kommer was instantly enslaved by Diana. From the moment of their meeting till his death in 1942 his proudest ambition was to serve her. His adoration contained nothing sensual. Diana was often afraid that sex might obtrude in their relationship. 'I'm so terrified Kätchen is going to declare his love for me,' she wrote from New York. 'He said, if I stayed much longer, he *might* fall in love with me. I can't face it, darling Mr Duffy Dumpling.' She had no need to worry. Kommer wished only to bask in the light of her countenance and would no more have laid a hand on her than he would have answered back when Reinhardt berated him.

Now he took Duff and Diana off to Reinhardt's baroque palace of Leopoldskron. Duff was disappointed by the food and still more the drink – beer alternating with indifferent white wine – but Diana was enchanted by the great candle-lit halls, excursions on the lake, endless teas on the terrace with their host while Kommer translated their banal chit-chat with a zeal worthy of the most sublime philosophizing. It was seven days before *The Miracle* was mentioned more than casually; then Diana plucked up her courage, tied her head in a pair of chiffon drawers and paraded for rehearsal. First Reinhardt expounded his version of the story and did it so beautifully that she broke down and cried. 'Her tears seem to have made a great impression on him,' noted Duff. So, presumably, did her acting. That evening she was told the job was hers.

The appointment was announced to a fanfare of publicity. Diana was to enter a convent to get the right atmosphere for the part; she was to receive the highest salary ever paid to an English actress in the United States. 'A stage star,' proclaimed one paper, 'possessed of $10m by ancestral inheritance, who lives in the famous Haddon Hall, England, and has seventy servants, is unique.' But Gest had a still more ingenious piece of promotion up his sleeve. From the 1912 production he resurrected Maria Carmi. She, it was rumoured, was truly to be the Madonna. 'Something else is needed for the part beside beauty and charm,' Carmi proclaimed, and threatened to sue Gest for £20,000 if anyone but she played the leading role: 'It is my life. Without me *The Miracle* would fail. It is fate.' Alarmed, Diana telegraphed to know if she was still wanted. 'Come to America and I'll treat you like a queen,' replied Gest. 'Which Queen?' Diana cabled back, 'Mary Queen of Scots?' The rivalry between the two Madonnas became headline news, but Diana refused to play the part allotted to her by Gest, declining his suggestion that she should announce the Virgin had appeared to her in a dream and insisted that she must play the part.

In November, 1923, Diana set sail on what was to be the first of many Atlantic crossings. Duff took some leave and came along to lend moral support; his presence did not prove enough to still Diana's fears of storm and shipwreck and she eventually had recourse to the ship's doctor for a calming dose of bromide. 'I suppose there are any amount of frightened people like me?' she asked plaintively. 'Sometimes a few emigrants in the hold,' was his unfeeling answer.

New York proved a treasure-house of new excitements. There was a telephone with 'a curious sort of dial typewriter attached to the apparatus which you work to get your own number without the operator'. There was a radio which, at the press of a button, would leap from Chicago to Buffalo. There was a Frigid Air machine which made ice by electricity; a device Diana coveted and eventually persuaded the manufacturer to give her on the grounds that she would publicize it widely. There were delectable cafeterias: 'I mean those places where you can see what you eat before you eat it.' Diana found everything extraordinary and relished even what she disapproved of, including the décor which Elsie de Wolff had imposed on Condé Nast – tiger-chintz curtains in an eighteenth-century library, and a bedroom like a tart's with red satin amchairs. She flung herself into local society with the same zest as she did into the local traffic: 'she understands neither the workings of the car, nor the traffic laws of New York,' wrote Duff resignedly, yet somehow she always arrived at her destination.

Rehearsals took up most afternoons and sometimes went on until 4 a.m. As a foreigner and an amateur Diana feared a frosty reception from the other actors, but Maria Carmi, by her vanity and arrogance, did much to make the way easy for her rival. Rosamond Pinchot, who played the Nun, was still more of a novice, and any resentment there might have been at the intrusion of society beauties was aimed at her. The only problem was Werner Krauss who played the *Spielmann*. Krauss delighted in baiting Diana, making her laugh at solemn moments, biting her neck, pulling her hair, predicting disaster and threatening to flee back to Germany on the eve of the first night. Diana endured the torment stoically and in the end Reinhardt called the troublesome *Spielmann* to order.

Reinhardt was greatly pleased by the prowess of his protegée. After a few weeks of rehearsal Kommer delivered a portentous message from the master:

'(1) He is positively delighted with your acting. You are *admirable*. He never expected that he would have so little work or trouble with you;

(2) He is deeply grateful with the intense interest you have shown during rehearsals and he will always be grateful for the devotion with which you are doing your work;

(3) He is particularly impressed by the unusual skill and great care with which you are already expressing, even in appearance, the part you are going to play;

(4) He would like nothing better than to have you as his Councillor Supreme in all questions of costuming.'

There is no reason to doubt that Reinhardt meant what Kommer said, though in a letter to Helen Thimig he was slightly less whole-hearted. Diana, he wrote, 'is not my Madonna. Too much statue, but because of it and as such simply perfect, by no means unintriguing. A living wax figure and therefore touchingly childlike.'

Reinhardt's accolade arrived just after Duff had left for England and did something to restore her battered morale. It took Duff's departure to make her realise how much she depended on him. 'My heart seems to tear my body with pain for the loss of you,' she wrote on December 8, 'I don't know how I am going to bear it'. Duff for his part went home and passed two evenings reading and rearranging the letters Diana had sent him during the war. They wrote to each other every day and Duff was delighted to find her new letters as full of love as the old ones. 'How little I deserve all that expenditure of love' – a reflection which did not curb his extra-marital adventures but was none the less sincere for that.

One of Duff's last acts in New York was to call on Gest and insist that Diana should play the Madonna on the first night. Gest winked and shuffled and hinted, but would not be trapped into a direct promise; the continuing doubt as to whether Diana or Carmi would have precedence was yielding far too rich publicity for him to cut it off before he had to. Carmi refused to admit Diana to any rehearsal in which she was acting but spies reported that her appearance was bizarre and her acting crude and vulgar. 'I'm ashamed to be glad,' wrote Diana, 'in fact I am not, for it's all very embarrassing.' In the end it was announced that the two actresses were to draw lots for the privilege of playing first and Diana was secretly assured that she was going to win. An elaborate charade was played out. Carmi, who had refused even to meet her rival before this date, arrived 'terribly flash in black and diamonds with a left-handed languid greeting,' making Diana feel like a gawky bumpkin. The lot was drawn and Diana duly won. She raged inwardly at the beastliness of it all; 'that she should lose and that I should look so foolish winning, and that I should have to suffer the embarrassment and humiliation of cheating'.

It was agreed that, after the first night, Diana and Carmi should
alternate in the rôle. Pinchot then decided she too should share the
rôle of the Nun. Various possibilities were canvassed and discarded;
finally Reinhardt pleaded with Diana to take on this part whenever
Carmi was acting the Madonna. Diana's first instinct was to refuse – 'I
haven't the lines or suppleness required, nor the nerves' – but as each
possible replacement proved more disastrous than the last, her resistance was worn down. In the end she agreed and went for coaching to
the great Boleslawsky of the Moscow Art Theatre. She sought to
model her performance on Pinchot's, until Reinhardt saw what she
was doing and remonstrated with her. 'Ecstatic I must be, not animal.
How the bloody hell am I to be ecstatic, I wonder?' As she gained confidence she began to regard the part as rightfully hers. When Randolph Hearst brought his mistress Marion Davies to a rehearsal, and
it was rumoured that she was to be offered the part of the Nun, Diana
was indignant and meditated a protest to the management.

By now the theatre had been transformed into a Gothic cathedral.
'We got a cathedral in New York,' remarked the under-stage-
manager. 'I had a look at it. Fine it was. Did *you* ever see a cathedral,
ma'am?' Diana loved all the stage-hands, in particular the one who
observed the ballet of nymphs with baleful disapproval and muttered,
'I don't think it fits in. Lesbianism don't fit in!' Once the problem of
Carmi had been solved Diana's worst difficulty related to the Christ
Child. The management proudly produced a gross, snow-white abo-
mination which was wired for electricity and glowed like a spectral
foetus. Diana substituted a simple doll but every time her back was
turned the foetus reappeared. Only a spectacular explosion which
even Carmi could not have bettered secured the banishment of the
offending baby.

The first night found Diana 'haunted, desperate'. The play could
be a disaster, her own part the most painful element. By the time the
show was over and the audience had clapped and cheered for fifteen
minutes she realised her fears were liars, but still dreaded next day's
papers. In the event even she admitted the notices were spectacular,
though she complained that they concentrated on how many feet of
wire cable were used in the theatre and the money taken at the box
office. The comment she most appreciated came in a telegram C. B.
Cochran sent Duff: 'Wife's performance exquisitely beautiful
unquestionable work of sensitive artist with many individual subtle-
ties the result of thought and complete mastery of rare resources.'

So many unbiased observers praised Diana's performance
that one cannot doubt it was in some way remarkable. It is harder
to decide in what the quality lay. For half an hour before the play

began and forty-six minutes thereafter she remained immobile in a stone carapace on her pillar above the stage. Even when she descended from her eyrie no wide range of movement or expression was called for. Competently directed – and Reinhardt was a more than competent director – almost any actress of beauty could have been modestly impressive in the rôle. Somehow Diana contrived to transcend this norm. She had that capacity to impose herself upon an audience which is something quite distinct from great acting but is enjoyed by many of the greatest actors. At eighty-eight she can still command the attention of a crowded room; in 1924, at the height of her beauty, her presence was almost overwhelming in its impact. At no time as the Madonna did Diana do anything out of the ordinary; she merely *was* extraordinary.

'I think I must go on the stage proper in England,' she wrote to Duff. 'I really think I could be good, if only for the reason that I can concentrate so easily and gladly on it, and am such a good learner.' Never did she delude herself that she was a great actress. She sat next to Stanislavsky and was quite unable to see what he was going on about. Nor did she much care. But she did believe that she could muster enough technique to make herself a true professional. No speech was called for in *The Miracle* and the thought that she would not often be so lucky deterred her greatly. For a while she took elocution lessons with the celebrated Mrs Carrington, who was said to have bestowed the gift of tongues on a hitherto dumb John Barrymore. Unfortunately this teacher believed that language must be approached through character, psycho-analysis must precede speech-therapy. 'She's going to explore baby's personality,' Diana wailed. 'Baby *hates* it.' She decided that this problem would have to wait until she confronted it on the stage. Meanwhile, playing the Madonna at one performance and the Nun at the next; leaping, sometimes within a few hours, from the statuesque to the hyper-active, seemed to her sufficient test of her abilities. She described a typical day to Katharine Asquith:

> 'Nerves start about five minutes before the opening. I've had to give up even the little cup of coffee which I relied on for keeping me awake because it makes my hand tremble so ridiculously through the long stand. During this I have a home programme thoughtage – Duff and you and others and towards the end Maurice [Baring] and Hilary [Belloc] and via them to the Mother of God. Three or four minutes I pray to her but I am not sure the prayer reaches her as I am past concentration by then. My turn comes, I get out of the stone and do it sometimes beautifully, I think, sometimes

atrociously, sometimes sincerely, sometimes not, but the audience never knows, I discover, and the pundits who watch every night will say "You never gave a better performance," when I know it was my worst. There is a long pause in the middle in which reporters come and ask me what I think of American men and what make-up I wear. The stage again to wrestle back into my sepulchre, home by 5.30 to a bath, for one is black after a minute in the theatre. At 6.30 a dreary little dinner of beef which I hope will fortify but never does. Back to the theatre, always too soon, dressed too soon, so that one has to wait with shaking knees and sinking solar plexus. Out on the stage for the Nun's part, no time for fear, only lightning plans for taking breath behind pillars, of getting rosin for my shoes, four full changes of sixty seconds each, dressing-rooms dotted around the theatre.'

And so to the inevitable supper-party after the theatre and bed, if she was lucky, at two or three. It was a gruelling routine, made tolerable by the friendliness of most of her colleagues at the theatre, the confidence that she was a success and the faithful service of adorers like Kommer and Bertram Cruger.

No one can have loved Diana more fervently than Mr Cruger. He was a middle-aged American of better family than fortune, his main source of income a somewhat ill-defined job on the Parole Commission. Good-looking in a conventional way, his rimless spectacles and stiff collars lent him an air of respectability tarnished only by the bouts of alcoholism which afflicted him every three or four months. Diana viewed him with mingled affection and dismay. 'If any of you saw him I should, I think, die,' she wrote to Katharine Asquith, 'with his incredible nasal twang, three-syllable words and invisible pinch-noses.' But for all his lack of allure he was incomparably useful; dancing attendance at all hours, providing sandwiches and hot coffee when rehearsals dragged on towards dawn, acting like a shadow-slave at parties, 'he truffles out champagne for me and fills my glass while all round are parched'.

Cruger never braced himself to do more than make furtive grabs for Diana's hand in a cinema. To worship and serve was all he wanted. When Diana asked him what he would do when she had gone, he replied, 'I will walk in crowds looking for people who resemble you'. On such terms Diana would have been happy to retain him in service, but unfortunately Cruger had a long-established mistress already, who did not take kindly to this English interloper. 'The other woman is completely off her head about it,' wrote Diana. 'He is livid to look at and frightening. I'm feeling unnecessarily responsible, sorry for her,

miserable for him, and want only to be out of it, and yet haven't the
heart to.' For weeks Diana meditated giving him up and finally found
the courage to tell him they must see each other no more. Cruger's
response was to plunge into a swamp of alcohol and threaten to drown
in it.

Diana was distressed. She was convinced she was bringing Cruger
much unhappiness yet feared for his life if she did nothing to rescue
him. She wrote to Katharine Asquith for advice. 'If it were an
Englishman, Scotchman or Irishman,' replied her friend, 'I should
say don't worry. Men have died and worms have eaten them, but not
for love. But these Americans! One is dealing with a completely
unknown factor. Impossible to make a forecast or prescription. It
would be like taking the pulse of a pterodactyl and ordering it a
bromide. How can you know? You can only act on some sort of ethical
principle.' Diana's principle was that the quality of mercy should not
be strained. Cruger, haggard and distraught, was given an interview.
'He was half-crying and twitching, a dreadful picture of misery, and
I'm ashamed to say I rather enjoyed a tremendous feeling of strength
and knowledge that I could get him right.' To Cruger's delight and
Diana's relief (for she had missed his company as well as the early
morning coffee) the relationship was resumed.

Bertram Cruger was not the only admirer to ease her passage in
those first few months in New York. George Baker Senior, a commodities millionaire, was at her day and night with senile fervour.
'The old bugger asked me to stay with him,' Diana told Duff. 'It
would mean a Rolls Royce at the door always but, I'm told, no hope of
a cent in his will.' She was tempted to move in all the same, if only to
tease Baker's daughter who was frantic with worry lest this adven-
turess should marry her father and make off with the family fortune.
In the end, however, the thought of holding him perpetually at bay
proved too forbidding; besides, the saving would not have been considerable for 'my publicity has become so colossal that I hope to get a
clean sheet for hotel bill'.

Her mother would anyway not have approved. Delighted at the
prospect of seeing her daughter starring on the New York stage, the
Duchess of Rutland had set off in pursuit and taken up residence in
the same hotel. Diana, anyway forlorn after Duff's departure, was at
first quite pleased by the visitation: 'She will make cocoa for me and
give me a tonic and chatter to Wade.' But soon the two women were
on each other's nerves. The Duchess was perpetually at the theatre,
sketching the cast, advising on décor, wandering around behind the
scenes. She seems in fact to have been generally well liked, but to
Diana it felt as if her mother was making her position impossible,

always 'tearing around, whining, crying, saying I am being outraged, put upon, overworked, and what not, till I am so ashamed of her I can scarcely keep from silencing her roughly'. The two women egged each other on to excesses of economy, eating, if at all, in the cheapest cafeterias and more often boiling up rice pudding in the apartment at their hotel. Marjorie Anglesey, alarmed at reports of her sister's loss of weight, sternly rebuked the Duchess. 'Diana's natural food, as mouse is to the cat or fish is to the seal, is lightly roast beef of Old England. She takes four heaped helpings if you give her the chance and you are feeding her on peptonised cocoa. This I know to be wrong considering the work she seems to be expected to do. It is equivalent to feeding said cat on mosquitoes or said seal on Gentleman's Relish.'

'Please Duffy Dumpling, get my mummy home, somehow, please,' besought Diana, after the Duchess had been on the scene for several weeks. Perhaps the Duke could be induced to cable saying that he was missing his wife and wanted her back? Duff consulted his brother-in-law, John Granby, who reported that the Duke had never been happier in his life and was dreading the day of the Duchess's return. It was more than four months after the arrival, and towards the end of Diana's first season in New York, that the Duchess finally put to sea. Then at once Diana was overwhelmed by contrition, seeing her sail away, installed as a final economy in a third-class cabin, 'some bolting-hole of beastliness among the lower barnacles,' leaving behind 'her last real fun in life and going back to grumpiness and monotony'.

Once she had gone Diana realised to the full how lonely she was and how much she was missing Duff. Everything suddenly seemed to be going wrong: 'I've a growth on the sole [or as Diana expressed it "the soul"] of my foot and the chiro buggered it up and I broke my record and couldn't appear yesterday'; it would take her four more weeks to pay off her tax; the Prince of Wales was in New York but he had never visited *The Miracle*; 'it's all black as night'. The best consolation she could find lay in assuring herself that to live in misery with some hope of future happiness was safer than to live in happiness with the constant fear of future misery. This thin comfort was supplemented by the arrival on the *Aquitania* of a Bedlington puppy called Major II after their dog in London. It took Cruger two days of negotiation to get Major II through immigration, since he had first 'to give a true account of his ancestry and his health, and what's more, he's got to promise not to roger while he's in the States,' but in the end officialdom was satisfied and Major II replaced the Duchess at the hotel.

Though Diana had innumerable acquaintances in New York and could dine out or go to parties as often as she felt inclined, she missed the hard core of intimates with whom she could relax. Most of all she missed Duff. 'I want you, Duffy,' she wrote. 'I need you. I'm famished for rocking and loving and being nonsensical and kissed and laughed at.' On April 1, 1924, Diana opened a letter from Duff and read:

'My dear Baby. I don't love you any more. I meant to have told you this before, but I didn't like to hurt you. The knowledge has gradually been forcing itself on me. Of course I shall always be very fond of you but ever since I met [end of page] Yah! Boo! April Fool!'

Diana would have found the joke funnier if it had not echoed her secret fears. Separated from Duff, she found it impossible to believe that he would continue to care for her. 'Do you still love me?' she once cabled anxiously. 'Her ladyship enquires whether you still love her,' the lugubrious voice of Holbrook informed Duff as he drank with his cronies at Buck's. She continued to grumble about Daisy Fellowes and Duff's other paramours. Duff professed great indignation at her accusations. Mrs Fellowes was at Monte Carlo, another candidate 'whore de combat,' if Diana would make a list of people he was to avoid he would be happy to obey. 'When I think of my bachelor existence and your vile suspicions, my blood boils. Last week I dined six nights at the club, the seventh was in the company of my sister Sybil. If I do so again you will no doubt begin muttering about Lord Byron and Augusta Leigh. You beast, you beast, you horrid little, dearly-beloved beast!' It was not so much the thought of other women that disturbed Diana as 'a feeling that I cannot dismiss that you are learning to do without me, that your pangs of separation are less sharp. What am I losing to gain this miserable triumph and these few dollars?' It was, she complained, a sailor's marriage with her the sailor; and Duff was not cut out to play the part of a male Penelope waiting dutifully for his Odyssean bride.

Meanwhile Diana addressed herself doggedly to the task of making the 'few dollars' needed for Duff to be able to throw up the Foreign Office and take to politics. Another £1000 a year would suffice, and 'if we can't pick that up with journalism, directorships, smiles, artful-dodging – we are not worth it'. Even with her mother gone she continued to scrimp and save, cadging the most unlikely perquisites in the name of publicity, ruthlessly beating down couturiers and hoteliers. The price of everything appalled her, taxis started at 19/6d, every dish – 'sole, succotash, gallumagetty grandmother style or veal cutlets' – always cost $2. Her life was transformed when she discovered a restaurant near the theatre where she could get a plate of spaghetti for ten cents. Meanwhile Duff week-ended in Paris, ate and drank lavishly, visited theatres, night-clubs, brothels; came back, went to Buck's, dined, drank a bottle of champagne, lost £8 at bridge; and was amazed at being overdrawn. 'It is most disheartening, I indulge in no extravagances.'

Diana's earnings were now expanding to a point where they could cover even Duff's most energetic economies. After a fierce battle with the management she got her pay raised by $150 a week, with $50 extra for each matinée. It was the extra-theatrical enterprises, however, that brought her the most striking rewards. Otto Kahn put her into property development in Florida and within a few months her $5000, anyway provided by Kahn, had swollen to $30,000. A flaw was that the money never actually seemed to be there if wanted, but the profit on paper appeared massive – 'So go ahead Mr Dumphy and don't deny yourself *noffing*.' A testimonial for Pond's Cold Cream was worth $1000, a signature at the end of an article for the Hearst press as much again. Diana speculated whether it could be right to sacrifice dignity in this way. Duff was robust: 'Cast dignity to the winds while in New York and get the Yanks' money so that you may be able to resume dignity in Europe!' It was Diana, however, who proved robuster when the depredations of the Inland Revenue were in question. She was outraged when it was suggested tax might be levied on her American earnings: 'I *won't* pay tax on this money. Why can't I say my salary was exaggerated for publicity purposes? They can't possibly look in Gest's books and I luckily have no contract.' This time it was Duff who had qualms. You must tell the truth, he urged her: 'otherwise we shall end in gaol as sure as eggs is eggs. Besides, it's very wicked to tell lies. When the poor unemployed do it they get sent to prison at once.'

By now it was clear that *The Miracle* would be revived the following autumn, so when Diana was asked to stay on for another month and add a further £1800 to the nest egg, she was inclined to refuse. Duff urged her to accept and promised to come out and collect her if she did so. Reluctantly she agreed; there was no one to talk to but Cruger and 'he's a slave lover, no fun, so I shall be deathly lonely'. Worse than the loneliness was the fear that Duff would have grown away from her and they would find it impossible to get on terms again. There was indeed some constraint at first but it soon wore off. Bertram Cruger's sister-in-law Pinna, a formidable beauty much courted by the Prince of Wales, meditated an assault on Duff's virtue. Then she heard the Coopers talking and laughing together in their bedroom. 'We sounded so happy,' recorded Duff, 'that she realised there was no place for me in her life.'

On May 30, 1924, came the last performance of the season. The whole company assembled outside the theatre to cheer Diana as she left. Gest told Duff that he had never known a star so unanimously beloved. His words were no doubt tailored to his audience, but Diana had won the affection as well as the respect of all involved. She had proved herself not merely a shining success at the box office but the equal of any professional in resourcefulness, stamina and cheerfulness under adversity. No one doubted that *The Miracle* would be gravely impaired if it went on tour without her.

Her respite lasted only three months before Duff and she were on the Atlantic again. This time the Prince of Wales was aboard, with the Mountbattens as escorts. Diana was assured by all the pressmen that she was a close friend of the Prince's and lived in terror lest he might fail to recognise her and send her stock tumbling in New York. This fear was soon dispelled, but she then found herself offered enormous sums to report to the Hearst Press on what he ate for breakfast, how long he spent in the lavatory and other such details of the royal life at sea. She refused, mainly because she could think of nothing to say. The only story of any note seemed to concern the tug-of-war team, of which the Prince and Duff were members and which Mountbatten organised on the most scientific principles. He challenged the American champions and was confident of victory but, alas for science, brawn triumphed over brain, and sceptre and crown came tumbling down in ignominious defeat.

For the next three autumns and winters Diana toured the United States in *The Miracle*. The reception was always enthusiastic, sometimes spectacular; she was fêted, mobbed in the streets, placarded across the newspapers; *The Miracle* transformed the life of every city in which it was performed and for hundreds of thousands of Americans *The Miracle* was Diana. She loved the glory and the money that came with it, but the pleasures of American provincial life soon staled and she hankered after Duff's love and the comforts of home. Cleveland, the first stopping-place, in some ways stood for the rest. 'It's worse than words have power to tell,' Diana wrote. 'To start with, climatically, it's polar-deep snow and blizzard biting across Lake Erie. This enormous hotel is fustier and mustier than an old Great Eastern compartment and the hall is like Liverpool Street Station on Whit Monday.' Every day the *Cleveland Plain Dealer* reported the mortalities from cold and fire. 'I die of both in a mild way – because I won't wear enough clothes and can't regulate the heating apparatus.' 'Cooked and coma-ed,' she would await Kommer's morning telephone call. 'That starts the melancholy day, and after a few moments groaning and complaining and upsetting him,' she would clamber from bed. In the afternoon, if there were no matinée, she and Kommer would go to the cinema. Then she would read Proust and he the scripts of plays, before a tediously teetotal supper. After the evening show would come milk and oysters in the hotel bedroom, then, just as she pined for sleep, an hour-long telephone call from Cruger in New York – 'I know it's costing him £5 for three minutes, yet if I cut the talk short he's hurt.'

Ten thousand people a night crammed the Civic Hall at Cleveland and four or five times a week there were luncheons with the city fathers in their pompous mansions or receptions at a Woman's Club where '1600 women passed in single file shaking hands and saying "I certainly am charmed, Lady Manners!"'

'In Cincinnati,' as Iris Tree wrote of a later stage of the tour,
'Everyone asked us to a party
Because we act in *The Miracle*
And Americans are so hysterical.'

Occasionally there were variations to this routine. Once it was Siamese twins in the audience. 'No one looked at the play and *they* couldn't see it, 'cos they sit almost back to back as if they were mad at each other.' At the end the half-dressed cast forced their way to the door to see the distinguished visitors depart, but somehow the twins had slipped away. At one matinée Diana began to sway on her pillar and realised she was about to faint. She bit her cheek until the blood came but could not clear her head. Pinchot heard her cry for help but could think of nothing to do and in the end Diana crumbled to the ground, missing by inches the spikes and candles that clustered round her eyrie. Within three minutes she was on her pillar again and that evening she acted the Nun. 'It comes, of course, from a healthy life,' she complained. 'Not a drink since I've been here! I feel ridiculously sick and miserable.' On another occasion an insect settled on Diana's face and tormented her by crawling up her cheek and around her eye. Fortunately it was an election night in England. Diana told herself that if she moved a thousand votes would be lost to Duff, and the insect did its worst to no avail.

Visitors from New York, or better still London, were vastly welcome, but Diana's morale was so low that she was unusually censorious. Gertrude Lawrence and Beatrice Lillie were in town. Bea was 'the sweetest woman' but Gertie was 'so common one feels that she has nits in her hair, so kitchen-maidy'. (The comment, it is fair to say, was made only after Diana had been subjected to a particularly exuberant Lesbian party which left her cowering in disapproval on a

stiff chair in the corner.) Lesbianism was always a threat. In Boston
Diana and a female admirer were being driven home by young Mr
Harvey Brown. The admirer swooped, head on Diana's neck, fingers
fumbling at her breast. 'You look more like a Madonna than ever',
commented Mr Brown as he tried to see what was going on in the
back. Although it was 3 a.m. her would-be lover insisted on coming to
Diana's room. Diana, who was preoccupied not so much by fears of
rape as her wish not to hurt anybody's feelings, was dismayed, but
luckily Kommer was in attendance. The admirer was eventually
despatched, satisfied that Diana had a prior and heterosexual engagement. "Poor woman, I think it was perhaps more drink than lust,"
was Diana's temperate conclusion.

Boston she hoped would be more congenial but her initial reaction
was as sour as it had been in Cleveland. 'We might as well be in Inverness for all the excitement or variety we get,' wailed Diana. Boston
was known by all connected with the theatre to be the vilest of cities.

Gradually the enthusiasm of the Bostonians overcame her doubts.
As she walked down the street florists dashed out to press roses on
her, many shop-windows were dressed Miracle-style, Morris Gest
was held by cultured Bostonians to be the only Jew of merit since
Jesus Christ. In the flamboyantly extravagant Morisco-style hotel,
everything was offered free and the rarest fruits and wines were
lavished on the honoured guest: 'The proprietor is a young successful
bugger. I shall have to give him a solid gold enema or something else
he'd really like.' The Duchess of Rutland reappeared, and took
Paderewski to *The Miracle*. After the performance he refused to go
behind stage, not wishing to break the spell: 'He thought it wonderful
and Diana most excellent. He was enraptured and said to me "She is
seraphic".' More than 120,000 Bostonians saw the performance and,
if the *Boston Sunday Post* is to be relied on, any lingering reservations
of Diana's must have perished on the last night when the vast audience cheered her so long and so enthusiastically that the cast joined in
and 'accorded the beloved star a farewell certainly greater than in any
other city'.

A long stay in Chicago was brightened by the presence of Noel
Coward. Two years later Clifton Webb found in his dressing-room
the grim graffito 'Noel Coward died here', but at the time he seemed
cheerful enough. He had his mother with him, and Mrs Coward and
the Duchess struck up an unlikely rapport, shopping busily for bar-
gains with which to cosset their children. Coward and Diana went
together to visit the house of a celebrated architect, rich with glass-
floored Turkish baths and black satin love-nests. They speculated on
the sexual proclivities of the proprietor and decided that a romp with

both of them had probably been intended.

What should have been another triumphant visit was marred by the curious affair of Dr Henry Schireson. Dr Schireson was a facial surgeon who specialized in removing signs of wear and tear from the faces of ageing beauties. Diana was only thirty-four but she was worried about a small patch of sagging tissue below the left eye. She believed that the doctor was to deal with this for love, or at least for the credit of having worked on so celebrated a beauty. Dr Schireson did not agree and duly put in a swingeing bill for $1000. Diana, according to the doctor, said there must be some mistake, smiled amiably, tore up the bill and promised to recommend him to her friend the Queen of Roumania. Dissatisfied, the doctor sued and the journalists buzzed thickly around Diana when she arrived in New York on her way home. She lost her head and denied that the doctor had ever touched her. 'There is nothing new about me!' she cried dramatically. 'Look! Am I any different from when you last saw me?' The journalists tended to give her the benefit of the doubt and her rapid retreat tourope nipped a promising scandal in the bud. That Schireson's charge was exorbitant and Diana to some extent misled seems clear; but so also does Diana's reluctance to pay out money if she could avoid it and the panic which led her to lie about her operation.

Even back in Europe for the summer she could not wholly escape *The Miracle*. In 1925 she went to Salzburg to play the Madonna in a Festival production. To create a Gothic cathedral and improvise an astonishingly complicated production within the space of a few days proved well beyond the powers of all concerned; only a few hours before the first performance Diana was wandering around the theatre plaintively demanding of everyone she met: '*Wird niemand mir ein Kind machen?*' On the night all turned out reasonably well: Duff thought the production worse, but his wife decidedly better, than in New York; the doyen of German actors declared that Diana could only be compared with Duse; while Gladys Cooper thought her Madonna 'a really fine piece of work' and tried to organize a London season in which she and Diana would alternate the two rôles.

English friends abounded, notably Maud – now styling herself Emerald – Cunard. Lady Cunard was at her most fractious; grumbling about the heat, the wasps, the theatre seats; complaining that the standard of the music was lower than that of Norwich. Duff charitably assumed that her ill-temper was caused by the change of life, but his tolerance was strained when she followed him to Venice.

He took her to a cabaret where a woman danced wearing nothing but a sanitary towel and a live snake. Maud 'cheered up wonderfully and showed symptoms of an incipient orgasm. When last seen she was asking the concierge for the number of the snake's room.'

Another visitor to Salzburg was Iris Tree; 'that perpetual renewer of spirits,' as Diana described her, 'that dearest romantic in clown's clothes'. Diana conceived the idea that Iris should return to America to act the Nun, overrode her objections, talked Reinhardt into acceptance, and the thing was done. To have an old and close friend with her when touring America made an inestimable difference to Diana. Iris Tree's Nun, said the Duchess, was gentler than Pinchot's, 'less athletic and tender, though in many ways doesn't come *near* Diana's rendering', but it was her company, not her acting, that was truly valued. Emotionally tempestuous; perpetually in love, though rarely with the same man for more than a few days; exuberant, extravagant, she threw a baked apple at Kommer when he complained about her endless long-distance telephone calls, followed it with a cup and saucer, burst into tears and ended in a paroxysm of laughter. She scattered her love-letters everywhere and left Diana divided between jealousy at her conquests and outrage at the untidiness of her life.

Together they toured the Mid-West and California. In San Francisco Noel Coward gave a party for them. In Los Angeles it was William Hearst who fêted her. She was sickening of her travels. 'I cannot shake off my melancholy and prejudice against everything around me here. The people are more common, worse dressed, less amusing, more mushy and soiled and tousled and unchic than is believable. All the women are blowzy blondes, all their hair is lemon-coloured and their faces pasty from lack of rouge.' She sat next to John Gilbert, super-star of the silent cinema, and found him 'good-looking and terrificly conceited. He called me "darling" from the start, but I liked that.' They drove to Taos to visit D. H. Lawrence but found him away. Brett was there, 'middle-aged, fat and rabbit-faced,' dismayed to find Iris and Diana were on the stage.

Iris's promiscuity filled Diana with vague discontent. She knew that it was not her style but rather wished it was. The material for romance was at hand. In Salzburg she had met the poet and librettist Hugo von Hofmannsthal; now his eighteen-year-old son Raimund arrived to delight her solitude. Slim, graceful, infectiously light-hearted; suffused by what David Cecil called 'an exquisite Rococo spirit of pleasure'; Diana found him irresistible. He returned her affection with alarming fervour. When Diana suggested he should join the party in San Francisco he cabled his father: 'If you met Helen and she asked you to go to Troy with her, would you send your son $100?'

The money came and Raimund went.

For a month he played the Rosenkavalier to Diana's Marschallin, without a suggestion of a Sophie to distract him. He was besottedly in love, asking no greater pleasure than to be allowed to run her bath, brush her hair, take off her shoes. He would sit all night outside her bedroom door, fill the night with the plangent fluting of his wooing. 'He tells me he can never love another woman and if I laugh it wounds him almost to tears.' Diana was touched and amused and slightly uncomfortable: 'I feel like Leilah, and old and ridiculously ashamed.' She would urge him to go and woo someone of his own age but her uring lacked conviction. She would not have banished him for the world.

Others were less satisfied. Bertram Cruger telephoned anxiously about 'the German boy'. Diana told him not to worry, she had never like German boys. 'Yes, but you will,' retorted Cruger. Kommer was 'green-tinged with raging, furious jealousy over the child-lover'; 'I'm through, I'm through' he would moan, threatening suicide or an immediate return to Europe. Even Duff showed mild disquiet. He wrote from London:

'I don't much like the sound of Mr Hofmannsthal. It is uncanny the fascination that German Jews seem to possess for you. But there's no accounting for tastes. Some people like Elizabeth Bibesco. She arrived the other evening to dine with Maud very late. She talked very loud during dinner and shortly afterwards became unconscious. Maud turned to the butler and said "Her Highness has fainted. Give Her Highness a little brandy," to which the butler replied in a resounding whisper, "Her Highness has had seven brandies since dinner."'

For one fearful week in February, Raimund, Kommer and Cruger were all with Diana in Los Angeles; all jealous of each other, all demanding exclusive attention. One evening she went to a party with Raimund, rang up Kommer on her return to try to placate him, failed, discovered that Cruger in the adjoining bungalow had over-heard the conversation, rushed round to try to placate him, failed, and returned to find that Raimund had stormed out in a fit of jea-lousy. 'I wasn't born for this. I was born to be held safely in Duffy's arms, to be soothed and comforted and loved.' Meanwhile Duff was on the rampage in Paris, where he had gone with Michael Herbert and Fred Cripps. The jaunt ended in near-disaster when they were all three arrested for stealing a taxi. Only Duff's repeated assertion: '*Je suis un député très important*' eventually secured their release.

As the end of her last American tour drew near, Diana began to speculate about the future. She was never going to be so long separated from Duff again, of that she was sure, but a short season in Canada might be a possibility. She was now determined to acquire another £2000 a year. Gest proposed she should do a round of the super-cinemas acting the Madonna coming to life against a drop-scene. Diana was revolted by the idea. She was more attracted by Diaghilev's proposal to give her the part of "Nature" in a new ballet he was putting on, but this came to nothing. Still more hopeful was Otto Kahn's promise to back her in any play she cared to put on in London. Reinhardt volunteered to produce it and Kommer to manage the theatre. John Barrymore was about to act in *Richard III* and urged Diana to join him as Lady Anne. More cautiously George Arliss said that she should do a year in provincial repertory before undertaking a major speaking part in London. 'I wanted to say "Balls to you, old fool!" but I agreed in word, while knowing it was foolish because it's too late. What's the use of starting at the bottom at my age?' Privately, though, she suspected that Arliss might be right. She was not qualified to act a speaking rôle on the London stage and had no wish to make a fool of herself in front of all her friends.

But there was life in *The Miracle* yet. In the summer of 1927 came a European tour. First stop was Dortmund, a visit made memorable by the fact that Diana had to play both Nun and Madonna in the same performance. Rosamond Pinchot was back in the cast – 'She's looking hideous and acting abominably but I like her all the same,' wrote Diana. Reinhardt was brutal to her and she responded by spraining her ankle at the last minute, leaving Diana to dash around the theatre as the Nun and then, under cover of darkness, to slip into the niche above the altar, freeze into immobility and finally make the gradual transformation and descent. The strain was crippling, but she survived. To make matters worse, she was convinced the drains were unhygienic and went everywhere with an orange pressed to her nose, like some medieval courtier.

A few weeks to recover, and the caravan was on the road again, this time to Budapest. Diana spelt Hungary "Hungry" and complained she always over-ate there. All the men had wives who shot themselves or were lovers who had shot husbands; all the aristocrats were Jews and anglophiles who read the *Sketch* and *Tatler* weekly; all the impresarios – and a surprising number of Hungarians seemed to be impresarios as well as aristocrats, Jews and anglophiles – flung themselves on their knees before her and treated her like the prima donna which she knew she wasn't but half wished she was. Diana enjoyed Budapest. She enjoyed Prague too, though she was shamed when Duff, as usual, remembered their wedding anniversary and she, as usual, forgot it. 'Is it eight years? Oh dear, how quick it's gone, and the rest will go quicker. Please always love me as you have done, I don't need more. I can never change. It is only with you I am happy, safe and not anxious or wondering if all's well. Hold me, hold me!'

Vienna, the end of the tour, should also have been the high spot. Diana filled Sacher's Hotel with close friends – Alan and Viola Parsons, the Hutchinsons, Iris Tree's husband Curtis Moffat – yet somehow the mixture failed to work. Tempers wore thin, the performances seemed threadbare, Diana's health never fully recovered from the exertions of Dortmund. She appealed to a doctor for something to stop her coughing on the stage and was recommended a long sea-voyage. Other prescripions proved more relevant but equally ineffective: 'The great Austrian Medical Faculty,' she wrote crossly, 'seems to me about as advanced as the Deauville one – leeches and cataplasms are this year's discovery.'

It seemed an inglorious end to what had been a spectacularly successful chapter in her life; but Diana would not accept that it *was* the end. *The Miracle* should be filmed; if it could not be filmed, then at least it should be staged in London. It had been a great success there before the war, why should it not be even greater now? C. B. Cochran agreed and wished to produce the play; after protracted negotiations Reinhardt accepted; *The Miracle* was to be revived. Earl's Court in 1930 was the original proposal, the Lyceum in April 1932 proved the final answer.

By the standards of the United States the production was done on the cheap – costing a mere £30,000. 'Hollywood Perpendicular,' Brian Howard described the decor; the cathedral 'more a triumph of the parrot than the Paramount mind'; the forest 'resembling an effeminate vegetable garden'. The cast, however, was more ambitious; Massine played the *Spielmann*, Glen Byam Shaw was the Cripple, and Tilly Losch, the talentd Viennese dancer-cum-actress, was cast as the Nun. Unfortunately Miss Losch proved as mischievous as she was talented. When Diana descended from her niche to put on the Nun's clothes she had devised graceful movements to fit the music, by which she slipped the habit smoothly over her head and emerged triumphant. Tilly Losch put the habit back to front so that, far from emerging smoothly, Diana was left thrashing around ingloriously looking

for the exit. Not to be caught twice Diana next time carefully inspected the costume, decided it was correctly placed, plunged in and
emerged to find two of the largest hairpins ever made hanging from
the veil so that they swung to and fro in front of her eyes. To her
credit, Diana neither complained to Cochran nor allowed the incidents to put her out of her stride. A complaint to Cochran would
anyway have achieved little; he was besotted by Tilly Losch and even
allowed her to rewrite the final scene so that the Nun died dramatically, making the Madonna's previous descent to take on her duties
entirely pointless.

'My lovie, my dovie, my duck and my dear,' telegraphed Lord
Beaverbrook. 'I am certain you will have a great success on your first
night and for ever after.' On the whole his certainty was justified. The
critics were somewhat less reverent than they had been in New York.
'A remorseless production,' the *New Statesman* described it, consist-
ing mainly of 'processions of what seem gleaming debutantes disguised as nuns, supporting electric-fixtures and intoning they know
not what.' A pageant, wrote *The Times*, which laid claim to a spiritual
beauty beyond its grasp. 'The play is full of ingenious substitutes for
the truth which, like the electric bulbs that do service as candles, are
enemies of the spirit while decorative of the substance.' But no critic
spoke harshly of Diana and some glorified her, notably *The Times*
once more:

> 'One thing stood apart from and above it, Lady Diana's represen-
> tation of the Virgin. There are long passages during which a wise
> man will look at nothing but this glowing stillness, this superb pass-
> ivity on which all action is gathered up and transcended. It is as if,
> coming in from a hot and turbulent street, one is resting coolly
> before the picture of a master.'

Friends rallied loyally to admire. Robert Bruce Lockhart was moved
to hot tears and was still more impressed when he found that Diana
had a huge mosquito-bite on her shoulder but had resisted the urge to
scratch it; was suffering from a cold but had managed not to cough.
The King, too, was more impressed by her immobility than her
acting. 'You played this part twenty-five years ago?' he suggested.
'No,' said Diana firmly. 'How's your broken leg? I remember you
broke it on our Coronation Day.' 'No, sir, on Peace Day.' 'Does it not
tire you to stand so long with your head on one side?' 'Yes, sir, it is a
little tiring.' 'But of course you have no words to say, and talking is
three quarters of acting.' Diana was little better pleased by Max
Beaverbrook, who did not come till the last night of the tour and then
arrived so late that he missed three quarters of the play.

After three months at the Lyceum the time came for a provincial tour. To act *The Miracle* in the United States had enjoyed a certain *réclame*. To appear in London's West End was perhaps less acceptable, but Diana was known to behave surprisingly and her friends marvelled and forgave her. To appear in Manchester or Glasgow was inconceivable, however; eccentricity carried to the point of lunacy. Tilly Losch made it clear that she would submit herself to no such indignity; Diana reached the opposite decision with as little hesitation. She wanted the money; she was loath to lose the glamour and the glory; but, far more important than either of these, she was at heart a trouper. She liked the company – particularly since Tilly Losch was to abandon them; she knew her presence would be an important element in its success; she was loyal to her fellow-actors, to Reinhardt, to Cochran. In early July she set off on the trail that was to wend from Manchester to Golders Green by way of Birmingham, Glasgow, Edinburgh, Southampton, Liverpool and Cardiff.

'Don't overwork,' urged Hilaire Belloc. 'I was distressed when I heard from you that you were going at it again, and with travel and the foul towns at that. Courage is glorious, but the Devil is the master of the world and when he sees anyone as brave as you are he makes them overdo it.' Belloc had earlier complained to Katharine Asquith that Diana should never have agreed to impersonate the Madonna. Katharine had passed on and perhaps exaggerated the rebuke. Hurriedly Belloc composed a sonnet sequence to appease Diana.

> 'Because I find foreknowledge in my soul
> Of your true sisterhood with heavenly things . . .'

he explained

> 'Therefore did I and therefore now complain
> That you're profound, and daily do renew
> To make your own resplendent beauty vain
> Through mimic beauty of what's likest you.
> This was my sentence. This was all my say;
> Mourning such light be clouded in a play.'

Frances Brett Young's 'votive epigram for the Madonna's shrine' was more approving, but the verse was worse:

> 'A miracle in Manchester! What manner
> Of miracle? Max Reinhardt's? No, Diana!'

No number of epigrams could have made up for the absence of her friends. Duff came to Glasgow for a long weekend, but his departure left her more disconsolate than she had been before. He wrote on his return to London:

> 'I don't think that I ever minded leaving you so much... My only consolation was the thought that our unhappiness was itself such a tribute to our happiness and love, and how much sadder it would have been had we parted with a sigh of relief. I don't think I ever loved you more than these days – the first was the best because it had the "first day of the holidays" feeling which only schoolboys know – the last was the worst because it was fog instead of sunshine and the approach of separation hung over it, darker than the fog.'

A new friendship was cemented during these weeks. Diana first met Evelyn Waugh at a luncheon given by Hazel Lavery. With *Decline and Fall* and *Vile Bodies* already published, Waugh was greatly in demand as a brilliant young novelist. Diana was enraptured by his wit, his sensibility, his gusto, his affection for her; dismayed by his black rages and cruelty. She called him her 'dear malignancy' and their relationship was punctuated by fearsome quarrels. Constantly she rebuked him for believing and embellishing stories that suggested she was speaking ill of him: 'You know perfectly well that you have no Baby as loyal as this Baby and if you believe anything else you are very foolish.' She was one of the few people who could to some extent call Waugh to order. In Birmingham, on the tour of *The Miracle*, they were walking together down a steep hill. A man came towards them, crimson and tottering under the weight of a heavy suitcase. He asked if he was going the right way for the railway station. 'Quite right,' said Waugh. 'Go the very top of the street and turn left.' They walked on, and then a thought struck Diana. Wasn't the station in a different direction? 'Certainly,' said Waugh. 'That'll teach that vulgar little man to address us!' Diana refused to speak to him again until he ran after the man, explained the mistake and even helped him some of the way with his case.

Such aberrations did not detract from the delights of his company. Many weekends and sometimes during the week as well he sought her out in her provincial hotel and devoted himself to entertaining her. From Manchester they drove together over the Derbyshire hills and visited the great houses of the area, on a rainy afternoon in Glasgow he read her *The Wind in the Willows*, a classic which incredibly she had never come across before.

In Edinburgh he introduced her to a Scottish Nationalist group. Eric Linklater, Moray McLaren and the like would gather in the Café Royal to discuss the destiny of the nation. Diana preferred the stained glass windows of sporting scenes to the political solemnities, but was entirely happy in this unexpected company. The provincial tour was not a high spot in Diana's life, but it would have been much less tolerable if there had been no Evelyn Waugh to comfort her.

The curtain went down for the last time on *The Miracle* at the Hippodrome, Golders Green, at the end of January, 1933. There was talk of revivals, even as late as the 1960s it was seriously suggested that she should return to the part, but the ideas never came to anything and she did not want them to. Duff was now in the Government, henceforth he would play the starring rôles. Diana's part, she was resolved, would be that of the loyal but unobtrusive supporter. It did not work out quite like that – unobtrusiveness was never Diana's forte – but henceforward it was Duff's career that preoccupied her, never her own.

SEVEN

'A Light World'

While Diana was winning glory on the stage, Duff was embarking on his long-meditated political career. He was not ideal material for a politician. His courage and pugnacity led him into rows with those who might otherwise have been his supporters. Though ambitious, he could not be bothered with much of the drudgery essential to the Member of Parliament and would spend drinking with his cronies in White's hours which would have been better devoted to cossetting aldermen or acquainting himself with local issues. He had an on the whole well-deserved reputation for idleness: 'And, Mr Cooper,' Lord Curzon had enquired when Foreign Secretary, 'in the intervals between entertaining your beautiful wife, how do you occupy yourself?' His friends loved him but tended to consider him a lightweight: 'We all,' wrote Harold Nicolson, 'think Diana will be a more serious candidate than Duff himself.'

Above all, he was singularly lacking in the common touch. He had no small talk and was shy and brusque except with those to whom he felt affinity. In 1925 Diana cross-examined Iris Tree on what she and other close friends like Alan Parsons and St John Hutchinson really thought of Duff.

> 'They admire you and are proud of you,' she told him,' but they are all frightened and none *loving* of you, because of your deathly coldness to them. They think it has greatly developed since you married. Iris feels you despise your companions of this order utterly. This may be true, but I hold it wrong that you should show it forth. I am very conscious and sometimes horrified at your lack of warmth to anyone, but have hugged the remembrance that to me you are different. Yet sometimes lately I have felt the habit, which is all it is, on myself and shuddered. Duffy, don't be deathly proud, my darling. You cannot have a completely different manner just for my group, and so you probably dish out the frozen mitt to all, and I want all men to love as well as admire you.'

Diana's letter shows well not merely Duff's deficiencies but also the ways in which her own strengths could complement him. Her political opinions, in so far as she had any, were instinctive and imprecise. She was for conservation, but not necessarily a supporter of the Conservative Party; a monarchist, but not automatically the champion of any individual monarch. On the whole she would have preferred to see the rich man remain in his castle, the poor man at the gate, but if the poor man by industry or sleight of hand gained possession of the castle, she would be perfectly ready to accept an invitation to dine there. What would have disturbed her most would have been if the castle had been demolished and a row of identical bungalows erected on the site, but even this would not have been cause for despair. Diana would have known that one bungalow would soon be larger and more luxurious, or at least more interesting than the others, and have felt confident that it was to that one that she would find her way.

Duff could not have espoused communism or fascism without changing his character so fundamentally that he would have been no longer the man she loved; but short of such excesses she was prepared to follow in whatever direction he pointed. No wife of a would-be member was less qualified to argue the rights or wrongs of her husband's position; what Diana knew, and was prepared, indeed determined, to say loudly, was that Duff was a good, brave and honourable man and that if he made half as good an M.P. as he was a husband then the electorate could count themselves lucky.

When Duff was selected as Conservative candidate for the Lancashire mill-town of Oldham, Diana hastened back from America to help him in the election. The local Conservatives were alarmed. Diana had no intention of dressing down for the occasion or in any way pretending she was different from what she was. What would the Lancashire mill-hands, famous for their bluntness and sturdy commonsense, think of this exotic celebrity? The *Sphere* had recently conducted a poll among its readers to choose the ten most remarkable women of the day. The Queen, Edith Sitwell and Tallulah Bankhead accompanied Diana to the top. Was this the sort of *galère* from which a member's wife should come? 'Make that hussy go away from my door!' had been the cry of an indignant voter in another by-election where Diana had assisted. Would this be the reaction of the inhabitants of Oldham? Diana herself was apprehensive and protested that she looked 'such a foolish bear, being led around to be looked at, given a bun-bouquet. Or is it useful publicity?'

It was, and more. Her attitude to the electors was perfect because it never occurred to her that any attitude was called for. She was totally unselfconscious, without any trace of patronage, friendly, interested and obviously delighted by her reception. She did not seem superior because she did not feel herself superior, merely different. 'There's no swank about her,' an old lady told the *Daily Express*, 'and, oh my, isn't she a beauty.' She genuinely liked the people of Oldham and they recognized her sincerity and liked her in return. 'I loved the mills,' she wrote in her memoirs, 'because the girls mobbed me and kissed me and thought me funny. I promised them a clog dance if they put my husband in, which I later performed as best I could.'

Duff won at Oldham with a small majority. To Diana it was self-evident that he deserved office as soon as possible. A year or so later a vacancy occurred in the Foreign Office and it was known that he was being considered as a possible candidate. Diana was acting in Boston, and as soon as she heard the news she telegraphed Churchill, then Chancellor of the Exchequer, 'Please look after Duffy'. Churchill never referred to the telegram but Duff heard of it through a private secretary. 'I am sorry you telegraphed to Winston,' he wrote. 'If one can get on without intrigue – and I'm sure I can – it is much better not to indulge in it.' Diana was chastened and pledged herself never to interfere again, but the resolution was not one she was likely to keep. Strings were there to be pulled, and never did pride or delicacy inhibit her from pulling them with a will when the need arose.

Diana was back in England in May of the following year, 1926, the month of the General Strike. To her this seemed the prelude to violent revolution and she passed unhappy hours badgering Mrs Churchill and friends in the Government for news. How soon could they leave the country with honour, she asked Duff. Not till the massacres began, he answered firmly, knowing well that he would be dead on a barricade or a tumbril long before he would take to flight. Diana's fears were multiplied when she realised that Churchill was virtually in control of the Government – 'that terrifies – with his "whack 'em on the snout" policies'. She urged Katharine Asquith to stay away from London. 'Don't imagine you could be doing any good here – one simply isn't wanted, though when the barricades and the shooting begin we may be.'

Her morale improved when there was more for her to do. First she taxied people to and from Hackney and Putney and Golders Green. Then Lord Beaverbrook summoned her to the *Daily Express*, where she succeeded Edwina Mountbatten on the telephone switchboard. Finally she moved to *The Times*. Duff foresaw trouble with the pickets and tried to keep her at home, but she slipped out of the house and spent till 4 a.m. each morning folding newspapers. The rights and wrongs of the dispute never concerned her; it was our side and their side, and though she felt no animosity against the opposition she had no doubt that they must be defeated. Then it was back to America to earn more dollars. By the time *The Miracle* ended its run

Duff was poised to enter the Government. Early in 1928 he was offered the post of Financial Secretary to the War Office, a post traditionally reserved for young men whom it is believed are destined to go far.

There were other changes too. In May, 1925, the old Duke of Rutland had a heart attack and died. Diana had long accepted that he was not her father, but in his detached and on the whole benign way he had not done a bad job of playing a father's part. Diana regretted rather than mourned him. The Duchess, after a brief pause for decorum, throve exceedingly. With relief she sold the house in Arlington Street for a satisfactory fortune and moved into the coachman's lodge. There was a sale of the contents in July which on the whole went well, though a portrait of a child believed to be by Reynolds fetched only £42. Diana slipped into the sale various pieces of furniture given her by admirers and no longer wanted, and was delighted by the results, particularly a rather ugly Italianate cabinet presented by Tommy Bouch which fetched £68. The only out-and-out failures were the Duchess's own drawings, on which she put high reserves and which all had to be bought in. 'It must have saddened and rather humiliated her,' commented Diana sympathetically.

With the Duke's death her brother John succeeded and Belvoir ceased to be home. Duff and she still slept in the same room, went there regularly for Christmas, yet now she was a guest where once she had gone of right. The 9th Duke's accession was not followed by any slackening of formality. Duff was required to wear tails for a family party of six in June, 1926. The new Duke's brother-in-law, Michael Tennant, asked whether they never wore a black tie in the country. 'Yes,' said the Duke. 'When I dine alone with my wife in her bedroom.' Even Duff, who throve on grandeur, was disconcerted. 'Your brother is really getting rather alarming, you know,' he wrote to Diana.

Things were very different at Aldwick, near Bognor, where the old Duchess presented Diana with the eighteenth-century farmhouse which the Duke of Portland had given her many years before. It was comfortable but never grand, tails were unheard of and even black ties a rarity. Instead it was a place of bathing and picnics and walks on the Downs, of Belloc reciting his latest ballad or Maurice Baring reading his new novel.

Belloc was among the most regular visitors. 'Children, I must have beer,' he announced one evening as he swept in, cloak billowing behind him and dinner already on the table. Beer was, with some difficulty, provided; a glass of sherry proffered and accepted; red wine followed white; then came port and brandy. The glasses accumulated in front of Belloc as he ate and talked and talked and ate, until when Duff rose to leave the table Belloc looked at them in surprise. 'God damn my soul, I must drink this up,' he protested, and swilled down the whole collection, with no perceptible effect on his sobriety.

Bognor also provided a haven for Major, the Bedlington, who was growing tetchy in London. Holbrook outraged Duff by announcing the dog would have to be destroyed as it had bitten a boy. 'It does boys good to be bitten,' protested Duff. 'He also invariably flies at "the girl". He doesn't, it seems, like youth.' In Sussex Major would be able to use up his surplus energy on long walks and worrying sheep.

For four years Diana had been complaining that acting in *The Miracle* kept her away from Duff, particularly at Christmas. Now, in 1928, when Christmas together was at last a possibility, she elected to go to Nassau with Sidney Herbert. The fact that she was ready to desert Duff in so cavalier a fashion shows how restless her theatrical life had made her. It was to be another twelve months before she found it possible to settle down to a normal married existence. Certainly this voluntary separation did not indicate that her marriage was under any strain, still less that she was having an affair with Herbert. Playing the copulation game, in which one had to list within ten minutes the ten people one would most like to go to bed with, Diana had tentatively come up with Jack Barrymore; Chaliapin; Reinhardt; D'Annunzio; Ivor Wimborne ('I'd hate it!'); Bendor, Duke of Westminster ('Phui!'); and Sidney Herbert's brother Michael ('I'd have to be driven to it!'). Sidney Herbert himself did not figure and was really more Duff's friend than hers, much loved by both of them and now seriously ill. Diana's rôle was in fact no more than to lend respectability to Sidney Herbert's affair with another woman; she was anxious to do him a good turn, delighted to have all her expenses paid, and hungry to set out on her travels again.

It was a model holiday. Diana described the perfect turtle dinner. Turtle-eating was a ceremony in Nassau, and when one was caught the turtle-cook was sent for. On this occasion turtle soup was followed by 'the freshest, most amazingly cooked' little mushrooms with a firm cream on them. Next came the turtle herself 'on her own hot shell and under a little roof of pastry; the best food there is, I think.' Then a froth of coconut ice, the coconuts so young they were still unformed, served with a cake of fly-away nuts and a compote of cumquats. Finally a Roquefort cheese was followed by 'the prettiest, reddest, most flavoured strawberries. It was a culinary masterpiece.' Next day she felt distinctly sick. Her first reaction was to blame the culinary masterpiece, but when it persisted she began to look elsewhere for the cause.

Diana's attitude towards having a baby had been curiously ambivalent. Shortly before she married she told Katharine Asquith that she did not think she wanted one. 'To have them seems purely egotistical and yet not worth it to oneself – more especially to me, who would fear for them so much.' It was something of a relief when the first few years of marriage did not produce one: first filming and then *The Miracle* made such demands on her time that the interruption would have been inconvenient. Duff tried to convince himself that he felt the same, observing the sins of his friends' children and congratulating himself that he was spared such tribulations.

Simultaneously, however, Diana was taking energetic steps to achieve the end she professed not to desire. In 1921 she had an operation to enable her to have a child. This gained nothing, and the following year a surgeon diagnosed a fibroid in the womb and said that it must be removed. Diana was alarmed and depressed, bolstering her morale by a massive intake of cocktails, and Duff went out to seek another doctor, who obligingly declared that a further operation was quite unnecessary. Instead Diana was packed off to the Pyrenees, to follow a cure that Eugénie had taken nine months before the birth of the Prince Imperial. In spite of so encouraging a precedent this too proved a failure. Diana now had recourse to Dr Arens, a celebrated gynaecologist who claimed personal responsibility for some of the noblest babies in Britain. Some said that his responsibility was more personal than was proper under the medical code of practice, others that he retained a squad of fecund footmen always ready to impregnate the aristocracy for a suitable fee. Whatever his methods, they did not work with Diana.

She turned to wilder schemes. Duff should have a child by a carefully selected prostitute and the infant would then be adopted into the family. The plan foundered on Duff's reluctance to cooperate. Diana tried again. Iris Tree was about to have an illegitimate child by her current lover. Diana knew that if she were to adopt the child overtly, Duff would complain about the bad Tree blood whenever it misbehaved. He must therefore remain ignorant of the child's ancestry. Iris was booked into a nursing-home in Gower Street and it was arranged that the baby should be left anonymously on the Coopers' doorstep. This scheme was foiled by Iris Tree, who decided she wanted to keep

the baby for herself. In despair Diana concluded that a boy would undoubtedly be a bugger and a girl a whore; she was better barren.

Then came the Nassau holiday. Diana's period was late, she felt
sick, she had toothache, she found a blue vein on her chest: all, she
was told, infallible signs of pregnancy. Nervously she wrote to Duff
of her symptoms. 'I'm sure it's climate or something wrong and not a
baby, because it never is a baby. And if it is a baby, it may be a nigger,
because who went even for a trip to the West Indies has nigger descen-
dants for ever, and don't tell me the Victorian wives did funny things
with niggy-wiggs, so it must be the climate and air that produces the
wool and ebony.' If it wasn't a 'niggy-wigg', she gloomily concluded,
everyone would assume it was a Herbert. 'I feel so frightened and so
disinclined for such things at my time of life.' In a moment of panic
she took a large dose of quinine, hoping to produce an abortion, then
rejoiced when the foetus appeared unruffled by this treatment. Her
mood now was one of exultation, coupled with doubts as to whether it
could really be true. 'It is so naughty of me to raise your hopes when it
may all be my giant nerves and my obedient imagination.'

It was not a false alarm. Exultation soon faded, to be replaced by resigned dismay. Diana disliked pregnancy, found her appearance grotesque and the delay interminable. Everything fed her fears. The
nurse advised her not to engage a nanny yet: 'Better see what
happens.' A hare got up in front of the car, a sure sign that the baby
would have a hare lip. She went to hospital to have an X-ray: would
she see a normal child or 'a kinkajoo or a big Buddha? I shall be surprised at nothing.' She went into labour, or thought she did, on the
road between Bognor and London and was delighted that she would
get it all over 'before they could sharpen their knives – but alas, the
little bugger gave one look and retired again. I guess he knows when
he's well off.' She had to wait another week before she went off to
Lady Carnarvon's nursing home, pale-faced, smiling gallantly,
casting a last, longing look at the house which she knew she would
never see again.

It was, in fact, a difficult birth. Her son was born by Caesarean
section – in honour of which Julius was added to the traditional
Manners name of John – and for several hours Diana's life was in
some danger. She quickly recovered, however, and settled down to
ensure her son a proper start in life. The richest among her friends,
including Lord Beaverbrook and the Aga Khan, were included among
the godparents. A 150-year-old cradle was refurbished for the lying-
in-state. And then, after all her trouble, the baby developed jaundice
just before the christening. A yellow baby would never do. John
Julius was powdered and rouged, doped, covered with a film of

muslin and exposed triumphantly at the ceremony. All agreed it was a great success and mother and baby were both exceptionally handsome.

With this behind her, Diana felt that her duty as a mother was largely done for the next few years. She had little enthusiasm for babies, nor indeed for children except her own. Her Paget nieces so disliked her when they were young that they wrote her name on the bottom of their boots and tramped to and fro on the beaches of Anglesey, hoping they would wear her out. They found her brusque, insensitive, intolerant of their efforts, indisposed to make concessions for their youth. 'Lady Diana, despite her innumerable social duties, visits the nursery regularly,' reported the *Sunday Express* reverently, but the visits were cursory and day-to-day management was left to nannies and nursemaids. The fact that babies bored her did not, however, stop her worrying distractedly if anything seemed to be going wrong. Duff did not share her concern. She rushed to him in anguish because John Julius was losing weight. 'So for God's sake stuff the little bugger up with nourishing vitamins!' Duff retorted.

Things changed dramatically once the child had a mind of its own. From the time that he was four or five Diana took a close, continual and passionate interest in John Julius's education. Greek myths and British history were the staples of good scholarship; Diana pounded these into her son whenever an opportunity arose and often when others might have said that it did not – in church, for instance, or during a dull play. Pictures of the English kings were cut from a book and pasted on a screen for easy memorizing. Learning by heart was all-important; pocket-money had to be earned by recitation. Geography was capital cities, in particular those about which she knew; she was keen on Quito but bored by Caracas. Arithmetic was no doubt useful but not a subject about which a gentleman need concern himself unduly. French was essential. The Duchess was outraged when Diana dragged her son off to France with a temperature and without Nanny. The noise and bustle, she feared, would 'tire that sensitive brain and start an inward fretting. It's not economy that makes her go without Nurse or Maid, but to make him have intensive French talking.'

The sensitive brain survived. At least once a week it was taken on an outing, to a cinema or perhaps the Aquarium. Diana did all the things that Nanny didn't do, like race John Julius down the street. She ran like the wind and won the parents' race at her son's school with hardly any cheating. All plans were abandoned if they were in a car and a fire-engine was seen. Diana would cling to its tail, helter skelter through red lights and one-way streets until the two of them could ooh and aah contentedly at the scene of the disaster. One thing she failed to instil in her son, however, was her arrant lawlessness. John Julius could never accustom himself to his mother's headlong charges across the Sussex downs, ignoring signs forbidding entry, pushing aside barriers, putting the sheep to flight; still less accept her conviction that in city traffic it was a case of *sauve qui peut* and damned be he who first cried, 'Hold, enough!'

There were plenty of people who alleged that John Julius was not Duff's son. It is curious how many of Diana's acquaintances, let alone those who knew her only through the newspapers, believed that she was sexually promiscuous, almost degenerate. Beverley Nichols described what he thought her to be in 1927 and the novel was sent to Duff: 'There is the old, old character of the heartless society girl who rogers right and left and thinks it vulgar to fall in love. That is what *they* think you are – poor oafs!' A constituent wrote to enquire about the forthcoming divorce in which the Duke of Kent was to be cited as co-respondent. Scandal-mongers delighted in putting Diana into bed with one man or another, sometimes two at once. Diana was mildly flattered by such *canards*. She did not wish to be accused of infidelities, but would have regretted it if nobody had thought her capable of them. Randolph Churchill was told by a woman in Algiers that Diana was a *grande amoureuse*. He passed it on to Evelyn Waugh, who laughed heartily. Diana was indignant. 'How the hell can he tell if I am or not? Just because I never responded to his dribbling, dwarfish little amorous *singeries*, he need not be so sure!' John Julius's birth after so many years of childless marriage was enough to set the gossips buzzing. Michael Herbert was one of the putative fathers, St John Hutchinson, Reinhardt; but most popular candidate of all was Conrad Russell.

Conrad Russell was first cousin to the Duke of Bedford, as individual as any member of that quirky family and far more amiable than most of them. Six feet, four inches tall, stooping under a thatch of white hair, huge feet splayed out in penguin gait, his features were noble and yet humorous, a fair indication of the strange intelligence that lay within. He had started life as a stock-jobber, made some money, disliked the process and retreated to the country, where he farmed with limited success but total dedication. He had a small house at Mells and from this base tranquilly cultivated his crops, his mind and his friendships. Himself ascetic, he was indulgent towards the self-indulgence of others. Wise without being worldly-wise, infini-

tely interested in the vagaries of others, protected by a shield of inno-
cence, he was almost unshockable: 'What strange and curious things
you tell me,' he would exclaim with mild delight. 'I love my Conrad
with a C because he is courageous and cuddlesome and courtly and a
charmer of charmers,' Diana wrote to him on his birthday. An aura of
charm hung around him, not the superficial charm that can be turned
on and off like a light, but the charm that stems from benevolence and
joy of life. He was a profoundly happy man and loved to make others
happy too. 'I think,' he once told Edwin Montagu, 'that one's first
duty is to make life as pleasant as one can for the people one is thrown
with.'

Diana had known his brothers for years but really became aware of
Conrad for the first time when visiting Mells during the run of *The
Miracle* at Cardiff. She liked him immediately and, on an impulse,
asked him to come back to Cardiff with her to see the show. To her
astonishment, he accepted. At once she lost her nerve. How would
she entertain this strange, silent man? She confessed her doubts to
Katharine Asquith and was reassured; Conrad was exactly the sort of
man she would like. And so they went off together 'and he loved *The
Miracle*, and afterwards we had a little supper, and in the morning we
walked the town and he held my hand in his pocket for it was so cold,
and he told me he loved me, and he told me the same every day until
he lost consciousness in death.' 'Cardiff is engraved on my heart,'
Conrad wrote to her on his return. 'You were so perfect to me and I
have no words to thank you for your sweetness.'

Diana's acceptance by Conrad was total. Within a few months she
received the ultimate accolade when Moonshine's heifer calf was
christened Diana in her honour. 'You can tell Diana by her white
rump,' was the future instruction to visitors. As well as this came a
constant stream of presents; jewellery for the most part but many
other lesser trinkets designed to please or amuse her. Diana constantly
reproached herself for accepting so much, but as constantly over-
ruled her conscience on the subject; 'I should help my fool and his
money to keep together – but there it is, I am weak as water and can't
but be excited to death about the present.' To have curbed Conrad's
generosity would have been to deprive him of a signal pleasure – 'just
about the most roaring, stamping, cracking, galloping fun I ever had
in my life,' as he told a censorious neighbour. His sisters, who felt
their bachelor brother to be their private property, deplored the relationship and tried to point out its dangers. Conrad was not
impressed. 'I suppose they see me as a besotted poor fool helplessly in
the clutches of a heartless, frivolous whore who is just amusing herself
by making a fool of me.'

They corresponded endlessly. Conrad delighted in long, gossipy letters; rambling idiosyncratically around the events on his farm, the movement of his shares, visitors to Mells, books, politics and the wonders of Diana. Diana's replies tended to be brisker and briefer except on her travels, when she would write diary-letters giving a detailed picture of her doings: 'You scribe in your day-book, *ja?*' as she was asked in Kiel. The arrival of one of Conrad's letters was always a moment for rejoicing. Diana slipped back gratefully into his tranquil world and persuaded herself that she would like to share it: 'If only I could live in this simplicity, how happy I could be – appreciative of all – smooth and collected – time for all – to read *The Times*, to read books, dream more agreeably, no stuffing, no boozing, no smoking, no pretending.'

> Give me, O indulgent fate!
> Give me yet before I die,
> A sweet yet absolute retreat
> Through paths so lost and trees so high
> That the world may ne'er invade
> Through such windings and such shade
> My unshaken liberty.

Diana, as no doubt the Countess of Winchilsea, would have been horrified if an indulgent fate had granted her request, but both liked to dream of pastoral felicity and Diana found it vicariously in Conrad's letters.

Conrad relished platonic flirtations with beautiful, high-spirited and usually high-born women. Daphne Weymouth, though second to Diana, was a warm favourite. 'I came up to London yesterday afternoon,' Conrad told Diana, 'and made a bee-line for Lady Weymouth's bedroom. It was unlucky that Henry her husband had the same idea. I mustn't complain. He has as good a right to be there as I have.' But with Lady Weymouth, as with Diana, the relationship stopped at hand-holding and friendly kisses. The fact that he wanted no more was one of the many things about Conrad which endeared him to Diana. He was loving but sexually unexacting. This was so obvious to most people who knew him well that it is surprising to find some of them firmly believing the contrary. Evelyn Waugh, for one, was confident there was more to the relationship than platonic love. Kommer, on the other hand, elected to be jealous of Waugh. 'If he has to be jealous of anyone it really might be me,' commented Conrad. 'It is galling to think that Wu is considered more dangerous than me.' Conrad himself was above jealousy:

'I believe in your affection for me, dear Diana, and I think you love me far, far beyond my deserts. I have not lost my surprise at it. I shouldn't wonder if you liked other men – some better than me possibly – but what can I do about it? And suppose you are Lord Beaverbrook or Albert's mistress? I don't see what I can do about it. You wouldn't be likely to give them up to please me. I should make myself ridiculous by asking you to.'

To those who were determined to find an alternative father for John Julius, and who rejected Conrad, if for no other reason than that he only came into Diana's life three years after her son's birth, Albert Ashfield seemed a hopeful substitute. Though born in England, Lord Ashfield had spent most of his life in the United States before he was called back to manage London's fledgeling underground system, and become celebrated as 'Lord Straphanger' and the creator of London Transport. Diana met him when she was hired by Kensitas to find captains of industry ready to advertise cigarettes. Beaverbrook introduced her to Ashfield, who in turn passed her on to Thomas Lipton but pledged himself to help her in any other way. He proved himself the staunchest of friends until his death. When she complained of a shortage of transport during an electoral campaign, he provided a motor-car and chauffeur which arrived every day with a white camellia for her to pin in her cap. But though Diana appreciated his wealth, his power, his determination to make all smooth before her; though, indeed, she loved him dearly; it was not a relationship with passion in it. Simply through his constant importunity, Lord Wimborne might have appeared a more formidable threat to her fidelity, but by now she had perfected her technique for keeping him at bay. The fact that Conrad did not include him with Ashfield and Beaverbrook in his list of putative lovers would have caused Wimborne great offence but was an accurate estimate of his position.

Beaverbrook was a more interesting case. Diana was fascinated by him, slightly frightened of him, very conscious of the fact that Duff could not endure him and finding this, in a perverse way, something of an attraction. The two men clashed most fiercely at the time of the Westminster by-election. Duff was champion of the official Conservatives supporting Baldwin; the press lords Rothermere and Beaverbrook mounted a spectacular barrage in favour of the anti-Baldwin Conservative, Sir Ernest Petter; no other candidate stood. The full ferocity of Beaverbrook's attack was, however, muted by his affection for Diana. At one moment he could have damaged Duff's campaign, perhaps even destroyed his career, if he had published some slanderous remarks Duff had rashly made about his opponent's war record. Diana went to plead with him. 'I know what you've come for,' he grunted, and promised not merely to suppress the news himself but to try to get the press as a whole to do the same. He succeeded. Another time one of his favourites produced some especially vituperative copy about Duff. Beaverbrook censored it. 'Do you love your wife?' he asked. 'Well, I love Duff Cooper's wife, so lay off him!'

With the official Conservative party in disarray, Duff needed all the help he could get. The Duchess of Rutland and Emerald Cunard attended all Petter's meetings, ostentatiously reading pro-Baldwin newspapers. Whenever they heard mention of Beaverbrook or Rothermere they would raise their eyebrows and exclaim, 'Degenerates, they're both degenerates!' A dignified butler informed one of Duff's supporters that he would be voting for Petter, since Sir Ernest was a man of title while Mr Cooper was merely a clerk in an office, and a foreign office at that. Butlers and the like were Diana's especial responsibility. She was delegated to address the housemaids at the Ritz – 'but I can't even address a golf ball,' she protested plaintively – and then held a meeting at 85 Eaton Square for the assembled domestic servants of the neighbourhood. Her message was admirably free of political content. 'My husband is a good candidate,' she told them. 'I don't know if any of my staff are here. They would tell you I've never had a bit of trouble with him.' The meeting was such a success that two more proved necessary. Duff triumphed over Petter and the press lords by more than five thousand votes.

Diana enjoyed the business of being a political wife, giving gracious little dinners for the Baldwins, with eggs provided by Conrad Russell, gardenias by Maurice Baring, caviare by Lord Ashfield and champagne by Lord Beaverbrook. She would do anything to further Duff's thriving political career, and knew her parties were relished by even the stuffiest politician. But political entertaining on a modest scale was not a full-time occupation. The revival of *The Miracle* temporarily filled the gap, but only for a few months. She dabbled in good works but her heart was not really in them; indeed she more than half approved of H. G. Wells's reply to her begging letter: 'I do not care a damn for the Westminster Church Mission for Sailors. Sailors ought never to go to church. They ought to go to hell, where it is much more comfortable. I love and adore you, but all the same I am sending nothing to your Anglican charity.'

She cast around for a job that would divert her and supplement their income. She went to Brighton by the 'new electric train' and thought of starting a restaurant in what was then a culinary desert. She lent her name to the promotion of various products which she had never sampled and would hardly have recognised. Briefly she was co-director with Gertrude Lawrence of a flower-shop. She was tentatively offered a job as editress-in-chief of a newspaper called *Eve*. The place was said to be worth £5000 a year but Diana found the chairman of the Illustrated Newspaper Group 'a common, stupid man' and rejected what anyway seemed an illusory prospect. She missed a chance of easy money when a syndicate offered her £10,000 if she could persuade Lord Wimborne to sell them his house. 'You had better get busy,' urged Duff, but she hesitated to bring too much pressure on the still besotted nobleman. Not paying one's bills was a sure way of economising. 'They had the impudence to ring up from Selfridges and say that you owed them £130,' wrote Duff indignantly. 'They are the most insufferable badgerers for money. I told them they could go to hell!'

Instead of earning money she took up with the Bach Choir. Vaughan Williams tested her voice and accepted her: 'He was an adorable man. I think he only let me in out of kindness – "She has tried, poor beast."' Diana was a contralto and for several seasons sang with great relish in the Matthew Passion. She was a pioneer of the cross-word puzzle and did much to make Mah Jong fashionable in Britain. The *Daily Express* even announced that she was taking flying lessons; Diana being far less likely than the proverbial pig to take to the air unless compelled to. But none of these diversions could blind her to the fact that she was not making full use of her talents.

Diana at forty was as beautiful as she had ever been. St John Hutchinson's daughter, Barbara, had a vivid impression of her in a hammock at their cottage in the country, sewing in an enormous hat, with a 'feeling of sun and blondness, very laughing and welcoming and golden; what I loved about her was the colour, white and gold and blue, blue eyes; and the sparkle'. Though her rasping, cracked-ice voice made the young Barbara Hutchinson think of the Snow Queen, in every other way she exuded life and warmth. Enid Bagnold modelled Lady Maclean partly on Diana in her novel *The Loved and the Envied*:

> 'No one liked to be excluded. No one could afford to leave alone such a dispenser of life: everyone fed at the spring. She seemed to develop, when in the company of those who enjoyed life as she did, a baker's yeast ... When she came into a room it was plain it was a spirited person who entered, a person with an extra dose of life. It was apparent on all sides how people were affected. They had a tendency to rise to their feet to be nearer her, not of course in her honour, but to be at the source of amusement, to be sure not to

miss the exclamation, the personal comedy she might make of the moment of life just left behind.' 'If she lives in a light world she does it with a splendour of spirit,' said Duke Alberti in the same novel.

Hilaire Belloc's small daughter made the same points more prosaically when she remarked at dinner: 'She makes everyone happier wherever she is.'

Inevitably she was sought after socially, and since she found it almost impossible to refuse an invitation in case she missed an unexpected treat, her life was crowded and complex. The twenties and thirties were a golden age for the party-goer. Fantastic sums were squandered on clothes and decorations. At Ditchley the Ronald Trees erected a great tent of white muslin on the terrace and Oliver Messel decorated it with negro heads sporting feathered hats and ropes of pearls. There were fireworks and flowers by Constance Spry. The ladies were asked to wear red and white and Oliver Messel arrived in a white suit with a red tie – 'Bugger ought to be thrown in the lake,' muttered an outraged peer. But extravagance was not essential, a few nights later everyone sat on the floor at Sibyl Colefax's while Rubinstein played Chopin and Noel Coward strummed and crooned. It was an exclusive society but beauty, breeding, money and the ability to amuse could all provide admission tickets: the more of these attributes one possessed, the more plentiful the invitations.

Even if very beautiful or very rich one had to sing for one's supper. 'The Game' had recently arrived from America and provided an opportunity for the cream of London society to make a fool of itself several times a week. 'A combination of Dumb Crambo and what we used to call Clumps,' explained Duff, 'and about as ridiculous and tedious as anything can be.' Diana adored it, as she adored dressing up. Sometimes she borrowed costumes of luxuriant splendour, but more often she would spend only a few shillings and much ingenuity. She went on the cheap as a French revolutionary to a ball at Hampden House. A team of youngish beauties came as the Eton eight, coxed by Duff, while Lord Blandford elected to be a female cross-channel swimmer.

Hectic motorised treasure-hunts were another of her delights. One typical example took her to the Achilles Statue ('A vulnerable point in Hyde Park'). A postcard of the Death of Chatterton then led her to the Tate Gallery where a messenger boy gave the next clue: 'Not far from here, the warriors of Crimea, have a garden.' From the Pensioners' Garden in Chelsea an anagram took her to the statue of Peter Pan in Kensington Gardens and thence ('Drury Lane. Look out for Nell

Gwynne') to Viola Parsons dressed as an orange girl and on to the treasure in a letter-box in Woburn Square. Diana completed the course in two hours ten minutes and came second.

Her appetite for such delights was inexhaustible. Time after time Duff would return home at 1 or 2 a.m., knowing Diana would not follow him for two hours or more. On three successive nights she was out till 4 a.m., 'very happy. She divided her time between Jack Barrymore and the Prince of Wales'; 6 a.m., dallying with Barrymore again; and a mere 3 a.m. when a party at the Embassy Club broke up unexpectedly early. But though she enjoyed her London life, it was in travel that she found her greatest pleasure. An avid sightseer, she would go anywhere with anyone, accepting luxury if it was available but undeterred if it was not. Duff's political duties and their differing tastes meant that they often went their separate ways. 'I shall be back in a jiffy,' Duff promised as he left for Cap d'Ail in 1932, 'and you will like me all the better, like one of those angel faces which you have loved long since and lost awhile. I promise not to fall:

(1) out of the puffer
(2) into bad habits
(3) for the girls
(4) by the way
(5) at the tables
(6) off the boat
(7) from grace'

He kept his word at least so far as the boat and the puffer were concerned. Throughout his absence Diana suffered agonies lest disaster overtake him. John Julius unwittingly fed her fears by seeking to appease them. 'Papa *will* come back,' he reassured her earnestly. 'I *know* he will.'

Some of Diana's more ambitious expeditions took place under the wing of Lord Beaverbrook. In 1927 she visited Germany with him, Venetia Montagu, Valentine Castlerosse and Arnold Bennett. Gross in appetite and appearance, with nimble wit concealed beneath buffoon's exterior, Lord Castlerosse was Beaverbrook's court jester. 'What is your handicap?' Nancy Cunard asked him on the golf-course. 'Drink and debauchery,' he answered sadly but correctly. Arnold Bennett was shocked by the coarseness of the conversation between Beaverbrook and Castlerosse in front of the women – 'I mean physical love' – and did his best to curb it. His gallantry was appreciated but not called-for; in Berlin, while he sought out a play by Bertold Brecht, Diana and Venetia went off with Castlerosse on a tour of the transvestite nightclubs. Bennett liked the two women. They 'really do their best to be agreeable and very well succeed, though Venetia has a darting tongue. However, with her stings, she really is witty. Diana less so, but Diana is kinder. We called in at the most footling party I ever was at last night, and Diana threw herself into the total inanity and tedium in a manner which proves she has a very serious sense of human duty.' Bennett was determined to go to *Tristan* and Diana seconded his efforts. 'The women know about music because it seems to be somehow their job to be companionable in everything, and they must have taken the hell of a lot of pains to be so, and I think they may be mildly interested.'

Sefton Delmer, then a junior stringer for the *Express* in Berlin, was summoned to the Hotel Adlon. He found Bennett 'sardonic, silent and sallow', Castlerosse 'fat, flushed and chortling', Venetia 'gracious, erect and smiling' and Diana 'brilliant, brittle and blonde, with the palest watery blue eyes'. They were in Berlin, he gathered, in connection with some film which Bennett was to write, Beaverbrook finance and Diana star in. In fact the idea was no more than an idle fantasy which none of those concerned wished to pursue with vigour.

A few years later came another expedition, this time to Brazil. Castlerosse was again in the party and this time Beaverbrook's mistress, Jean Norton. Things went wrong even before they set off, with Diana determined not to fly over the Andes but equally determined not to be the scapegoat for the others. She was quite happy to remain behind in Rio while the others flew wherever they desired. Jean Norton begged her to be more cooperative. 'Max doesn't the least want to fly, is very frightened of it, but must be allowed to say it's my fault that they didn't soar over the Andes.'

Beaverbrook was cantankerous from the start. On the way to Paris he settled down with his secretary and began to go through the household accounts. 'What's this? Three dozen eggs, one dozen eggs and a further two dozen eggs? Will you tell me what the hell I keep a chicken-farm for? Tell the Leatherhead Gas people I'm not going to pay tenpence a therm for my gas – the gas is not worth that money. Tell them Lord Beaverbrook is very dissatisfied with their rates. What are Canadian Tabs [they were calendar refills]? I'm not going to be charged 1/3d for Canadian Tabs, whatever they are.' He was authoritarian, even by his own standards. When he emerged from the eggs and Canadian Tabs he announced Diana would like some champagne.

'No thank you, Max.'

'Of course you'd like some.'

'Thank you, no; I don't want any champagne.'

'You must want some champagne.'

'But Max, I don't like champagne.'

'Of course you like champagne. Waiter, some champagne for Lady Diana.'

Lord Castlerosse came in for still rougher treatment. It was discovered that he was writing a novel and he was told he must read it aloud after dinner. 'Can Valentine read well?' asked Diana. 'Like hell he can, the worst in the world!' Castlerosse spluttered through the 8000 words he had written. 'Not worth a damn, is it,' said Beaverbrook triumphantly.

When they got to Rio there was said to be yellow fever, typhoid, cholera and leprosy rife in the city. Castlerosse was made to put on gloves before handling banknotes. Diana was in an agony of apprehension, scarcely sleeping at all. 'I look like an old, coarse, wrung-out cloth – grey-white.' She had also decided that Duff had met with some disaster and, every time she saw Beaverbrook look gloomy, assumed that he was about to break the news. Since Beaverbrook was gloomy much of the time, her alarm was constantly revived. Beaverbrook's depression deepened when Jean Norton fell seriously ill and all trips from Rio had to be cancelled. As soon as she recovered enough to travel, the disgruntled party took the first boat home. 'Personally I would rather spend six weeks in Wormwood Scrubs,' Duff commented as he sped Diana on her way. By the time she got back she would almost have settled for the Scrubs herself.

The Coopers made many trips together. In 1930 they set off for Canada with Lord Dudley and his young son Billy. It was a camping holiday deep in the country, sleeping on a bed of spruce branches, riding, fishing, canoeing. For Duff it was flies, fleas, indigestible food and a lack of hot water; for Diana the romance of open spaces, still waters, sunrise and sunset in the wild. Duff bore it nobly, but never were their differing views as to what constituted an ideal holiday more dramatically displayed.

Duff's reputation as a coming man had grown steadily over the previous years. So also had his renown as a writer. His study of Talleyrand, one of the best-written and mostly brilliantly perceptive short biographies of the twentieth century, had come out in 1932. It brought glowing reviews and a satisfactory flood of royalties. It did not, however, win Diana's unquestioning reverence for all Duff wrote. When they went to Sweden, where Duff was to lecture, he meticulously kept a diary. Diana read it, found it dull and decided in future to dictate its contents. It at once took on a new tone. At Flushing the tickets were mislaid: 'He always loses the tickets and even when he doesn't he sends me nearly mad by fumbling in all the wrong pockets before he finds them.' On the train to Stockholm, Duff read peacefully: 'Duff never notices anything, he might as well stay at home. I noticed there were no motor-cars and no roads.' Duff met the Swedish press 'to whom he said a great many silly and indiscreet things. He was sorry afterwards when I pointed them out to him.' At Gävle Diana first tested schnapps and spent the rest of the evening with her arm round the Governor's neck. Duff did in fact make one observation of sociological import while in Sweden:

> 'To speak with your mouth full
> And swallow with greed
> Are national traits
> Of the travelling Swede.'

Diana was still dictating the diary when they set off for Venice later the same year with St John Hutchinson by way of Paris and Annecy. At Paris she softened up the men with cocktails in the Crillon and then set off for Sèvres where she had heard there was a good restaurant with a terrace overlooking the river. 'It is true the food was not very good and one saw nothing from the terrace but a large, disused factory. However, I think the men were grateful to me for taking them there.' They returned by boat. 'Duff had a suppressed *fou rire* because Hutchie, doing the highbrow, said Degas was a very witty painter.' There were terrible scenes in the Berkeley that night because the chef stuffed the grouse which Duff had brought with him. 'It did spoil them, but not sufficiently to excuse the absurd fuss that Duff made about it, refusing to touch them and shrieking for cold ham.'

At Annecy they found the Baldwins. Diana insisted the Conservative leader should be asked to luncheon. Duff grumbled but gave way on condition Diana did not wear trousers. After a battle he conceded even that point, against a promise Diana would say nothing embarrassing. Diana expressed dismay that Duff should even envisage so absurd a possibility. Baldwin duly arrived, hotfoot from a crucial conference with Ramsay MacDonald, the Prime Minister. 'Come on now,' said Diana. 'Tell us every word Ramsay said, for Duff tells me nothing.' Duff blushed, Baldwin grunted, Mrs Baldwin observed: 'My husband tells me nothing either, but then I would never ask him.' The luncheon was not a total success. The Baldwins, Diana recorded, 'are a boring couple, slow in the uptake and no sense of humour. They didn't laugh even at *my* jokes.' Walking off the effects of lunch, Duff tripped over a bush and fell flat on his face. 'He was covered in blood and dirt and obviously in severe pain. I roared and roared with laughter. He was rather annoyed with me for laughing. Some people are quite extraordinary.'

Venice was visited almost every year. Cecil Beaton first saw Diana there, in an enormous apricot-covered garden hat. 'Surely she must be the most beautiful English woman alive today. I stared in awe. Her lips were japonica red, her hair flaxen, her eyes blue love-in-the-mist.' With her were her regular courtiers: Lord Berners, 'who looks more like a figure in a tailor's shop than a composer'; St John Hutchinson, 'huge, jocular and Regency in his arty clothes'; and Maurice Baring, 'who I believe writes novels'. Beaton saw her again a few nights later at a fancy-dress ball given by Baroness d'Erlanger in honour of the Crown Prince of Italy. Diana's first costume had to be ruled out as it involved wearing a mask, something which Italian etiquette forbade in the presence of royalty. Undeterred, she reappeared half an hour later wearing crinoline and Turkish turban. 'She looked furiously beautiful now, sitting in her box.'

Social life was as hectic in Venice as at the height of the London season, the participants slightly nastier. Laura Corrigan was at the heart of it. Immensely rich, a Mrs Leo Hunter of the most luxuriant order, she lived in a world of frenetic entertaining. Diana took some coaxing before she would settle in the Palazzo Mocenigo, where Byron had lived for two years and Mrs Corrigan now gloried and drank deep, but once there she relished the opulence, the hubbub and even the vulgarity. Mrs Corrigan delighted in royalty above all things and turned her palazzo upside-down to accommodate some Greek princes. 'But Sir,' she expostulated when they arrived, 'where are the servants?' They had none. 'Why I, Sir, have *two* body-maids and Mr Corrigan never crossed the Atlantic without two body-men.' Raymond Mortimer, Clive Bell and Frankie Birrell were staying in a flat on the Zattere. Diana insisted that Mrs Corrigan should ask 'the Bloomsberries' to a meal. Her hostess complied, supposing that three brothers called Bloomsbury were coming to the house. Dutifully Diana introduced: 'Mr Raymond Bloomsbury, Mr Clive . . .' Lytton Strachey also crossed her path. He found Diana very agreeable: 'but I had, as I always do with her, the sensation of struggling vainly to show off that I'm not a fool – mysterious, because really her own comments are very far from being out of the ordinary.'

It was with Mrs Corrigan that Diana first met Chips Channon. He was everything she liked in an admirer: rich, good-looking, amusing, devoted and unlikely to make any sexual demands. 'You will be sorry to hear Chips has become my "inseparable",' she told Duff, 'follows me like a little dog, and is a great solace.' A regular feature of the Grand Tour which the Coopers undertook every summer became the

Channons' idyllic Austrian *Schloss*. 'Everything here is quite Utopian,' she wrote to her sister Marjorie. 'Naked brown peasants and orchards and cows and mountains and early hours and blazing sun and swimming-pool and gaily populated lakes and strawberries and visits into the Balkans, brigands, passes and Zendan prisoners.' She would get up at 7.30, swim, read till breakfast at nine with Viennese ham, honey and coffee, more reading and swimming till lunch, post-prandial doze in a hammock in the orchard, then a drive or walk, dinner, backgammon or paper-games and an early bed. All was of the most sybaritic and relaxing, ahead stretched 'Venice for a few days, then driving back via Germany, a glimpse of baby, to the Wallaces in Scotland, then off in a yacht with Loel Guinness.' Could life hold more, and yet: 'I have a sick mind and am melancholic and always worrying myself to death about Duff or John Julius or Mother or something.'

Time had not cured her vulnerability to bouts of melancholy, particularly in August when her birthday was approaching. Once she appealed to a specialist in nervous disorders. He recommended hormonic treatment. This did not often produce cancer, he said, and when it did you could be sure the disease was latent anyway and much better brought to the surface. Diana was not so much deterred by this as by the fact that the injections would make her fat as a eunuch. She took her custom elsewhere and was told that her troubles were sexual. Since what she wanted was a cure, not an explanation, she moved on again and was issued with some pills which at least dulled the sharp edge of her agony.

Skiing worked even better. 'How can I be so absurdly and acutely miserable in England and so conscious of the weight of misery falling away?' she asked Duff shortly after arriving on the Swiss slopes. 'It's perplexing and despairing – for I want to love my life as it deserves to be loved. Age doesn't worry me, deterioration of lovers, death of friends. It's introspection, apprehension, disease and lack of interest.' In Switzerland too Chips Channon was a regular host. She preferred the weather and the atmosphere of skiing to the activity itself. 'Fair and determined,' Channon called her, but she herself said, 'the moment there's a little *piu di velocita* I lose my head, forget my morning instruction and come down on my face or bum.' Once she was abandoned by the guide and Chips's wife, Lady Honor, and had the most painful descent, humiliated, nose-bleeding, cold and lost. When at last she reached the bottom she was told the guide had said she had turned back. 'Well, one *can't* turn back,' she commented plaintively. 'At least I can't.'

One of the pre-requisites of really enjoyable travel for Diana was that somebody else should pay for it. Some of the best holidays arose out of Duff's job as First Lord of the Admiralty. So did the most notorious, the cruise of the *Nahlin* with Edward VIII and Mrs Simpson on board.

EIGHT

Royal Circles

Since childhood Diana had been on the fringes of the royal family. She had always been known to them by name and by reputation, the latter being viewed with some disfavour by the starchier members of the court. Then it began to be said that she would make a good wife for the Prince of Wales. That the King and Queen ever seriously contemplated this possibility seems unlikely. Certainly neither Diana nor the Prince was enthused by the idea. It was still gossiped about in a desultory way until the moment of her marriage, but no one in the know, least of all the two leading figures, took the gossip seriously.

The Prince of Wales re-entered Diana's life in 1920, at a small luncheon given by the Laverys. 'I found him quite wonderfully charming,' wrote Duff in his diary. 'Of course there is a leaven of snobbery, or I should prefer to call it loyalty, which magnifies the emotion one feels about him. He is shy but has beautiful manners. Diana was singularly self-possessed, considering how nervous some things make her.' She was self-possessed because she did not find the Prince in the least intimidating. The King could inspire awe; perhaps when the Prince succeeded to the throne some of the mystery of majesty would wrap around him; but for the moment she found him agreeable and mildly pitiful. A few days later they met again at the Sassoons'. The Prince had Mrs Dudley Ward with him. Duff was in splenetic mood. 'Philip Sassoon and his cousin Mrs Gubbay brooded over the scene like a couple of conspiring pimps, which they are. It made me shudder to see their evil, scheming, semitic faces always watching those two sweet little Christians.' He went on to attribute this astonishing outburst to the fact that Philip Sassoon had refused to lend him his car at the end of the evening.

Though they met occasionally over the years, Diana and the Prince never became close friends. The nearest approach to a real rapport came when they were both staying at the Angleseys' house, Plas Newydd. The Prince poured out his heart over dinner, complaining of his miserable life. He never had a minute to himself; when at last he had arranged a day's hunting Bonar Law was inconsiderate enough to die and do him out of it. 'He described the gloom of Buckingham

Palace; how he himself and all of them "froze up" whenever they got inside it; how bad-tempered his father was; how the Duchess of York was the one bright spot there. They all love her and the King is in a good temper whenever she is there.' Possibly he regretted his indiscretions next morning; certainly he never repeated them. As the Nazi threat began to emerge and London society divided into the 'sound' and the appeasers, the Coopers, staunch champions of the sound, looked with some doubt on the allegedly pro-German tendencies of the heir to the throne. Duff never had cause for any confrontation with him, but the knowledge of their differences put a slight distance between them.

Though Diana had less in common with his brother Albert, future King George VI, she approved of him more whole-heartedly. Their first encounter had hardly been propitious. After a dance the Coopers swept into a car standing by the door, which they thought belonged to their friend June Chaplin. A few minutes later the Duke of York emerged, asked for his car and was told that it had been commandeered by Lady Diana Cooper. By the time it was returned the atmosphere was cool. Diana grovelled and got a most forgiving response, but still felt uneasy about future relations. She had no cause to worry; the Yorks went out of their way to be friendly when they met at the theatre and the Duchess noticeably took to Duff. 'They are really a rather sweet little couple,' wrote Duff. 'They reminded me of us, sitting together in the box having private jokes – and in the interval when we were sitting in the room behind the box they slipped out, and I found them standing together in a dark corner of the passage, talking happily. She affects no shadow of airs or graces.'

By the time that George V died, the Prince of Wales was inextricably involved with Mrs Simpson. Diana already had had a brush with Mrs Simpson's husband. He lured her on to the terrace at Blenheim after dinner, pawed her hungrily, called her his goddess and made a number of suggestions on how they might pass the night. By the time she escaped and got back to the house, all the other women had gone to bed and Duff was fuming, not so much from jealousy as because he felt he had been made to look a fool in front of the other guests. It was shortly after this that the Prince took them up again; probably because they were one of the few couples of position and respectability who fitted into the somewhat raffish ambience of Fort Belvedere. They were several times invited there for the weekend and were classified by London society with Emerald Cunard, Chips Channon and a few others, as being members of the 'Mrs Simpson camp'.

In fact Diana did not warm to Wallis Simpson. She found her lively and entertaining but never for one moment felt she was suitable as a

wife for Edward VIII, let alone Queen of England. Indeed it did not
occur to her that the threat was a real one until after most of her
friends had debated the issue exhaustively for many weeks. She did,
on the other hand, relish the fun and the consequence of weekends at
Fort Belvedere. She first went there in July 1935, staying 'in a pink
bedroom, pink-sheeted, pink-Venetian-blinded, pink-soaped and
pink-and-white maided'. Everything was done American style with
vast dinners and light forage-for-yourself luncheons. The Edens
arrived for tea at 6.30, and the period between 8.30 and dinner at ten
was filled with endless drinking. Diana stuck to gin and pineapple but
the Prince and Mrs Eden downed vast quantities of 100% proof
whiskey. 'It's a menace, there's no saying no. The Prince prepares the
potions himself with his own poor hideous hands and does all the
glass-filling.' Diana found endearing the Prince's consciousness of his
own ignorance: 'What's *'ad hoc'* mean, Duff? You can always tell me
the things I don't understand.'

Little changed superficially when he became King. On Sunday he
wore the kilt and marched round the table playing the pipes, 'Over the
Sea to Skye' and one of his own compositions. 'It's clever to have
chosen the pipes as one's show-off,' Diana wrote to Conrad, 'for
which of us can detect mistakes or know good from bad artistry?' But
the relationship between prince and paramour had evolved significantly. The King danced attendance on Mrs Simpson with disturbing
zest. 'Wallis must not get too bossy,' wrote Diana. 'I had rather she
had not said to him at dinner that she wanted to encourage his *reading*
his papers and documents, that he was inclined to have them read to
him – but that it was essential he should learn to master the points in
them. She is right of course, as he made haste to say. "Wallis is quite
right. She always is. I shall learn it quite soon."'

In August, 1936, Duff and Diana were summoned to join the
King's yacht, the *Nahlin*, on a Mediterranean cruise. The first indication they had that this might differ from other royal tours came
when they saw the King scrambling down the gangway, naked but for
straw sandals, grey flannel shorts and two crosses on a gold chain
round his neck. Ominously, Mrs Simpson wore duplicates of the
crosses on her wrist. The royal couple, as it became increasingly difficult not to consider them, were in the best suite at one end of the
yacht; all the guests were at the other. Diana was not impressed by
her companions. When they approached Ragusa after two or three
days dawdling around the islands the women exulted at being at last
near a civilized city. With field-glasses clapped to their eyes they
scanned the waterline: '"I don't see any hotels. Do you think that's
one? Can you read the name on that building? Could it be Excelsior or

Diana's mother, Violet
Duchess of Rutland

Henry Cust, a drawing of 1892
by the Duchess of Rutland

Diana with the Duke of Rutland at Arlington St in about 1916

Diana's sister Marjorie Manners, who became Marchioness of Anglesey

Diana's sister Violet, 'Letty', Manners, who became successively Lady Elcho and Lady Violet Benson

Belvoir Castle, dominating the Vale whose name it bears

LEFT: *Diana a year or so before the end of the Great War*

BELOW: *Duff Cooper as a young diplomatist in the Foreign Office*

Edward Horner, 'six foot four
inches tall with muscles and
shoulders to match, strikingly
handsome and with a good nature
and bonhomie that shone from his face'

Patrick Shaw-Stewart, 'pallid,
freckled, red-haired'

Raymond Asquith—'Most noble
in presence and with every grace
of voice and manner,' wrote John
Buchan, 'he moved among men
like a being of another world'

Diana and Duff on their wedding day, June 4, 1919

Diana as Lady Beatrice Fair in her first colour film, The Glorious Adventure, *1921*

*Duff at the seaside with Viola Parsons
(formerly Tree) and her son David*

Raimund von Hofmannsthal in 1926. 'Slim, graceful, infectiously light-hearted . . . he played the Rosenkavalier to Diana's Marschallin'

Carl Burckhardt shooting near Danzig in 1938

Diana motoring in France with Lord Wimborne in 1921

Feodor Chaliapin

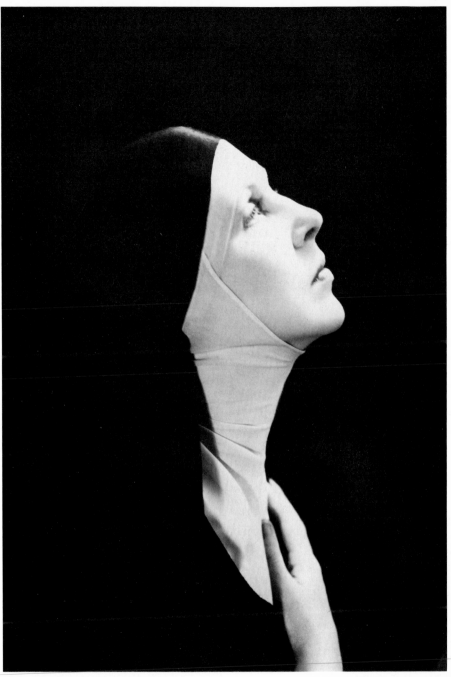

Diana as the Madonna (left) *and as the nun* (above) *in* The Miracle.

A group in California in 1926 at the time of The Miracle. From left to right: *'Kaetchen' (Rudolf) Kommer, Iris Tree, Max Reinhardt, Diana, Morris Gest*

Diana at the Lido

Conrad Russell in Home Guard uniform outside the Manor House at Mells

Duff at work in the cottage near Bognor

Diana electioneering, with her son, John Julius, voicing opposition

Diana rusticating at Bognor

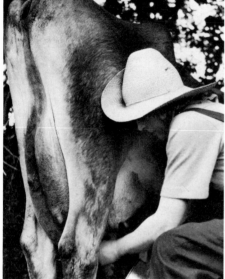

Duff with Louise de Vilmorin in Paris

Diana and Duff at the British Embassy in Paris

The Chateau de St Firmin, Chantilly, 'an eighteenth century house of exquisite dignity and serenity'

At the Embassy with the Ernest Bevins

*John Julius and Anne Norwich with their daughter, Artemis,
in Beirut in 1950*

Diana in Venice, dressed for the Bestigui Ball

Diana today, in front of an early portrait of her by Ambrose McEvoy

Imperial?" for all the world as though they had just come off the Gobi desert after weeks of yak-milk diet. The King seemed pleased with the place. "I think we'll stay here a day or two and relax." I longed to know what we'd been doing the last two days.'

As soon as the *Nahlin* had anchored Edward VIII went off in a rowing boat to look for a good sandy beach. By this time the boat was surrounded by curious sightseers, but they never guessed that 'this hot tow-headed little nude in their midst' was the King of England. Mrs Simpson 'looked a figure of fun in a child's piqué dress and a ridiculous baby's bonnet. As her face is an adult's face *par excellence*, the silly bonnet looked grotesque.' Next morning Duff and Diana were up at dawn sight-seeing; the rest of the party surfacing at noon for a bathe. In the evening the King and his guests managed a cursory stroll round the town. The King walked ahead with the Consul and Mayor. He was, wrote Diana, 'utterly himself and unself-conscious. That I think is the reason why he does some things he likes superlatively well, but it means he can't act, and therefore makes no attempt to do a thing he dislikes well.' The party's appetite for baroque churches proved limited and soon they took refuge in a hotel garden where the King sent to the yacht for whisky, lemon, gin, vermouth, ice and a shaker and settled down to make cocktails. Diana found peculiarly irritating his habit of apologizing regularly for the boat, the food, the company and most of all for himself. 'How he spoils everyone's fun.' She had decided that the King loathed her, but since another of the women on board believed the same was true of *herself*, she decided she might be exaggerating – 'anyway, it doesn't grieve me'.

At Corfu Duff and Diana were again away from the boat in the early morning on an expedition to the other side of the island, returning to dine with the King of Greece and his 'six common English intimates, including a very good-looking mistress called Mrs Jones'. Edward VIII paid particular attention to the last and charmed her totally, while Mrs Simpson's rasping wisecracks delighted the King of Greece. Diana felt the evening had been a success but trouble started when the party was back on board *Nahlin*. The King was fussing proudly over Mrs Simpson, and went down on his hands and knees to pull her dress from under the chair feet. She stared at him as one might at a freak: 'Well, that's the *maust* extraordinary performance I've ever seen'; and then she started to criticize his manner, the way he had talked to Mrs Jones, his attitude to the other king. Edward VIII began to look irritated and sad, and Diana left almost in protest, guessing the scene would continue for hours. 'I feel the sooner the trip ends for us, the better,' she wrote to Conrad. 'It's impossible to enjoy antiquities with people who won't land for them and who call Delphi

Delhi. Wallis is wearing very very badly. Her commonness and Becky Sharpishness irritate.'

The relationship between king and mistress was the principal fascination of the trip. On the whole Diana felt it would soon die a natural death, not from doubts on Edward's part but because Mrs Simpson was losing interest in the affair. 'The truth is she's bored stiff by him,' wrote Diana, after Wallis Simpson had refused, with some tetchiness, to go on a bathing expedition, 'and her picking on him and her coldness towards him, far from policy, are irritation and boredom.' As soon as the Coopers got back to London they were assailed by their friends, clamouring for news of the projected marriage. When they said they knew nothing at all about it and did not believe it anyway, they were greeted with incredulity. Obviously they had been sworn to secrecy. The *Nahlin* trip confirmed the popular belief that they were in the King's camp in what Chips Channon saw as 'a war to the knife between the past and the present'. Then, at a dinner for the Cavaliers – the supporters of the monarch, right or wrong – Channon found that Duff was a doubtful ally, 'revolted by the King's selfish stupidity'. Were the Coopers waverers, spies within the city walls? In fact they were as muddled as most people: loyal to the legitimate King; dismayed at the thought that he might insist on placing a twice-divorced American beside him on the throne; ready to consider any compromise that would avoid direct confrontation between crown and people. They differed from Baldwin only in that they did not rule out the possibility that one day, perhaps a year or more after the Coronation, the people might come to accept that Mrs Simpson could make a queen.

On November 17, 1936, Duff was called to the Palace. He concentrated on arguing that, if catastrophe occurred, history would put the blame on Mrs Simpson. He painted a lurid picture of the existence led by ex-monarchs, citing the misery of the King of Spain. 'Oh, I shan't be like Alfonso,' said the King. 'He was kicked out. I shall go of my own accord.' 'But how will you spend your time?' 'Oh, you know me, Duff. I'm always busy. I shall find plenty to do.' He winced when Duff referred to Mrs Simpson as 'twice married' and said that the first marriage hadn't really counted. Exactly what he meant by this Duff did not enquire.

Two days later Duff went to pick up Diana from the Channons', where the King had also been dining. He found him in high spirits, though complaining about the failure of the Government to control the BBC. Duff tried to explain about its independence. '"I'll change that," he said. "It will be the last thing I do before I go." He said this quite loud and with a laugh,. as though he was looking forward to going.' By this time both Duff and Diana had resigned themselves to the fact that abdication was the inevitable, perhaps even a desirable solution. Duff was moved but unshaken when Winston Churchill harangued him. 'What crime,' asked Churchill, 'has the King committed? Have we not sworn allegiance to him? Are we not bound by that oath? Is he to be condemned unheard?' Duff in the Cabinet still pleaded for delay but not in any real belief that the situation could be saved. On December 5 he and Diana lunched with Emerald Cunard, whose house was one of the last redoubts of the Cavaliers. 'It was curious,' Duff remarked drily, 'how everyone who had sought the views of taxi-drivers, hair-dressers, hospital nurses, clerks or servants, had heard exactly what they wanted to hear – that is to say their own opinions.'

After the abdication there was much talk of a black list; friends of the Duke and Duchess of Windsor who were not to be asked to royal functions. The newspapers were full of reports that Diana had curtsied to the Duchess of Windsor; a social misdemeanour which made it seem still more likely that the Coopers would be dropped. Diana was surprised how much the thought distressed her. Royal displeasure could be damaging to Duff's career, but her main regrets were less practical than that. She disliked the idea that she was going to be excluded from a privileged minority, cut off from a circle to which she had the entrée as of right. The court of King George VI might not offer much in the way of fun, but it was still the court; she might grumble at having to go there, but the injury to her pride would be considerable if the opportunity to grumble were denied her.

She had no cause for concern. In April, 1937, the Coopers were summoned to Windsor for the weekend; 'So much for the black list, anyway,' wrote Diana in triumph. It was the first time she had spent a night at the Castle and she marvelled at the encrustation of Victorian relics which adorned the vast building. Their sitting-room had thirteen oil-paintings of royalty including a Landseer sketch and 'about a hundred plaques, miniatures, intaglios, wax profiles etc of the family in two Empire vitrines and two bronze statuettes of King Edward VII in yachting get-up'. Diana's bedroom, 'throttlingly stuffy', contained nine more oils and the bathroom added a further eight dating from 1856 with a bronze statuette of Princess Louise on horseback and of Princess Beatrice on the moors. She sat next to the King at dinner and talked busily of the Coronation and the Castle; then plunged boldly and asked if he had heard of a supposed visit the Coopers were to pay to Ernest Simpson. The question did not go down particularly well, nor did Diana's sympathetic: 'How awful, it's a life-sentence for you.' 'Oh well, we all know that,' he replied frostily, but then came the question '"When did *you* first know about it?" From then on it was jabber, jabber, jabber. Lady Desborough on the King's left and Sir E. Ovey on my right got no conversation at all.'

After dinner Duff was closeted with the Queen for more than an hour. 'It's a bit of bad manners,' was Diana's first reaction; then, after midnight had struck, 'It's d'Artagnan (no! Buckingham), it's Bothwell; it's Potemkin, it's Lancelot, it's *boring*.' Duff emerged rosy with satisfaction but with no very clear memory of what had passed and the Coopers left Windsor with the impression that things would do a lot better under the new régime. Diana told a wistful Chips Channon how very different the atmosphere at Windsor had been to the old days at Fort Belvedere: 'That was an operetta, this an institution.'

Duff's career was at a point where the hostility of the royal family could have been most damaging. Many of his own party believed that he had been at best indiscreet, at worst mischievous, and that no sensible minister should have become embroiled in the scandal of the *Nahlin*. There was what Duff described as 'a whispering campaign' against him. His forthcoming dismissal was freely talked of, and when he was offered a lucrative contract to work as political adviser to the *Evening Standard* he was tempted to accept. 'I suppose that I shall never know who was behind this campaign,' he wrote in his diary. 'From two or three sources I learnt that it was Anthony Eden.' Diana believed the same and conceived a fierce dislike of Eden which lasted till he died.

Duff had become Secretary of State for War in November, 1935. He remained at the War Office for eighteen months. He himself felt that he was a success and that the army as a whole would share his view. Many disagreed. He had criticised Neville Chamberlain, then Chancellor of the Exchequer, for blocking certain desirable if expensive reforms. He had been intemperate in his attacks on Bishop Barnes and other pacifists. He had confirmed his reputation for indiscretion, and his ability as an administrator was open to doubt. He offended his more sober colleagues by his taste for parties and pleasure. Even the Queen had been quoted as saying that he ought to be careful not to burn the candle at both ends. 'I ought not to go to parties,' he resolved. 'I ought not to be seen having supper at restaurants. I ought not to drink too much.' He proved no more able to put into effect these very proper sentiments than he had been twenty years before.

Diana was his most energetic champion. Beaverbrook instructed Robert Bruce Lockhart to write an article denouncing Duff's tenure

of the War Office. Bruce Lockhart pulled his punches but made it
evident he felt Duff had been a failure. 'I can only tell you,' wrote
Diana, 'that the Government (P.M.s, two of them) never meant there
to *be* an army, nor that it should be equipped with armaments...
The money was never given out. What meagre equipment there is
today is due to three years' struggle of Duff's.' It was, indeed, Duff's
successes rather than his failures that led to his unpopularity with the
Conservative leadership. When he was summoned by Chamberlain
during a Cabinet reshuffle, he suspected that he was about to be
dropped. Instead he was offered the post of First Lord of the Admiralty. Diana was away in France and he wrote to her in ecstasy:

> 'How very fortunate I am. I have been tapping wood and cross-
> ing fingers. No money troubles, no health troubles, no love trou-
> bles, no political troubles and a perfect job. Can it last? I think even
> a few weeks' separation from you is a good thing. It makes me
> realise how much I love you, how much I miss you, how you are
> the backbone and the bottom, the beginning and the end of me.'

Diana was delighted because Duff was, but there were other reasons
for welcoming his transition. Ships were romantic things; the office
had a pleasantly heraldic ring about it; best of all, it carried with it
one of the most splendid houses in London. Admiralty House, built
in the late eighteenth century, looks out over the Horse Guards
Parade to St James's Park. It was already more than adequately furnished, but Philip Sassoon, now Minister of Works, indulged all save
her wildest fancies. A bust of Nelson was produced, a set of pictures
illustrating Captain Cook's voyages placed in the dining-room and a
large Guardi banished from it as being too sombre. Sassoon drew the
line, however, at a grand piano. Diana put an advertisement in the
personal column of *The Times*, was offered several, and triumphantly
installed the best of them in her drawing-room. On an expedition to
Copenhagen with Conrad Russell she bought a large and extravagantly naked mermaid which her companion was made to clutch to his
breast while tottering through Customs.

Admiralty House already possessed a fine set of dolphin-legged
chairs and tables made for a Mr Fish in 1815. Inspired by this, Diana
plunged into aquatic riot. She bought mirrors held by Neptunes or
nymphs, a dinner-service of Wedgwood shells, a tankful of sea-horses.
John Julius's schoolroom was transformed into a repository for
anchors, compasses, nets, binnacles and other maritime delights. To
Dirksen, the German Ambassador, 'a slow, dense, humourless, typically thorough scientific type', she poured out the details of her
pastime. '"Zo," he said, staring at me through his glasses with a look

both penetrating and alarmed. "Zo – you have a feesh complex!" I felt he knew more Freudian lore than I did, and shuddered to think what admission I had unconsciously made.'

As always with Diana's houses, her bedroom was the heart of the establishment. The bed itself rose sixteen feet from a shoal of gold dolphins and tridents to a wreath of dolphins at the crown, while ropes made fast the sea-blue satin curtains. Here she would hold court every morning; seeing friends; dictating letters; planning a raid on some Ministry of Works storehouse; reading or listening to music. She visited the room again in April, 1940, to find all the trimmings swept away and the new First Lord, Winston Churchill, using a narrow, curtainless pallet bed. Something of her presence perhaps lingered on, however. Many years later a maid at the Admiralty burst in on Mrs Healey and cried that she had seen a ghost, 'a lady with a very beautiful white face and staring blue eyes was lying in the state bed'.

'Luncheon very nasty, house superb,' commented Evelyn Waugh. His bile had perhaps been stirred by the fact that everyone was discussing a new play of which he had never heard, called, it seemed, 'a morning with the electric'. 'Diana', he complained, 'made me feel a bumpkin and wanted to.' He was unusual with this complaint; Diana's greatest strength as a hostess, indeed as a guest, was her ability to make bumpkins feel sophisticated; schoolboys mature; scholars, wits; and wits, profound. It was the first time that she had been able to indulge her appetite for entertaining in a way that was both formal and fantastic; the rooms of Admiralty House were admirably designed for the grandest of occasions, Diana's contribution was to leaven grandeur with fun, so that the dignity of the rooms was not lost but was never allowed to grow oppressive.

Another delight of the Admiralty was the yacht *Enchantress*, a thousand-ton sloop at the disposal of the First Lord. Their first expedition, in September 1937, was close to being the last as far as Diana was concerned. *Enchantress* took them from Anglesey, through the Minch to Uist and then on to Stornoway and round Cape Wrath. Stornoway was Stormoway and Cape Wrath so true to its name that the First Lord was tumbled out of bed and bounced about his cabin like a die in a dice-box. They joined the fleet at Invergordon, Duff inspecting the ships while Diana fraternized with the crew. 'Duff is thrilled all day and doing his stuff with enthusiasm and therefore doing it well,' she wrote to Conrad. 'They must like us better than the Hoares, mustn't they – but not I suppose as much as the Winstons.'

Bad weather had almost wrecked the trip, but that, felt Diana, could hardly be repeated in October's cruise in the Mediterranean.

They were picked up at Venice and sailed down the Dalmatian coast to Skyros, where they deplored the memorial to Rupert Brooke. 'It represents a huge nude man and when I say nude I don't mean maybe. It is like some ghastly advertisement in a German bugger-journal. How can Eddie Marsh have allowed it?' From there it was by way of Rhodes to Cyprus, where Diana delighted in a Turbaned Turk whose command of idiomatic English was more extensive than accurate. 'I am,' he assured her, 'hand in blouse with Lady Leconfield.' Cairo proved 'the hell of a town – loud and crude and common,' while the pyramids were much as might have been expected on the outside and inside pervaded by an asphyxiating smell of elephants. For one who habitually responded excitedly to the monuments of antiquity, Egypt's relics left Diana curiously cold. She was far more moved by the state of the sea, which defied propriety by producing a 105 m.p.h. gale:

> 'Water is everywhere,' she wrote to Conrad at the height of the storm, 'tearing down the passages, bearing the ship's treasure to and fro – silver candlesticks and (O! bad omen) the bugle. I look like a Dalmatian dog because my bureau has also broken loose and covered me with ink. I am on my knees as usual, praying without knowing how to make myself heard. The ship seems without a crew. No sailor or steward is seen or heard above the roar of waves and shivering of timbers. I look through the porthole once, and see mad milk boiling over and no sky. I bang the shutter with a vow not to look again.'

Lord Gage, a guest aboard, sought to cheer her up by giving her a roaringly funny description of the Admiral sitting nervously in his cabin with his life-jacket laid out like a boiled shirt on the bed in front of him. Diana failed to find the story even faintly cheering.

The third of the cruises in the *Enchantress*, in August 1938, was to the Baltic; to Kiel, where Duff had to propose Hitler's health and Diana drank it in water; to Lübeck where Brendan Bracken insisted on the band playing '*O Tannenbaum*', a tune equally well known as 'The Red Flag'; and on to Danzig. It was there that she got to know Carl Burckhardt, the League of Nations High Commissioner. Burckhardt had been brought up by Hofmannsthal, and so was almost an elder brother to Raimund. Diana had met him once before at Venetia Montagu's, had dismissed him as a slightly arid highbrow and was at first inclined to stick to her opinion. Then came an after-dinner shooting-party with no shooting but a lot of dancing in the dark. Brows fell, aridity diminished, 'I felt that Carl is to be a friend at least,' Diana reported to Conrad. Soon it was 'my dear, beautiful

Carl'. They disappeared together for a few days, allegedly to visit an exhibition of Velasquez's paintings; they roistered in Paris; they corresponded with romantic precautions, Diana's letters being signed '*ta nièce Inez*', Burckhardt addressing his letters to Phyllis de Janzé formerly Boyd. Diana, conscious of the fact that she was now forty-six years old and as always sceptical about her beauty, was flattered to be wooed so ardently by a man of Burckhardt's brains, good looks and international standing. She also enjoyed his company, though regretting the fact that they always spoke in French. 'What is so amusing is that his advances of courtship are identical with Raimund's,' she wrote to Duff in the early stages of the affair. 'The latter must have asked Carl as a boy for lessons and tips, but my new lover has it over Raimund every time for one reason, his hand is not like a hippopotamus's tongue. I could almost fall for him if I wasn't always in an agony of not understanding.'

In part, Diana's fling with Carl Burckhardt was spurred on by a hope that Duff would feel some anxiety. She relished the idea of getting something of her own back for Duff's long sequence of amatory escapades. In this she was wholly unsuccessful. 'Duff will never listen to accounts of my amours,' she wrote crossly to Carl. 'I fear it's genuine boredom, not a kind of delicacy.' Conrad, on the other hand, responded with amused outrage. 'Oh, what a story of lechery and of lasciviousness and lickerishness,' he wrote after Diana had described an outing to Paris. 'And to think you look so pure and good!' Early in 1939 she put off a projected meeting. Conrad accepted the delay with resignation but regret:

'And the reason!' he protested. 'Oh, dear! It's just a regular thing in your life now. If it isn't Geneva, it's Montreux, and if it isn't Montreux it's Calais or Boulogne. And always hotels and always two geese. I wonder what you'd think if Lady Weymouth and I carried on in that way. But it's no use pretending. Carl is madly in love with you and Lady Weymouth is not even mildly interested in my wooing. And it's clear you take a much, much deeper interest in Carl than ever I do in Daphne. Sometimes you say it'll be a relief when the war has actually started. Well, I feel I may be less unhappy when you and Carl have actually gone off together. It's the anxiety and suspense that kill.'

There was no question of Diana and Carl 'going off together' in any permanent sense, and Conrad was well aware of it. There was an element of play-acting about the relationship even at its most extravagant, and both protagonists would have been dismayed if they had been required to take it seriously. The war put a natural term to it. Burckhardt, a Swiss, paid a last visit to London in October, 1939 and distinguished himself by failing to turn up for his final assignation with Diana. 'I think he was probably in bed with another woman,' commiserated Conrad with some satisfaction. 'If ever there was a treacherous, lecherous, bawdy villain in this world I know where to find him.' Diana was more relieved than distressed. As she had found with Chaliapin nearly twenty years before, a little passion went a long way; and besides there were other, more important things to think about at the end of 1939.

The old Duchess of Rutland had died two years before. Diana had been abroad at the time of an earlier illness and Duff had written to warn that her mother's life was in danger. 'I could so well bear her death,' Diana replied. 'I am quite resigned and disgustingly selfish enough to hope it could happen when I was away, and this confession I am more ashamed of than any cowardly thought that ever passed through my distorted brain – but I cannot bear her to be anxious, or linger or suffer mentally.' In the event she did none of those things, but Diana was still shaken by the strength of her regrets. She did not go to Belvoir for the funeral but, when she knew that the ceremony was over, 'I got sad, sad, sad and had to crush surging memories and heartrending sentiment'. She had been at her mother's deathbed. The Duchess had seemed tranquil, resigned, then a few moments before she died she tried to struggle from her bed and had to be held down. '*Elle fuyait la mort*,' as Diana's French maid said grimly of another such scene. It happened just before Christmas, and her son John decreed that the festivities at Belvoir should not be disturbed. Anyone who rang to enquire was told that the Duchess's condition was unchanged, an elegant playing with the truth reminiscent of Franz Joseph's courtiers who for ten days after their master's death assured the world that the Emperor had left the palace for an un-named destination. From December 22 until December 27 Diana kept vigil at the Duchess's home in Chapel Street, alone with the corpse of her mother. Then she fled to Mégève to ski with John Julius. 'All these days I receive sad letters from Diana,' wrote Duff. 'She doesn't easily get over her mother's death.'

The Duchess left her house in Chapel Street to Diana, which meant that Gower Street, already deserted while the Coopers were at the Admiralty, was now obviously unneeded. To Diana's regret, they decided that it must be sold. There was no house in which she had been more happy and to abandon it was to put her youth finally behind her. Most of all, she regretted the loss of the drawing-room decorated by Rex Whistler with Roman plaques and vases in *trompe l'oeil*. For Duff the sacrifice involved a more immediate inconvenience. On several occasions he had used the empty house as a rendezvous for his illicit love-affairs. Once he was ensconced there when a party of potential buyers arrived with a key and demanded to inspect the property. Only with the greatest difficulty did he persuade them to go away and come back later. 'They must have suspected the worst,' he wrote in his diary, 'and they were right.'

Increasingly their life was being dominated by the coming war. The Coopers had had their first encounter with Nazi Germany in 1933 and had disliked intensely what they saw. Dismayed by the crowds at Bayreuth they took refuge in what should have been the quiet country town of Berneck. To their dismay they found themselves at the centre of what seemed to be an incipient Nazi rally. Seeking to distract them from an ill-cooked chicken, the waiter told them that Hitler was staying at the same hotel. Duff asked for an interview, and for half an hour Diana was left downstairs, praying that he would not lose his temper and put a premature end to their holiday. In fact he was fobbed off with Rosenberg, who said nothing of interest but offered them places for the Führer's forthcoming speech at Nuremberg. The speech bored them so much – mainly, no doubt, because neither spoke German – that they left half way through, but Diana at least got to within two feet of Hitler.

> 'His dark complexion had a fungoid quality, and the famous hypnotic eyes that met mine seemed glazed and without life – dead colourless eyes. The silly *mèche* of hair I was prepared for. The smallness of his occiput was unexpected. His physique on the whole was ignoble.'

Duff's bad opinion of the Germans was confirmed when he found that the barman was unable to mix a gin-fizz. He got still angrier when Diana tried to explain how it was done. It was no good, he felt, trying to improve people. Diana disagreed. She felt it was her mission in life to educate the world.

By 1936 the Coopers were prominent in the still small group which opposed Nazi Germany clamorously and urged rearmament. At a supper-party at Emerald Cunard's – 'a really magnificent stew of

Germans and French Jews and gentiles and Jockey Club stewards, tarts and duchesses and MPs and idiots' – Diana was sitting next to the German Ambassador, Ribbentrop. He asked if she had been to Berlin lately. No, she said, but she was going to Paris next day. To buy dresses? asked the Ambassador archly. '"No, to Flanders to see the war cemetery," I said, with a brave stare into his treacherous little eyes.' Usually, however, Diana left the more belligerent pronouncements to her husband. At a dinner-party given by Venetia Montagu, where Chips Channon found the company sadly pro-semite and out of touch, 'Crinks' Johnstone toasted the death of Ribbentrop. Diana thought this was going too far, but Duff added the rider that he should die in pain.

She did not much like the Germans she knew and was therefore all the more prepared to condemn the Nazis. The Italians she liked. Dino Grandi, the romantically bearded Italian Ambassador, wooed her fiercely. At dinner, while Diana made polite conversation about Whipsnade and Sir Oswald Mosley, he interrupted with hot whispers: 'We are just play-acting with this talk, Diana. Why do we have to do it?' 'Quite,' Diana replied politely, 'why indeed?' But she did not feel she was play-acting at all. She successfully kept the ardent Ambassador at bay, but 'old Wopping' amused and pleased her. He represented Fascist Italy; there must therefore be something to be said for Fascism, Italian style. Duff, more rationally, felt that it was folly to quarrel with Germany and Italy at the same time. When Italy invaded Abyssinia he found himself on the other side to his usual allies, Eden and Churchill. Politically he regretted Eden's resignation and feared the advent of Halifax: 'He knows very little about Europe, very little about foreigners, very little about men. He is a great friend of Dawson, whose influence is pernicious, and I think he is also a friend of Lothian, who is always wrong.' Personally, he was not sorry to see Eden go, believing him to be an enemy. Diana actively rejoiced at Eden's departure and hoped that it would clear the way for Duff's eventual succession to the Foreign Office.

It was the Abyssinian crisis that inspired Diana's solitary foray into high diplomacy. At a dinner-party in the House of Commons, attended, *inter alia*, by Winston Churchill and Lord Tyrrell, Permanent Under-Secretary at the Foreign Office, there was much debate about how Italy was to be persuaded from her adventurist course. Diana was due to leave next day to attend the canonisation of Thomas More – lover of Italy, wife of a senior Minister, who better could warn the Italians that they risked creating bitter resentment in Britain? She gamely undertook the mission but achieved nothing. It is doubtful whether anyone in authority was even aware of her presence and the only noticeable mark of her passing was a turbulent scene at Lord Berners's luncheon-party. The Princess San Faustino was so offended by Diana's well-intentioned political homily that she stormed from the table before the meal was over.

Diana was in Geneva in September 1938 when it was announced that Chamberlain was to fly to Germany to try to secure a settlement to the problem of Czechoslovakia. She was sitting next to de Valera at a British Empire dinner when the news came. 'This is the greatest thing that has ever been done,' pronounced de Valera. Diana was sceptical, but more preoccupied by doubts as to whether her neighbour would stand up for the national anthem. She had promised to get him to his feet, and was ready to take a pin to him if necessary. Eventually she plucked up the courage to ask him his intentions and was relieved to find that it had never occurred to him not to stand with the other guests.

Diana had gone to Geneva for a quiet holiday with John Julius but soon found herself caught up in a League of Nations Conference, acting as unofficial hostess to the British delegation. Halifax was there briefly, the young R. A. Butler, Litvinov smelling strongly of garlic, Carl Burckhardt. Diana gave a party in the deserted Villa Diodati, a rococo pleasure-house overlooking the lake where Byron had once lived. She lit it with candles and filled it with flowers; Maurice de Rothschild produced the wine and Chips Channon most of the food – 'It cost a fortune,' complained Diana. Burckhardt produced a bevy of Swiss beauties and R. A. Butler lured the wife of the consul on to the balcony and began to recite Lamartine to her. When he got to the end of the poem he looked round to find that his partner had fled and the balcony was bare.

And so back to a London where trenches were being dug in the London parks. Diana had made herself absurd two years before in the eyes of many of her friends by taking a Red Cross course in the treatment of gas-victims; now first aid was the rage and the threat of war a staple of conversation. In office or out, Duff Cooper, with men like Stanley, Cranborne, Hore-Belisha, looked to Churchill for leadership. Admiralty House was a centre for their plotting. Oswald Mosley was their *bête noire*: 'Canting, slimy, slobbering Bolshie,' Duff had described him in 1923, in 1938 he would have substituted Nazi for Bolshie but otherwise kept the description unchanged.

Soon after Diana's return came Chamberlain's meeting with Hitler at Munich. As soon as he heard the full terms of the settlement, Duff decided that he must resign. Not all the 'sound' were ready to go so far, and his action surprised many of his friends. Harold Nicolson saw the headline 'Cabinet Minister resigns' and assumed that it was Lord

De la Warr. When he heard the truth he was impressed: 'That is fine of him. He has no money and gives up £5000 a year plus a job that he loves.' Though not everyone regretted his departure – 'Good riddance of bad rubbish,' remarked Alexander Cadogan tartly – there was agreement on every side that he had behaved with dignity and self-sacrifice. 'Most honourable conduct,' Sir Odo Russell found it. '*She* won't like it! She won't like giving up Admiralty House and the yacht.'

Nor did she like it. Duff at least had the consciousness of duty done, and the heady if fleeting delights of being feted as a hero. For Diana it was all loss: loss of the house she loved so much, loss of the perquisites, the holidays at sea, the consequence, the money. Some acquaintances like Odo Russell assumed that she would plead with Duff to change his mind, or at least would silently disapprove. They were wholly wrong. Diana never for a moment questioned Duff's judgment and supported him wholeheartedly. On many things she held her own strong views but on matters of politics, as on money or learning, she felt that Duff knew best. On this occasion her instinct had brought her to the same conclusion. She loathed Nazi-ism, was sickened by the stories of the persecution of Jews which were beginning to filter out of Germany, feared war but was prepared to risk it rather than suffer abject humiliation and the triumph of tyranny. Her views were unsophisticated but not without courage and generosity. History proved her right.

For the moment she was sustained by the enthusiasm that her husband's sacrifice engendered. Four thousand letters were received in the first few days, almost all of them supporting Duff. Answering these, training John Julius to forge his father's signature, concealing this convenient technique from Duff, took time and energy. 'Duff will get a swollen head if people don't stop treating him as the Saviour of Honour,' she wrote to Katharine Asquith. 'For the moment he's good and serene and free of conscience. I'm proud and not the least regretful – only bewildered by an entirely new future.'

Leaving Admiralty House and moving into her mother's house in Chapel Street was one troublesome part of that future. Luckily money was not a problem. A lucrative contract with the *Evening Standard* meant that Duff was better off as a result of leaving office. In theory he was pleased to be able to devote more time to his writing and to escape the pressures of politics. In fact he fretted in the wings, longing to be on stage where the action was. Diana fretted with him. 'Duff Cooper and Eden, who resigned but won't fight, expect to be re-called to the Cabinet for being good and causing no trouble,' wrote Cecil King cynically. Diana knew well that Duff was bent on causing all the trouble he could and that it would take something near a miracle to persuade Chamberlain to invite him back. Churchill told her that he would certainly be in any future War Cabinet and that Duff should 'wait patiently for he would not fail him'. But how long would the wait be, and who could be patient at such a moment? The *Express* ran a competition to select the ideal cabinet. Diana urged her friends to enter. 'Put Duff as Home Secretary,' she urged Conrad. 'I don't think I could face moving back to the Admiralty again.'

1939 began. Diana took John Julius skiing in Italy. At the frontier a great banner proclaimed: *'Mussolini a sempre ragione'*. 'I told John Julius never to forget the idiocy of those words.' Much of that last summer was spent at Bognor. Diana was in richly apocalyptic mood. 'The days were long and, as I see them now, particularly radiant. I remember feeling that all they lit had the poignancy of a child that has to die.' She was convinced that war would come, that Duff would go to battle, that most of her friends and relations would follow him, that even John Julius – then ten years old – would eventually fall victim. She meditated a suicide-pact with Duff and even propounded it to him in all solemnity, only to be laughed out of it by his robust belligerence. One spring day they lunched off lobster, cold grouse, Montrachet 1924 and Chateau Yquem 1921. Duff noted that they were all in excellent form, 'except Diana who, poor darling, cannot face the war at all'.

Through the summer came the count-down to war. The German ultimatum on August 31 demanded the virtual dismemberment of Poland. To Duff's dismay Diana could not see why it should not be accepted. 'I felt that the reactions of millions of people might be the same as hers.' Diana he could convince of the real truth, but who would do the same for the people of Britain? Next day she took John Julius into Bognor to buy fresh prawns for lunch. They saw a little crowd clustered round a motor-car and, on principle, joined in. From inside, a car-radio was announcing the invasion of Poland. Diana took John Julius's arm and led him away. 'You can't imagine just how important this is going to be for everyone,' she told him. 'Nothing will ever be the same again.'

NINE

First Years at War

The outbreak of the First World War had found Diana excited, exhilarated even; mildly irritated at the disruption of her social life; confident that all would be over in a few months before any of her dearest friends ran serious risk in battle. It was some time before she realised the enormity of the catastrophe that was overtaking her world. September, 1939, in contrast, found her in black despair, convinced that London would shortly be destroyed by bombardment, its people choked by gases, famine and disease rampant among those who survived. It was some time before she realised that nothing of the sort was going on; that things, in fact, were remarkably unchanged.

By the time the phoniness of the phoney war had become apparent, she was, indeed, already far away. Duff had long been pledged to go to the United States in October 1939 on a lecture tour. When war came he hoped for employment, but though Churchill, now back in the Cabinet, muttered that all would be well, it did not seem as if anything was in the offing. In America he would make some money and have a chance to put Britain's case. Chamberlain was grudgingly acquiescent, sending his private secretary to Duff the night before he departed with the almost incredible instruction that, during his tour, he was to avoid saying anything that might smack of propaganda for the Allied cause. To this Duff resolved to pay no attention.

Duff and Diana left Southampton on October 12. Preparations had been chaotic, largely thanks to the ministrations of a lunatic butler who packed for Duff as for the Hunting of the Snark. There were fifteen small valises, half of them empty and the other half packed for single one-legged men. Each contained a suit and collar, one shoe, the top of a pair of pyjamas or the bottom, one handkerchief and a sock. 'It is too peculiar,' said Diana sadly. Photographers swarmed around the ship but she pleaded with them not to photograph the former minister in case the Germans assigned a special submarine for his destruction. Her precautions did not comfort one gloomy fellow-passenger who had been a survivor of the *Lusitania* and now announced that she would have cancelled her passage if she had suspected so obvious a target would be on board. Diana's own spirits remained high. 'I feel

that this is the first time I have been part of real life,' she told Conrad.
'I was going to say "except when John Julius was born" but even that
wasn't very real. Artifice, science and drugs veiled the reality.'

Her cheerfulness did not long survive arrival in New York. Ill
health, reaction from former excitement, guilt at leaving Britain at a
time of crisis, a bout of irrational melancholia, all contributed to her
determination to view everything with a jaundiced eye. She was
staying with the Paleys, rich, intelligent, successful. He was President
of the Columbia Broadcasting System and she found him 'very, very
attractive. 100% Jew but looking more like good news from Tartary' –
everything she most liked in men. Yet the luxury was too stifling, the
taste too exquisite, the wit too sophisticated and sterile. People rarely
seemed to read and never to write. When Duff said he must write
some letters, 'the footman was asked to find all the necessities, as if
one had asked to make toffee on a wet afternoon'. Diana knew that she
was being carping and ungrateful, but she could not feel content.

The Coopers were fêted at a series of parties, each more elegant
than the last. The Americans were extravagantly friendly, but their
preoccupations were not the same. At the Cole Porters': 'They all talk
of war, but I have a feeling it is because it comes under their duty to
us, that really the interest except to keep out has died in them.' At
luncheon with Mrs Ryan: 'I felt I should have to leave, I was so ill and
irritable.' Under the surface sympathy anglophobia still ran strong.
The only book widely advertised was Louis Bromfield's *The Rains
Came*, a novel about India sharply critical of British rule.

Diana found that she could not enjoy the New York life which once
had seemed so delectable. She was taken to the smartest nightclub,
boasting what was said to be the best swing orchestra in America. 'A
room the size of the two Bognor sitting-rooms with a band composed
of sixteen assassins, bursting their cheeks and guts and bladders
with blowing and banging and stamping and blaring. I got home at
three and couldn't sleep with the horror of it all, and the hideous
expense [Diana was outraged to find the dollar had risen to $3.90 to
the pound], and the great war, and the heart pounding against the
electric air. The fire engines screech through the streets as soon as one
drops off, and whine and yell like hell's special sirens.'

A nightmare weekend with the Averell Harrimans provided little
relief. There were thirty guests, mostly writers of one kind or another
– Robert Sherwood, Harold Ross, George Abbott, Charles Mac-
Arthur – but as they passed their time drinking and playing endless
games of dice, cards or mah-jong, they might as well have been the
most illiterate philistines. Any conversation was drowned by the
thunder from the bowling-alley which adjoined the one vast drawing-

room. There was no fixed time for meals; they were late or later and uneatable when they came, so that Diana was forced to creep into the kitchen and beg for a piece of cake. Charles MacArthur, then one of America's most successful dramatists, passed out in the pantry three nights running and had to be carried upstairs to bed. 'Why does Charles always choose the pantry?' the guests asked crossly. 'I thought it showed discretion on his part,' commented Diana to Conrad. Duff managed to find a four of bridge but nobody paid the slightest attention to Diana and she spent most of the weekend in her room trying unavailingly to sleep.

Her spirits were not improved by her suspicion that nobody but Duff and herself were making any attempt to put over the British case. Apart from 'a few cultural sods sent over by the Ministry of Information to talk about Swinburne,' the official voice was mute. Propaganda was believed to be vulgar, probably counter-productive. Those Britons that *were* to be heard said the wrong things. Freddie Lonsdale was a menace, 'always saying Germany was sure to win and had been driven into war'. His camp followers were even worse. Duff berated them and they drifted on to Diana to complain. 'Duff says we're traitors,' they protested. 'That wouldn't matter much,' said Diana. 'It's the Americans saying it that riles me.' They protested that everybody had a right to speak out, whereupon Diana asked why they had been asking people not to pass on to Duff what they had been saying. 'They looked awfully guilty and slunk away much upset, but they will not profit or change their behaviour a jot. Only fear could do that, and we cannot frighten them.'

Her health did not make things any better. She went to a doctor to have wax removed from her ear, rashly admitted that she suffered also from chronic lumbago and, over her feeble protests, was stripped, X-rayed, stethoscoped, weighed and sent forth into the world swathed in twenty layers of white adhesive plaster. With the aid of Benzine and chloroform the mummy eventually managed to extricate itself from its carapace, but scarlet, covered with a rash and as sticky as fly-paper. At that evening's dinner, given by Hamilton Fish Armstrong; 'I dared not shake hands or pick anything up and my dress was stuck to me like rind to an apple.' Perhaps in part because of this treatment, she passed the next few weeks in increasing discomfort from a skin disease and was reduced eventually to swollen, spotted shame. Dr Ludwig Loewenstein, America's leading dermatologist, 'put my head in a steaming machine, then under an X-ray, then under a violet ray, giving me injections in the bum and ointments and all the rest of it. Tea, out of the pot, has to be applied every morning and evening.' The ointment, which smelt of dung, turned out to be the same as that used by would-be nigger-minstrels so, next day, 'Poor Black Joe looks at me from the glass, underneath was lobster-red. Since applying the dregs of Duff's morning tea it's turned Hindoo. The smell of dung persists.' Only her faith in Dr Loewenstein induced her to continue with the treatment, but she did, and faith was justified.

In Washington things began to go better. Duff was doubtful what sort of a reception they would get at the Embassy, but Lord Lothian welcomed them enthusiastically. 'Giggly and pleasant and badly-dressed,' Diana found him. He gave a dinner in Diana's honour in which she sat next to the poet Archibald MacLeish. She delighted in him, and equally in his disconcertingly frumpish wife who won her heart by proclaiming after dinner: 'The trouble about Mr Woollcott is that his flies are always open.' Joseph Alsop met her at lunch at the Embassy and can still recall her piercing blue eyes and the white Molyneux dress with coffee-coloured trimmings which she wore on that occasion. It had been feared that the Ambassador might try to sabotage a proposed meeting with the President but, on the contrary, he expedited it. 'He'll say he's met you before,' he warned Diana. He did; the first words Roosevelt uttered were: 'Lady Diana, come and sit next to me. I haven't seen you since Paris, 1918.' The President was gleeful over the recent repeal of the Neutrality Bill and made no pretence of being neutral himself. Perhaps deliberately he concentrated on Diana and avoided a tête-à-tête with Duff; the only direct question he asked him was the name of the Head of Naval Intelligence, and as Duff could not remember, the conversation did not develop. 'I was a bit nervous and didn't do very well with him,' Diana told John Julius, 'but he did well with me. If his legs had not been paralyzed he'd have danced a war-dance.'

From that moment all seemed to change. Diana felt as if some poison had mysteriously drained from her system. 'My heart is no longer dead within me,' she told Conrad. 'It is heavy with sunk ships and a child and a lover I miss, but it's alive again.' She seemed too to sense a different spirit among the Americans. At a large luncheon given by Tom Lamont, an eminent banker, Mrs Lamont got to her feet and announced a toast which she said no one need drink if they did not want to: 'Here's to the victory of the Allies and to hell with neutrality!' Everyone drank, though some with more enthusiasm than others, while Diana wept in gratitude. When Duff lectured in Brooklyn, trouble was predicted and five hundred police were posted around the auditorium. In the event only a handful of dispirited demonstrators appeared, carrying banners reading 'We won't be dragged in' and 'Send Duff home!' 'It merely gave Duff a chance to do a turkey-cock about the last stronghold of liberty being none too impregnable when you get demonstrations (there wasn't one) and picketing (that hadn't come off) against a man speaking his mind.'

For three months the Coopers were ceaselessly on the move. South Bend, Indiana, was the worst place they visited; Toledo, Ohio, the most agreeable. At Akron, Ohio, Diana was delighted by a bar with a panorama on one wall of a sandy bay edged with palm trees. Suddenly the view darkened, thunder pealed, lightning flashed, torrential rain descended. 'It was all operated from a tiny magic electric box by two aborigines who were enjoying it madly.' Outside snow lay thick. At Chicago there was a St Andrew's night dinner with a ram's head, haggis, reels, sword-dance and Auld Lang Syne, but not a drop to drink. 'What is the idea? Prohibition is dead. Is it a legacy? Why do they all have to drink behind closed doors? I can't make it out.' Dining in Boston she sat next to an American who told her he used to live in London, in Oxford Square. 'To me,' said Diana, recalling afternoons spent there with the Asquiths, 'Oxford Square means painting a gigantic map on the wall. I wonder if it was washed out by the next tenant?' 'No,' said the man. 'I varnished it.' Barbara Hutton arranged the list of those invited to Duff's lecture in Palm Beach. Joseph Kennedy was not included, and when pressed for an explanation, Barbara Hutton explained that while he had been Ambassador in London she had found herself there, abandoned and unhappy. Kennedy was eager to help, but the help was to consist mainly of setting her up as his mistress. 'I gather some pouncing accompanied these propositions,' Diana wrote to Conrad. 'How amusing, and how little I would have thought of it! Mr Asquith and Lord Wimborne, to think of only two old gentlemen, both put forward more or less the same plan to me, and I thought it so flattering. While poor Barbara feels she can never look Kennedy in the face again. She is probably right and I am wrong.'

At Fort Worth, Texas, they stayed with Amos Carter, 'far and away the greatest boaster and god-darned bore we've hit yet'. Over the huge log-fire was the stuffed head of a steer, his eyes flashing with red electric wrath, his nose snorting little puffs of smoke. Amos Carter disappeared and shortly afterwards the steer delivered a speech of welcome. Mr Carter possessed a collection of hats belonging to celebrities, including Lord Rothermere and the Prince of Wales, and a life-size wax nymph with eyelashes and real hair. The lecture that evening was introduced by the President's son, Elliot Roosevelt, who opened question-time by asking, 'Hasn't the British Empire been built up by deeds similar to Hitler's?' Hardly, felt Diana, the question to be expected from your own chairman. It was at Fort Worth, too, that Duff was told of the appendicitis victim who pleaded that his navel should not be cut into. When asked why, he explained: 'There is nothing I like better than lying naked on my bed eating celery, and I always put salt in it.' At Oklahoma City they went to see *Gone With the Wind*. When they entered the theatre everybody stood and sang 'God Save The King'.

Hollywood was the furthest point of their expedition. They stayed with Jack Warner, richest and most powerful of the Warner brothers. 'Diana is never happy in great comfort and longs to take me riding in the desert,' noted Duff. But though the sybaritic luxury grated, she took a childish delight in meeting the stars. Dietrich came to dinner with Erich Remarque, author of *All Quiet on the Western Front*. She was wearing a black trouser-suit made of velvet with Fauntleroy jabot and cuffs; 'her face is really lovely,' wrote Diana, 'but she took so little interest in Duff and me that we are not very gone on her'. Errol Flynn she disliked intensely; apart from being anti-British and thinking the war foolish, he was vainer than any actor she had met. Charlie Chaplin she knew already. He was in the middle of making *The Great Dictator,* but though he said it was going to be magnificent, Diana had her doubts. She had an interminable conversation with him afterwards: 'I did not think he made very much sense – who knows that the boot was not on the other foot!' Of all the stars she met, her favourite was 'a young man called James Stewart'.

Diana was more to Duff on this expedition than just a companion. He acclimatized well to his surroundings: 'He has given up carying a stick or umbrella,' Diana told John Julius. 'He is very energetic and full of hustle as though he thought "Time was Money". He speaks through his nose and soon he will be wearing pince-nez and smoking a cheroot, and may even grow a little goatee beard.' But though he had complete confidence on the lecture rostrum he found the necessary conviviality before and after the event a painful duty. He had no small talk and relied on Diana to ease his passage, in the same way as he had relied on her to make a success of his parties at Gower Street and Admiralty House. The lectures would have been well received in any case, but the affection that they left behind them was largely Diana's doing.

Only the most churlish denied that the visit had been worthwhile. No dramatic shift in American policy ensued, but many people in a position to shape public opinion understood the British position better and felt more sympathy for it. Financially it had been less of a triumph. They had expected to make a minimum of $15,000 from the trip, but the expenses had been so great that they ended up with barely half that amount. Diana would not have cared if they had actually lost money, so pleased was she to be going home. She had as yet hardly adjusted to the austerity that lay ahead for Britain. Home thoughts from abroad in February 1940 included speculation as to where the Easter holidays should be spent. 'Bognor will be frightfully cold. I have no servants but Wade, Nanny and the two Joneses. Can we run it on that? I don't see why not, on lobsters, pâtés, salads, tinned stuff, baked potatoes. Then there is honey and cheese and prawns and tunny fish and foie gras that needs no cooking.' A slight flavour of Marie Antoinette still clung about her a few weeks after her return. She speculated on why people would talk all the time about the food shortage. 'I can't think why, because there seems to be masses. The poor still refuse to eat all the things I love – hare, rabbits, venison, trout etc.'' Such attitudes were not long to survive the opening of the total war.

The Coopers returned to find their Bognor cottage 'dense with child-refugees,' the unfortunate exiles digging in the chilly sands with gas-masks dangling around their necks. Duff and Diana perched uneasily in Chapel Street but the house was too big, too difficult to run in wartime. Duff was unemployed and restless, Diana suffering with him, unable to settle to anything.

'What a hopeless hell is it,' she wrote to Juliet Duff, 'so much worse than 1914 when there was a fanfare and a display of courage and high-spirits, cheering, boozing. I'm taking it like the lesser breeds are supposed to take danger – but don't – with a drawn ghastly face no paint will disguise, wet hands, despairing lassitude. I'm deeply ashamed and feel it would be much better if I had anything to do, but I haven't even a house to run. Two families with four children each are in occupation here, but they 'do' for themselves and are no trouble at all. I've rung up the Labour Exchange about helping with the harvest but they say they know nothing about it. We can't plant spuds till spring. Duff is, I can see, in a state of concealed restlessness. He has no job, he the great fire-eater – if I leave him for a second he'll go to France as an interpreter or liaison man and I shall go out of my mind.'

At one point Duff actually set out to re-enlist in the Grenadiers. He had his old uniform altered, donned puttees and Sam Browne and set off for the wars. It was a gallant but abortive effort. The generals called him 'Sir' and it soon became clear that no one had a job for a fifty-year-old second lieutenant with several years of Cabinet service behind him.

Then came the invasion of Norway. In 1917 Duff had bet Patrick
Shaw-Stewart £1500 to £100 that Winston Churchill would never be
Prime Minister. In May 1940 he lost his bet. Chamberlain's Government fell, Churchill replaced him, and Duff was invited to serve as
Minister of Information. It was not a post in which he was ever to feel
at ease. He found his duties ill-defined and distasteful. Unjustly, he
was attacked by the press for seeking to suppress their liberties, and
found it temperamentally impossible to establish a relationship with
proprietors or journalists that would remove the misunderstandings.
To the public he was an ogre, none the less repellent for being slightly
comical – 'Cooper's Snoopers' became a by-word for official interference with the freedom of the individual. With little support from
the Cabinet and less from his staff, his remedy was often to retreat to
White's and play bridge. 'More impotent, more negligible and more
defeated than one would have thought possible,' was Cecil King's
judgment; and though it was unfairly harsh it was not wholly beside
the mark.

Diana did her best to make things work. Eminent American journalists like Vincent Sheean, who might have been riled by the inevitable
censorship, were lulled by her into a mood of acquiescence. Walter
Monckton, one of the few wholly capable organizers on Duff's staff
and meditating escape to greener pastures, was surprised to get a
'rather miserable' letter from Diana begging him to stand by his minister. Her role was never more than peripheral, however; she hardly
visited the ministry and knew little of Duff's work. 'Papa tells me
nothing,' she complained to John Julius. 'It's been a grievance for
twenty years.' Knowing that Duff was unhappy and disaffected, she
suffered with him but could do little to help. 'It's a hard life, politics,
and you must have most of the things in "If". Papa has most of them
and is unaffected by bludgeonings, but your poor Mummy has none
of them.'

Her own wartime activity was helping in a canteen at the YMCA.
Every morning she would rise at six-thirty, put on blue overalls and
yachting cap and with tin hat and gas-mask over her shoulder make
her way to the canteen. There was often no hot water, so the problem
of giving breakfast to four hundred men could be considerable; but
somehow it was managed. Cooking, serving and washing up took till
mid-day. Then it was home for a bath and usually abortive telephoning, and off to Chapel Street to pack up books, pictures and china for
eventual storage at Belvoir. Most dreaded disturbance of the routine
was the periodic giving of blood. The process filled her with horror,
not least because her veins seemed to be abnormally slim and the
doctor would have to battle with his 'big, blunt bodkin' to secure an

entry. 'The tears run out of my eyes in torrents. "Does it really hurt so much?" asked the doctor, but I couldn't answer for tears.'

After the evacuation from Dunkirk Diana was asked to work with the Free French who were billeted at Olympia. This soon palled, however. All she was given to do was sew tricolors on soldiers' caps, 'speak French to them in my inimitable way, sell them toothpaste and bootlaces and seek out girl-friends for those who seemed most deserving'. Washing up four hundred breakfasts in cold, greasy water seemed a better use of her energies.

She was filled with plans for aiding the war-effort. One problem that concerned her was how British soldiers were to be distinguished from German parachutists. Badges or armlets would not provide an answer since they could be taken from the dead. Suddenly she thought of war-paint. 'Paint all our boys' faces blue one day, scarlet the next, tiger stripes another day or snow-white. I don't see how the enemy could catch up on that.' Another brainwave which she hastened to pass on to the War Office provided for 'some very strong magnates [*sic*] in open spaces – parks and even squares – to attract the land mines that come down slowly by parachute'. The authorities wrote to assure her that 'a great many of the suggestions they received were far more foolish than hers'.

She was swept away by the mood of defiant patriotism that consumed Britain in 1940. The Duke of Windsor outraged her by allegedly saying that the English must be mad not to see they were doomed: 'Well, maybe we are, but I'd rather be mad than turned slave by fear or reason.' But she could not go so far as those of her friends who hungered for the Germans to come so that they might be defeated. 'Your poor mother was never as brave as that,' she told John Julius. 'I would rather victory was achieved by famine and revolt in Europe than by hideous hordes in England.' She was confident that God was on the right side. 'It's difficult, I find, to pray about the war, one feels both sides are praying equally hard. Still, I think that is the best we can do. He knows we're fighting for all that Christ taught us was good and that the Huns are not. I love God and greatly rely on him.'

Her son's safety preoccupied her and when Joe Kennedy, the American Ambassador, offered to procure him a passage in a neutral ship to the United States, she leapt at the idea. She realised that to some this would look like cowardice and was disturbed by Churchill's disapproval – 'I hate these little Ambassadors,' he snorted – but the counter-arguments seemed to her too strong. She was haunted by the vision of Britain over-run, Duff with the Government in Exile and John Julius held by the Germans as a hostage. Duff initially resisted the idea but allowed himself to be overborne. Possibly he suspected that, if necessary, Diana would have had John Julius passed from hand to hand like a recusant priest and shipped illegally from the country. If he had pleaded that his son's evacuation would damage his career, Diana might have yielded, but arguments based on the national interest seemed to her unconvincing. They had to weather a certain amount of hostile comment, and Diana got a brief flurry of indignant letters and telephone calls, but the matter was soon forgotten in the larger crisis.

John Julius left in July 1940. The *Daily Mirror* carried a picture of him 'sitting on your pathetic bottom on your pathetic trunk. You looked like all the refugees of the world rolled into one wistful little victim of the Nazi follow-my-leader. I nearly howled.' He was carried to America on a tide of exhortations. Kaetchen Kommer, who was charged with his welfare, was to make sure that John Julius was never spoiled. It was to be buses, not taxis; drug stores, not restaurants; clothes from Bloomingdale's, not Saks. If he was rude to Americans, imitated their accent or behaved less than perfectly, he was to be severely reproved. To her son she wrote: 'Remember always that you represent England in your way and that you must be respected by all the boys and masters as much as you want them to respect and admire our adored England. Don't forget that there's a war being fought and that it's *got to be won*, and that your contribution towards winning it is to be better, more hard-working, more thoughtful and braver than usual.'

She was very aware that she was depriving John Julius of an experience which he might come to regret. The old gardener at Bognor underlined this poignantly. 'Wouldn't John just love it,' he said repeatedly. 'There's a German plane lying at Rose Green and another in Pagham Harbour. The dead Germans are still lying there. Smell something frightful, they do. Wouldn't John just love it!' John would just have loved it, but there was time enough for that. Whatever the course of the war might be, Diana knew that it could not possibly be a short one. Her son, she decided, should come back when he was thirteen. 'Thirteen I feel to be an age of grown-upness when you are no longer to be treated as a baby that must have bangs and alarms and disease and hunger kept from it. At thirteen you will feel perhaps that you must share in the struggles of other English boys who are here.'

By now they were installed in a bilious-coloured suite on the eighth floor of the Dorchester Hotel. They got it cheap, because few others wanted rooms so close to the roof. Otherwise the hotel was much favoured among the homeless rich, its ultra-modern wind-resistant steel structure offering, in theory at least, protection against acts of God or man. The place seethed with friends and acquaintances; Emerald Cunard, the Halifaxes, Ann O'Neill were permanent residents; Evelyn Waugh, trying to spend a night near Diana, was offered the choice between the Turkish baths and St. John Hutchinson's bed if neither he nor his daughter were using it. Cecil Beaton left a vivid impression of life in the hotel lobby one September evening in 1940:

'The scene is like that on a transatlantic crossing, in a luxury liner, with all the horrors of enforced jocularity and expensive squalor... Diana is nervous: she darts, every so often, with enquiries to the hall-porter. As she staggers down the lobby like a doll with its leg put on sideways, the fellow-passengers point, "That's Lady Diana. Doesn't she look Bohemian!" Duff is late. Why hasn't he come home? Has he had a heart attack, been run over, bombed? [Duff returns.] Diana totters towards him. Instead of saying "Evening darling" she stands at bay ten paces from him and snorts and snarls while he snarls back. They throw a few statements at one another, then dash lovingly into the elevator.'

Life in a grand hotel, indeed any hotel, suited Diana well. She felt singularly little of the nesting instinct common to most women. In the Dorchester all was uncluttered: 'I feel as free of possessions as a bird – just the clothes I am wearing, the book I am reading, the letter that has to be answered.' Provided she could be surrounded by her friends she would have been almost as happy in the park or in a public lavatory. In the Dorchester she could hold court. Conrad complained bitterly about 'that horde of hard-faced tipsy women who occupy your sitting and bedroom from 6 pm onwards.' Regular habituées were Ann O'Neill, Phyllis de Janzé, Maureen Stanley, Venetia Montagu, Juliet Duff, Moura Budberg, Virginia Cowles and Pamela Berry – some harder-featured and some no doubt tipsier than others.

There was always something going on in the Dorchester: half a dozen tables of friends to join in the restaurant; a party at Emerald Cunard's. She saw in the New Year on December 31, 1940 with Ann O'Neill. There were pipers downstairs and one was kidnapped, 'a god of beauty seven feet high, golden haired with skirts skirling, bonnet at a brave angle, ribbons flying and that appalling noise coming from the pigskin under his arm'. Everyone swooned and said there was nothing like the pipes ('There isn't, thank God!' was Diana's comment) and then someone asked him to play the tune he had just played, which did not surprise him in the least since no one could ever recognise a tune on the bagpipes. So round and round he tramped, and then he played a reel and no one could dance it except Diana and her hostess, 'so the old girl swirled and the weight lifted from my heart for a while. So maybe there is something to be said for the pipes after all.'

That autumn the blitz burst over London. Diana telephoned Kommer. He was to approach the President, who in turn was to urge the Pope to call on the belligerents to stop bombing capital cities. Somewhere along the chain of command the message faltered and was lost. The disadvantages of the top floor of the Dorchester now became apparent as incendiaries thudded on the roof above, the building quivered as bombs fell all round and the anti-aircraft guns in the park seemed to be firing a few feet from the window. Duff slept peacefully through the worst of it, Diana was in an agony of apprehension from the first wail of the siren. After several prolonged arguments Duff finally agreed that they should sleep in the gymnasium, which had been turned into a dormitory. Night after night they shuffled down, to lie hugger-mugger with all that was most distinguished in London society. Everyone had their own torch, 'and I see their monstrous profiles projected caricaturishly on the ceiling magic-lantern-wise. Lord Halifax is unmistakable.' In the end Diana plucked up her courage and decreed that they should defy the Germans and remain in their own beds. The bombing began and Duff, seeing how his wife was suffering, insisted they should abandon their resolution and go downstairs. Diana refused. To encourage her, Duff went off alone to the gymnasium; Diana obstinately stuck it out; and the night ended with Duff fuming below and Diana in an agony of fear above.

Diana longed to leave London, if only Duff would come too and the retreat could be arranged with dignity. A chance seemed to offer when Lord Lothian, British Ambassador in Washington, died in office. Might Duff get the vacant Embassy? 'I'd ring Winston up and say please,' Diana told John Julius, 'if I didn't know that Papa would throttle me.' In the end the job went to Lord Halifax, and the occasional weekend in the country was the only escape from the blitz that Diana could contrive. Several times they went to Ditchley, home of the Ronald Trees, where Churchill used to pass the Saturdays and Sundays of full moon. Armed guards were at every door, the house swarming with DMIs and AOCs and other incomprehensible sets of initials in medals and red tabs. It was a great deal better than London but hardly relaxing.

Other friends offered temporary refuges. They spent weekends with the Rothschilds at Tring and Waddesdon, Lord Dudley at Himley, the Wallaces at Lavington, the Gilbert Russells at Mottisfont. Only when she got away from the bombs did she realise how much she hated them. 'It's still pouring, but I wouldn't mind if it was snowing ink,' she wrote from Lavington. 'Anything, anything, not to be in London. I don't think I shall ever want to live there again – never, never.' Friends suggested that she should stay with them when Duff went back; there was just as useful work to be done in the country. 'I can't desert Mr Micawber,' Diana concluded sadly; and back they would trail at dawn on Monday.

At Ewhurst, staying with the Duchess of Westminster, Diana retreated to bed while the others played bridge. The planes buzzed overhead and she felt scared and lonely. Discovering an empty bedroom directly above the bridge-players she crept along to it, jumped heavily on the floor and then rushed back to bed. One of the guests, Ian Fleming, came up to find the incendiary bomb. He agreed with Diana that they were absolute shits to leave her alone, and went happily back to finish the rubber. Diana let fifteen minutes pass, then went back to her bombing range, this time clambering on to a table before jumping. The crash shook the house and the whole party rushed upstairs. 'Was that you, Diana?' asked Duff suspiciously, but she seemed to be fast asleep and having got so far the bridge-players decided to go to bed.

At Tring she discovered a deserted folly not far from the house and tried to persuade Lord Rothschild to let her take it over. She could rent it, she calculated, for £1 a week, as against £15 at the Dorchester, feed herself and Duff for £3 a week, 'and wash him and soap him and light him to bed and give him Vichy water and his *Times* for another £1.' She would plant vegetables and keep hens, feed such friends as would venture down from London, and even be able to pay off the outstanding taxes. The idea enraptured her, and when it came to nothing she looked elsewhere. They had a cottage at Bognor; why should she not set up a farm there and provide a base where Duff could sleep away from the intrusive bombs?

Bognor was not what it used to be. The evacuees had gone but monstrous accretions of barbed wire prevented access to the beach, a concrete pill-box and gun blocked the gate into the wood, and there were ARP workers sleeping in the stables. The land was still there, however, and any other problem could be overcome. Diana flung herself energetically into her new activity: buying bee-hives, a butter churn, a henhouse, four goats, a cow; building an outdoor fireplace 'on which to bubble my trouble for the piggywigs'; poring over manuals on fowl-pox, fowl-pest, white diarrhoea and various unmentionable diseases of the udder, puzzling over the arcane lore proffered by Conrad Russell.

Conrad made the exercise possible. Every week he deserted his own demanding occupations and spent a minimum of ten hours in the tedious travail of wartime railway journeys, so as to pass a night at Bognor and help with the farm. 'Sweet Conrad, help me with my farm! Help me until it hurts, as Wilkie says. I'm sure you will!' He did, profligate as ever in energy, advice, admiration and love. His sisters complained that he was being exploited. So he was, but to be exploited was his delight. 'I love Bognor and your goodness to me in letting me come so often,' he wrote, and when the farm was closed down he lost the greatest pleasure of his life.

Princess, the cow, was the most valued member of the menagerie. The first night after her arrival she escaped and ambled off to rejoin her old friends at a neighbouring farm. Diana recaptured her and began to lead her home, taking with her a bag of cattle-meal as bait. All went well till they were passing the local shopping-centre, when Princess struck. 'I pulled from in front and kicked from behind and hullaballooed and shouted and threatened and cursed and even pretended to eat the meal myself to show how good it was.' Literally and metaphorically, Princess was unmoved. Eventually, a group of soldiers arrived and more or less carried the cow to its yard. There Diana milked and left her, but within a few minutes she was on the move again. Mrs Barham saw her go, but Mrs Barham was from London and thought all cows were dragons and refused to venture out until she was out of sight. For a few days Princess, consumed by nostalgia, sought endlessly to rejoin her former cronies, but then she settled down; a feminine equivalent of 'Ferdinand', Cecil Beaton described her, 'for there never was so clinging and affectionate an animal'.

Princess produced twenty pounds of cheese a week, as well as plentiful milk and butter. Diana was 'white-fingered', said Daphne Fielding, 'so that milk in her hands turned serenely to golden butter and ambrosial cheese'. The goat proved more troublesome, tearing its udder on the barbed wire and trying to bite Diana when she milked it. It was part of the establishment, however, and she was proudly loyal to it. She got a peremptory note one morning from the head of the ARP workers who shared a stable with the goat. The smell was unpleasant, could the animal please be removed. It was a funny thing, replied Diana, but only that morning the goat had made the same complaint about the ARP workers. It was well known that nanny-goats didn't smell, but she was going to get a billy goat if she could, and then the ARP workers would have something to complain about. 'They ought to have a spell in London and smell burnt flesh, instead of lying in a comfortable room and smelling through their snores the smell that every farmer loves because it means produce and wealth and nourishment.'

There was no Marie Antoinette posing about the farm. Problems proved endless. She had rations for only half her hens, so begged stale bread from the local baker. She was taken to law for her pains but fought the case and was acquitted with honour and a guinea costs. She had no pond for her ducks and bemoaned the fact that they were nevertheless saddled with 'those awful feet. It seems dreadfully cruel, like taking the snow but leaving our skis on.' The pigs grew large as ponies, knocked her over and trampled on her. The queen bee stung her on the nose. Misled by her Shakespearean recollections, she grasped the nettle danger and plucked from it not safety but a bad case of nettle-rash. She treated herself with morphine, which only doubled the agony because to some people the drug was an active itch-promoter. Princess developed rheumatic fever and had to be fed by hand. 'Farming has got beyond me,' she complained. 'The crisis of high summer gives me no time for lunch even.'

With it all she was sublimely happy. She had found a means of escaping from London with honour. She was doing work which she found unexpectedly fulfilling. She was making a real if small contribution to the war-effort. Duff got catarrh and urged Diana not to catch it too. Who, he asked, would run the farm if she did? 'Oh, *I* shan't be ill,' replied Diana with less than her usual tact. 'People with something vitally important to do never are ill.' She had succeeded in creating a productive and efficient smallholding on relatively small expenditure. Princess was in calf; the goat giving rich, good milk; hens and ducks were laying; seven pigs 'like dreadfully castrated little sods fat and white on tiny feet' were fattening for the market; thirty-five rabbits of different ages followed the same course and provided gloves for airmen into the bargain; she was self-sufficient in everything but bread. For someone with no help save Conrad's occasional visits and with no previous experience of any kind, it was an impressive achievement.

'I did not dream last winter,' she told Kommer, 'in my very acute misery, that I could be happy again, and here I find myself beginning my fourth month without once leaving the country, as happy as I have been for so long a period for years and years. I always knew London was not for me. I never want to see it again, poor city. It is a seat of nervous futility to me, while the life of an intelligent rustic labourer suits me to perfection.'

When Diana was still dreaming of her pavilion at Tring she explained to St. John Hutchinson how nice it would be for Duff to be able to come home to the country every evening. 'You wouldn't ask Duff to do *that*, surely?' said Hutchinson in dismay.

'Why not?'

'Well, you can't expect him to spend every evening alone with you. He likes bridge and fun.'

'Yes, but he likes the country and reading and quiet from bombs also.'

'Well, I think that's *really* asking too much of him!'

Diana was humiliated and alarmed. Would Duff so dislike the life of a wartime commuter? If he did, he concealed it. He kept a room in the basement of the Chapel Street house, where Daisy Fellowes was now ensconced, but most evenings made the journey to Bognor and seemed to thrive on it.

Life in fact offered more than the secluded tranquillity that St. John Hutchinson envisaged. Evelyn Waugh came for the weekend to find the Duchess of Westminster already there, 'Diana with grimy hands fretting about coupons and pig-swill. Fine wine. *Vice Versa* read aloud, gin rummy.' He returned in mid-week to find Desmond MacCarthy, Katharine Asquith and Maud Russell staying. Diana enlisted them all to help with the chores on the farm and managed to convince them that it was fun. Emerald Cunard descended in her country clothes – leopard skin coat, pearls, *béret basque* and exceed-ingly high-heeled shoes. She teetered around: 'Oh, Diana, this is very interesting! How do you do it? These are your pigs? Very interesting pigs! How *can* you milk that cow?' She insisted on carrying the milk and was butted to the ground by Princess, who evidently took except-ion to her leopard-skin. Food was always excellent, wine good and plentiful, one evening Ronald Storrs came down with Duff and the three of them consumed four bottles of claret and one of port.

Duff was all the more ready to leave London because his work at the Ministry of Information filled him with chagrin and distaste. Eventually his resignation was accepted and he was appointed Chan-cellor of the Duchy of Lancaster, traditionally the odd-job man of the Cabinet. The first odd job was already awaiting him. Churchill was uneasy about the state of preparation of the British in the Far East. Duff, it was decreed, was to go out there to take a look.

TEN

Asia and Algiers

While Diana had been rusticating at Bognor, the war had taken a decisive turn, with Hitler's attack on Russia. There were many of her class who viewed Communism with such loathing that they would almost have made common cause with Nazi Germany rather than welcome Russia as an ally. Diana had no such inhibitions:

> 'People hate Russians because they are Communists,' she explained to John Julius, 'and have done atrocious things to their own people and would like to convert us all to their highly unsuccessful ways, but I prefer Russians infinitely to Huns and fear their creed so much less than Nazism that I have no swallowing trouble over fighting on their side. Communism has at least an idealist aim – men are equals, no nations, all races are brothers, share your cow with your neighbour. Never be caught by people who say that Russia is worse than Germany – just consider if they are rich or poor.

Now another extension of the war was threatening. It seemed inevitable that Japan would soon be fighting against us, and Duff's new mission was therefore overdue if not already too late. It never occurred to Diana that she should not accompany him: if her husband were going into any sort of danger, then of course she must go too. Anyway, she had never visited the East and greatly looked forward to the experience. There was less enthusiasm among officials and military. A single V.I.P. could be shuttled to and fro with comparative ease; accompanied by a wife the problems were worse than doubled. 'That is bad,' commented Oliver Harvey severely, when he heard Diana was to join the trip. 'It will create the worst impression among the poor soldiers and sailors who cannot have their wives.' Duff must have been aware of such feelings, but he seems to have made no attempt to dissuade Diana. He probably thought the objections nonsensical – knowing as he did that Diana would not expect anything in the way of special treatment – and reckoned that, anyway, once she had made her mind up it would take more than her husband and the combined Chiefs of Staff to stop her.

For Diana the only real deterrents were her affection for her animals and her horror of flying. The previous year in Texas she had for the first time been coaxed into the air. The weather was perfect, the aircraft both luxurious and secure, the pilot skilled and sympathetic, the country flat as a pancake, and Diana hated it more than anything she had done in her life before. 'Your mother is a shuddering funky, old mouse and you must make the best of it,' she wrote dolefully to John Julius. Now she was confronted by a vista of almost endless travel, much of it in dangerous conditions and under threat of enemy attack. Crowning offence, Imperial Airways had just been rechristened B.O.A.C., removing any tincture of romance that might otherwise have flavoured the projected flight.

At least the first leg of the journey took her to New York and a brief reunion with her son. Her presence was needed. Mrs Paley had advanced ideas about education and brought up her own children at arms' length with the help of stiff Austrian nurses in white coats who were regularly changed in case the children became attached to them and a psychiatrist to oversee their play-pen. John Julius had arrived with a nanny to whom he was devoted. Mrs Paley was dismayed by this and blamed on it every defect in her English visitor, even down to his occasional car-sickness. Nanny must go. Diana pleaded that in England middle-aged men still loved their nannies and would confide in them. This confirmed Mrs Paley's worst suspicions. 'Although I like her and admire her enormously,' Diana told Conrad, 'I had to refrain from saying that anyway the result was a brave race, not a cissy lot screaming "Don't send the boys over!"' Eventually compromise was reached: Nanny was exiled, but only to the secretary's house at the bottom of the garden.

All too soon for Diana they moved on. The last lap took fourteen hours, and Claire Booth Luce, a fellow-passenger, brightly announced that typhoons were predicted. She also reported that all white women were being evacuated from Singapore. Duff was reading *War and Peace* and was entirely happy throughout the flight, but Diana was reading Virginia Woolf's *Between the Acts* and found it insufficiently gripping to distract her from the horrors ahead. In the event both Mrs Luce's predictions proved false and the Coopers arrived safely in Singapore in early September.

It was the city of her dreams: 'no trams, nothing of Birmingham or Kansas City or smoke and squalor of ports.' It was full of character and charm, with endless fascinating streets of indefinable period crumbling under her eyes. The street-restaurants smelt better than Prunier's, with succulent little baked crabs and delicacies in *sang-de-boeuf* bowls. The atmosphere was Sino-Monte-Carlo with flashes and whiffs of Venice 'most frail, tarty and peasant-pompous – there is the working life of the Chinks going on before your eyes down every street – coffin-making, lantern-painting, a tremendous lot of shaving. I never tire of strolling and peering and savouring.'

She settled down to learn Malay, so as to be able to communicate with the servants, but since most of them were Indians or Chinese, the incentive to study hard was limited. Ah-hem, the amah, could not speak to the cook, who in turn had no language in common with the gardener. A police chauffeur called George, who looked like Genghis Khan and wore a red badge meaning that he could speak English, was the only link with the household. Sen Toy, the butler, was particularly hard to make contact with: once Duff asked for his driver and got a bottle of crème-de-menthe. Diana had elegant lanterns painted with Chinese characters and hung round her bedroom, but had no idea whether she was 'advertising trusses, or aphrodisiacs, or the price of a roger for all I know'. The house was delightful, a villa but open to the winds with a rough garden of flowering forest trees and neatly clipped cypress and hibiscus hedges. All the walls seemed to fold back and there was only a minimum of furniture. To complete the décor she bought a jade-green parakeet with scarlet cheek and nose. Diana would slip the ring of his chain on to a long bough of hibiscus and perch him on a flower-vase, where he glowed like a rare jewel.

As a holiday home it would have been idyllic. Unfortunately Duff had a job to do, and a job that led inevitably to irritation and frustration. His powers were no more than inquisitorial; enough to cause suspicion and alarm, yet too little to do anything about the deficiencies in Singapore's defences. Sir Shenton Thomas, the Governor, and Air Chief Marshal Sir Robert Brooke-Popham, the Commander-in-Chief, considered him an ignorant mischief-maker; he felt them to be complacent and negligent. To add to his problems, Anthony Eden was sniping at him from London, sending offensive telegrams urging him not to interfere in matters beyond his sphere. Duff replied in a fury, saying that he would return at once if the Government's confidence in him was anything less than complete. 'Anthony has always been Duff's thorn,' commented Diana. 'He's a shit!' His outburst temporarily soothed Duff, but he was worried and fretful and for once in his life slept badly. One fearful night a 'brain-fever bird', whose speciality was uttering a single gloomy note at two-second intervals, perched on the tree outside their bedroom window. Duff was quickly hysterical with rage and soon Diana, half in tears, was imploring him not to bombard the darkness with the Ming pieces which she had lovingly acquired.

Though she knew that he was delighted she was there, Diana was

uneasily aware that her presence in some ways made things more difficult for Duff. Thomas and Brooke-Popham, who insisted on regarding his visit as a fleeting one, took the fact that she had accompanied
him as proof of the Coopers' frivolity and amateurishness. It was still
worse when Diana made it clear that she expected to accompany her
husband on his journeys around the area. A brief trip across the straits
to Johore was considered in order, though even that almost ended in
disaster when the Sultan's baby elephant reached out affectionately
with its trunk and tried to rip her skirt off, but things were different
when it came to flying to Java in a Hudson bomber. No place for a
woman, said Brooke-Popham firmly; no time for joy-riding either, his
attitude implied. Duff concurred. Diana fought the decision and, at
midnight on the eve of his departure, Duff decided that peace at home
was more important than a sense of injury among his colleagues and
ruled that she should come after all. She almost rued her victory when
the Dutch Governor held forth about the variety and venom of the
local snakes. 'Do they come into the house?' she gibbered. 'Not into
this house,' said the Governor consolingly, 'but into the guest house
many times.' She would be ill-advised to pick up anything unless
quite sure that it was not going to move.

The same battle took place when Duff was to visit Kuala Lumpur
by train. Urged by his staff he turned on her. 'I make everything more
difficult – don't I know that I'm only here on sufferance? I mustn't
lose face everywhere by not giving warning of my visit.' Diana sulked
and once again 'sweet Duff showed remorse and said I could do what
I liked always'. So along she went in the imperial train – yellow and
chocolate with crowns all over it. Joe Alsop boarded the train at 5.30
a.m. at a wayside stop, having no idea she was aboard, and blundered
into her cabin to find a chalk-white-faced mummy swathed in netting
and not at all in a mood for visitors.

After this it was taken for granted by everyone that she would
accompany Duff on all his journeys. Burma and India were next. In
Rangoon Diana caused deep offence by removing her shoes and stock-
ings and paddling off into the Shwe Dagon pagoda while Duff and the
other dignitaries hovered nervously outside. Such conduct, the
Governor explained, was most improper for a sahib, let alone a mem-
sahib, and could well lead directly to the loss of Burma. Diana was
unimpressed. Even her spirits, however, were somewhat daunted by
the pomp of vice-regal Simla. It was the combination of grandeur and
discomfort which most disconcerted her; regiments of servants in
sumptuous uniforms, yet nobody prepared to clean a pair of shoes.
Nor was the Viceroy's idea of camping quite what she approved of,
though Duff liked it exceedingly. 'It was what a camp should be,' he

told Venetia Montagu. 'Dozens of servants, a hot bath in your tent, and an observant orderly ever at your elbow with a gimlet or a chotah peg.' Lord Linlithgow advised speaking to a visiting maharajah 'as you would to a *very nice* local parson'; which seemed to Duff sound counsel. But Duff was preoccupied by his future and the problems of his job. To him, too, Eden seemed a perpetual threat: 'I sometimes feel, probably without cause, that certain people will try to do me down in my absence. A.E. is the worst.'

Soon after their return from India, Duff prepared and despatched his report for the Cabinet. His chief recommendation was that a Commissioner General should be appointed, to co-ordinate all British policy in the East. To Diana it seemed alarmingly likely that such an office would be created and Duff picked to fill it; an appointment that would condemn them to exile for the duration of the war and perhaps longer. Only when faced by such a possibility did she realise how much she hankered after England, her friends, her cow. 'The future is made of terror this morning,' she told Conrad. 'Soon our fate will be in the balance at 10 Downing Street.'

Meanwhile they planned their longest visit, to Australia and New Zealand. Diana was apprehensive about Australia. A lady from the *Sydney Post* had been to see her and had warned her that she should expect a rough reception. Noel Coward had been there recently and had been asked in so many words whether he was a bugger. 'You're nothing but a bloody queen,' another journalist had told him. The Australians, Diana had been assured, were labouring under an inferiority complex; were determined to be high-hatted and Ritzed, and even called their farmers 'graziers'. She was in dismay as their aircraft neared its destination:

> 'What is there as a reward for the flight? No pagodas, no anthropophagi, nothing but ugliness and discomfort. I am writing now with Australia laid out beneath me for seven and a half hours. I have not seen one human habitation. Nothing but utterly arid plain without tree or river. Perhaps it is seasonal. One can only hope so — but the lack of humans can't be.'

Her sourness did not survive the beauty of the country and the warmth of their reception. 'Papa and I have had a triumphal procession through Australia,' she told John Julius. 'They were crazy about us; don't ask me why.' Everywhere she met people who had crossed her path in England: at Belvoir, at Rowsley, at Bognor; filled with questions, goodwill, warmly inaccurate remembrances of the past. Robert Menzies particularly impressed her; bone-idle, she was told, but head-and-shoulders above the other politicians. Diana had met

him in London with Chips Channon and had been delighted at his
amiable mockery of their host. 'Never knew such a fellow for royalty,'
he said. 'He's like a water-diviner. He'd smell out a prince anywhere.'
As Channon laughed rather hollowly the butler arrived to announce
that the Duke of Kent was on the phone. In Australia Menzies was
quite as refreshing. Best of all, when Duff sounded him out about the
possibility, he made it obvious that he would relish the post of Commissioner General if it were offered him.

New Zealand was another matter. It seemed to her to exemplify
every English attribute which she most disliked – smug, insular,
mediocre. 'The blood of New Zealand is so stale that they are revert-
ing to type,' she told Marjorie Anglesey; 'Maori-type – growing
longer torsos and weeny legs, and you can't get a bed in a loony bin.'
They had imported all the English pests so as to feel at home – spar-
rows and starlings and gorse and newspapers that looked like *The
Times* of forty years before; their houses were smothered in roses;
their patriotism was touching; their gentility painful; oh, for a little
honest vulgarity: 'I suppose they are happy. I couldn't bear it.' The
Governor General epitomized the mediocrity of the country, and his
wife was embarrassingly arch. 'What book are you going to write next,
Mr Cooper?' she asked. 'Do make it about a lady next time.' And
then, more daringly, 'Do you and Mr Eden play much Chinese che-
quers together?'

Back in Singapore it was clear that war was imminent. 'There
seems to me no defence at all,' wrote Diana, 'but I expect I'm wrong.
Today a little fleet arrived to help.' The 'little fleet' included the
Prince of Wales and the *Repulse*. Six days after she wrote, the Japanese landed in the north of Malaya. A few hours later Singapore was
bombed. Three days later the two great British ships were sunk. It
was not to be much longer before Diana's view of Singapore's
defences was proved tragically correct.

The next few weeks were rich with muddle and alarm. The Japanese attack came before Duff's report had been properly considered,
long before it had been acted on, and Churchill's decision to appoint
him Resident Cabinet Minister with authority to form and preside
over a War Cabinet was a belated emergency measure, not a piece of
considered policy. Duff tried hard, but there was precious little to be
done. Diana's main fear was that there would be evacuation of women
and children. If this were ordered, she resolved, she would not argue
about it, merely wait until the last minute and then hide. Short of
being carried forcibly up the gangway, she knew that the only thing
that would get her aboard was a reasoned appeal from Duff to her love
and loyalty. If she were in hiding, such an appeal could never be de-

livered. In the meantime she launched a campaign for blood-donors and settled down in Duff's office to help with the secret work of some of the female secretaries who had left for Australia.

'I hate being behind the scenes,' she told Conrad on December 28. 'Office mismanagement plus Whitehall muddle breaks one's faith, and the waste of money in cabling and decyphering! No private business would dream of such squandermania. And O, bless me! The flaps from Ambassadors! They are always in a flat spin, and ne'er a decisive thought. A scream of "While not...", a yell of "At the same time we agree..." The Governor and Colonial Secretary grow daily in black, obstructive defeatism plus foxy eelishness. They are violently anti-Duff and do all they can to undermine his powers and push, but the country, the towns, the press and business are against them and the Services are leaning that way, so I think all will soon work with greater dispatch.'

Early in 1942 Diana deciphered the telegram which informed Duff that Wavell was appointed Supreme Commander in the South West Pacific and that his work was therefore at an end. A few days later Wavell arrived. Diana was disconcerted by his silences, but struck by his obvious courage and integrity. 'The impression he gives is not brightened by his being very deaf and by having one wall-eye drooping and sightless. I suppose he can smell and feel still.' At least his presence gave her a chance to be indiscreet about the leadership in Singapore, while Duff looked on, half disapproving yet relieved to have the story told in terms more crude than he would have cared to use himself.

Diana had no illusions that Singapore would long survive their departure. 'The Germans don't look too healthy,' she told John Julius, 'and we don't worry about the Wops, but those slit-eyed dwarfs from Japan are a pest.' The inhabitants would undoubtedly desert at the first bomb and who was to blame them? 'These poor natives have no traditions and not much understanding, no Nelson to turn in his grave, nor a flag that generations have died to hold high, nor anything to make them face up to fear and sacrifice.' Nor, she admitted, much reason to risk their lives to defend their white masters. She told herself that she was sad to be deserting the city at its most perilous moment. So she was; she would have been insensitive indeed if she had not felt regret, even guilt, at leaving behind so many people whom she had grown to like. Her servants were touchingly sad to see her go. And yet her main sensation was relief, tinged with exhilaration at being on the move again. Her sensations were, in fact, blurred at the moment of departure. 'A last gin-sling', she demanded, as the cars waited. The Chinese butler thought she said 'A large gin-sling'. Diana's gin-slings were always large, this one was enormous.

It was a protracted return, including in the itinerary a stop-over in the penal settlement of Port Blair, in the Andaman Islands. Surrounded by 'surly filthy Indians and bad Burmen, criminals to a man', in a house without light or mosquito nets, deprived of sleep and with no hope of breakfast, Diana passed a night of exquisite discomfort. Then it was on to New Delhi – 'In our passage we are asphyxiated by the smell of elephant. It may be a dead one in our wing somewhere; it may be dead Viceroy' – and endless delays at Cairo. Duff was depressed by the fate of Malaya and his own association with it. 'Papa did an amazingly good job against obstruction from all sides,' Diana wrote loyally to John Julius, but failure was failure and she knew that it could do no good to his career. 'It may after all be that the home Government think he has made an appallling balls of it.' Would he be offered another job or left to fret in semi-retirement? They would find out only in London and they could not get there quickly enough for Diana. On February 16 she stepped from the train at Paddington in white fur coat and Royal Yacht Squadron cap. It was cold, it was drizzling, no one of consequence was there to meet them, but they were home.

Duff did not find himself in disgrace, but nor did he return in triumph. 'You were the man in charge,' Churchill told him reproachfully. 'Why did you not warn me what was about to happen?' Duff's resultant explosion did something to clear the air, but it was several months before he was employed again and then only in a secret, backroom job that kept him well out of the public eye. Ministry of Information followed by Singapore; he knew that the stigma of failure was marked on his career. Diana resented the unfairness more than he did, and did not scruple to plead with Churchill that her husband should have some more dignified employment. At one point it was suggested that Duff should succeed Oliver Lyttelton in Cairo, but the idea died young – mercifully, in Diana's view, since the three weeks she spent in Egypt on the way back from Singapore had been more than enough for a lifetime.

For a few months they lived in London, squatting in a flat lent them by the novelist A. E. W. Mason. 'It smells dreadfully, and artistically it leaves me low, but it is free – Freemason – so we are lucky, as ends simply won't meet.' Diana worked by day making camouflagenets on the top floor of the Army & Navy Stores. The task kept her hands occupied, no doubt to the benefit of the war-effort, but it left her mind idle and even the physical demands were limited. She hankered for the farm at Bognor and soon was there again, restocking with rabbits and goats and gradually annexing nearby building sites on which she grew illicit crops of kale and mangolds. Chips Channon visited her and was recruited to drive the pigs, still wearing his Lobb shoes and his Leslie and Roberts suit. They walked to the water's edge and surveyed the formidable array of barbed wire and spiked ramparts. 'If only Singapore had been like that,' said Diana sadly. Then they moved on to admire the latest boiling of pig-swill. 'To think,' gushed Channon, 'the world's most beautiful woman showing off her swill.'

John Julius returned from the United States in the summer of that year. The temptation to keep him in safety across the Atlantic was a real one, but Diana had no doubt that it must be resisted. When Kommer protested she replied firmly: 'For his character and his fame he must be in his country now he is no longer in his babyhood . . . to be part of it all, to breathe the same air as his people and generation have to breathe, to fight the same fight and not be in Canadian cotton-wool.'

She was literally ill with apprehension while he was crossing the Atlantic, but a warship delivered him safely and he was despatched at once to Eton. Her fears were by no means at rest, however. She was haunted by the memory of two Eton boys who had been burnt to death forty years before. Lord Wimborne, a man terrified by fire, used always to take with him a Gladstone bag containing a long rope with a hook at one end. This seemed to Diana a sage precaution, and John Julius was thus equipped when he arrived at Eton. His house master was not amused and returned the paraphernalia next day. Elaborate plans were made on this and similar occasions to avoid his travelling by way of London, but she was determined that her son should not be cosseted. 'I like him to have as much discomfort as possible,' she told her sister Marjorie, when he was going to stay at Plas Newydd. 'No feather-beds or painted rooms. Give him a soldier's bed in a loft or basement or under the wide and starry.'

In August 1942 Diana had her fiftieth birthday. She did not look her age. The lines of her face were a little sharper, more rigidly defined, but they had lost nothing of their arresting splendour, the love-in-the-mist blue eyes struck home as forcibly as ever; the radiance, the inner glow still burnt fiercely. Nor did she feel fifty. All the old vitality was there, the hunger for new experience, the determination to turn every expedition into an adventure, every meeting into a joyous party. Yet in some ways she had changed. She was more tolerant than thirty years before; no more ready to suffer fools gladly, yet less ready to dismiss a person as a fool merely because he differed from her. She accepted people for what they were, rather than condemned them because they were not what she felt they ought to be. She was less egocentric, still single-minded in pursuit of her ends but more apt now to pursue those ends in the interests of Duff, of John Julius, of one of her multitude of friends. She admitted a wider responsibility towards the world: in the past there had been an inner élite of those she loved and the rest for whom she cared nothing; she still cherished her friends above all things, but she now admitted that the rest too had a right to exist, even that she had a duty to help them on their way. She was wiser; more ready to come to terms with her limitations, more prudent in her judgements, less disposed to rail against a malign and perversely hostile fate.

In other ways she was the same. No one who had known and understood the little girl scrabbling around the turrets of Belvoir would have failed to recognize the same traits in the great lady of 1942. No *grande dame,* indeed, could have been less grand, more impetuous, more informal. There was the same assertiveness, the same outrageous demands on friends and acquaintances, the same generosity and total loyalty. She had no more respect for authority, was no more disposed to trust dogma because it had always been accepted. Loving tradition, she remained the least conservative of women. The circle of her interests had widened, but the same limitations, the same prejudices flourished. Moral judgments still meant nothing to her; she either liked people or as far as possible ignored them; and if she liked them then they could commit almost any iniquity without forfeiting her affection. She still swung between black gloom and lyrical high-spirits; rejoiced in a place in the limelight and was crippled by painful shyness. Life was still far more fun when she was around. Middle age had not withered her and her infinite variety was still a delight to all who knew her.

The Coopers spent eighteen months in England while the war swung gradually in favour of the Allies. Then in October 1943 Duff was offered the post of British Representative to the French Committee of Liberation in recently-liberated Algiers, with the probability that in due course he would proceed as Ambassador to Paris. All his life he had longed to fill this office. He almost lost his chance when Churchill discovered that he was an ardent Gaullist but Alexander Cadogan, the Permanent Under Secretary at the Foreign Office, was detailed to brief him on de Gaulle's iniquities and the Prime Minister allowed his affection for Duff to overcome his doubts.

It remained to tell Diana. She knew that the appointment would make Duff happy and so gallantly put her best face on it, but the idea filled her with dismay. 'Flustered, hysterical, funky and giggly,' she described herself to Bridget McEwen, wholly unsuited to the pomp and circumstance of a great Embassy. Her stumbling, schoolgirl French, 'the loss of my cow, my plot so lovingly mulched, my few fast-ageing friends, my child, this Eton, this England'; the terrors of flight, all made her feel that she was the unluckiest woman on earth. The diet in Algiers, she was told, was spam and lemons, the lemons no sourer than Algerian wine – what of the cream, the eggs, the cheese, the rabbits of Bognor? French women intimidated her: 'they make me feel at any time a smelly, untended, untaught, uncouth, dense bumpkin.' What must be must be, however. For the second time Cincinnata put away her plough, dispersed her pigs and chickens and girded her loins for battle.

Duff and Diana arrived in Algiers on January 3, 1944. For the next three months Diana's correspondence was an almost uninterrupted cry of woe. Their house was the first and most enduring grievance. Evelyn Waugh described it as 'a charming Arabesque villa', but to Diana it was the epitome of vulgar ugliness; dark, musty, squalid. The sitting-rooms looked as if they belonged to an inferior brothel; the chimneys smoked, if any fuel could be found to burn in them; the beds were damp and broken. There was no stove, no telephone, no linen or plate. Duff was little help since he was almost blind to his surroundings, though he did join in deploring the lack of hot, or even tepid water. 'All goes worse than I have power to tell,' she wailed to Conrad. 'I have felt for the last three days that once the fearful flight was over nothing else would disturb my mind, and I really believe that it has taken this house, and this house only, to do it.' Almost their first night Charles Codman from Boston arrived to dinner. Diana, still suffering the after-effects of the drugs she had taken to calm herself for the journey, made matters no better by stoking up on many cocktails and much Algerian wine. 'She got in a state of exaggerated depression about the ugliness of the villa,' wrote Duff in his diary, 'and the impossibility of improving it owing to the complete absence of any commodities in Algiers.'

The house had been found for them by their comptroller, Freddie Fane, formerly Secretary of the Travellers' Club in Paris, a Mephistophelian figure whom Diana at first distrusted. He would not make the grade, she told Conrad, he was close to collapse, 'the cold, the shame, his impotence and incompetence are getting him down'. He bought three thousand eggs on the black market, which, as they cost sixpence apiece and there was neither ice nor isinglass in the house, Diana reasonably felt excessive. Gradually he began to prove his resourcefulness, he found prisoners to clear up the house and garden, raided a local cellar to provide drinkable wine. His methods were eccentric, but agreeably flamboyant; when he caught a young Arab stealing from the orchard he crucified him against a stone wall in the full sun. The punishment cannot have been very fearsome, for within six hours of his release the Arab was in the orchard again. 'I'm getting very fond of old Freddie,' Diana confessed, after she had been there a month or so. 'My first impressions, I ought to learn, are always wrong.'

She did not change her first impression of the Rookers. Kingsley Rooker was Duff's deputy, and not the last of Diana's grievances was that the two couples had to share the house. In normal circumstances she would probably have found the Rookers harmless if not congenial, but living cheek-by-jowl in acute discomfort proved a strain on everybody's nerves. Hostilities grumbled for weeks, then erupted when Diana proposed to open the villa gardens to the employees of Duff's office. Rooker vetoed the idea; one wanted the grounds to oneself, one would get an awful crowd. Duff advised Diana to give way and avoid any more rows. Fuming, she acquiesced, then revived the idea when the Rookers at last moved off to a house of their own. The staff flocked to the gardens and the experiment proved a success. 'I'm surprised at my own energy and confidence,' she told Conrad proudly.

Diana's irritation at the squalor in which they lived was heightened by the comparative luxury enjoyed by their colleagues. The Americans had heat, light and even a sofa; the Russians disposed of three comfortable villas. Down the road, Harold Macmillan, Minister Resident with Allied Headquarters, lived in considerable style. He asked Duff and Diana to many meals, but Diana felt he might have invited them to stay, he had no wife with him and four or five empty rooms. She still liked and admired him, however. Randolph Churchill, when he came to stay, said that he was going to run Macmillan as next Prime Minister: 'Anything is better than Anthony. You must think so, darling.' Diana did think so: 'There's more life and vision, less die in his wool, than there is in Donkey's ears or Sir J. Anderson's warts.' He was her horse in the prime-ministerial stakes and she backed him loyally till he finally came home.

Gaston Palewski, 'my old grinning, spotty friend', now *chef-de-cabinet* to de Gaulle, met them on their arrival and was their principal ally among the French. Occasionally Diana found him too much of a good thing with his endless '*O, la joie de vous avoir ici*', '*la première femme civilisée*' and so on *ad nauseam*, but she appreciated his high spirits and his affection. He could do little to influence his intractable leader but at least his heart was in the right place and he would do all he could to ease Anglo-French relations. General Giraud, 'a more wooden Kitchener of Khartoum', would have liked to be friendly too, but he was so preoccupied by the crumbling of his position in face of an implacable de Gaulle that not much could be expected from him. De Lattre de Tassigny seemed to Diana the pick of the bunch, 'spirit and wit, strength and fun'. Her personal favourite was probably d'Astier de la Vigerie, a 'spell-binder and no mistake', Diana called him, a romantic hero of the Resistance with whom every woman in Algiers was in love. She felt no similar enthusiasm for the worthy René Massigli, future French Ambassador in London, in spite of the fact that the local gossip had it that she was a *grande amoureuse,* sleeping regularly with Palewski, Massigli, and some third lover not yet identified.

De Gaulle, himself, was the reason for their being in Algiers. 'Wormwood,' Diana called him. Before she met him she called on his wife and babbled on about her life in England. The word reached Wormwood: '*Qu'avez vous fait de votre vache?*' he asked at their first meeting. When in doubt Diana always talked about her childhood, which lasted for a meal or two; but the thought of a procession of meals in Algiers and Paris beside this iceberg filled her with dismay. She cast around for new subjects and tried Australia: '*Il parait qu'il y a des kangarous,*' Wormwood observed gloomily. Fortunately for Diana, though sadly for Duff, de Gaulle was usually in such a rage with the Allies about their treatment of what he held to be the only legitimate French Government that social occasions were rare. Diana in fact sympathized with him. What she felt to be the persecution of the French seemed to her ill-judged and absurd. 'I feel ashamed now to talk to the French about the situation, or would be if they were not all confident that Duff was doing his best for them whole-heartedly.' Though she never learned to enjoy de Gaulle's company, she equally never lost her romantic vision of him as liberator and superman. It was typical of her that, during the July 14 celebrations, even though due to meet him at tea, she insisted on joining the crowds and running after his car, cheering and clapping. 'I like my celebrities seen through difficulties,' she told Conrad, 'and I like to run for them, not sit and speak with them.'

Her French was an added hazard in these relationships. Diana possessed a wide vocabulary but even less control of grammar than in English. Tenses and genders were a vexatious barrier to self-expression, to be knocked over if they could not conveniently be jumped. She had discovered the essential truth: that the French do not much care whether you speak their language correctly provided you speak it fluently. 'It's nerve and brass, *audace* and disrespect, and leaping-before-you-look and what-the-hellism, that must be developed.' At first she 'tutoyéd' de Gaulle, because that was the only construction she had learnt in her nursery; her use of the wrong word sometimes caused embarrassment; yet she got by and the French loved it. Duff, with twice her control of the language, was stiff and tongue-tied, afraid of making a fool of himself. Half aghast and half admiring, he listened as Diana rattled on, and thus won for himself a reputation for stony taciturnity.

Shortly after their arrival the Coopers were summoned to Marrakesh where Churchill was recovering from pneumonia, for what was to be a critical confrontation between the Prime Minister and de Gaulle. The meeting went well and Churchill was in uproarious form. They talked about the future. Mrs Churchill was tranquilly concerned that her husband would not long survive the war. 'You see, he's seventy and I'm sixty,' she said, 'and we're putting all we have into this war, and it will take all we have.' Diana was moved but unconvinced. She believed that the only thing that would kill Churchill off before extreme old age was some lethal disease. 'He is too interested in other things. The peace will absorb him while he's part of it, and he'll be fighting like a champion to get back to the helm if he loses it.'

The party went on an elaborate picnic in the hills about eighty miles from Marrakesh. Churchill was settled on a long chair and fed a succcession of brandies, each one accompanied by an elaborate charade of consulting his doctor, Lord Moran, first. Churchill insisted on pounding down a steep slope, then staunchly confronted the climb back. Diana seized a table-cloth and looped it behind him, and a group of men towed him puffing to the top, with Lord Moran walking behind carrying the great man's cigar and at intervals taking his pulse. Mercifully, Churchill took an interest in their sad plight in Algiers, and a stream of peremptory telegrams went off, insisting that the British Representative must be better housed and served.

From then on things began to mend. China, silver and glass arrived in large quantities; linen too, floridly marked 'Empire Hotel, Bath'. Lord Portal was enlisted to bring a four-branched candlestick, Sergeant-Major Bright scrounged a new boiler, Diana 'borrowed' blue paint from the military stores. Rifleman Sweeny, formerly from the household of Lord Gretton, lent tone to the establishment. He remembers above all the unexpectedness of Diana. She was always having new ideas, goats in the dining-room, meals in the garden. You never knew where you were, but could be sure at least that life would not be dull.

For almost the only time in her life, Diana had started off in Algiers by being bored. She moped for hours on her bed, slept late and went to bed early. 'In any other place I have been – Geneva, Singapore, New York, Midwest towns – I always found something: learning the language, exercises for the hips, riding. Here nothing that I can find makes sense.' Then abruptly she pulled herself together. The villa began to function properly. Guests flocked in. The Embassy, as it was usually known, became a place to which people competed to go. The official French welcomed invitations, the unofficial too. André Gide came to lunch. 'I expected an old Frog in a skull cap and velvet collar covered with scurf; instead I found a very clean, bald, gentle-manlike man dressed in a good brown tweed suit with brown shoes and spats. His only eccentricity was when he saw there was a fire in the dining-room and exclaimed, *"Ah, je vais ôter mon sweater"*, which he retired to the hall and did.' Martha Gellhorn was called in to enter-tain him and 'swept the old sod off his feet'; indeed he enjoyed himself so much that he refused to leave until Miss Gellhorn was on her way.

English friends came thick and fast. Victor Rothschild arrived; 'On no account unpack his Lordship's bag,' Duff warned Sweeny. 'It's full of bombs.' Randolph Churchill and Evelyn Waugh were frequent guests, spitting venom amiably at each other. Churchill later had a non-malignant tumour removed. 'What a triumph of modern science,' commented Waugh, 'to find the only part of Randolph that is not malignant and remove it.' Evelyn Waugh haunted the house, slumped in black misery alleviated only by sudden rages. Diana asked what was wrong. Nothing, said Waugh in surprise; he was rich, he was success-ful, he loved his wife and children. Then could he not look a little happier? Waugh was struck by the suggestion, which people, he said, had sometimes made before, but did little to act on it. Randolph Churchill arrived to nurse his injuries after the aircrash in which he and Evelyn Waugh had come close to being killed in Yugoslavia. He seemed to settle in almost permanently and proved a wearing guest:

'Randolph chain-drinks from noon on, it's quite alarming. He does not seem to get any tighter. I should think he must go through two bottles of gin a day. I wouldn't mind if only he were better house-trained. He staggers into my room at about 9.30 and orders his breakfast. His coughing is like some huge dredger that brings up dreadful sea-changed things. He spews them out into his hand or into the *vague* – as soon as I get up he takes my place in my bed with his dirt-encrusted feet and cigarette ash and butts piling up around him. He is cruelly bored and leaves his mouth open to yawn.'

Another constant visitor was Bloggs Baldwin, second son of the former Prime Minister, who attached himself to Diana as a cross between aide-de-camp, lover and court jester. Turnip-white-faced, ginger-haired, heavily bespectacled, ill-at-ease in society, he was not a glamorous figure; but he was a true original, uproariously funny when relaxed with a few close friends, with a streak of poetry and a sense of beauty. He was a perfect companion for Diana when Duff was preoccupied by business; as ready for adventure as she was, as unconcerned about decorum or discomfort. Devoted to his wife and son in England, he was forlorn and lonely in North Africa and found in the Coopers' house a home where he could feel appreciated and at ease. 'We go and picnic and read Browning,' Diana told her sister Marjorie, 'and talk interminably about our childhood and our families.' Diana approached the Secretary of State for Air, Archibald Sinclair, and suggested Bloggs Baldwin should be promoted. Not surprisingly her proposal met with no success.

Diana was still not wholly happy in Algiers – she did not feel she had a proper role to play, slept badly, was bored by the official dinners – but life had many compensations. There was a freedom to life which she feared would be lost in Paris. 'Duff allows me to be eccentric in clothes and deportment and behaviour. I thought he just put blinkers on but I discovered the other night when there was a row because I broke his last pair of spectacles, that his leniency is a policy. So good he is.' Martha Gellhorn was summoned to help entertain important visitors and found her hostess in full Arab dress. Lunching with Sir John Slessor Diana wanted to bathe but had no costume. Rejecting all offers of a loan she plunged into the pool in her lettuce-green lunch dress and Chinese coolie hat and swam to and fro at a stately breast-stroke. She lunched in underclothes and Sir John's macintosh, looking ravishing.

She found activities to fill her day. At 8.30 every morning a forceful lady in white trousers arrived to put her through a routine of exercise, bending and stretching and puffing and panting. Two or three mornings a week were devoted to packing Red Cross parcels at a particularly sordid convent. She acquired a cow called Fatima, from the *franche comté,* with a white face and brown body. She was asked £170 for it, an impossible price; then a rich French *colon* offered to buy it and leave it with her on extended loan. 'I said I couldn't allow it. Then I said I could.' Second thoughts proved best. There was also a tame gazelle that fed on rose-petals and cigarettes, a peacock that periodically visited the drawing-room and lay with tail extended on the sofa, two partridges, some hens and a family of hoopoes.

From time to time she escaped officialdom to undertake the sort of expedition she adored. Often Bloggs Baldwin came with her. She dragged him once to the famous market at Michelet, a journey that involved a night in a bug-ridden hotel. They started too late on the return journey and darkness found them still in the mountains. Trying to remove the blackout-masks from the head-lights, a relic of wartime London, Diana removed the entire light by mistake. She was delighted since it gave her an excuse to invade a nearby hamlet and curl up on the first verandah she came to. At her feet slept a cat, by her side a pariah dog; only at dawn, when it took off and harooshed over her, did she discover that an enormous hen was roosting a foot from her head.

A still more perfect afternoon was passed after she escaped before the coffee from a stuffy lunch given by their Russian colleagues. 'Bognor clothed, kerchiefed head and cowboy hat, I walked off into the hinterland, adventure bent.' She infiltrated through the vineyards to a neighbouring convent and snooped around the farm, talking to the Arab cowman. Diana asked if she could milk them some time; the cowman was agreeable to the idea, but explained that the morning milk was at 3 a.m. Diana said that in England she always milked her cows at 7 a.m. The Arab saw nothing surprising about this apparition being a milkmaid but found her schedule grotesque – '"*tordant*"; he laughed and laughed and had to go to tell his chums of this English eccentricity.' She rambled on happily in search of an old palace she had glimpsed from a distance. Encouraged by a No Entry sign she pushed on until she reached the front of the house. At this point the U.S. military arrived and asked what she was doing. She apologized for losing her way; as she had got this far could she perhaps see the other side of the house. 'Certainly not,' said the soldiers: a restricted area. Charmingly Diana surrendered, walked back out of sight, then darted through a hedge, across a ditch and into a farmyard. In a few minutes she would have reached her objective but the military police, now thoroughly suspicious, were on her track, and a jeep intercepted her. 'Have you come to arrest me?' asked Diana. The answer was clearly that they had: 'So in I got, delighted that I was to see my house, and from the inside too.' For an hour they incarcerated her, uneasily conscious that they had got hold of something not covered by the military manuals: 'They'd caught something odd, like the clowns in *The Tempest* finding Caliban.' Eventually they took her name and let her go. 'I hope Duff won't be serious,' wrote Diana nervously. She had little cause for worry: it had all happened many times before and Duff knew that nothing he could do would stop it happening many times again.

The end of the war was drawing near. The flying bombs were now hitting England – 'terrible news from London,' wrote Duff. 'Wilton's gone, and before the end of the oyster season.' Life ebbed from Algiers as the war moved up Italy. Winston Churchill paid a brief visit in August, 1944. Randolph, 'all smiles and love and as irritating as possible,' elected to take Duff's side in support of de Gaulle and pontificated as if he were the elder statesman and his father a foolish young man. 'Shut up!' shouted Churchill, finally enraged. 'I will not be lectured by you.' Lord Moran, in attendance as usual, thought that Diana looked as lovely as ever but exhausted. 'When a beautiful woman begins to lose her looks she needs something else to keep her afloat. When the time comes, Diana, who is still beautiful, will, I think, be saved by her character. Meanwhile, she is one of the few women who is not intimidated by Winston.'

Rome was liberated and at once Diana began to dream of a visit. It seemed likely to remain a dream, then suddenly it became reality. A passage was available, room could be found for Bloggs Baldwin as well, Churchill would be there and had said he was particularly anxious to see her. Jock Whitney, who had fallen from a table in Rome on which he was dancing and broken his glasses, had told her that never had licence and brothelry gone further. The prospect sounded delightful. It turned out less well. Bloggs fell ill shortly after their arrival. 'Unforgivable,' Diana stigmatized his conduct. 'People have no right to be ill on three-day trips.' Every time Churchill saw her he thought of de Gaulle and became apoplectic. Randolph Churchill fêted her energetically for the first day or two, then moved north with his father. Evelyn Waugh was at his most amiable, very much at home and clearly considering the Roman Catholic church his private property, but Diana declined to join in his enthusiasm for Pio Nono – Pope Fanny Adams I was Bloggs's name for him. The Canadian George Vanier, too, was wild in his enthusiasm for the Roman Church and its Pontiff – 'Please talk to George after dinner,' pleaded Mrs Vanier. 'I think he's gone mad.'

Diana was in Rome when news came of the liberation of Paris. Years later she wrote to Evelyn Waugh: 'I remember to my shame the stab of personal anguish the news gave me.' Algiers, once a hell-hole, now promoted to paradise, was behind her. The postwar was beginning. Shades of the prison house began to close. By the time she wrote the letter they had long closed. 'It's very dull now (my life I mean). It's what *you* like. Calmly planned – unhurried – no adventures – no milking – no interest to me at all. *I* am to blame, but I was born and bred an adventurer, with a great zest for change and excitement.' In fact, as always, she was to create her own adventures as she went along; but in Rome in August 1944 the future seemed depressingly taped and ticketed.

She went back to Algiers for a few final days. 'I feel sad,' she told Conrad, 'because it can never be again, and because it has been sunlit and strange and unlike real life.' The last night she dragged her mattress to the garden, tethered her mosquito-net to a tree and tried to sleep. Within an hour she was woken by a cloud-burst that soaked her and ripped away her net. 'I fled whimpering to the house,' she wrote in her memoirs. Whimpering she left Algiers and, with a brave smile but inwardly whimpering still, she went to Paris.

ELEVEN

Paris Embassy

'I quite agree with Diana that she is not cut out for an Ambassadress,' wrote her old friend Bridget McEwen to her husband. 'Although she is capable of great heroism and devotion she is not capable of enduring boredom: and to endure boredom with the good manners that don't show it is half the duty of an Ambassadress. To be a successful Ambassadress means having a very considerable sense of public duty and public spirit unless you are uncommonly limited yourself. Diana will be no good at all. She will be rude to the bores, and she will wear trousers because they are comfortable, and offend everyone. Only if there is an earthquake or a revolution will she show her true mettle. But who knows, there may be both.'

Whether or not Diana could be called a successful ambassadress depends on what one believes an ambassadress is supposed to do and be. Some expect her to be a benevolent mother hen, clucking lovingly over the migraines of the secretaries and the table-manners of the Head of Chancery. This certainly Diana failed to be. She knew the names of hardly any of Duff's staff and tended to ask to the Residence only those whose company she enjoyed – a practice vexatious to the senior members who found themselves neglected. If a typist had been knocked down at her doorstep she would have coped with kindness and competence; but it would never have occurred to her to enquire after the typist's welfare if the accident had happened round the corner. Somebody else would cope with that side of Embassy life and, if they didn't . . . well, a grown human being should be able to look after itself. They gave three large parties the first Christmas: 'one for some French friends and the principal members of the staff, "*très digne*"; one for the whole embassy staff and their friends, a nightmare; one for four hundred little British children, a bad smell.'

Nor was she any more enthusiastic about her rôle as shepherdess, taking her flock of Embassy women to diplomatic soirées, conducting the wife of a newly-arrived member of the staff to call on the other ambassadresses. It was a dreary chore, certainly, and one which gave pleasure to nobody concerned, but her failure to play her part caused embarrassment to younger members of the staff who knew that they ought to be doing *something* but did not feel that they could set about it on their own. Diana's grisliest memory was of a tea-party with Mme de Gaulle. Dutifully she led her crocodile of diplomatic wives into the Elysée Palace, only to find that not one of them was prepared to say a word to their equally taciturn hostess. Then the 'exceedingly vulgar Consul's wife' plunged into the silence and asked Mme de Gaulle whether she had ever been to the Marché aux Puces; if not, she would be delighted to take her any morning. Mme de Gaulle received the overture with disdain and 'a rocket of a look'.

Still less was Diana one of those formidably well-equipped ambassadresses who knew the difference between the ICPU and the SGMP and never forgot that the Permanent Under Secretary of the Ministry of Power had to be cosseted because an important contract for a new hydro-electric scheme was shortly to go out to tender. If the Permanent Under Secretary had wit, charm or good looks he would be well received, but bores – however influential – got short shrift at the British Embassy. Her habit of saying the first thing that came into her head could cause much offence. Talking to a young Frenchman from the Quai d'Orsay called Couve de Murville, she referred to a new book by Paul Reynaud and said that the only sensational and funny part was the title. '"What is the title?" froggy asked. I saw then and, seeing it, could feel my torso and feet flushing and quickly diverted the subject to a headline in the newspaper, for the title was *La France a Sauvé l'Europe*.'

She could not bring herself to take seriously the French preoccupation with *place à table*. At a grand dinner Princess Radziwill conceived herself ill-placed and lit a cigarette before the fish to signal her displeasure: her neighbour, Gaston Palewski, thought this entirely proper; to Diana it seemed insane. 'As the French undo their napkins,' she complained, 'they take a look round two tables of twenty in hopes of seeing something wrong.' She never bothered with the orthodox chains of command when she wanted something done. Nor was she much more concerned with the protocol of British officialdom. When one of her favourites was threatened with transfer, Diana wrote direct to the First Lord of the Admiralty to get the posting cancelled, without consulting Duff or the Naval Attaché. 'Very naughty of her,' Duff remarked mildly.

But though she was something less than a copybook ambassadress, she gave the Embassy a glamour that was enjoyed by no other mission. Fierce resentment was caused among those who were not invited, those who were invited often disapproved of their fellow-guests, but the British Embassy was the place to be. There was a flavour of the unexpected about any occasion there, as if Diana was intent on seeing how far she could go without causing disaster. She could go far. Chips Channon, effetest of ultra-Tories, found himself confronted by a young communist trades-unionist; the two got on famously and after lunch the communist took Channon off to a place where he could buy cheap silk for his shirts. Before an opera gala Clement Attlee met Noel Coward, Jean Cocteau and the Spanish-American multi-millionaire Charles de Bestigui. 'Rather an odd dinner-party to my mind,' wrote Harold Nicolson, who was also there; but Attlee seemed to enjoy it greatly.

Diana's capacity to get on with people and convince them that their meeting was a memorable occasion for her as well as for them, now became a tool of real importance. To be with her gave great pleasure to many people who it was important should be well-disposed to Britain and British interests. Diana would hardly have seen it like that – she talked to people because she enjoyed their company and was interested in their affairs – but she was also a professional doing a good job of public relations for her husband's sake. A bizarre illustration of Diana at work came at a grand banquet at the Quai d'Orsay in July, 1945. She was sitting next to the guest of honour, the Bey of Tunis, and Duff, who knew the Bey spoke not a word of French or English, feared she would have a dull evening. From the other end of the table, however, he caught occasional glimpses of the couple apparently in intimate conversation, roaring with laughter and digging each other in the ribs. She explained her method to Conrad:

'I was determined to have some communication with him and managed, by boring guests and waiters, to get a fountain pen to draw my mute some pictures. I drew him a very pretty Tunisian mosque. Palm trees shaded it. He was so pleased he grabbed the pen and added dates. Then I drew him Othello, then the New York skyline, then three fishes. He drew a smart Tunisian lady, with no top to her head at all, and he added a flag and crescent to the mosque. All this time he was too busy to eat and the hundred diners were being held up so I signalled to the waiter to remove his untouched plate and started on folding caps and a boat to float on his forbidden champagne. Great fun. We then exchanged our hideous trinkets of jewellery, a diamond bird of mine, and all his rings were taken off. We gasped our admiration. I discovered later he was a professional jeweller and he promises to make me a ring of a serpent. So we'll see what the word of a mussulman is worth.'

Diana's own parties were occasionally disasters but they were never dull. People went to enjoy themselves but with the pleasing reflection that they might be outraged as well. Duff knew well how much he owed her. In her absence he had a dinner of what should have been merry young people: 'I didn't think it went very well. I can't entertain without Diana.' Another time there was lunch for M. Massigli, French Ambassador in London: 'It didn't go very well, I thought. These things never go well without Diana.' It was his constant refrain. From time to time she could be an embarrassing liability but his mission would have been a tougher and bleaker one without her.

The Coopers left for Paris on September 15, 1944. A farewell luncheon was given at Wilton's by Lord Sherwood and Daisy Fellowes, but though many of those she loved best were there, Diana's spirits remained low. They flew to Paris in a private Dakota with an escort of forty-eight Spitfires. At the last moment Diana contemplated smuggling John Julius aboard 'and could have with a little more courage – foolishly I asked Duff not to look and he stared it out of countenance'. The arrival at Paris itself was equally grandiose: a motor-cycle escort with klaxons blaring; ceremonial wreath-laying at the Arc de Triomphe, flags flying, crowds cheering. The Embassy was still uninhabitable so they went to the Berkeley Hotel – small, undistinguished but much loved by Diana as her and Duff's Parisian base for many years. The sitting-room was bulging with orchids – a curious phenomenon in a Paris almost entirely deprived of heating: 'There must have been £500 worth, and we know only coal grows them.' Food was delicious – 'O.K. for us; spam for the staff; beans only for the left bank.' Virginia Cowles, Martha Gellhorn, Victor Rothschild, Raimund von Hofmannsthal and other old friends were there to welcome them. A glimmer of light began to appear on the horizon.

It was quickly extinguished. The Berkeley was insufficiently grand for a British Ambassador and Diana found herself translated to the more palatial but chillier Hôtel Bristol. 'I was so cold today,' wailed Diana. 'No bath, no heat, no fire. One is driven to the whisky bottle.' And this was in the comparatively low and small rooms of the hotel; could life survive at all in the vasty halls of the British Embassy? After they had been at the Bristol a few days it was discovered that P. G. Wodehouse, then in disgrace for broadcasting on the German radio during the war, was also ensconced there. Duff, who adored Wodehouse's novels, nevertheless thought that his presence was an insult and he should be evicted. Diana, who found his books unreadable, felt a lot of silly fuss was being made about nothing and that it was indecent to hound an old man in this way. In the event she won, or at least Wodehouse was still in residence when they moved on to the Embassy. It was an unpleasant foretaste of the problems that were to embitter much of their first year in Paris.

The British Embassy in the Rue du Faubourg St Honoré is one of the noblest public buildings in Europe. An eighteenth-century palace in the grand manner, it yet is workable on a domestic scale, and, except in the pompous nineteenth-century additions, contrives to be gracious without being stuffy. Diana was aghast when she saw its condition: no water; no electricity; the bedroom floor in ruins; the ground floor littered with the possessions of thirty-two British families who had fled the Germans. The wartime debris was swiftly cleared away, and with Cecil Beaton in attendance she settled down to imprint her personality on the building, scattering books and candlesticks, hanging a favourite Victorian picture on a red cord over a mirror, propping silhouettes, wax masks and family photographs along a shelf – 'humanizing the grandeur of the Embassy,' Beaton called it, 'spreading a warmth of character to these frigid rooms of state'. There was precious little other warmth and though gradually most of the more frequented rooms were properly heated, a year later a guest was still complaining about having to play bridge in a 'great cold drawing-room untouched since the days of Wellington'.

The problems of moving in, Duff wrote, were not being helped by 'the recalcitrant military, who try to rule the country with a touch as delicate as a sledge-hammer'. He hoped, however, that a projected visit from Churchill would frighten them into action. Typically, Diana saw the same visit as reason for dismay rather than hope. 'If Duckling [her nickname for Churchill] comes in a fortnight as he threatens,' she wrote, 'he'll find us in the same whiney, impatient state as he saw us in Marrakesh about the Algiers house and will think me a muddler and Duff weak.' He did come, and though he stayed in the Quai d'Orsay, the Embassy was burnished and swept clean and opened its doors for its first post-war dinner-party. For a time the tired old man was morose and pathetic; then the table was brought out for bezique 'and he laughed, and brightened up and the whisky warmed and the old magical splendour and jokes shaken up and frothing poured over us all.'

Pauline Borghese's bedroom in the Embassy outdid even the splendours of Admiralty House. The great *lit de parade*, supported by Egyptian caryatids, crowned by a golden eagle, was both a spectacular piece of décor and also a comfortable study. 'Like Milton's Vallombrosan leaves,' wrote Peter Quennell, 'innumerable letters and papers

lay scattered thickly all around; and the Ambassadress continued to
distribute her attention between some half-dozen subjects... At the
same time, a maid was preparing the tented alcove that had replaced
the much simpler bathroom where Pauline Borghese had once washed
in milk; and, having tapped on a hidden door, a minute yellow-
skinned personage would silently slip across the carpet and, intro-
ducing himself as *"Pédicure Chang"*, move reverentially towards the
bottom of the bed.' Diana derived enormous pleasure from these
rooms. 'As I get older I get more susceptible to beauty of surroundings,' she told Conrad. 'It's strange how exaggeratedly it affects me.
Hence the love of Algeria.' Paris itself she did not love, nor London.
She craved the exoticism of Singapore or Venice and found it in
Pauline Borghese's bedroom.

Uncertainty over how much money the Foreign Office would make
available curbed her more ambitious projects. She called on the authorities and explained that Churchill wanted Duff to do a good job, for
this purpose a generous allowance was necessary. When she was told
that the Treasury would first want to see detailed accounts she was
scandalised. In her memoirs she complained that, while everyone else
in Paris exchanged their money on the black market, she alone was
forced to buy shoes at £30 a pair and pay £70 for a lunch for eight. She
did less than justice to her ingenuity. The Embassy subsisted on
barter, exchanging soap, candles or whisky for wine, meat or clothes.
Nor was the black market wholly debarred. When Evelyn Waugh
wanted to change money he was led off by John Julius to find an
emigré Pole who, Auberon Herbert said, gave 1000 francs to the
pound. Only 720 were offered and the money-changer asked whether
Waugh was disappointed. He denied it. Then it came out that he was
staying at the Embassy. 'Oh, then you *are* disappointed,' said the
Pole. Diana's translation to the highest reaches of the official establishment did nothing to curb her buccaneering instincts or her belief
that the law was an ass, to be flouted or evaded. That winter she
wanted to visit Katharine Asquith at Mells. 'Do you know of any
black market petrol?' she asked. 'I'll gladly buy it. No shame.' When
Diana said the Lord's Prayer she always omitted the phrase 'Lead us
not into temptation'. 'It's no business of His,' she declared roundly.

'The old girl still cries when we mention Algiers,' wrote Duff in
September. The first three months in Paris were not happy ones – the
first three months anywhere were unhappy for Diana but Paris presented special problems. 'I ought to be so pleased,' she wrote to Juliet
Duff on 1 January 1945. 'In the fairest capital, with husband and non-
combatant child, plenty to eat, hot baths, gilded rooms, a self-driven
little car for independence – yet you can hear my groans from England

to Algiers. It's not sleeping ever, and no memory for faces or names or what I did yesterday.' Her circle of courtiers had temporarily disintegrated and she felt lonely; alarmed too, lest she had embarked on the sad downhill trail to zestless senility. Worst of all, she felt she was doing her job badly and letting Duff down. They had had a cocktail party for the Andersons the night before and it seemed to Diana that it had been a macabre failure. 'Anxious as I am to make a success of things, it looks to me as if it will be impossible. Everything is criticized, there is a lot of jealousy and backbiting. They are sure to be saying, *"L'ambassade n'a été jamais si moche"*.'

Duff's problems and his own sense of failure added to her woes. 'Anglo-French relations could hardly be worse,' wrote Duff gloomily. Things had improved slightly after Churchill's visit and the recognition of the French Government, but de Gaulle resented his exclusion from the Yalta summit and in the summer of 1945 an Anglo-French clash over Syria meant that for a time the Embassy was almost boycotted by French officialdom. Duff being away, Diana decided that she could take liberties which the Ambassador would never have permitted himself. 'My idea was never to let a corridor get blocked, open at all costs even with loss of prestige.' She invited her old friend Gaston Palewski, now in high importance at de Gaulle's right hand in the Elysée, to lunch *à deux* at the Embassy. He grumbled about the tremendous concession that was being asked of him but came nonetheless. Then she expounded her plan. On July 14 the Embassy garden should be covered with a huge dancing floor, the trees bedecked with lanterns, a band installed, and the gates flung open to the Parisian crowd. Palewski smiled and nodded, but clearly thought the idea a disastrous one. Diana attributed his doubts to a fear lest the British should prove more popular in Paris than the French Government cared to admit. She could have been right, but July 14 was, after all, Bastille Day. More probably Palewski feared that the Parisians might follow the precedent established by their ancestors and burn the Embassy to the ground.

Though the man-in-the-street knew little of it, the British Embassy was viewed askance by the more ardent Gaullists for another reason. Fairly or unfairly, the Embassy, and in particular Diana's inner redoubt, the *salon vert*, was held to be a haunt of traitors and collaborators. Some people were predisposed to expect this even before the Coopers arrived in France. 'Duff and Diana went to Paris last week,' wrote a senior official in the Foreign Office. 'I fear the worst from her, that idle useless woman who scarcely speaks French; she will collect round her all the old fifth-columnists.' The problem for diplomats who were even mildly venturesome in their social contacts was that, in Paris of 1944 and 1945, it was extraordinarily difficult to identify fifth columnists, old or new. Only the Gaullists who had spent the last few years abroad were automatically exempt from any taint of collaboration. Those who had stayed behind were intent on establishing their good behaviour, and one way to do that was to besmirch the reputations of their neighbours. Paris was a welter of accusation and counter-accusation, with anyone who had treated a German for ulcers, acted before him, sold him a fur coat or served him a meal, vociferously proclaiming that he could not possibly have done anything else and that, anyway, his colleague across the road had behaved much worse.

Diana put her faith in Gaston Palewski, arguing that, if a man as close to the General as he was, considered that somebody could properly be invited to the Embassy, then no one else had any business to complain. 'Palewski is our pilot fish,' she explained, when justifying her presence at a concert featuring the somewhat controversial Maurice Chevalier. 'Where he goes we feel ourselves safe.' Palewski, however, was more relaxed in his standards than some of his compatriots and prepared occasionally to let the charms of society or a pretty face modify the rigour of his judgments. He must have been in particularly benevolent mood if he authorised the presence at an Embassy dinner of the notorious M. Patenôtre, something that so outraged François Mauriac that he stormed from the house without waiting for his meal. He was not consulted at all when Marie Laure de Noailles was invited and seated next to an ardent Gaullist called Oberlé. Mme de Noailles had had an accident during the occupation while driving with a German officer and was looked at askance by the stauncher patriots. M. Oberlé turned his back on his neighbour and addressed not a word to her from soup to nuts.

Diana herself sometimes put friendship before the dictates of discretion. When the daughter of Daisy Fellowes was released from the Parisian prison where she had been incarcerated for her relationship with a German officer, she was at once invited to the Embassy. Diana was fascinated to know how she had got on with the four prostitutes with whom she had shared a cell for the past five months and who were apt to stand by the window with bared breasts waving to passersby. 'I asked if she had got fond of any of them (I know I should have). She said *no* emphatically. She's an unlovable woman and I hope I never go to prison with her.' Behaviour like this provided fodder for the gossips; and in London Mme Massigli, wife of the French Ambassador, spread the word about the riff-raff to be met in the salons of the British Embassy.

She found plenty prepared to listen and such talk did Diana con-

siderable harm. Venetia Montagu arrived from London to spend a few
months and help in some unspecified way with the running of the
Embassy – 'the witch of Endor,' Diana described her appearance,
'long blue locks, dreadful little hat awry, long blue face, multi-
coloured shirts and coats, blue boots; she did look a fright.' She came
with alarmist reports of what was being said in London and urged her
hostess to be careful and to occupy herself more conspicuously with
ambassadorial good works:

> 'Well, I don't know what to do,' Diana complained to Conrad.
> 'There are no British things now in Paris, no hospitals, no colony
> even. I've inspected the Wrens because they asked me to, I can't
> now offer myself to the Ats or Waafs. There isn't a day that I don't
> have Ensa or ecclesiastics or commercial representatives to meals.
> If we get these grim entertainments over with laughter, it doesn't
> mean that they are enjoyable. Anyway I can't bear a "breaf of criti-
> cism". I'm sure Venetia did it for the best, but I suspect the chan-
> cery wives here said something to influence her unreliable
> judgment. They wonder what sort of people we have, and why and
> when, and condemn with looks and shrugs and "I could and
> woulds". I shall have to appease these boring wives who are
> absolutely useless. They never try to be agreeable to the French,
> are dumb at table, and are trained not to get on intimate terms with
> those to whose country they are accredited.'

In January 1945 she dined at the Spanish Embassy and found the
place filled with notorious collaborators, including at least three who
had been imprisoned for a time and let out only for want of evidence.
All of them came from aristocratic or at least plutocratic families, and
nobody seemed to see anything surprising about their presence. 'It
seems it's only the writers and journalists who ever get sentenced,'
commented Diana, 'for there is black and white as evidence, but vile
denouncing traitors and traitoresses get off scotters.' It was in part
this feeling that the artists had been unfairly victimized, coupled with
her pleasure in their company, that led her to fill the *salon vert* with
the brightest – if not necessarily the longest burning – stars of the artistic firmament. She created a group which in some ways seemed
meretricious and certainly won little favour in the eyes of the staid and
the conventional, but was as lively as any that could have been found
in Europe.

Christian Bérard was one of the most talented. He was France's
leading stage-designer, a scruffy, shambling creature of enormous enthusiasm, perpetually suffused with excitement, convincing whoever
he was with, and indeed himself, that they were the most intelligent

and stimulating of people. 'Oh, but he was loveable,' wrote Diana to John Julius when Bérard died. 'I see him most vividly coming for the first time to the Embassy; hair streaking over his scurfy collar, shaking little face as clear as a shower in the middle of the old birds' nests and beaten eggs and ash and scent that his beard was stuffed with; septic trousers, their flies undone.' Diana was always berating him for drinking too much, neglecting his work, looking too slovenly. He was abashed, loved her for caring, but did nothing to mend his ways. '*D'où as tu ce noir pour tes ongles, mon chéri?*' asked Jean Cocteau, surveying his grimy hands. '*De Londres*' answered Bérard glibly.

Like Bérard, Cocteau was introduced to Diana by Cecil Beaton. A man of alarming versatility, a verbal juggler of transcendent skill, he lacked Bérard's warmth and spontaneity. Diana relished his company but felt no love for him. His behaviour during the occupation had been equivocal but his sins had been more of omission than commission. The Gaullists felt for him contempt rather than hatred: '*Ce n'est qu'une danseuse*' was the answer when someone contemplated prosecution. To be received at the British Embassy was important for him and all his British friends were called on to smooth his way. Harold Nicolson listened to his explanations of how he had owed it to his art not to join the Resistance, and how ill-treated he had been by the fascist *milice*. 'Somehow it was not very dignified or encouraging,' he commented.

Edouard Bourdet, director of the Comédie Française; Drian, the artist, Georges Auric, the composer; Jacques Février, the pianist: these were the other stars of *la bande*, as Diana's group was christened. They came to the Embassy because they liked the warmth and the whisky; because they knew they would find their friends there; above all, because they appreciated and enjoyed Diana. 'It was extremely moving to see Diana presiding over this gathering,' wrote Violet Trefusis. 'There was something mythological about her appearance, she could so easily have burst into flower or into leaf; her moth-like, myth-like pallor stamped her as a being apart. Only goddesses have the right to be so pale.' No goddess would have been so ribald, so vivacious, would patently have been having so much fun. Her vast enjoyment of the band in its turn fed their pleasure in being together. She flattered them, amused them, bullied them. Once she decided they did not know enough about Britain at war and forced them to sit through Noel Coward's *In Which we Serve*. Whether through real enthusiasm or nervousness about Diana's reaction if they were seen to be unappreciative, the French hailed it as a masterpiece; 'never were there so many boo-hoos and manly snuffles'.

But the heart of *la bande*, the member closest to Diana's heart, the woman who made the *salon vert* 'sing with laughter and song, wit and poetry' was Louise de Vilmorin, poetess, minor novelist, but supreme in the social monologue, the dinner-table fantasy, the art of making the trivial seem profound and the profound exquisitely trivial. Diana's first reaction was of caution. 'A long evening with a certain siren past her earliest youth called Lulu Vilmorin,' she reported to Conrad, but even at that first dinner at Verrières she was enchanted by Louise's wit, her songs and her 'winning, unaffected ways'. 'Unaffected' was not a word that even her admirers often applied to her; her enemies – and she had many – considered her a monster of artifice whose every spontaneity was carefully rehearsed and every indiscretion calculated. 'An egocentric maniac with the eyes of a witch,' Evelyn Waugh considered her. 'She is the Spirit of France. How I hate the French.' She was an accomplished entertainer and one who craved the limelight; within it, she could blossom into wild and captivating originality; excluded, she grew morose and bitter. Her admirers relished her fine flights of fancy, to her critics they seemed like the most maudlin whimsy. She was in her fashion beautiful, slightly lame, delicately built with sharp, distinguished features. Like her or not, she could not be ignored.

Unfortunately her war record was open to question. Duff at one point was given a list supposedly emanating from the Sûreté of 'pederasts and collaborators' who were alleged to haunt the Embassy. Louise de Vilmorin's name was prominent as having lived during the occupation with a German called Stuazi. In fact she had spent most of the war in Hungary with her then husband Count Palfi, and 'Stuazi' was probably a confusion for Prince Esterhazy to whom she had once been engaged. The fact that she was of French birth but, being married to a Hungarian, had travelled freely across Germany during the war, was however enough to wake the darkest suspicions of the authorities. Duff dismissed the list as reading more like a gossip column than a police report, but French efforts to eject her from the Embassy continued. The Préfet summoned Victor Rothschild and asked him to tell the Ambassador that his consorting with a notorious collaborator was causing great offence. Duff greeted the emissary with one of his celebrated 'veiners', a rage so violent that the veins stood out on his forehead. For several days Lord Rothschild was banished from the Embassy, until Sweeny telephoned to ask when the nightly games of backgammon were to be resumed. The Préfet then tried to enlist Gaston Palewski, who considered him to be so unbalanced on the subject as to be hardly worth attention. Palewski retorted that the authorities could prosecute Louise if they wished but that until they did so he would continue to be seen with her. Palewski, or so Louise told Duff, tried to enlist her as a spy to report on Duff's activities, but if he really did so he sadly misjudged her powers; anyone less competent to elicit political or economic secrets could hardly be imagined.

Duff's defence of Louise de Vilmorin was not disinterested. 'Duff is deeply in love with the spell-binding Lulu,' wrote Diana, 'which is nice for him and good for his prestige, as she is acknowledged to be the most remarkable and attractive woman in Paris, the most eloquent and witty.' But Duff's love for Louise was far from being the whole story; soon there had developed a triangle of affections that to some seemed bizarre yet to the protagonists was entirely natural and proper. Duff recorded in his diary how, after he had spent an afternoon making love to Louise, he and Diana had discussed their new friend. They had agreed that she was the most attractive woman they had ever met; 'Diana was overcome by her charm'. Diana in fact adopted towards Louise an attitude of touching reverence; she was 'more attractive than any woman I've ever seen anywhere,' but it was absurd to think that she might become an intimate friend. 'I'm too old and shy to make a friend of a poetess . . . I'm not *"de son hauteur"*.' She wrote to Conrad speculating about the homosexuality of one of her friends. 'My ways are going a little unnatural too, I fear,' she told him, 'all for the sake of Lulu.'

Louise de Vilmorin craved warmth and light and flattery. All these she found at the British Embassy in quantities far greater and quality richer than were to be had elsewhere. At the beginning of 1945 she almost took up residence, had her own room reserved for her, was present at every meal, slept there for a fortnight at a time. 'She is an adorable companion,' wrote Duff. 'I don't think I have ever known her equal – except Diana, who is almost as fond of her as I am.' To some of Diana's friends it seemed that Duff was too enraptured by his new mistress and would rudely neglect his wife so as to concentrate on Louise. If he did so, Diana was hardly aware of it. It was as happy and well-balanced a triangle as could have been contrived.

'What an extraordinary element to come into a couple's life at our age!' wrote Diana gratefully. 'This forty-year-old genius (genius she is, mark my words) loves us both with so much passion, tenderness, monomania, that her friends think she's mad. We are really rather dull, though good old things, but still, dim water to her fountain of rainbow waterdrops.'

Triangles are awkward relationships to sustain; and the more intense the emotions, the more likely the structure is to crumble. It was predictable that Duff would be the first to grow restless – his hungers were intense, his surrender to them total, yet he soon got bored with anyone except Diana. He began to complain that Louise took their love too seriously; she showed her affections ostentatiously; she was *accaparante* – monopolizing; when Daisy Fellowes arrived in Paris she became ridiculously jealous. 'It is strange that so clever a woman should not understand that it is a mistake to telephone *every* morning, to want to meet two or three times *every* day. No friendship can stand such a strain.' Why could she not be more like Diana?

Feeling that Duff was slipping away from her, Louise redoubled her efforts to retain him and in so doing made his desertion all the more certain. Diana suffered with her. At dinner one evening Duff devoted more attention to Daisy Fellowes than Louise thought proper. She rushed from the room in tears, and thence to the house of a friend. Diana at once followed her there and tried to persuade her to come back. She failed, whereupon she returned to the Embassy herself, collected Duff and went once again to the Rue de Bellechasse. 'We found her in bed, poor darling', wrote Duff. 'We had a great many tears, but she was fairly calm before we left. It was charming, if rather odd, to see Diana trying to comfort her and assuring her that I really loved her.'

Perhaps unfairly, one suspects an element of play-acting in Louise's distress. There was none in Diana's. Her tolerance of her friend's histrionics was infinite, her affection without restraint.

> 'Lulu looks like death,' she told Conrad. 'She cries all the time she is with me. I am the only one she can talk to about her mad and most unfortunate love for Duff. Duff belongs to the sense school, she to the sensibility. I fear she is on his nerves, or rather, being very masculine, he probably prefers bitchy women and cannot carry the weight of her adoration. I am frightened she will die of love and decline, or even kill herself. I love her so much, yet I dare not add to Duff's coldness by worrying him to be nicer to her.'

Diana's freedom from jealousy was awe-inspiring. She had usually condoned and sometimes encouraged Duff's extra-marital adventures. The Duchess of Windsor once remarked that she would never have an affair with Duff because it would mean having Diana around the house day and night being nice to her. The notoriously promiscuous wife of a prominent politician came to stay just before the Coopers left for Strasbourg. Diana's only concern was lest people should think she had removed her husband to protect him from the visiting harpy. 'Indeed, indeed, I have not. I would love him to have a tumble with the pretty little fool.' Louise was something totally different. With her

Diana was prepared to share Duff's love, to accept that Louise should play in Duff's life a rôle comparable in importance to her own. Louise could never have done so and Diana soon realised the fact, but she would have been ready to make the sacrifice of her own unique position.

She was not invariably tolerant of Duff's relationships. While his affair with Louise was settling down into tranquil friendship, Duff had a short but passionate fling with a tall, slender seductress who also played an uncommonly fine hand of bridge. Diana was outraged. The woman was not worthy of Duff, she was vulgar, coarse, her flamboyance would compromise his position. More than her own injury, she resented the fact that Louise was ousted to make way for so contemptible a rival. Duff was indeed far more apprehensive about Louise's reactions than about Diana's, and was disconcerted when his wife abandoned her usual acquiescence for violent opposition. 'Diana has one of her obsessions and can think of nothing else,' he noted in his diary; and then a few days later, 'Diana in floods of tears, I think she needs a rest'. Duff's therapy was to recite *Modern Love* to her; a disastrous remedy since 'she saw in it many allusions to our own troubles which led to endless argument'. In the end he promised to abandon the woman, to whom Diana usually referred as the 'Whore of Babylon'. Several times in the next few months he was tempted to break his word; 'but I didn't dare – or rather I would not willingly do anything that could give pain to Diana'.

Louise de Vilmorin was a mistress whom Diana adored, but of whom Duff grew bored; the Whore of Babylon was adored by Duff, yet resented by Diana; last in the triptych of Duff's Parisian loves was a woman who fitted smoothly into the Embassy scene and made herself appreciated by husband and wife alike. Susan Mary Patten was the ideal mistress. Like Louise she was in love with the establishment as well as the individuals, but unlike her she had no wish to do more than bask in its warmth and splendour, no ambition to impose her personality upon it. Diana first saw her when she had bicycled to a grand cocktail-party in bright red macintosh and blue plastic hat. She was enchanted by this gay, waif-like figure, discovered that she was the wife of Bill Patten, an attaché at the American Embassy, and asked them both to dinner. As the wife of a relatively junior official, Susan Mary's proper place was near the bottom of the table, but on a whim Diana put her next to Duff. It took him a year to get her into bed, mainly because of her loyalty to her husband, who was fatally ill and in almost constant pain. Even when he did it was a comfortingly tranquil business, a refuge after the emotional storms of Louise and tempestuous orgies with the Whore of Babylon. It lasted until his death. 'It is a strange, imaginative affair,' Duff wrote, 'very flattering to me but a little disturbing. She is a very sweet and charming girl whom I find most attractive.'

Susan Mary was a monument of discretion. Her husband never knew of the liaison, her children were frequently at Chantilly. She idolised Diana, thought her the most romantic, daring, splendid woman she had ever met, never for a moment doubted that his wife would always be first in Duff's affections. Duff wrote to her about Diana's melancholia and the ways in which they might together cajole her out of it; Diana enlisted her as an ally who might persuade Duff to have a cup of tea instead of a dry martini. She made a most important contribution to Duff's happiness in the last years of his life, and did so in a way that gave almost as much pleasure to Diana.

La bande was in its fullest glory one cripplingly cold night in January, 1945, when Diana stoked high the fires in the *salon vert* and invited a bevy of poets to eat, drink and recite their works: 'O the poor cold poets were so pleased, and the food too, and the wine – how they guzzled and gurked. There was Eluard, a new genius said to have outstripped Aragon; Vercors, author of *Le Silence de la Mer*; Max Fouchet, editor of *Fontaine*; Jean Cocteau, 'world-renowned for I don't know what'; Hugnet, communist, surrealist, and hero of the Resistance. Hugnet presented her with a volume of his poems, printed on japanese paper the thickness of cardboard, with more margin than print. 'The poems are of tomorrow, I prefer them of yesterday. The illustrations are by Picasso, a drunk baby's scrawl would be better.' (Diana continued to abhor the modernism of several of those who came regularly to the *salon vert*, while relishing their company.) Much later they moved on to a restaurant in the Palais Royal. There was an electricity cut and Diana sent off to the Embassy for candelabra. It was the sort of gesture that delighted her, and the power to make it was the aspect of an ambassadress's life that pleased her most.

At other times the life of the Embassy became rather too much of a good thing. She loved to have her friends to stay but recognized an unpleasant flavour of truth behind the joke when Cecil Beaton discovered, copied and sent her an Internal Memorandum signed by the Unit Production Manager of London Film Productions. Mr Beaton and Miss Vivien Leigh, it reported, were to visit Paris in connection with a new film. They would be staying at the British Embassy Hotel. Miss Leigh had already made the reservation. Diana did not mind being a hotelier but wished her patrons would behave in a more orderly fashion. 'The guests eat up our substance and make whoopee and ask *their* guests in our absence – as they did in the house of Ulysses,' she told Conrad. 'All goes worse than I have power to tell.'

The closer the friend, the wilder the whoopee they seemed to make. Randolph Churchill caused his own particular kind of stir when a film of the 'trial' and execution of Stauffenberg and the other July conspirators was shown after dinner in a special theatre. 'Exactly what we are doing in Nuremberg today,' announced Churchill. Duff, who was sitting behind him, was so incensed by the remark that he slapped his guest hard on one side of the head with a folded programme and then still harder on the other. Diana besought him to make it up when the film was finished, but instead Duff launched into a diatribe on Churchill's rudeness, drunkenness and immorality and sent him storming from the house. Evelyn Waugh was another mischief-maker. He had difficulty in getting his transit-visa for Paris, since the only evidence he could show that he was invited to the Embassy was a telegram reading: 'O yes please Stitch.' Once there he settled down to bait the other guests. Julian Huxley he insisted on treating as a crypto-Communist zoo-keeper with no interest in life beyond the diet of his panda. Speaking of Peter Quennell, wrote Diana, 'a good and harmless man, fond of pretty girls, he painted something so foetid and sinister that it will colour most unfairly my sentiments for him'. Later the same evening he got drunk and talked unsuitable sex in front of John Julius. 'Poor Wu – he does everything he can to alienate himself from the affection he is yearning for.'

The Embassy was no place for the over-sensitive or the faint-hearted. Diana had high standards and harsh judgments; if people failed to contribute they would rarely be offered a second chance. The grandest celebrities were dismissed with a terse phrase. Ernest Hemingway was 'the greatest bore to end bores we've ever struck; gigantic, ugly, spectacles with fairy glasses'. He insisted on reading a 'twenty-page chaos of dirty words and surrealist sentiments called a "poem". Poor man; well disposed and a good novelist – but woof!' Cyril Connolly was, 'an ugly man. He has not even got the splendour of Beast – like Edwin [Montagu] or Jimmy Rothschild or Caliban. He's disgustingly ugly in a fat yet mean way. I don't derive any pleasure from his company.' Julian Huxley was 'curiously common in taste and accent.' Of T. S. Eliot: 'No one with sensibility or imagination or the art of stringing words together could be capable of administering such a dose of tedium as he did for one hour.' But she could relent. Charlie de Bestigui outraged Diana by enquiring of the heroic General Marshall, *'Est-ce qu'il est de bonne famille?'*; but she soon grew to appreciate him. 'The despised little worm I have known on

Lido beaches for thirty years has become a distinguished, good-looking genius.' Cyril Connolly became a close friend and she was godmother to his son; presenting him for his christening with a hand-some silver cup engraved with his name but marring the gesture by spelling both surname and Christian name incorrectly.

The Windsors were a constant embarrassment, because of the ambiguity of their status and the uncertainty of their pretensions. Diana was loyal to old friends and defied etiquette by curtseying to the Duchess, but she got little pleasure from their company. She first met them again in September, 1945. 'The two poor little old things were most pathetic. Fear, I suppose, of losing their youthful figures, or homesickness, has made them both Dachau-thin. She is much commoner and more confident, he much duller and sillier.' Second impressions were slightly less unfavourable – the Duchess was 'slim and svelte as a piece of vermicelli'; the Duke 'common, of course, and boring, but not so puppetish as I thought' – but no sort of rapport was established. Diana did not imagine that the Duke found her any more congenial than she him. He saw her, she felt, as a sort of *Folle de Chaillot*; 'It can't be helped, we do very badly together.'

Carl Burckhardt was in Paris as Swiss Ambassador, slightly more pompous and portly but still romantic. He had been thinking about Diana for six years, he said. His one desire was to renew the fires of their love. 'We'll see, but I don't think we'll see much,' Diana told Conrad drily. 'We've both got our cats away – Duff and Elizabeth – but I don't think Mr Mouse has much courage, nor Mrs Mouse much heart to put into an escapade.' They went off on a picnic together; Diana nervous because she knew Burckhardt would want to talk about love and she found the subject embarrassing. All passed off well and their relationship settled down into amused and sympathetic friend-ship. He passed on to her Parisian gossip about doings at the British Embassy. 'Messalina is quite a common comparison, insatiable sex-ually and ruthless. I made a lover jump out of a fifth-storey window in Venice on to the *pavement*. Lesbian too, now intimately enlaced with Lulu. One who takes more than two to make love – husband and husband's mistress preferred. Duff the greatest of all ambitious egoists knocks me about something cruel – yet I made him.'

By now the Embassy was fully operational. For Diana no party was just a party; each had to be in some way special, so that the guests were surprised and flattered and would remember the occasion as extraordinary. For Montgomery the dining-room was transformed with flags and laurels into an anteroom for Valhalla. A thousand red roses were imported from Verrières. She found the guest of honour 'slim and straight, smiling and talkative and charming'. Cocteau and

Bérard were offended at not being asked to dinner and failed to turn up at the reception that followed it, but Diana had invited a girl who had fought with the resistance and now sang ballads on that theme. 'The candles were burning low and the band had gone. She sat on an aristocratic marble console beneath the flags, this tough girl dressed in skirt and shabby black shirt, and sang everyone to tears and exultation. She made her guitar into a muffled band or a clandestine tramp of feet, or what she willed. Monty glowed.' At the end of the visit Diana asked her visitor to give her a motor caravan. He smiled politely and proffered instead three photographs of himself, all signed 'Montgomery of Alamein, Field Marshal'.

It was not merely for grandees that she would put herself out. Charles Ritchie was at that time a relatively junior official in the Canadian Embassy. He complained wistfully to Diana that, though he had a lot of interesting and important things to say, nobody ever paid any attention to him. Struck by this misfortune, Diana set to work to organize a 'Ritchie Week'. Parties were given in his honour and at his arrival a band played a hymn composed for the occasion by John Julius. Everyone telephoned everyone else to ask 'Have you heard about Ritchie?', 'What's the latest about Ritchie?'. Nancy Mitford painted five hundred balloons with the slogan 'Remember Ritchie!' and they were ceremoniously released from the Embassy courtyard with postcards attached asking the recipients to return them to Ritchie with their good wishes. Several came back from East Europe and one from Norway. It was an absurd waste of time, unjustifiable by any rational standards, but it gave great pleasure to everyone concerned, Charles Ritchie in particular.

In her entertaining Diana relished skating on the thinnest ice. A somewhat stuffy dinner to say farewell to the Head of Chancery, Patrick Reilly, was drawing to a close when a telephone rang. Lady Pin was said to be calling. Lady Pin turned out to be Lady Peel, or Bea Lillie. Delighted, Diana asked her round at once. 'But darling, I'm stinking!' 'Not so good,' reflected Diana. 'Bea can sure stink', but undismayed she sent a car for her. Half an hour later Lady Peel swept in; hair like a bird's nest, monkey clinging to her back, swathed in a huge blood-red swastika flag which she had acquired on the way. She rushed to the piano and tried to sing and recite, 'remembering no words and never being within two tones of the note, but so funny and charming that no-one was embarrassed'. Eventually she developed atom-splitting hiccups and had to be carried home. 'The foreigners said they'd never enjoyed themselves so well, *"tout à fait comme en famille"*. Not my idea of life at Belvoir.'

Anything might happen at the Embassy. An elderly and distinguished Frenchman arrived at the start of a reception to find Diana in the centre of the salon, unbuttoning her trousers preparatory to putting on a skirt. 'And what can I do for you?' she growled. Guests were dragooned into playing acting games and Laurence Olivier sharply criticised for his inept rendering of *Remembrance of Things Past*. When Julien Green lunched at the Embassy the conversation turned to Bresson's new film *Anges du Péché*. Luncheon was interrupted while a scene from convent life was acted out: Louise de Vilmorin as the mother superior, Diana as a postulant flat on her face before her. 'Every meal, even lunch with two guests,' wrote Susan Mary Patten, 'was a piece of theatre for Diana, one never glimpsed the effort or machinery behind the scenes.' She asked her once what her secret was. 'Oh, just give them plenty of booze and hope it will go,' Diana answered vaguely.

Diana herself saw her entertaining through less rose-clouded glasses. A dinner for Sir John and Lady Anderson was hailed as a great success by the guests, but to Diana, in atrabilious mood, it was a squalid failure. Ava Anderson was 'not altogether unamusing because of her very subtle beastliness about people, but when she leaves the acid for the cloying sweetness, one wants to throw up'. Sir John 'has warts you can see through all over his face and is as dour and stuffy and graceless as a methodist elder'. The other guests included Pleven, Mendès-France – 'a water-drinking melancholic', Count d'Ormesson of *Figaro* and François Mauriac. All were 'very boring indeed. How can one write about such doings? The table-cloths are always stained with gravy and coffee, the napkins are soaking wet from their last rinse, the towels in the bedroom are like those we have used night after night in the *wagon-lit*.'

This jaundiced view of her own activities was characteristic of her first year in Paris. In spite of the glamour, the excitement, the acclaim, she was not content. Partly she was disturbed by the criticism of those she entertained; not disturbed enough to change her ways but worried lest she might be compromising Duff. Partly she took a long time to settle down to any new existence, and now regretted Algiers as she had regretted Bognor when in Algiers, or Singapore when in Bognor. Partly the life genuinely did not suit her. A grisly evening in March, 1945, ended with Duff reducing Louise de Vilmorin, Lady Baldwin and Diana to tears in a mere forty-five minutes. 'Too much nervous strain with work and feasting, we're both fretful and when I am lethargic he becomes more choleric.'

Duff throve on the relentless pressure of social life. Diana resented it. She wrote to announce to Conrad that they were about to have their second meal *à deux* in more than twelve months, but even before she had finished the letter the telephone rang to announce that the Ambassador would be bringing friends home to luncheon. The Travellers' Club in the Champs Elysées was never as close to Duff's heart as White's but he still relished it and would usually go there if nothing else was on; to Diana it was 'the cesspool of Paris where old drunks sozzle and cheat and scrap and calumnize'. In London she could forgive Duff's clubland life; in Paris, with so many other demands on his time, it was harder to condone.

The press was a constant source of irritation. Diana and her doings had been excellent copy for more than forty years and the journalists were not likely to forget her now. She had barely arrived in Paris before there were wild reports of the company she had brought with her: African body-servants, apes, peacocks, a tame gazelle. Her parties were headline news, any extravagance in running the Embassy led to angry mutters about misuse of tax-payers' money. 'Find out if you can who writes the rot about me in the *Evening Standard*,' Diana wrote to Juliet Duff. 'It's most mischievous and has happened repeatedly.' In the past she had often courted publicity, now her chickens had come home to roost.

She had always enjoyed dressing-up, but even on the grandest occasion her appearance was apt to be unconventional and for the rest of the time she rarely bothered to look more than moderately tidy. Now she found formality and correctness were expected of her. She did not meet those expectations but the fact that they existed was a worry to her. She disliked the Parisian fashions: 'I never saw such dreadful Aunt Sallies, nor more hideous clothes. Not a touch of imagination, femininity, glamour, history, just ugly stuffy garments made by sods to make women ugly.' But she must be fashionable. Molyneux dressed her for almost nothing, which gratified her instinct for economy, but the results still dismayed her. In the end Cecil Beaton took it on himself to write to Captain Molyneux, telling him that Diana's clothes were a disgrace and she was being made the laughing-stock of Paris. 'He meant it kindly, but I wish he hadn't,' wrote Diana forlornly. Embarrassment all round ensued, and the clothes remained much the same. Diana decided that it was not Molyneux who was to blame but her own fading beauty. She went to a fashionable Swiss beauty specialist who examined her carefully and announced that Diana was suffering from suppressed acne; 'so I bought a pot of expensive skin-educator, learnt a jaw-exercise which consists of saying "U" with a fish-like projection of lips, followed by "X" japanese-wise, and set her down as an ass'.

As usual when she was bored or depressed, her health sprouted a crop of sympathetic ailments. The trouble started with abscesses in the teeth which she treated by neither eating nor drinking for several days. Not surprisingly this did little good, either to physique or morale. The doctor who eventually treated her was foolish enough to tell her that her heart missed every fifth beat. Thoroughly alarmed, Diana lay awake all night counting her heart beats and would break off a conversation in the middle of dinner with a worried expression and one hand clasped to her breast. Then she had her stroke, the right side of her tongue was numb and tingling, the same sensation creeping down her arm, 'partial obstruction of vision, fiery cressets etc'. Duff was summoned, told her it was nerves and was grateful to find her all right by lunch-time. But Diana knew that she was merely putting a good face on it. 'It's the thin end of the wedge that will end me,' she wrote direly; then, with a brave attempt to seek a silver lining: 'It might be worse, cancer or foetid bronchitis.'

Worse was to follow. A month later she had leprosy. Father Damien, she remembered, had discovered he had contracted the disease when he spilt boiling water on his leg and felt nothing. A similar test disclosed there was still life in Diana's limbs. 'What can it be?' she asked Conrad Russell. 'Paralysis? It worries me. Ask your doctor.' She asked hers, complaining of legs stuffed with half-dead ants. The doctor laughed heartily and proclaimed her in perfect health, 'but a victim of nerves, hallucinations, phantasmagoria, *fata morgana*, mirages, delusions and the rest of it – the Poet Cooper in fact. I feel splendid now.' The reassurance soon wore off, however, and she went to Lourdes to see whether a miracle could be arranged. Dutifully, she doused her leg in holy water and found immediate relief. 'I have thanked the BV in a very incapable way. I don't know how to pray. I'm sure my efforts never leave the earth. Yet she has sent me peace of mind after many weeks of neurasthenia.' Alas, the cure once more proved short-lived; a month later she was in London being prescribed pills for low blood-pressure.

This catalogue of woes was not the whole story. She enjoyed the travel round provincial France with cheering crowds and affection so warm that she could almost see it in the air. She loved the peace celebrations. She coaxed Duff into an open car and drove down the Champs Elysées. In no time there must have been thirty people clinging to the car, singing '*Tipperary*' and '*Auprès de ma Blonde*'. It took an hour to get from the Etoile to the Place de la Concorde. 'Our team was so proud of us, they'd hit by chance a star for their bandwagon and would not leave us till we got to the Embassy door. Poor Duff, it was not really up his street – his street has the silence of a Mayfair Sunday – but it *was* my street and he bore it sweating and smiling and once over felt it wonderful.' She delighted in darting round a Paris still largely free of motor-cars in her tiny Simca, dodging the bicyclists, slithering in and out of what traffic there was, defying signals, mounting pavements – 'On the bat's back I do fly' – with her chauffeur in the back leaning panic-stricken out of the window yelling '*Méfiez-vous, messieurs*' to passing pedestrians.

She enjoyed the perquisites and the privileges. 'You get more presents as ambassadress, and amongst these poor givers I have an embarrassing pull, with my car at the door, sending it to and fro for lifts or to the Embassy for a guitar or a coat.' Power was delightful, and she used it with zest for others as well as for herself. She was energetic in getting the Hertford Hospital on its feet again, shameless in her importunities on its behalf: 'Let's think who's cadged on us so we can cadge back,' was her ruling precept. She would devote an entire day to bullying, bribing, cajoling until at last she found a dose of penicillin for a dying girl whose mother had appealed for help – 'It makes me quite happy, as a rule I feel so useless here.' When Louise's brother was dangerously ill she motored through the night with the vital medicine. When Susan Mary Patten rashly offered to organise a charity ball, only to find the Parisians far too snobbish to attend something proposed by somebody so insignificant, Diana took the enterprise under her protection. She dragged Susan Mary around the leading dress-makers, demanding to see the models for the masks at the great ball to be held at the Pré Catelan, reserving materials for the bevy of distinguished visitors from London who would be arriving for the occasion. Not one couturier had heard of the ball, not one dared admit the fact. They passed on the word to their clients and within two weeks every ticket was sold and a black market was developing. It was fun to provide food, wine, warmth, treats for less fortunate friends; fun to play Lady Bountiful, especially when effort was all that she was required to put into it.

There were, in fact, many compensations for the pains of Embassy life. She only realised how many when it seemed likely that she would lose them altogether.

TWELVE

Paradise Lost

In July, 1945, came the first post-war General Election. Until the votes were counted it was taken as a foregone conclusion by most people that Churchill and the Tories would coast home to an easy victory. Diana felt her first doubts when she went to a political meeting addressed by Beaverbrook and was disconcerted by the hoots and hisses he provoked. She reflected that he must be the most hated man in England. The electorate's reaction showed that they could recognise real malignancy when they saw it, not that they favoured the Labour cause. Still, 'he must be losing our party a rare number of votes'. Diana felt sorry for him, 'a fireless, impotent little creature, bent with loose-hanging clothes', but rejoiced that she did not have to take part in the election herself. Duff, she felt, still hankered for the battlefield.

When the results were announced, Diana was aghast. Quite apart from the fact that the wrong party had won, what seemed to her the country's ingratitude sickened her. She met Churchill shortly after the election. He was very affected, even stunned. 'I'm told it's a blessing in disguise,' he said to Diana. 'If it is, it's very well disguised.' Little Winston Churchill, then aged five, was brought over to Bognor for tea. Duff asked him kindly whether he knew what had been happening. He replied that he gathered he had a new grandfather.

As a political appointee it was reasonable to expect that Duff would be removed by the new Government. Lindsay of Balliol was said to be favourite for the job. The *Observer* announced that Halifax and Duff Cooper would both be moved in a matter of weeks. Foreign Office officials were unlikely to fight hard to preserve a non-career diplomat. Duff decided that he would be regretful, but not extravagantly so: 'Curiously enough Diana would mind much more than I should. She loves Paris now, although she was not prepared to and didn't at first.' The French were perturbed at the thought that they might be going to lose an ambassador so conspicuously well-disposed to their cause, and Gaston Palewski, with a certain amount of prompting from Diana, wrote informally to a friend in the Foreign Office to say that the General would be delighted if Duff were to be left in Paris.

Duff claimed to want to stay for Diana's sake, Diana was equally sure she wanted to stay only for the sake of Duff. Both in fact recognised that they would never find a position half as desirable. A fortnight after the election, rumour reported that Halifax was to stay in Washington. Diana exulted. 'If this is true it should likewise apply to Duff who is less politically tainted than Holy fox, is newer to the job, more popular in the country to which he is accredited and loses more by dismissal.' Next, Duff was summoned to London to see the man Diana for the first few months invariably spelt as 'Bevan'. The interview went well but Ernest Bevin was non-committal. The new Foreign Secretary gave the impression that personally he was well-disposed but that powerful elements in the Labour party felt that Duff should be removed. It was another six weeks before Duff was called again to the Foreign Office and told that the Embassy was definitely his for a year and perhaps for longer.

Bevin soon became a staunch ally of Diana's. He first visited the Embassy for the Peace Conference in April, 1946. Diana was amused and impressed by this hulking uncouth figure, 'the size of three Buddhas, hardly hewn at all'. His appearance was squalid – 'Ernie's nothing but a large spot of grease,' explained Mrs Bevin; his manners were spectacular in their lack of polish; his courage, commonsense and self-confidence were evident in all he did and said. 'He laughs uproariously,' noted Diana, 'and is nicely naive and quite uninhibited – a bit of a gurker too.' At the first session of the Conference, Duff went peacefully to sleep. Bevin was most struck by this behaviour. 'Tell Duff I'll call 'im if anything 'appens,' he said, and added, ''E's the most sensible man in the room. It's all a waste of time.' (The habit stuck. When Diana went to a session of the Conference in August, Duff again dozed off and caused some alarm by almost pitching forward over the low balustrade which separated the Distinguished Visitors' Gallery from the body of the hall. She shared Bevin's view of the usefulness of the proceedings: 'A more grotesque performance I never witnessed. I think the world should be put into women's hands. We would never allow such foolery.')

At the first dinner the Coopers held for Bevin he ate enormously, drank deeply, talked without pause and showed every sign of having the time of his life. He ended by singing a few songs – cockney, 1890 type – 'My old Dutch' and 'Two Lovely Black Eyes'. Diana retaliated with 'Wotcher, all the neighbours cried'. 'He has neither ear nor articulation,' wrote Diana, 'and my rendering wasn't much better.' At 11.30 his private secretary suggested taking him home. 'No,' he said. 'You go. I'll stay. I'm enjoying myself.' Next time he came to the house Diana invited to meet the proletarian hero Lord and Lady

Rothschild, Lady Crewe, Lord Pembroke, the Cavendishes and the Marquis and Marquise de Noailles. Bevin was delighted and thoroughly at home, 'stroking and pinching and laying down the law and congratulating himself throughout dinner'. Someone asked:

'Will you seek election again, Mr Cooper?'

'Oh no,' interrupted Bevin. 'We're going to send Duff to the 'Ouse of Lords.'

'Oh, please, please not,' cried Diana.

'Why, don't you want to be a Viscountess?'

'No, indeed, I'd lose my rank. Besides, it would mean his job was over.'

'You don't think I'm a big bad Bevin who's going to send you 'ome, do you?'

Meanwhile Duff sweated with nerves and shame. Luckily Bevin had to leave for a meeting before things went much further. 'I think he was pretty tight,' observed Diana. 'I know I was.'

Susan Mary Patten was at the Coopers' house near Chantilly when Bevin arrived to take some country air. He again talked ceaselessly except for a half-hour break after lunch when he went to sleep, made bad jokes, told dirty stories. 'He is clearly in love with Diana, whom he addresses as "Luff", and implored her to come to Durham for the annual miners' gala.' At the end of the day the chef was packed off to Paris in the Rolls while Bevin was loaded into Diana's open Simca, with Duff and the detective perched uncomfortably in the back. The last words Mrs Patten heard from Ernest Bevin were: 'Please, Luff, drive a little slower. You drive so well, but you frighten me more than the most 'ideous terrorist.'

In a light-hearted way Bevin was indeed attracted by Diana. 'Go the 'ole 'og, darling,' was his advice when she asked him what she should wear at some reception, and the remark is typical of the relaxed, ribald relationship which existed between the two. In March 1947 he was again dining at the Embassy and as his private secretary, Pierson Dixon, had temporarily vanished, Diana took him to the lift:

'What was my surprise when he suddenly clasped me in his arms with the strength and immobility of a bear and buried his pudgy face in my neck. So we stood for a full minute, or an eternity: then, with a very slow, utterly relentless gesture, he shifted his mouth to mine. No struggles could have affected the situation, as well stand against the mountain weight of lava. I was agonized at the thought of Bob Dixon coming in and writing me down as an office-hunter seducing the boss, but as far as I know he didn't see anything, unless it was the lipstick that transformed poor Ernie into an end-of-the-evening old clown Joey. He asked me to stay the night. Could he have thought I would? Still, there's life in the dear old dog and courage and character and humility and a lot of other nice things, and if he likes to be foolish late at night, he should be indulged.'

There were those who said Duff owed his job to Bevin's affection for Diana. That is nonsense; the matter was decided long before they got to know each other and the most that Diana can have done was to convince the Foreign Secretary that the Embassy was a pleasant place to visit. Bevin was too shrewd not to realise that in part at least Diana's attentions were aimed at protecting her husband's future, and though he in no way resented her somewhat transparent scheming, he was equally not greatly influenced by it. He counted himself a friend of the Coopers, though, and in that friendship Diana more than played her part. Over the next two years Duff was going to need all the friends he could get among the Labour ranks.

It would be foolish to pretend that Duff was temperamentally well equipped to represent a Labour Government. It was more a question of personalities than of principles. As a conscientious ambassador, he gave a party for delegates to an international Trades Union Conference, greeted them affably enough, but that night entered in his diary: 'It was a strange spectacle – the dregs of all nations eating and drinking as though they had never had such an opportunity before, scattering the remains on the floor, pushing each other about as though they were on the platform of a railway station.' He did his best to hide his feelings but a marked unease characterised his relationship with working-class – or indeed middle-class – socialists who were less robust and self-confident than Ernest Bevin. Diana was far better than he at getting on with people of different habits and outlook, mainly because she found such differences a source of curiosity and wonder rather than disdain. People were condemned for being common, but Bevin was not to be classed as common, and few were quite as common as the Duke of Windsor; her judgments were based more on idiosyncratic whims than social strata.

Even if he had been the very pattern of proletarian bonhomie, Duff would have found opponents in the Government camp. A. V. Alexander, the First Lord of the Admiralty, came to Paris and interrogated the Naval Attaché about Duff's weaknesses. The worthy officer was outraged at such incitement to disloyalty and refused to say a word against his Ambassador. Maurice Edelman was heard to boast that he would get rid of both Cooper and Franco before 1946 was out; in neither case was he conspicuously successful. Harold Laski dined and made the sinister comment: 'Your party badly needs you in the House of Commons.' 'I don't like him,' noted Duff. Diana did her best to soften the visitors. John Strachey and his wife came to stay. 'He a brontosaurus and she a squirming go-by-ground,' Diana told her son. 'I smelt hostility but have been able to dispel it. He is here to talk about cereals to others of his own ilk, and she to irritate me. I can see no other reason.' The wives always seemed to fall to Diana and heavy going she often found them. Mrs Bellenger, wife of the Secretary of State for War, was 'very German and very disagreeable. In Labour circles the female is usually more deadly than the male.'

Duff had little use for Clement Attlee. 'Less impressive every time one sees him . . . really a poor specimen,' he commented disdainfully. Diana was shrewd enough to suspect that Duff was missing the point of the Prime Minister, though she herself still hankered for the colour and panache of Churchill. A few months after the election the old man announced he was to visit Paris. The Coopers were determined to do him all the honour he deserved, but were equally aware that, as loyal servants of a Labour Government, they could not show them-selves too partisan. They arranged a dinner at the Elysée at which de Gaulle was conspicuously affable. The women 'coiled about Winston, and cried a lot and kept cigar-stubs and matches in memory. He quite enjoyed the emotion.'

He enjoyed it so much, indeed, that soon he was back again, this time with his daughter Mary. A dinner for the grandest French poli-ticians was organised at the Embassy and a merry evening for Mary Churchill laid on by Duff's drinking crony from White's and private secretary extraordinary, John de Bendern. Churchill, however, announced that he was too tired for a formal dinner but instead would take his daughter to the Folies Bergères. Both dinners were therefore cancelled, the de Benderns' cook gave notice, and a reduced party as-sembled at Maxim's. 'Having possibly endangered international re-lations,' recorded Duff, 'and certainly caused immense inconvenience to a large number of people, he seemed thoroughly to enjoy himself and was with difficulty induced to go to bed soon after midnight.'

For the two years after the fall of Churchill Diana was intermittent-ly in an agony of apprehension lest Bevin should change his mind and Duff be dismissed. Rumours constantly crossed the Channel that so-and-so was being considered, that someone else said Duff would be out by Christmas. In June 1946 Duff asked Bevin bluntly whether there was anything in the stories. Bevin shuffled uncharacteristically. Personally he had a soft spot for Duff; he thought he was doing a good job; he would like to keep him on for a time at any rate; but there were difficulties; he could make no promises; Herbert Morrison, it was suggested, was a difficulty. Diana's fears were augmented. A few weeks later a young Frenchman, stuck for conversation, enquired politely: '*Vous partez en vacances, madame?*' Diana clasped the mantelpiece convulsively. 'Me go away!' she cried in horror. 'If I don't hold on with both hands they'll take the whole thing from us!'

'The whole thing' had now grown significantly. Wandering round the great park of the Château de Chantilly, Diana pushed through some rusting gates and found herself beside an eighteenth-century house of exquisite dignity and serenity, looking down the lawns to a lake and thence to the ornamental cascades and a hierarchy of stone gods and goddesses. A window ajar provided further temptation; she forced her way in and wandered entranced through a series of light, spacious, graceful rooms. They were almost wholly unfurnished, though an empty bottle of gin on every mantelpiece suggested recent habitation. Enquiries revealed that the house was called the Château de St Firmin, that during the war it had been lived in by the German Ambassador, Otto Abetz, that it belonged to the Institut de France but was leased by a former American Ambassador to France, William C. Bullitt. Bullitt had no wish to return to Chantilly himself and still less need of rent. He said that the Coopers could live there if they would provide linen for the house. Linen was unobtainable in France. Diana arranged with a friend to 'liberate' some in Germany, but when the consignment arrived it was found that all the sheets were designed to button on to blankets and were useless at Chantilly. Diana was in despair; then Bullitt suddenly lost interest in whole affair and abandoned the lease. The Coopers took it on for the modest rent of £100 a year.

St Firmin became the house that Diana loved best in the world. Almost every weekend they would move down there, and their Sunday lunch-parties became part of the Parisian scene. She loved picnics and the park at Chantilly, vast, deserted, romantic, filled with unexpected and dilapidated pleasure-houses, was a picnic-lover's paradise. One Sunday a party of guests was led away on what was alleged to be a brief pre-prandial sight-seeing expedition to a park belonging to an unknown Baron. They advanced to a round glade, where a folly-cum-boathouse stood beside a lake surrounded by classical statues. Shots were heard. 'The Baron must be shooting today,' said Diana casually. Then someone saw some bottles of sherry. 'They must belong to the Baron,' Diana suggested. 'Let's drink them.' Shocked but amused the guests sipped the sherry. Someone ventured inside the folly and found it spread with rugs, wine in coolers and delicious food. 'The Baron's shooting lunch!' cried Diana. 'Let's eat it.' This time she had to overcome strong protests but she had her way and the party nervously set to. Only when one of the guests spotted that the silver came from the Embassy did they realise that they could eat and drink with a clear conscience: the Baron would not be coming that day. Another picnic was at night beside a lake, in a fairy-tale building called the Pavillon de la Reine Blanche. The table was laid on the landing-stage, candlelit with a splendid array of silver and china. As the moon rose over the towers of the Château de Chantilly, someone began to sing French ballads to a guitar. Fantasy, beauty and a proper respect for the creature comforts created a blend which even the most austere could relish, in which even the most formal could relax.

Chantilly was where Diana was most at home, and where she felt least doubts about her capacity to make others contented. She told Duff that she would be happy to lose the Embassy provided Chantilly could be retained, and though she deluded herself, her heart still soared whenever she passed its gates. In Paris she shone, she was admired, she was noticed and remarked on, she was happy, but she was never wholly at ease. François Mauriac wrote a celebrated passage about her in *Figaro* which both Duff and Diana quoted in their memoirs but which bears repetition for the way in which he evokes not merely her beauty but also the slight sense of alienation from the surrounding scene which hung around her.

> 'A une fête de ces derniers jours, où les visages fermés des Slavs glissaient, tous feux éteints, à travers les groupes, j'observais L'Ambassadrice d'une nation amie, cette figure de Pallas Athénée qui épandait sur ce troupeau sombre et méfiant l'inutile lumière de ses yeux, statue encore intacte, témoin des époques heureuses, sa beauté adorable se dressait en vain, comme un dernier appel à la joie de vivre au dessus d'une humanité sans regard.'

'un dernier appel à la joie de vivre' – Violet Trefusis called her 'the radiant incarnation of all the French had been deprived of during four long years'. Some she irritated, some she shocked, but she was a presence to be reckoned with and for the most part to be wholeheartedly welcomed.

Her last year at the Embassy was clouded with unhappiness. Conrad Russell had been ill even before she went to France, his never robust health strained too far by the rigours of wartime. By April 1947 he was dying, his grasp of reality slipping away; for an hour on end he sat with an imaginary book on farming in his hand, reading

aloud with perfect lucidity, turning over the pages at the right intervals. His last conscious words were: 'Tell Diana how much I think
about her.' A few days before he died Katharine Asquith wrote in
mingled grief and triumph to report that Conrad had been received
into the Roman Catholic Church. Diana wrote to Mrs Asquith that it
was a miracle, she was 'deeply impressed and moved and glad'. Her
real feelings were somewhat different. Conrad had frequently talked
to her 'about the Papists, and never without contempt or jeers'. The
Russells were born and raised as Liberal free-thinkers and the more
Conrad had read on the subject the more sceptical he had become.
Was his conversion no more than a deathbed vote of thanks to
Katharine Asquith for so much love and care? Was he willed into it
while hardly conscious? 'We shall never know. I hope in my heart that
he knew what he was doing, and that it has brought him peace and
resignation as true faith does.'

She herself found that faith came no easier as she grew older.
Evelyn Waugh urged her to join the Roman Church as being the only
discipline firm enough to overcome what he saw as her fatal restlessness, her irresolution. She was attracted by the idea, in one way
longed to be swept up in something stronger than herself, but knew
she was incapable of it. 'One cannot join something so serious as the
Church for a whim, or as an experimental medicine. I must wait for
the hound of heaven – or some force, some insistence.' The hound
never bayed, and she would have been disconcerted if it had. If
pressed she might have admitted that she found undue preoccupation with the state of her own soul a little common. But this
squeamishness did not preclude recognition of the value of faith and
envy of those of her friends who enjoyed it. She had never included
Conrad among them, and she found it difficult to conceive that he had
somehow slipped away at the last moment into that charmed but
mysterious band.

On April 28 she tried to tell John Julius what Conrad had meant to
her:

'My darling Conrad is dead. I cannot be too unhappy. He was
longing to throw off his weary, disobedient body and the sooner his
humiliation was over, the better pleased we should be. He was so
wise and sound and uncensorious of morals, and his own rare
humour was better than any other – angle, fancy and delivery. O
dear, O dear, I don't think I'll write any more or think, when low,
of the check suit, the turned-out toes, the stoop, the haircut by the
ploughman with the help of a pudding basin, the deer-stalker cap I
gave him, the zip-bag that brought his modest accessories and a

pound of butter, eggs, the first primroses, the "short-legged hen" and some pretty little kickshaw.'

The jokes; the endless curiosity; the quizzical intelligence; the tolerance for others combined with the most exacting standards for himself; above all, the certainty that there was somebody who cared about her more than all others and was insatiably interested in her doings: all this Diana lost with Conrad Russell's death. She was never to be short of friends but Conrad, she knew, was irreplaceable.

Even before Conrad's last illness, her sister, Marjorie Anglesey, was seriously ill. The doctors professed themselves baffled. Lady Anglesey was indifferent; she felt that she was dying and that it was high time too; the cause of death was a secondary consideration. Diana was dismayed by her abandonment of hope and tried to rally her. 'My darling Marjorie, where is your spirit?' she asked. 'Your letter came from *my* craven head, not yours, though I could not have made it so beautiful. *Pas de faiblesse*, no babbling o' green fields. If it's anaemia we'll cure it with liver-extract. You are too old for T.B. We'll cut out growths. Death is always outside the door, but don't O don't let me hear you say "come in". You can't leave us behind.'

Lady Anglesey could and did. By October, 1946, she was clearly close to death. Raimund von Hofmannsthal, who had married Marjorie's daughter, Elizabeth Paget, tried to persuade Diana that it was her duty to rush to Plas Newydd to join the mourning children. She was revolted by the idea. 'I deplore the theory and practice of the wake,' she wrote firmly. Grief was something to be endured alone, not shared or exhibited before other people. When her sister at last died, her predominant feeling was relief. Marjorie's misery of mind and pain of body had haunted her for many months. 'I think she was afraid, and this fear horrified me most because she was, as a rule, fearless and certain of being fearless, ready to laugh at me for my cancers and hypochondrias. Now, so far as we can imagine, she is no longer afraid or groaning.' She was in London when her sister died. On her return, Duff summoned Susan Mary Patten to help cheer her up. Susan Mary arrived at the Embassy, brimfull of sympathy and anxious to offer such comfort as she could. 'My darling, I'm so sorry!' she cried, embracing Diana. 'Never had such a crossing in my life,' replied Diana gruffly and embarked on a lively saga about the battles she had had with various importunate officials.

By the spring of 1947 enough straws were in the wind to make it clear that Duff's position in Paris was once again becoming insecure.

The two names principally canvassed as successors were Oliver Harvey and Gladwyn Jebb. Duff knew them both well. He thought Harvey would make a respectable ambassador, industrious but dull. Jebb on the other hand, might be exceptional: 'There is more life in him, but the Foreign Office will think he is too young as he has only reached the age of Napoleon and Wellington at Waterloo.' Then the rumours died down again, and the Coopers decided they were probably safe until 1948. It was a halcyon summer, the more so because it seemed likely to be their last. In May there was a luncheon party for Churchill at Chantilly. The old man started the day surly and depressed, greeting the overtures even of his beloved Odette Pol Roger with a churlish 'Gwumph!' Luncheon improved things greatly and by the time of the brandy he was launched into a passionate speech in defence of a united Europe. Then the party straggled down towards the lake. Churchill insisted on jumping a brook that stood in his way. Susan Mary Patten, who for some reason Churchill pretended to believe was French, took off her shoes preparatory to following him. Churchill waved her on with an encouraging flourish of his cigar: '*N'ayez pas peur. Suivez-moi!*'

After the party Mrs Churchill wrote to Diana: 'How I do hope you will soon be assured of a calm, permanent tenure of your lovely Baby Palace with its cool crystal waters and its emerald lawns and pastures.' She could not have wished it more fervently than Diana. But would the French Government allow them to stay on once the Embassy was lost? Might Duff conclude that they must return to England? Apprehensively, Diana began to look around for a house in London. To make matters worse, the Foreign Office had recently cut their allowances to pre-war levels and they were £4000 overdrawn. Poverty and squalor seemed to lie ahead, certain to descend as soon as an unkind Government struck the fatal blow.

Early in September the blow duly came. Duff and Diana were not expecting it, certainly not expecting it in the shape of a somewhat bleak letter from the Secretary of State rather than a personal message. As soon as he had read it Duff hastened to tell Diana. 'She took it superbly,' he wrote in his diary, 'as she always takes bad news.' Duff's former secretary, Daphne Wakefield, was staying with them at the end of a honeymoon trip. Dinner that night was in honour of the newly married couple and was particularly cheerful. Only next morning, when Diana had already left Paris on a provincial visit, did Mrs Wakefield receive a note telling her that the Coopers had not wished to spoil her last evening but felt she should know that they had been dismissed.

From that moment life was a fever of preparation. Diana resolved to go out with a flourish and held a farewell ball in December. Churchill was among the many English friends who flew over: 'Winston was there to lend lustre to the feast,' Diana wrote in her memoirs. 'I lent it a skeleton.' The skeleton rattled its bones merrily enough; only those who knew Diana particularly well would have detected that the occasion was not the happiest of her life. Every candle was lit, every piece of the great gilt service was gleaming on the tables, it was 5 a.m. before the last guests filtered from the courtyard. For some of them it was a farewell to the Embassy as well as to the Coopers, for no new broom sweeps cleaner than that of an incoming ambassador, and the intoxicating free-for-all of the *salon vert* had gone for ever. For Susan Mary Patten it was one of the most beautiful parties of her life, yet 'Diana and Duff had been so beloved that the party was bitter-sweet as it meant farewell'.

A few days later a large proportion of the guests streamed to the Gare du Nord to say yet another farewell. Diana was in tears, Duff was in tears, Cocteau was in tears, Gaston Palewski was in tears; it was a richly lachrymose occasion. Louise de Vilmorin was so overcome by emotion that she impulsively clambered aboard the train and proclaimed that, since the Coopers could not stay in France, she, a Frenchwoman, must go to England. The spontaneity of this moving tribute was hardly marred by the fact that her suitcase turned out to be on board already.

And so these three romantic years ended with a splendid, if slightly spurious flourish. It had been a great theatrical performance, and it was right that it should end with a melodramatic gesture. Diana had set an impossible standard for her successor to attain; a challenge which that successor very sensibly met by doing something entirely different. Diana had chosen her own battlefield and had triumphed on it. It was not the only battlefield, possibly it was not the best battlefield to have chosen, certainly it was not a battlefield that accorded well with the image of an austere and socialist Britain; but on it she performed as well as could have been required of her. It is doubtful if any other woman could have won for herself the position that Diana achieved in her three years at the Embassy in Paris; the fact that many women would not have tried or wanted to need not detract from her achievement.

THIRTEEN

'Neither Queen nor Tramp'

It is a convention in the British Foreign Service that a retiring head of mission should not visit his former post until a year or so after his departure. Life, it is felt, is difficult enough for a new ambassador without the previous incumbent in the background observing that that is not how things were done in his day. The Coopers accepted that this was desirable in principle but felt that in their case the practice must be different. Most retiring ambassadors had a home awaiting them in England; they only had the house at Bognor, now rapidly disappearing beneath the suburban tide. Most ambassadors had no especial stake in the country in which they had last served; they had Chantilly, which the French Government was prepared to let them keep. Duff would pay far less in taxes, cling on to many of his diplomatic privileges, enjoy the status of an '*ancien ambassadeur*'; it seemed to them inconceivable that they should abandon all this to return to England, where politics seemed closed to them and no other job immediately offered.

Within a few weeks of their departure from the Gare du Nord, Duff and Diana therefore found themselves packing for the return journey. It was hardly a propitious start to their new life. By the evening before their departure from London Duff was already fuming over the barriers which officials were erecting in his path. Diana and Louise de Vilmorin disturbed his concentration with their conversation and 'he lost his temper, head and good manners and flounced to bed, red with rage and refusing to wish Lulu goodnight'. Diana, as white as Duff was red, soon followed, but was so indignant that she refused to speak to him. 'I know I'm spoilt,' said Duff contritely, 'but I *am* sorry.' 'One can't cure hurts with apologies always,' retorted Diana, and they went to sleep in grim silence.

Next morning was still worse. Either through fear or rage, Duff did not call Diana till eight, and the Golden Arrow left at nine. Pandemonium ensued, porters sitting on trunks that would not close; Diana, almost naked, barking instructions at anyone within earshot; parcels in one direction, cases in another, this to be sent to Belvoir, that to be left with Lady Cunard. Some ferocious telephoning delayed the train and they scraped aboard. Duff was more than ever in the dog-house. 'I let him out on the SS *Invicta*. We couldn't arrive in Paris like two sticks.'

The first night back in Paris was an awful presage of the future. '*Je me sens un peu perdue*,' she admitted to Gaston Palewski. '*Pauvre Diane*,' he replied, and a great lump welled up in her throat. They had borrowed the Military Attaché's car all day but had sent it away in the evening. When they decided to go out to a restaurant for dinner they went on foot. It was cold and raining. The first restaurant was closed. So was the second. They were wet before they found one that was open and wetter still by the time they got back to the flat Loel Guinness had lent them in the Rue de Lille.

> 'When we were in bed I found that Diana was crying,' Duff noted in his diary. 'She is really unhappy about the fall from grandeur and the evening's walk brought it home to her. I was deeply touched and surprised. I have many weaknesses but have never cared for being grand. I liked living at the Embassy, which she made very comfortable, but I always felt as though I was living in a hotel. I suppose that Diana enjoyed the position and enjoyed entertaining, though she often complained of it at the time. One always enjoys doing what one does well. To me the restoration of liberty makes up for everything, but I am sad that she should be sad.'

It was several weeks before they moved back into Chantilly and even then they were met by a chaos of packing-cases, books stacked on the floor, pictures leaning against the walls, all the old copper pans covered with verdigris, 799 bottles of champagne with ten magnums and one rehoboam to be stacked in the white wine cellar, servants absent or incompetent, the only food in the house porridge and tinned pilchards. Even the crocuses seemed bowed and mutilated, 'none of that looking joyously to a new heaven of a million straight little throats that one gets in St James's Park'. Instead of being stimulated by the challenge, Diana was depressed; for the first few days she was frequently in tears. 'I do so hate the *maîtresse de la maison* life,' she complained to John Julius. 'I like to be a Queen or a tramp.' She was bored, she was fretful, she felt herself ill-used. The scene was set for conflict with those whom she felt had supplanted her, 'the horrible Harveys'.

Ambassadors traditionally disapprove of their successors; with the wives disapproval is often elevated to hatred. Usually, however, an ocean or at least a frontier divides the rivals; the previous incumbent is either savouring the delights of retirement in the Home Counties or organising coffee-mornings in Tegucigalpa. Diana was on the spot, rancorously disposed, ready to view any alteration to *her* Embassy as a slight, surrounded by friends who delighted in passing on or inventing offensive comments which the Harveys were alleged to have made about the old regime. Relations would have been difficult between the Coopers and any new arrivals, with the Harveys they were quickly strained to and beyond breaking-point. Diana considered Lady Harvey dull, insipid, bourgeois; Lady Harvey felt Diana to be a frivolous and flashy wastrel. Each saw the bad side of the other and made no attempt to appreciate the qualities. To apportion blame would be a fruitless task, but greater understanding on either side might have avoided a world of chagrin. It would also have deprived Parisian society of a most enjoyable scandal; one which Lady Harvey hated and Diana more than half enjoyed.

From a few days after her return to Paris Diana began to conduct raids on the Embassy to collect items of furniture which she claimed belonged to her. Lady Harvey would notice a chair or chandelier had vanished, ask where it was and be told that Lady Diana had called for it that morning. Then came the day of the Harveys' first grand luncheon-party. Diana chanced to call at a quarter to one in search of more of her possessions. The guests arrived to find her in the hall. '*Chère Diane!* How lovely to see you here. We didn't know you were coming to lunch.' 'Oh *I'm* not invited. We never are. You'll find the Harveys up there somewhere,' with a gesture upstairs. The guests clustered around her while upstairs the Harveys waited and wondered. Diana extended her attention to the staff as well. The chauffeur left to become Duff's valet. 'He has never valeted but it's such a pleasure he wants to leave the Embassy for the Chantillians.' Diana, of course, was quite taken aback when the proposal was made to her. 'True, I'd seen him yesterday when I went to collect some leavings and asked him if he knew of anyone of about his age who would like the job. True, I elaborated on the charm of the situation – good food, foreign travel, smart car, etc. etc.'

Everything Lady Harvey did was analysed and triumphantly ridiculed. She was said to have told the Bishop of Tanganyika that the library was a beautiful room *considering the books*. Could illiteracy be more clearly proven? She exhibited Diana's Napoleonic bathroom with the comment that her predecessor had decorated it because of her love for North Africa. Could idiocy be more complete? She 'hung a sparse row of her own pictures round the green salon's walls as though for sale; a Segonzac and a Derain etc.' Some might have thought that even a sparse row of Segonzacs and Derains was an enviable possession, but Diana would have scoffed at a gallery of Rembrandts or Leonardos. It was, however, somewhat provocative of

Lady Harvey to change the colour of the carpets and curtains in Duff's library. This exquisite room had been designed by Charles de Bestigui, filled with Duff's books and donated to the Embassy: 'that those ignorant, execrably tasted Harveys can have had the nerve to touch it entirely passes forgiveness.'

Diana's tendency to abuse the Harveys to anyone who would listen could cause embarrassment. Lees Mayall joined the Embassy as First Secretary, an old friend of the Coopers but very properly loyal to his Ambassador. By the time he arrived things had gone so far that it was tacitly accepted no member of the Embassy staff would visit Chantilly. Repeatedly he refused invitations, then one day Diana arrived uninvited at his house when mutual friends were staying there. She ate and drank nothing but talked merrily. As she left she said: 'Now I've been to your house, you must stop refusing to come to mine. I promise not to say a word against the Harveys.' From then on the Mayalls went regularly to Chantilly and Diana kept her word. All the same, they thought it best not to mention their visits at the Embassy. Then came the time that Oliver Harvey, who had hitherto refused to ask the Duke of Windsor to the house, was ordered by Churchill to repair the omission. He obeyed under protest and showed his feelings by inviting only members of his staff to meet the guests of honour. The Duchess walked round the circle in a frigid silence; then at last came to a face she knew and cried: 'Lees, how lovely; that was fun at Chantilly last Sunday, wasn't it?'

Royal visitors provided a tasty bone to be fought over between the rival establishments. The first time Princess Margaret visited Paris, Diana, who had not been invited to the Embassy, left word that she was at Chantilly and would love a visit if the Princess had time. The message was not delivered and when Diana saw her at the opening of the British Hospital, she said that she had felt certain it had gone astray – 'this last was not said naughtily. I meant in the general brouhaha it was natural.' To Diana's great satisfaction, Princess Margaret insisted on rearranging her schedule to include a visit to Chantilly. Nobody was there except the Coopers and Nancy Mitford. 'Off home she drove, gay, and I'm sure delighted with the outing. It had the tang of the Forbidden. She had clearly been genuinely appreciated by disinterested people – there was fun and the three hosts were in a sense famous. Eric [Duncannon] told someone that she had said it was what she had most enjoyed in Paris.'

Next time the Princess came to Paris, this time for a Hospital Ball, Diana arranged an evening at Chantilly – 'not more than twenty or thirty, all young, in order to keep away my frog friends and Maudie Harvey.' Cecil Beaton was there – hardly notable for his youth – and

Greta Garbo; John Julius played the guitar, two American folk-singers provided a cabaret, Princess Margaret sang and played the piano for an hour, the park was floodlit and the party ended at 4 a.m. eating roasted chestnuts round a brazier. It could hardly have been more successful, and like most of the best parties, its informality concealed careful organisation. Months before Diana had written to Cecil Beaton: 'The point of this letter is to beg you and Greta to come and stay with me when Princess Margaret visits Paris. The Hospital Ball she may like or hate, but *I'm* throwing a party on the 22nd.'

Princess Elizabeth visited Paris in May 1948, shortly after Diana had heard the dread news of the Harveys' plans for the Embassy library. 'She was really deeply hurt,' wrote Duff. 'She thinks it was done out of spite and swears she won't go to the reception for Princess Elizabeth.' She was still more put out when Oliver Harvey cut several names off the list of guests submitted by the French authorities on the grounds that they had been collaborators, including two who had regularly visited the Embassy under Duff. Curiosity and propriety triumphed over indignation, however, and in the end she went, making her point by the chilliness of her manner; 'the frights got the frozen mitt, not a smile broke from me'. Needless to say, everything seemed badly done: the Borghese candle-sticks had been suppressed and no candles were used; 'the gloomy hosts stood looking ghastly under the deforming light of a much brighter candelabra'; the band was inaudible; the flowers were arranged by somebody imported from Constance Spry; it was all safe, unimaginative, dull. Duff was less discriminating or more objective: 'I am bound to admit it was a good party and well done.'

The feud soon became part of Parisian folklore and many of the more colourful incidents related to it are apocryphal, or at least exaggerated almost beyond recognition. Nancy Mitford, prominent in the British colony in Paris, took particular pleasure in fanning the flames and dining out on the stories that arose from it. In *Don't Tell Alfred* she wrote a novel about a former ambassadress in Paris who secretly took up residence in a gatehouse of the Embassy, thereby causing confusion and chagrin to the new incumbents. The incoming ambassador and his wife bore little resemblance to the Harveys but Lady Leone was very evidently modelled on Diana. Miss Mitford sketched out this character to Diana while still working on the book. 'As it might be me?' asked Diana doubtfully. 'Yes, Tee hee hee hee!' was the reply. Diana certainly did nothing to discourage the enterprise and paid for her failure when the *Evening Standard* published an article alleging that she knew all about the book in advance, had given her permission and had even suggested some refinements. The Coopers, said the article, had set up a rival Embassy and split the British colony into squabbling fragments. Diana contemplated a libel action but was advised to forget the matter.

For Nancy Mitford it was an amusing game, for Lady Harvey unmitigated pain. For Diana it had something of both elements. She enjoyed baiting the Harveys, criticising their activities, frustrating their projects. Many people would have said that the vendetta was a light-hearted affair for her, a stimulating entertainment. The real depth of her bitterness was shown only when Duff died and Diana flew back to Paris with his body. Lees Mayall was sent out to the airport with messages of sympathy and promises of help from the Ambassador. Diana emerged for an instant from her shocked apathy. 'You can tell those bloody Harveys to go to hell!' she snapped.

Meanwhile life at Chantilly was settling down. Diana took it for granted that bankruptcy lay ahead. An interview with her solicitor confirmed her fears. 'We'll not be able to live in France,' she told John Julius, gazing far into a dismal future, 'and I and Papa will drive to your home to ask for shelter, and your beastly tart-wife will be like Goneril and Regan merged and bang the flimsy door in our nose, and we'll get a hulk on Bosham marshes as Peggotty did before us, and Papa will make love to the paid help and I will be Mrs Gummidge.' Duff saw the same solicitor and emerged altogether more ebullient. His writing was earning him several thousand pounds a year. He joined the board of Wagons Lits. Alexander Korda appointed him Chairman of the Paris subsidiary of London Film Productions at £2500 a year – 'I like and trust Korda,' Duff not surprisingly noted. They paid practically no taxes. 'It all seems to me quite satisfactory but Diana never stops worrying.'

Cecil Beaton took Greta Garbo to Chantilly while the Coopers were in England. 'Even in her absence she loved Diana; for she said she must be a woman who loves rural things.' Memories of wartime Bognor had inspired Diana to repeat her farming triumphs. The first her friends knew of it was when Chips Channon heard what sounded like quacking coming from his extravagantly sumptuous blue and silver Amalienburg dining-room in Belgrave Square. Investigating, he found twelve ducklings which Diana had put there to rest before taking them on to Chantilly. A few days later a cow and four pigs were also on their way to France. They were supposed to arrive at 10 p.m. and Diana spent the whole night fully dressed in a fever of excitement. In the event, they did not appear till breakfast on the following day. The pigs lacked charm but Diana was quickly seduced by the cow, who was 'very small, very thin and as gentle as a sleepy baby – tiny undangerous horns, a very pale face with Panda eyes'.

The routine of life at Chantilly quickly adjusted to accommodate the farmyard. A dinner-party was disrupted when the mother-goat gave birth to kids, the Beits were almost sent packing back to London in disgrace when they let the cow escape from the orchard and Diana got badly stung pursuing it through a nettle-patch. The French shared Diana's pessimism about the future, which did not suit her at all; what she wanted was cheerfulness against which she could react. They made a lot of hay and, as she tottered under a heavy load towards the stack, she asked Quarmi, the gardener, whether he thought the cow would like it. *'Je ne le crois pas,'* he answered gloomily. Quarmi had a fine line in the ghoulish, mitigated by a cleft palate which made most of what he said unintelligible. One of the few episodes which Diana understood in full was his account of his daughter's visit to hospital with a fibroid in her womb. Diana reassured him that the condition was not serious, common in women, one she had endured herself. *'Oui, mais Madame n'urine pas noir,'* said Quarmi with some relish. *'On peut uriner jaune, rouge et même bleu, mais Madame n'a pas uriné noir.'*

Diana was determined that the wedding bells must chime for Caroline, the sow. She was loaded into a trailer and taken to a neighbouring farm where there was said to be a suitable mate. Frustration; 'a furious daughter, the kind that will grow up a *tricoteuse* of the Communists', shouted from an upstairs window that the hog had been castrated. On they went to a second farm, only to find that this hog had been despatched to a happier rootling-ground. The third farm belonged to an ogre whose first words were 'Fee Fi Fo Fum' but who eventually admitted that he had a fine boar. It proved too fine for Caroline. The farmer cast one scornful look at the poor creature and ruled that her teats were badly hung, she was undoubtedly diseased and sterile. The only hope was that she might make acceptable pork for Christmas. 'We got home in darkness, having given poor piggy a tiring, costly and abortive wedding trip.'

Diana's English friends were relieved that she was resorting once more to this healthy and relatively harmless pastime. She, for her part, longed for their visits but found that they did not always make life easier. The comings of Evelyn Waugh, in particular, tended to be beset by fearful rows. Diana once went to the airport to meet him, having deposited her other guests at a circus in the town. At the interval she was back, looking gloomy. 'Evelyn's plastered,' she reported. There he was, in cloth cap and loud tweeds, clinging on to a guy-rope so as to remain on his feet. As the rope was at an angle of 45°, so was Evelyn Waugh. Diana took him home and shut him in his room to sleep it off, but by the time the party got back from the circus he had escaped and was annoying Lady Juliet Duff, who was trying to do the crossword.

Next day he was still drunkish. Duff endured him with sinister calm until, at lunch, he made some offensive remark about Mountbatten. This provoked an explosion: 'How dare a common little man like you who happens to have written one or two moderately amusing novels, criticize that great patriot and gentleman? Leave my house at once!' Evelyn Waugh left the room but not the house, and next day told Rupert Hart-Davis, a fellow-guest: 'Don't really like Cooper. Very fond of his wife.' For a time he kept away from Chantilly, but Diana delighted in his company. Once he took her to the Ritz in London, even though she assured him that it was no longer what it had used to be. He asked for a wine list. '"Red or white?" said the waiter. "What do you mean?" said Evelyn. "Well, you can have a carafe of either," said the waiter. Before Evelyn had time for his stroke, he added "O, I see, you wants it bottled." "Is there no wine-waiter or wine list?" gasped Evelyn. All this a great joy for me. Poor Evelyn doesn't *know* and is too proud to realise his ignorance and learn.'

They went together to stay with Somerset Maugham at Cap Ferrat. Alan Searle, who was filling the role of hostess, offended Diana by giving Waugh the better of the two rooms and offering him rather than her a sprig of heliotrope. Waugh had vitamin tablets in his bathroom, while Diana merely had aspirins. Evelyn Waugh called Somerset Maugham 'Doctor' every other sentence and read his new novel aloud for more than two hours after dinner. Diana did not find him altogether easy to travel with. He objected to her habit of dropping in at every hotel where she had ever stayed to gossip with the proprietor, and hated having things pointed out: '"Don't miss the swans," sort of thing; so it's sealed lips when I see the spring's pageant.'

When he began to come to Chantilly again things for a time went more smoothly, though abuse still flew on occasions. Cecil Beaton heard 'Diana and Evelyn being appallingly rude to one another – really vilely, squalidly rude'. Diana took particularly vigorous offence one day when the maid was ill and she 'in my dressing-gown, barefeet and nightcap,' took Evelyn Waugh breakfast in bed. He surveyed the tray and commented disapprovingly that it 'wasn't properly furnished'. 'Well, I let him have it. I said "Really Evelyn, it's too much to put on such an act!" and I gave him the full benefit of everything that

I'd been bottling up about his pretentiousness. It really rankled with him, but it'll do him good!' Waugh was disconcerted but not discomfited. 'Goodness the Coopers were crazy,' he reported to Lady Mary Lygon. 'Both Sir Alfred and Lady Diana fell into the most alarming rages. No self-control at all, it comes from living with the volatile frogs.'

A few months before Duff died he had another flamboyant set-to with Evelyn Waugh. 'Duff has a well-known weakness for uncontrolled rudeness,' wrote Diana to Waugh. 'We all have grave weaknesses. Baby's is melancholia and cowardice. You have some too.' Waugh left in dudgeon, was persuaded to return and passed a further happy week at Chantilly. After he had left, Randolph Churchill showed him a letter which Diana had written, describing the row with Duff. Waugh, offended, wrote Diana a letter 'coldly aimed to hurt – arrows heavy as lead, curare-tipped'. She was deeply distressed. 'Baby is *not* rude,' she wrote, 'but both men in this story are exceptionally rude in their cups. Since recriminations are the note, neither Baby nor Duff would have told all and sundry that their hosts were trying to poison them. She will not write again, it's too painful to face the leaden answers devoid of understanding or love.' For once the element of farce that pervaded her rows with Evelyn Waugh was lacking – 'Oh, Evelyn, Evelyn, how can you have done it to me?' A reconciliation of a sort was patched up, but it was not till after Duff's death that they really renewed their friendship.

Graham Greene was another author who visited Chantilly at this period. She greatly admired his writing and was fascinated by his tormented relationship with his faith. 'I think it's guilty love which has put him all out,' she concluded; hence *The Heart of the Matter* which had just been published. He had been to Padre Pio's mass but had feared to talk to him afterwards in case his life might be altered as a result. Hugo Charteris bombarded him with questions: 'Would you welcome death, Mr Greene?' Mr Greene admitted that he would, though Diana could not decide whether he was prompted by alcoholic depression or a wish to be free of Charteris's interrogation. 'I think Graham Greene is a good man possessed of a devil,' Diana concluded, 'and that Evelyn is a bad man for whom an angel is struggling.'

When remonstrating with Evelyn Waugh for picking quarrels, Diana complained that she had only a handful of men friends left in the world, one of them 'the frog who people can't endure'. The intolerable frog was Paul Louis Weiller, 'Poor Louis' as Diana habitually referred to him, a man of great wealth, power and generosity. Cecil Beaton remarked shrewdly that Diana combined a gift for using her friends and the amenities they had to offer, with a complete lack of selfishness. Paul Louis Weiller exemplified this admirably. Diana relied on him for food, drink, every kind of entertainment; he was constantly making available his Rolls Royce or one of his many houses – 'I've cost him a pretty penny and he can afford it' – and yet in return she defended him loyally against his legion of enemies, gave him real affection and procured him the entrée to many places where he would otherwise never have penetrated. Thirty years later, when he had almost ceased to be of use to her, she was still writing to the British Ambassador to get him invited to a party for the Queen Mother. She was not in the least embarrassed by him, or his generosity. He gave her a mink coat from Dior worth – in 1951 – £4,500: 'I like people to know he gave it to me,' wrote Diana. 'I consider it does him credit.' 'The coat of shame,' she christened it. It proved something of a liability. 'It entails being chained to it, insuring it, not sitting on it, having to have better hats and gloves and bags, always thinking it's lost or stolen, storing it all summer, ultimately being murdered for it.'

Her gratitude for Paul Louis Weiller's attentions was the greater since she felt that she had been to some extent dropped by her French friends since she had left the Embassy. 'I know something of the sag in one's social shares when you've no longer a Government background,' wrote Ronald Storrs, 'but I shouldn't have thought that would have affected *them*.' Nor did it to any great extent. The Coopers remained an ornament at any party and only the drearier official invitations no longer reached them. But there was a big difference between dropping in at the *salon vert* to see your friends and have a drink with the British Ambassadress and trailing all the way out to Chantilly to do the same thing with Diana Cooper. Diana had vaguely assumed that *la bande* would remain faithful and reconvene in fresh surroundings. That they did not was due more to geography than to lowered status, but they did not, and the fact distressed her. Even so close a friend as Louise de Vilmorin came far less often to see her. She was confirmed in her dislike of the French. In *Panegyric* Ronald Knox had suggested that the Reformation destroyed good fellowship. Diana disputed this hotly. 'There's good fellowship in the U.S. There are no nastier people than the frogs who were little affected by it, while the Scandinavians are comparatively pure; less wily than wops, less cruel than Spaniards.' Duff preferred the company of his English cronies, and more and more Chantilly became a redoubt of foreigners; cosmopolitan certainly, but where the French rarely went unless soaked in alien culture.

Diana was lonely, and the state was one for which she was ill-equipped. Three years in the social turmoil of Paris had weakened her aptitude for amusing herself. 'I have no life, no beckoning delights, no admirers (there's the rub),' she wrote to Evelyn Waugh. 'Duff scribbles and I'm left to Mrs Dale's Diary or the Benvenuto Cellini-ism of the Third Programme. There is no sap in nature, or in me – not in pain or acute melancholy, I languish dully, not happily re-signed.' This vision of the housewife solacing her long hours with soap-operas from the BBC was a caricature of the reality. By the stan-dards of most fifty-six-year-old wives of retired husbands her life was one of spectacular gaiety, crammed with incident and colour. But it was not what she was used to, and she found no comfort in the reflec-tion that the lives of others were drab compared to hers. Duff was puzzled and a little irritated by her appetite for society, complaining that three nights running she had dragged him to Paris when he would rather have been dining peacefully at home. Diana knew that her restlessness was irrational but could not control it: 'I'm bored, John Julius. Sad, isn't it? This is not a life I could ever tolerate – from early childhood I was always praying for excitement.'

In *The Loved and Envied*, Enid Bagnold presented what was intended to be a faithful portrait of Diana in old age. Diana was grati-fied by the attention, and told the author it was a striking likeness, but when she came to consider the noble, serene shadow which Enid Bagnold had discovered, she wondered whether a few more sittings might not have yielded a truer picture. Ruby Maclean is 'almost my opposite,' she told her son, 'with no fears and frailties, panics and pains'. Panics and pains were particularly evident in the first few months after their return to France. Boredom and discontent became translated into imaginary illnesses. By the summer of 1948 Duff was worried enough about her state to pack her off to an English doctor, who recommended a plethora of drugs. Diana, who distrusted all drugs except those she prescribed herself and procured illegally, had little faith in his proposals.

She pinned her faith on a man who cured anything except cancer and V.D. – the latter being about the only disease from which she never thought she suffered – by a system of footbaths. To supplement this she also consulted the immensely aged Dr Salvanoff, Professor of the Universities of Moscow, Paris and Berlin. To follow his course in its entirety would have been a full-time job: seven pills to be taken half an hour before every meal; constant hot baths with a secret fluid added; private parts thickly greased with vaseline before immersion; hot water bottles to be laid on the liver for forty-five minutes three times a day. Meanwhile, the chauffeur, Jean, was vomiting contin-ually. 'I do think servants should not be ill,' wrote Diana peevishly. 'We have quite enough illness ourselves without them adding to the symptoms.'

'She hates old age and she fears death,' wrote Duff in his diary. 'I wish I could help her but I don't seem to be able to.' She was distressed that she could not do everything she had been used to, and refused to admit that this was so until the facts compelled her to face them. She fought old age by taking greater pains to preserve her beauty. The *Evening Standard* gleefully reported that she was having a face-lift; she had visited a plastic surgeon before going to the clinic; she wore dark spectacles and her face was swathed in light bandages; 'then my *age*, which I resent (stupidly) and a bit about my rheumatic legs – altogether too horrible and malicious'. The worst of it was that she was not having a face-lift anyway: 'the spectacles were put on to hide a cyst, the bandages my poor little bald-pate nightcap.' She met Sam White, the *Evening Standard* representative in Paris, and more in sorrow than anger, complained about this unfair concentration on her doings. 'I suppose if I had piles you'd put *that* in,' she concluded sadly. It was not as if she was habitually preoccupied with her appearance. Often she looked strikingly unkempt. Malcolm Muggeridge saw her at Ann Rothermere's 'looking quite extraordinary with blond wig and sinewy bare legs, a more prosperous version of demented women to be seen on benches in Regent's Park muttering and going through wastepaper baskets in the early morning'.

Drugs, footbaths, face-lifts may have contributed, but the main reason for her regaining her spirits was that she grew used to her new condition. By the autumn of 1948 she was herself again. The cure seems to have started in Milan when she appeared in a vast hat and sunglasses and was hailed as Greta Garbo. A week or two later she told Duff that she felt really happy. 'Pathetically, she said, "I feel like other people: you can't imagine how heavenly it is."' Duff believed one of the causes was that Auberon Herbert had asked her to bathe with him. 'Accustomed all her life to such attention, she has been missing it.' Certainly she blossomed on this holiday. At Aix they spent a riotously successful night with Winston Churchill. Mrs Churchill had left that afternoon for London; 'I am afraid her absence increased the gaiety of the evening,' noted Duff. Churchill had recently been taught Oklahoma and abandoned a quarter of a century's addiction to six-pack bezique. He played very badly but with enormous relish till the early hours of the morning. Diana's confidence, never more than frayed, had now returned in full. 'I keep the table in roars,' she told John Julius. 'I'm considered the wittiest, funniest, most original angel that ever visited this dull earth. It puts up the morale splendidly.'

The fact that Duff so obviously welcomed old age did much to soothe her. He was entirely without regrets for lost consequence,

enjoying his writing, relishing his liberty, a model of elderly contentment. 'Duff's Sir Deaf Cooper now,' wrote Diana, regretting the way
in which he would lose track of a general conversation, then catch at
some half-heard remark and join in with an irrelevance. But Duff did
not seem to care a scrap, so why should she? Most important of all, he
loved her and depended on her as much as ever. On the twenty-ninth
anniversary of their wedding he presented her with a set of verses:

> 'Fear not, sweet love, what time can do
> Though silver streaks the gold
> Of your soft hair, believe that you
> Can change but not grow old.
> Though since we married, twenty-nine
> Bright years have flown away,
> Beauty and wisdom, like good wine,
> Grow richer every day.
> We will not weep, though spring be past,
> And autumn's shadows fall,
> These years shall be, although the last,
> The loveliest of all.'

The poetry may not have been his finest, but he never wrote from a
fuller heart.

Duff's satisfaction was still greater when, after the return of the
Conservatives in 1951, he was made a peer. To him this meant not
only a coveted honour but also a forum for his speechifying in the
House of Lords. For Diana it seemed only retrograde. All her adult
life she had been Lady Diana, daughter of a duke. Now she was to
submerge her identity in that of a mere viscount. She suggested hopefully that Duff might style himself 'Diana' or even 'Ladydiana'. Lord
Ladydiana would sound nice. Duff countered with 'Marrington'.
John Julius and Diana scoffed at this leaden flight of fancy and came
forward with Unicorn, Lackland, Sansterre, Erewhon, St Firmin, St
James, St George, St Virgil, Templer. Still more adventurous, Diana
tried Love-a-duck and Almighty. Duff was not impressed. 'One can
make a joke but one can't *be* one, not from choice anyway,' he
observed cogently. He brooded, then, without consultation, settled
for Norwich. 'Of all names Norwich is the most horrible,' wrote
Diana in dismay. 'Porridge' would have been better, a word which
seemed to her to be spelt much the same way. '"Man-in-the moon"
better still, though coarse, me being Diana the moon.' 'A little
Norwich is a dangerous thing,' was Duff's retort to this barrage of
wit, but he failed to convert his wife to the beauty of her new style.
She always disliked the name, was surly when congratulated on what

she considered her demotion, and swiftly followed Duff's ennoblement with an announcement in *The Times* that she wished to retain her former name and title.

She hankered after England, though her visits seemed increasingly connected with the deaths or diseases of her friends. She went to Breccles to visit Venetia Montagu, who was given only a few weeks to live by her doctor. At the end of the First World War and for fifteen years thereafter, Breccles had been a favourite resort – a place of comfort, beauty, gaiety, shoots, fireworks, picnics, rest. 'This last visit was like an old woman looking in a glass and seeing her youth's radiance. Very agonising.' Emerald Cunard died the same year. After her first heart-attack she told Diana that it was 'extremely pleasant – one was floating among clouds,' and her end now seemed equally peaceful. She left Diana a third of her estate, but this was to amount to little beyond debts. Diana did not mourn her dying; it came, she knew, at the proper time, and in the proper place. It was right to die where one had spent most of one's life. She knew that she, too, wanted to die in England.

Duff's new jobs involved much travel; to Venice for the film festivals, to various European capitals for meetings of the Board of the Wagons Lits. Diana's sight-seeing remained as voracious as ever. In Rome, when she went with the Altrinchams to the Vatican, she was outraged to find it closed. They battered their way past successive Swiss Guards, then met what seemed an immovable barrier. She recounted her eventual triumph to John Julius:

'I said Count Sforza [the Foreign Minister] had given me a name to ask for in case of trouble and I'd forgotten it. No good. I asked them to telephone the Count. They saved me by saying the Foreign Office would be shut. I told them to imagine I was Winston Churchill. What would they say then? They said *"Chiuso"*. It took the old trick of us not moving and the three of us forming an obstacle in a bottleneck to get us moved on to the next barrier. Suddenly tedium is stronger than guardianship, the morale gives, the pass is sold. The same thing at the second gate, this time with a senior man in civvies. I got as far as a laughing *"Siamo molto, molto importante"*. This shook him into telephoning to some higher power or principality, which produced a tiny little priest carrying the key of the Sistine Chapel.'

Eventually another priest appeared, who took them into parts of the Vatican not normally seen by the public and gave them tea and biscuits. It was a most satisfactory demonstration of the fact that her powers were not yet fading. But, 'You can see why I was glad Papa hadn't come.'

Her morale needed some such boost, for on a short visit to Holland earlier that year with her son, she had been disconcerted to find that her knee hurt and she grew tired. Duff wished that she would recognize she was growing older and could not do all she used to do. Diana would not accept defeat so meekly. Defiantly, she went to a monster exhibition of Flemish art and did not skimp a single picture. The European-American hand, she decided sadly, had lost its cunning. The Chinese, perhaps, could still do work of quality but we 'have pressed buttons for too long now, tapped type-keys, used machinery whenever possible and got used to "the pot of paint thrown in the public's face"'.

Rich friends continued to lavish hospitality on them. They stayed with Daisy Fellowes on her yacht and had their car pushed into the harbour; by drunken sailors, thought Duff; by Communists, Diana told the press – 'They hate my husband!' They stayed on Loel Guinness's new yacht too. There was debate about the name. *Diana? Gloria*, after his wife? *Gloria Mundi?* Better *Sick Transit*, suggested Diana. Bestigui's great ball at the Palazzo Labia in Venice was the apotheosis of rich friends' entertaining. Even the Aga Khan said he had never been to a better party. Costumes were to be of 1743. 'We can always be cheapjacks (what are they?)', mused Diana, 'or itinerants, or blackamoors or tumblers, or Ambassadors from Lapland or the Gobi.' In the event she was the centrepiece of an Antony and Cleopatra tableau after Tiepolo's mural in the same palazzo. She was dressed by Oliver Messel and Cecil Beaton, while herself feverishly sewing at a sack for Duff so that he could take a flask of brandy with him – Bestigui parties being notoriously short on alcohol. She arrived by gondola to find four thousand people massed outside the Palazzo Labia cheering each new arrival. She stepped out assisted by her negro pages, wrote Susan Mary Patten. 'I don't think that I ever saw anything more beautiful than that – the light from the palace windows falling on her face and the pearls and the blonde hair.'

John Julius was by now twenty and up at Oxford. The year before he had been sent to improve his French at Strasbourg. His mother warned him not to get engaged or married. 'You must see a world of women before you pick one and *don't get picked yourself*, especially not in the street or bar. They'll contaminate and deceive you and most probably give you diseases of all kinds, and so *méfiez vous* now you're on your own and keep yourself and your love for somebody almost exactly like me with a happier disposition.' Dutifully he kept free from the harpies of Strasbourg, but long before he had seen even a village of women he was engaged to Anne Clifford, a talented artist and daughter of Sir Bede Clifford, former colonial governor and member of an old Roman Catholic family. Duff and Diana approved of Anne but deplored the timing; insisting that at least the wedding should await the end of John Julius's period at Oxford. 'Good and pure and strong,' Diana found Anne. 'I admire her very much for her beauty and her sense and her not smoking or drinking or *lolling*, for her uprightness and her fun.' Her only faults were her mother and her Clifford voice, for neither of which, Diana charitably conceded, could she properly be blamed. Her Catholicism left Diana unmoved; indeed, the only person to be disconcerted was Evelyn Waugh, who had expected indignation at the thought of the noble house of Norwich falling to the papists and instead found acquiescence, even approval.

Her friends assumed Diana would be jealous at the thought of her only child being removed from her so young. Diana was herself uncertain about her reactions and relieved to find that she was already resigned to John Julius's marriage. 'Once he made his own friends I knew my day was over and accepted it easily,' she told Katharine Asquith. If loss there was, she had lost him when he went to Oxford. Besides, he was being particularly nice to her: 'I don't know if it's pity for the old girl or feeling loving and tender all round.' She reassured her son that she did not feel even a flicker of resentment. 'Jealousy is very rare in my case and is reserved entirely to sex.'

She found some attractions in the role of mother-in-law, with the chances it offered for giving advice to all and sundry. John Julius was urged at all costs to avoid being *common*, for instance by calling Anne 'darling' or pet names, or showing any intimacy in public. 'In private *la question ne se pose pas*,' she added somewhat ambiguously. She offered useful tips for married life. 'A man's strength with a woman is her terror of *losing* him, irrespective of how much she loves him.' John Julius should bear this in mind if Anne came over acid at any point. Anne found her warm and welcoming, though making it clear that in John Julius she was securing a treasure whose worth she must realise and whose happiness must be her chief concern. Anne was slightly alarmed by her, but much more amused and stimulated. The first time she saw her mother-in-law-to-be in full cry was at dinner with Louise de Vilmorin. She was struck by the way Diana encouraged her to exhibit her talents. The older woman so stage-managed things that she was soon sitting with a waste-paper basket on her head while Anne sketched her as the Madonna. Anne recognized what she felt must be the most important single reason for Diana's social success; the fact that though she loved to be the centre of attention, she felt any occasion less than a success if others present did not also show themselves at their best.

John Julius married in 1952. A few months before, Diana stated the credo by which she felt their future relationship should be governed.

'Whenever you are in pain of heart or body,' she told her son, 'or in despair of jams, dishonour, disillusion, nervous apprehension, drink or blackmail, you may rely on your old mother trudging the snow and through bars to perjure and to betray, to murder or – most difficult of all – to behave courageously to help you. But in your smooth days I must be courted and petted and needed, or I can't react. I was ever so with lovers too – neglect never roused me, only true love and cosseting got good exchange. I'm thankful that you have not turned out a pederast and I suppose I'm glad not to be Mrs Coward or even Mrs Beaton, but they have recompenses.'

There were times when Anne was to think the terms a little stiff but on the whole she felt that Diana gave a great deal more than she received or expected to receive.

Duff had become sixty in 1950. Diana felt that even his resilience could hardly survive this awful trial. 'I can't bear you to mind,' she told him. 'I'd much rather mind myself than see you sad over a matter of days. Dear love, you're always telling me the best is still to come.' So he was, and so, to his mind, *it* was. He found himself as happy as he could remember having been in his life, concerned only that Diana was less content. The solitary flaw was his health. For most of his life he had lived intemperately, he had eaten and drunk too much; now it was beginning to tell. 'I study his every gesture, gurk or twitch, determined with dread to find him in bad health,' wrote Diana, and though she was perfectly capable of manufacturing major tragedy out of a cough or itch, hard evidence in the shape of headaches, indigestion, sleeplessness, was accumulating to support her fears. In May 1953 he was taken violently ill in the night, uncontrollably vomiting black blood. He was rushed to hospital and the haemorrhage stopped, but not until he had lost a dangerous amount of blood. When Diana saw him the next morning she was dismayed by his appearance – 'bleached he was – with hands like plaster-casts and face of wan ivory' – but he was cheerful, even ebullient, and seemed to be enjoying the experience. The only thing that dismayed him was that his diet was confined to milk, boiled rice and asparagus – a régime that convinced him he must recover and come home as soon as possible.

Meanwhile there was the Coronation taking place in London. Diana's first instinct was to stay in Paris with her husband, who was clearly too ill to travel. Duff insisted that he was in no sort of danger and that of course she must go. Coronations did not happen every day and provided exactly the blend of pageant and romantic flummery which she loved most. Diana did not need much convincing. She felt for the royal family and the institution of monarchy that combination of irreverence and passionate loyalty that is so often found among the British of every class: the royals were there to be gossiped about, mocked affectionately, sometimes sharply criticized, but they were a vital part of national life. When Lord Altrincham published a modestly critical article about the monarch in 1957, Diana was warm in the Queen's defence. 'Have you ever heard of "tweedy" as an adjective?' she asked her son. 'Is it pejorative? I should have thought it meant sensible, flat-shod, wise, honourable people who work in the country, die in the wars, save what they can for their many children.' When Princess Margaret renounced Peter Townsend – 'I blubbed. I think it's noble and splendid of her if she's set on him, as I was told by inner rumour that she was.'

Though nagged by constant fears for Duff's well-being, her morale soared as soon as she arrived in Coronation-struck London. The decorations she found at first disappointing but they grew on her 'with the English faces which were the great decoration. Finest hour over again; 1940 at its rarest, nothing too difficult for anyone, all for all and wild gaiety and cockney jokes.' The night before the ceremony she walked down the damp, chill Mall to see 'the Belsen camp of happy sufferers – giant French letters spread over them, sou'westers, Everest equipment'. Then it was back for brief sleep, a struggle into 'a dead lady's ducal robes patched up', and dawn departure for the Abbey. One by one the great ones arrived: Princess Margaret, 'rather dusky and heavy featured'; the ducal husband, 'bigger, better, newer robes than the others, padded to a François 1er width by admiral's epaulettes.' Then the touch of bathos, the emergence of seven maids with seven mops, dressed 'as in smart American Hot-Dogs stands in hygienic white overalls and caps. At circuses they sweep up elephant droppings but what could those fairy royal feet have left – soles that had not left red carpets since birth?' At her side Lady Mowbray twittered in panic because her husband had to walk backwards down the steps with a long train. 'He'll never manage. He has to put on his spectacles to read the Oath and with them on he can't see the floor.' 'Couldn't he snatch them off?' asked Diana, ever helpful. 'I told him to, but he's so dreadfully obstinate,' whispered the despairing Lady

Mowbray. Lord Mowbray survived his ordeal and Diana's heart leapt as the ceremony moved towards its climax: 'It could not have been more moving and true and touching because of the size and grace of the central figure.'

She returned to Duff enthused with the delights of London and more convinced than ever that this must eventually be her home. She found her husband better than she had feared but not as well as she had hoped. Over the next few months he gradually picked up his strength and by the winter seemed almost himself again. 'I am so glad the darling old hot-cross-bun is really better,' wrote Lady McEwen from Marchmont, where they went to shoot in December. Then it was on to the Michael Duffs' at Vaynol for Christmas. A cruise to Jamaica was to complete the convalescence; arranged with great difficulty and now dreaded by Diana. Duff had a heavy cold when they left Vaynol and was coughing painfully by the time they reached the *Colombie* at Southampton. It was eleven on a cold, wet night when they boarded, to be greeted by a bevy of captains, pursers and other magnificos. 'Get rid of them all, I feel rather sick,' muttered Duff. Diana made everyone go away, then pleaded with him to give up the trip and get off the boat. It was impossible, said Duff. The luggage was aboard; there was no tolerable hotel in Southampton; besides, sea air was just what he needed to cure his cold and set him up.

Diana was by now haggard with worry, but forced herself to remain silent and not irritate Duff by asking constantly after his health. Next morning he seemed a little better but was obviously restless and uncomfortable. At last Diana asked him how he felt. 'Not really right,' he answered. 'And at noon it happened,' she told Cecil Beaton, 'a rush to the bathroom and a bigger, redder haemorrhage than he'd had before. "Poor child," he said, "you said you couldn't go through it again." I regretted then so often having whined if Duff drank so much as an extra glass of red wine – "Please not, I can't go through it again."'

Diana found the ship's doctor and Duff was given morphia and the drug with which their French doctor had equipped them. With proper hospital attention he might have pulled through, but at sea, and with the boat now tossing severely, there was little hope of checking the loss of blood. 'I became uncommonly calm and executive,' wrote Diana, and, 'I recognised this calm as a fatal sign.' Though she could not admit it even to herself, she had decided that all hope was over, 'hence the calm – it's hope that makes one hysterical'. The doctor and the jolly old *Infirmier* scoffed at her fears, there was no question of Duff dying, he was not even seriously ill. 'Do they think I am going to die?' asked Duff, with the same calm as he would have enquired whether dinner was ready. With relief she told him that they had pooh-poohed the idea. 'It was true, true, but I think if at that moment they had told me his end was so close I would have told him.'

Duff, white and frail, was now being sick every two hours. 'His trouble was torturing thirst – he was allowed no water, for the bleeding *had* to stop and I could only give him drops on my fingers, and he said once "It's *you*. The others would give it me."' It was December 31. As Diana sat by her dying husband, the clamour of singing and laughter floated up from the dining-room where the passengers were celebrating the *Réveillon*. It was a macabre backcloth for the tragedy, and for the rest of her life the sounds of New Year's carnival – the laughter, the music, the popping of corks – were to haunt her with signal potency. In the early hours the sickness stopped, 'but what was left? Not enough to colour his flesh or turn his heart into beats; no hope of transfusions of another's blood – the sea still rolling – his breath shorter – no pain – no consciousness.'

He lasted through the night and the next morning but slipped away with the daylight at 3.30 p.m. the following day. Diana spent the last hours in the adjoining bathroom, slumped in exhausted apathy. The doctor urged her to come to the bedside. She refused. If Duff recovered consciousness she would be there, otherwise she would leave him to die alone. '*Un peu de courage!*' urged the doctor. 'It was not a question of courage. I did not want to watch him *unconsciously* die. I greatly hope no one but strangers will watch my last breath. I heard no sound though I was within three yards or less. I dreaded the groans – no sound – he faded like the day and left me the night.' She could not even bring herself to look at him, though before she left the cabin she bent over his sheet-swathed body 'and kissed what I felt was his brow and said "Good-bye, my darling, my darling."' She was physically exhausted, emotionally void, and yet in a curious way felt a sense of liberation. 'Looking back and writing about it all makes me realise that never in my life have I felt more *natural* – perhaps it's not strange, but I'd imagined myself a grief-stricken woman feeling embarrassed or savage or shy. None of these things.'

The ship docked at Vigo and a charter-plane flew Diana and Duff's body back to Paris. 'Diana came down the steps looking like an angel from Chartres Cathedral,' wrote Susan Mary Patten, 'very beautiful, very calm.' Photographers and journalists thronged around but another close friend, Kitty Giles, flung herself against Diana, arms outstretched, and walked backwards to the car, shielding her from intruders. An evening followed of bright chatter at Chantilly, before Diana fell into drugged sleep. She woke at seven the following morning and insisted that Mrs Patten should identify a quotation for her – 'I wish I could remember it,' wrote Susan Mary, 'for it was lovely – about being very cold and alone but it not mattering, because the Elysian fields are warm.' Then Diana sat up, practical as always. 'This is no good, Susan Mary, you and I reading poetry. It would be better to have breakfast.'

The cortège moved on to England. Duff was to be buried at Belvoir, but Diana stayed in London. A few months before she had told John Julius that she almost never went to funerals. 'Public ones I grace by official duty, but not the burials of those I love. The idea jars upon me; exhibition of grief, the society duty side, does not, in my heart, fit.' Till the last moment she was uncertain whether she would react differently when the moment arrived for Duff to be buried. She did not. 'I did not want to hear the clods fall or be the central tragic figure, to court or dodge photographers.'

In London, she spent a few days of fierce sociability, finding in an endless procession of friends and acquaintances some relief from the pressure of her own misery. Great offence was caused by a letter of condolence beginning 'My dear Diana' and ending 'Yours sincerely, Evelyn Waugh,' but word of her indignation got back to the author and he made amends with a hurried note to 'Darling Baby' from 'Bo'. He visited her next day to find her in consternation because Lady Juliet Duff had taken it on herself to ask Lord Salisbury to read the lesson at Duff's Memorial Service. Diana at once telephoned him to insist that he must not be embarrassed by the request, she would never have dreamed of asking him herself. Only when she checked her flow of apologies did Lord Salisbury get a chance to say that there was no task he would be more honoured to undertake. 'She was very wild and witty, full of funny stories,' Evelyn Waugh noted in his diary; and everyone who saw her in those few days remarked on her febrile animation.

The Memorial Service was the day after the funeral. Diana lurked in a side chapel and saw almost nothing but Churchill with tears streaming down his face, heard little except for the murmur of surprise when *The British Grenadiers* was played as a voluntary. 'The obituaries treat Duff as a mixture of Fox, Metternich, Rochester and the Iron Duke,' wrote Evelyn Waugh. Only *The Times* was sharply critical in its final judgment. Few widows need expect to hear their recently-perished husbands treated with scorn or hostility, but Diana had more right than most to find comfort in the press and letters of condolence.

'A sort of shout of praise went up for Duff,' she told Cecil Beaton. 'He would have been so triumphantly pleased with it all; pleased with me too, I think.' As *The British Grenadiers* died away and she prepared to leave London, she congratulated herself on having survived a painful ordeal with courage and fortitude. She suspected that the true ordeal was just about to begin.

FOURTEEN

'What's That Lady For?'

For the last thirty-five years, Duff had been the centre of Diana's existence. All her activities had been subordinated to his, even when she had pursued her career in the cinema and theatre it had been with the aim of making enough money to launch him as a politician. Half the pleasure she derived from her friends, her sight-seeing, her social life, lay in the sagas into which she would weave her doings for Duff's entertainment. When they were apart no day went by without her writing to him, even after a few hours' separation they would meet to an explosion of talk and laughter. In his absence she felt herself no more than half a person. She could discern no purpose for her life. She had once heard a child peer in wild surmise at Lady Juliet Duff, turn to its mother and enquire: 'What's that lady for?' Now she asked the same question about herself and could find no satisfactory answer. She wrote to Evelyn Waugh a few months after Duff died:

'You have never, I think, known real grief. Panic, melancholia, madness, night-sweats, we've all known for most of our lives, you and me particularly. I'm not sure you know human love in the way I do. You have faith and mysticism, intense inner interests, a diverting, virile mind, gusto for vengeance and destruction if necessary, a fancy, a gospel. What you can't imagine is a creature with a certain incandescent aura and nothing within but a beating, frightened heart built round and for Duff... I have had as you can imagine since January a lot of the solitude that you advise. The "reflection" alas! is as it always has been, morbid, unedifying – vain and dangerous unless made healthy by the company of friends. For two days I am quite alone in these empty rooms with one thought, one prayer – "Let it end now"; an absurd feminine desire to die in the same way exactly as Duff. The "good account" grief has turned me to is fearlessness of death, so let it come now before custom of living disinclines me for dying. The summing-up is that one survives as best one can, either by spiritual or worldly ways. I imagine as a rule by one's habitual ways. My way has always been friends and distraction, you have always disliked it and condemned it, but

in these dreadful days one must be thankful and lenient to the way
found, for really there is no choice.'

'Friends and distraction' were Diana's formula for survival; distraction mainly in travel. Friends clamoured for the privilege of helping
her. Her instinct was to run away, but she needed people to run with
her. 'They pass the old torch from hand to hand,' she wrote: Alastair
Forbes to Enid Jones to David Herbert to Jenny Crosse to Paddy
Leigh Fermor. With Ali Forbes she paused briefly at Chantilly where
another group of the faithful had gathered. It was the place she most
feared to revisit, but though her time there was bad, it was not as
impossibly bad as she had dreaded. Paul Louis Weiller gave a luncheon for her – 'I, of course, splendid – but I can't think how, unless
Duff is helping. I really think he must be.' Then she was off on her
restless ramblings: to Madrid with Ali Forbes; Gibraltar with Enid
Bagnold; Tangier with David Herbert. 'I'm all right,' she told John
Julius. 'Don't worry for me. It's only sometimes I can't bear it and
talk aloud, but I'm not mad or drunk or drugged or suicidal, all of
which I'd expected.' If only she could run fast enough, then somehow
she would contrive to out-distance her memories; yet wherever she
arrived she found her memories awaiting her. She was in Bologna for
Duff's birthday with Jenny Crosse – journalist daughter of Robert
Graves. 'He'd have been sixty-four – too young, my darling, too
young. If I could get the cabin out of my mind it would help. Meredith says the past is blotted out, and if you taste oblivion of an hour,
so shorten you the stature of your soul, but those two days obliterated
would strengthen *my* soul, I'm sure.'

   With Paddy Leigh Fermor she went to spend a night with Berenson
in the villa where she and Duff had passed part of their honeymoon.
'Tell me, my darling, how it happened,' the old man asked. Diana
told him how calmly and painlessly Duff had died, 'and he put his
frail eighty-nine-year-old hands over his face and cried large tears'.
Then Susan Mary Patten took on the torch. 'Dope her with Chianti!'
had been Jenny Crosse's advice, and at every station a bottle was procured and poured into the acquiescent victim. In Rome she had been
sad and tired, but in a little Greek coaster bucketing out to Corfu she
began to revive. Her recovery was further encouraged when the
ambassadorial Rolls Royce failed to collect them from a remote village
eleven hours from Athens. 'Now we shall really travel,' announced
Diana exultantly. She persuaded the local hotelier to write on a sheet
of paper: 'We do not speak, understand or read Greek and we must
get to Athens. Can you help us?' Armed with this they embarked on a
series of uncomfortable journeys on local buses along lamentable

roads and in a heavy storm – 'Diana particularly pleased because the bus was jammed and every time it stopped the engine failed.'

It was material worthy of a saga for the delectation of Duff, but there was no Duff. Every so often the recollection of her misery would catch up with her. At Olympia the beauty of the ruins broke down her reserve and she walked along sobbing piteously while Susan Mary tried to soothe her by reading from the guidebook in her most monotonous voice. 'I had a bad cry because great beauty makes loss too near,' she told Leigh Fermor. This letter provoked the complaint that even by her own standards it was exceptionally difficult to decypher. A letter to Jenny Crosse inspired still more offensive congratulations on the speed with which she had mastered Greek writing. 'You can't call that a good sign,' Diana wrote plaintively to John Julius. 'Can you explain? Is it not re-reading them? Pam Berry used to say my letters made her very anxious.'

It was May before she finished her Greek travels. Enid Jones suggested that she join her in an expedition to Basutoland, where she would find quiet at the top of a mountain. Diana knew this would not suit her. 'It's not in my nature to be quiet. I have no wealth within me. All stimulus has to come through my eyes and ears and movement. Once still, I'm listless and blank and tortured by dread thought.' She could have spun out her odyssey by a few more visits, but it was six months since she had spent more than a single night at Chantilly and she hardly dared think what state the house and gardens were now in. As she grew nearer she prayed the journey would never end, knowing that the quiet of the house, Duff's deserted desk, the empty bedroom, would bring home to her, as nothing else could do, the loneliness that lay before her. 'It's arriving that's the rub,' she told John Julius. The Italian servants were dreaming of making their life in America; a new gardener had to be found; her tenancy was in question; a vista of domestic disorder opened before her as the train drew into the Gare de l'Est and she prepared for the last lap of her journey – 'Good morning Arturo. Good morning Percy. Bonjour Paris. Christ have mercy!'

A new gardener was indeed a first essential. The garden had been transformed into jungle: 'It's as dense as virgin forest in Sumatra. Great gourds rot on the ground, Jerusalem artichokes, grown to monstrous height, meet across its vast width.' Quarmi, the drunken incumbent, seemed hardly to have put his nose outside the local bistro. Now carbuncles sprouted from his head so that he looked like a monstrous pumpkin, his thighs had shrunk to nothing through colic and diarrhoea. 'No one will go into his room,' wrote Diana in despair. 'Have I got this stinking albatross round my neck for life? Must I abandon the place to be free of him?' She washed him and got him sober and took him to another potential employer, but when it came to the point he burst into tears and said he couldn't bear to leave. So back he came, and Diana resignedly began to advertise for an under-gardener.

She endured Chantilly for two months before she fled to England. The craving to be constantly on the move had now diminished; she could endure brief inactivity, time for reflection. The next few years, however, were above all ones of travel. 'You are such a kingfisher,' complained Lady McEwen. 'A flash of blue, a swirl and you are gone. "Diana is in London!" "No, where, where?" "I think she is leaving this morning." "She may be back for one day next week." "She is staying with Chips" – "No, with Oggie" – "No, on top of the Monument." Always poised for flight from your own sad heart.'

An expedition to North Africa with Ali Forbes and Iris Tree was marred by cold, wet weather, but at least got Diana away from Chantilly for two winter months. They made valiant efforts to drug themselves with hashish but achieved nothing by puffing innumerable pipes. Then Albert, the Arab guide, told them the rich ate it in a syrupy cake. Diana gave him ten shillings and he returned with a boot-blacking tin filled with the foetid mixture. They ate it with white sugar. 'It tasted rather good, of fig paste, and Iris wrote incomprehensible poems all night and Ali had bad dreams and I had my usual horrid one.' She was in a mood to find degeneracy in all she saw: the architecture, contaminated by Western fashions; the food – 'half a burnt sheep, schlocky puddings eaten with wooden spoons, then artichokes smothering what we've got used to calling somebody's feet'; the sordid beggars; the tasteless dancing.

'What happened to the Arabs?' she asked indignantly. 'They could once build and decorate and calculate, write and fight. We know Empires have lost their dominance, but Portugal is there, and Holland and Greece and Rome and France and poor old England, searching for beauty or some palliative or new morality. These hopeless Arabs search for nothing, a radio perhaps if you are a townsman, a street arab. Their women are beasts of burden, without a line or a harmony, huddled into shapeless sacks, with no idea, let alone hope of emerging from their muffled chrysalis. Ugh! I've had Arabs.'

Hardly returned from Africa she was writing to Stavros Niarchos to ask whether he would charter his boat to her. Niarchos did better and offered it free of charge. For several years a Mediterranean cruise in his yacht was part of the summer schedule. Paul Louis Weiller was another rich friend who put himself out to entertain her. Every summer she stayed at La Reine Jeanne, his house near Le Lavandou, 'a Babylon of beauty and shame and flesh and hedonism'. In 1955 Queen Soraya was the main attraction with 'an invalidish senator, son of Ambassador Kennedy' in a supporting role. The following year the Charlie Chaplins and the David Nivens were in the party. Diana felt ill at ease: 'I don't swim, except alone, I don't sunbathe, and I can't cha-cha and rock and roll as all the girls and Paul Louis do.' Instead, she sat in a corner and read Iris Murdoch's *The Sand Castle*; 'excellent. It saved my reason.' She was even more depressed when Onassis turned up in his yacht, though her reputation rose when she announced Greta Garbo was a guest, and soared when the actress fell on Diana's neck and wouldn't leave her. Twenty-seven guests from La Reine Jeanne went to dine aboard the *Christina*. The fountains played, the Hi Fi reverberated, and the pool changed its vivid lighting from scarlet to emerald to blazing white 'so that the all-but naked swimmers darted and dived like terrified goldfish'. Once Diana would have relished it, now she felt sadly out of place. 'I never got going at all. I had a strange aloof feeling that I was dead and watching the next century.' She concealed her misery well; to at least one person on *Christina* that night she seemed radiantly beautiful and the liveliest, most interesting person there.

At sixty-five she found, almost to her surprise, that the bourgeois virtues of Switzerland suited her far better than these meretricious splendours. She appreciated the order and the prosperity, the clean old men, the little girls with proper plaits and bows. All the animals were sleek and cared for; the cats never strayed; the cows were shaggy and serene, 'with graven bells on handsome collars fastened with buckles worthy of a bishop's shoes. I love the wholesome goodness of it all, rich earth and care, especially after the exquisite disorder of Italy.'

But it was Italy that she visited most often. In Rome she found again *'La Bande'* of the Paris Embassy, this time predominantly English but providing the same blend of artists and writers, talented, light-hearted, determined to enjoy life to the full. There was Jenny Crosse, married to Patrick Crosse, of Reuter's; Judy Montagu, Venetia Montagu's daughter, now married to the art-historian, Milton Gendel; Derek Hill, painter and Director of the British School; Iris Tree, with a one-room flat eight floors up above the Spanish Steps; Nigel Ryan, Crosse's younger colleague, who was to become one of Diana's closest friends in later years. They welcomed her as if she was their dearest friend and the fact that she was thirty years older than most of them was treated as a fact of entire irrelevance.

With Jenny Crosse she went on what she knew would be a farewell visit to Berenson. Spirits were always hard to find at I Tatti, so Diana stoked up with gin in the car before they arrived. At lunch the old man complained that he felt ill and low.

'Why don't you get drunk?' asked Jenny Crosse.

'I'd much sooner die,' he answered. 'I've never been drunk.'

'Nor have I.'

'Have you?' Berenson turned to Diana.

'Constantly.'

'But you always appear to be in good spirits. You don't need stimulus.'

'Perhaps you've never seen me sober,' suggested Diana.

He was delighted by this idea. 'I loved him as always,' Diana told John Julius. 'It's so disarming a man of ninety-two being so demonstratively affectionate. I suppose it's the same with all of us, but he makes you feel that he needs to hold your hand and that he must have one more embrace.'

More and more she began to treat Rome as a second home, without the burdens of Chantilly and with her friends on the doorstep. With John Julius she went to visit the Pope and took him a cross to bless. Only afterwards did it occur to her that the cross was hardly suitable for the honour, made as it was out of the plaited hair of King William IV, his mistress Mrs Jordan and five of his illegitimate children, from one of whom Duff was descended.

Wherever she went, however delightful the surroundings, congenial the company, black gloom would suddenly strike to dispel all pleasure. In October 1959 she spent what should have been an idyllic holiday in Ischia. 'It's too much for my familiar, my possessor,' she told Paddy Leigh Fermor. 'He creeps in through any cranny, black and stinking, and persuasive and plausible about life's futility. Even drink failed me. I mustn't go on holidays.' The mood did not last long, within a few weeks she set out on her travels again, but it was painful while it lasted and grew no less so with the years.

From about this time her journeys began often to be influenced by the whereabouts of John Julius and Anne, now in the Foreign Service. The relationship between mother-in-law and daughter-in-law is rarely a wholly easy one. If Anne had been meek or irresolute Diana would have overwhelmed her; but Anne was not, she was as strong-willed and as individual as Diana herself. While Duff was alive and Diana was both dependent on him and preoccupied by his needs, the two women had little over which to clash. When Duff died and John Julius was invested with much of the importance that his father had enjoyed in Diana's life, some element of conflict became inevitable. Fortunately each respected the other's qualities and a *modus vivendi* was not too painfully worked out.

An indication of the squalls that might lie ahead had come at Vaynol the Christmas before Duff died. On Christmas Eve, when everyone moved off to bed, John Julius announced that he was going to help his mother for a few minutes. Anne felt that at such a time some attention ought to be paid to her and asked her husband to join her quickly. He did not appear for two hours, by which time Anne was thoroughly upset. Next morning she wept and hid in her room. Diana had been quite unconscious of hurting Anne by absconding with her husband; had merely felt she wanted some affection and found Duff temporarily unavailable.

With Duff dead her needs became immeasurably greater. If John Julius and Anne neglected to write to her when separated they were bombarded with reproaches: 'Surely one of you could remember that I am an anxious creature and one lonely for family ... I am cruelly preoccupied by your silence and lack of heart'; 'Can your good generous hearts never understand how cruel it is to let me wait daily for the post and suffer morning and evening disappointment?' Anne could understand her requirements but found them sometimes oppressive. When they were on holiday with the Leigh Fermors on Hydra, Diana would arrive at their bedroom door every morning at 8 a.m. 'Come on, John Julius, Anne wants to sleep on,' she would call, and take him off to breakfast in the village. At first Anne saw in such demands a battle for the soul, or at least the body, of John Julius, but gradually she accepted that Diana's needs were not so extravagant; her mother-in-law was lonely, unhappy, craved attention and loved her son. Once back in London they came to an amicable if unspoken understanding. John Julius would be shared: if Diana wanted him for the evening and Anne for dinner then he must be returned promptly at 7.45. Eternally obliging, John Julius achieved the by-no-means easy feat of convincing both these forceful women that he was not sacrificing one in the interests of the other.

The only time John Julius felt his mother had gone too far arose over his first diplomatic posting. A fluent Russian-speaker, he had hoped to be sent to Moscow. To his delight he was offered the chance, then suddenly Belgrade was substituted. He told his mother, who was horrified. 'I meant you to be posted to Paris,' she said. Only then did it come out that she had approached Eden and begged that John Julius might be sent to Paris or somewhere near. Eden had refused to interfere but had said he would come to the rescue if John Julius were despatched too far afield. This aid she had invoked when the posting to Moscow was announced, only to find him sent somewhere which seemed almost as distant and was certainly far less welcome to her son: 'boring, music-less, only colleagues, no house, a landrover essential, no nurse will go with a child of one', she told Paddy Leigh Fermor bitterly.

'Are you pleased?' asked Lady Eden with a bright smile.

'How could I be pleased?'

'Oh, we thought we'd done right. Not too far and not too near.'

'How, not too near?'

'Well, we didn't think it would be fair on them.'

'Can you beat it!' Diana asked Katharine Asquith indignantly.

Diana never became resigned to Yugoslavia. She disliked Belgrade, resented being dependent on John Julius's friends for company, was irritated at not being able to make herself understood in French or English. 'I sure got a rough deal when they sent you there,' she was complaining eighteen months later. 'I'm despicable with self-pity, seeing all my contemporaries busy with their children and their grandchildren and their villages and their social activities and duties and good works and comforts. The science of living seems to have deserted me. It can't go on.' Nevertheless, it did go on, and became easier. Eden's decision, however little Diana was prepared to admit the fact, forced her to make her own life independent of her son's and, in the long run, proved a blessing. She made the best of a bad job. Tito visited Paris and a grand reception was given at the Quai d'Orsay. Diana got herself invited, with the help of General Catroux infiltrated the holy of holies where Tito was holding court, cornered his wife, Madame Broz, and told her firmly about John Julius and his guitar and pretty wife. Then she advanced on Tito himself with an inaudible mumble about a message from Churchill, threw in Fitzroy Maclean and Randolph Churchill for good measure, and once again dilated on the splendours of her son. 'I can't say he was interested by me,' she admitted, 'but I didn't care. My objective had been reached.'

The unfortunate consequences of her earlier intriguing did not deter her from further efforts. Harold Macmillan's appointment as Foreign Secretary raised her hopes but he soon moved on to be Chancellor of the Exchequer. 'I can't get over the bad luck of losing him as your boss,' she wrote with mingled pleasure and dismay. 'He looks so old and he shambles badly, but it is promotion and makes him nearer premiership.' Selwyn Lloyd took his place and Diana spent a weekend with him at Petworth. 'A little shy on arrival,' she noted. 'Out to please, not bad-looking, engaging, could be common. I wouldn't put a dirty story past him, though he did not deliver himself of one.' He spoke of the horrors of his life, his fear of flying, the fact that Eden had talked to him on the telephone the night before from 10 p.m. to 2 a.m. ('Harold would have hung up on him!' muttered their host, John Wyndham). He was put out because the *Daily Express* had photographed him at his desk, including in the picture the pad on which he jotted down things he had to remember – The Yemen, Cyprus, Beaverbrook etc – and blown it up for the entertainment of their readers. 'Lucky, really, that I hadn't written "Remind Anthony not to fuss so much"', observed Selwyn Lloyd.

To Diana the main significance of the Suez crisis was that it brought about the destruction of the detested Eden and the promotion of her favourite Macmillan to 10 Downing Street. Yet she deplored the means to this desirable end. Sturdily patriotic, she knew what she instinctively felt herself, but was dismayed to find many of her friends saw things differently. 'I need Papa to give me my lead,' she told John Julius. 'I'm desperately sorry for that donkey Eden. Being an objective old girl, I thought it was a clever, courageous plan, but like anything else we do, it was at dictation speed. Time is given for U N O gibbering, and though totally impotent it can blackmail. Now everyone seems pleased that we shall retire, tail between battered legs, and give what little we gained to a handful of Eskimos, Costaricans and harmless Laps with batons. It's wrong, no doubt, to go against U N O, but if U N O is wrong, is it wrong to go against wrong?'

With Macmillan Prime Minister and her new friend still at the Foreign Office, she had high hopes that John Julius might after all be sent to Paris when he had finished with Belgrade. Sir Frank Roberts had recently gone there as Ambassador to Nato and she persuaded him to plead her case in London. Eventually he spoke to the Chief Clerk in the Foreign Office, who was cautiously encouraging but raised the old objection. 'What was that?' demanded Diana. 'Too near his mother.' 'Honestly,' Diana wrote to John Julius, 'you'd think I was infectious or a witch or unfit for trust!' Instead, he was posted to Beirut; a more agreeable place certainly than Belgrade and offering greater possibilities for enjoyable sight-seeing, but still sadly far from home. Regrets became terror when civil war broke out in the Lebanon. Diana was on a ship sailing to Beirut at the time and took advantage of a stop at Athens to telephone her son. After hours of frustration in a suffocating booth she finally got through, to hear him say: 'Mummy, haven't you heard? I've been shot.' Diana's voice was inaudible in Beirut but John Julius guessed she was asking where he had been wounded and went on: 'In the head. The head! Like Anthony!' The fact that he could make puns slightly reassured Diana but not enough to calm her when the call was abruptly cut off. '*Au secours!*' she bellowed at the operator. '*Mon fils a été fusillé et il ne peut pas m'entendre!*' Eventually it became clear that the wound was a trifling one, and Diana returned to her ship.

> 'We seem to have no radio communication with land,' she wrote a day or two later. 'That's perhaps why we sang "Eternal Father" yesterday at evensong in the lounge, pronounced by the most unctuous, fat, self-indulgent padre. In spite of his shortcomings I cried my way through the service and thanked God that he had spared you death – but had to add a little something of disappointment that my nightly prayers for your protection from any harm had failed.'

One compensation for the Norwichs' far-flung postings was that their daughter Artemis spent much time in France. When it was first suggested that Artemis – whose very name was a compliment to Diana – should spend the summer of 1955 at Chantilly, her grandmother was acquiescent. 'Perhaps it will touch my heart,' she wrote to Katharine Asquith. 'I doubt it, poor Artemis. My heart and mind are as empty and heavy as a broken sarcophagus, and for all my praying aloud in night hours, nothing comes to fill it.' Though she had enjoyed bringing up John Julius, Diana was generally shy with children, disconcerting them by her brusqueness and irritated by their failure to respond as grown-ups. At first Artemis conformed only too well to this pattern. 'When this little girl looks at me she whitens, petrifies and then bursts into hysterical tears,' Diana complained to Evelyn Waugh. But familiarity quickly banished alarm, Artemis got used to being treated as a grown-up and began to enjoy the barrage of questions and instructions with which Diana larded her conversation: 'Who was Medusa?' 'What is seventeen minus two?' 'What's the capital of Denmark?' She was subjected to the same cross-examination on English kings and foreign capitals as her father had once endured and like him discovered that learning could be fun when the teacher enjoyed irreverence, originality and a sense of humour. Commonness was rebuked in all its manifestations: saying 'Bye-bye', going to the lavatory, catching cold. Artemis grew to adore her grandmother and Diana felt for the little girl the same affection as she had felt for John Julius twenty years before.

Anne was slightly irritated by the advice that would descend on her when Artemis returned from a visit to Chantilly. She was apt to giggle, a vice that verged on commonness: 'So reprove it.' She could not recite a single nursery rhyme, 'so do make her learn poems – too old for her but with simple metre. "Come Live With Me and be My Love" for instance.' Her wider education must not be ignored: 'What

about piano? Can you begin?' Diana complained about Artemis's hairstyle. 'She looks like a prissy miss if trapped into her futile grip, and
like a beatnik if it is loosened. This may be her prettiest year. Why
spoil it for me, who has her with me day in day out?' Though the
advice was not always welcome, most of it made sense and Anne
usually acted on it.

Any mother who sees her child so strongly influenced by another
woman – especially, perhaps, when that woman is her mother-in-law
– is likely to feel some jealousy. Anne was not wholly free of this, but
she was too sensible not to appreciate the value of what Diana gave
Artemis and to feel gratitude for it. Artemis's brother, Jason, was at
this stage too young to be exposed to his grandmother's attention. It
was not till they were all back in London that she came to know and
appreciate him.

Most of Diana's friends had assumed she would return to settle in
England. 'The peculiar beauty of [Chantilly] has a melancholy of its
own which is sapping to the vitality and must enhance your permanent ache,' wrote Pamela Berry. In London she could live in less grandeur but greater comfort, surrounded by her friends, close to all the
things she enjoyed most. At first Diana thought she agreed; she told
Ronald Storrs that she planned definitely to abandon France. She
played with the idea of settling somewhere near Stratford, involving
herself with the doings of the Royal Shakespeare Company, becoming
'relied on for something trivial and adored by cast and electricians
alike'. And yet when it came to the point, 'I have got attached to the
house and see Duff everywhere'. Besides, there was still a chance the
Foreign Office would send John Julius and Anne to Paris.

So she lingered on, though finding little pleasure in so doing. 'I do
nothing worth while and don't suppose I ever will,' she wrote sadly in
1955. What she hopefully told herself was no more than a phase
threatened to become a lifetime's pattern 'I read little, sleep little, go
out seldom in Paris, thank God, do the minimum of gardening and
dressing. I don't fear or fret much, or enjoy much.' Two drawings of
her as a baby by her mother crashed inexplicably to the floor in the
middle of the night. 'If it presages my death I don't really think I
mind,' she wrote with perceptible relish; her melancholy was wholly
genuine, yet she never failed to derive a certain pleasure from demon-
strating it to others.

Her life was made tolerable by the presence of Nora Fahie. Miss
Fahie had been intrigued by an advertisement for a secretary-cum-

Girl Friday with, among other qualifications 'a deep knowledge of the laws of growth'. She applied for the job, was engaged and from that moment became indispensable. When Duff died she moved into the chateau and tended her employer with mingled love and firmness. Diana believed that without Nora Fahie she might have lost her reason. She underestimated her own toughness but did not exaggerate Miss Fahie's devotion.

Otherwise domestic disasters multiplied. New servants were hired just before Harold Macmillan came to stay; then the morning he arrived the French maid was removed by the police and the Italian manservant announced he had to return home to stand trial for murdering his former employer. When Joe Alsop came to dinner it was to find that the cook had just been shot to death on the streets of Paris. Quarmi, the drunken gardener, was at last bribed into retirement and returned to Holland, only to reappear within the week pleading that he be allowed to set up camp in the stables. 'I found strength and cruelty to say no, so the poor *clochard* went off with a £10 bonus to Versailles. Is it not tragic? I feel like jelly masquerading as a stone.'

The cold in the winter of 1955 was so fearsome that Diana's bedroom was the only spot in the house of tolerable warmth. Paddy Leigh Fermor, rigid with lumbago, smoking five cigarettes in ten minutes, took refuge beneath her fur counterpane. 'I stuck to my night cap because I hate floating hair. The communal bed was smothered in dictionaries, Shakespeare, Quotes, genealogy books, novels, plus trays of old snacks, gin, red wine, dregs and dusty telephone-wires, radio moaning overlapping programmes, more sweaters to fight the cold of a dying stove.'

But with it all, life was slowly beginning to be fun again. Solitude was still hard to bear, but provided there was plenty of coming and going, friends thronging around her, Artemis to bring up, quick darts here and there, then things were tolerable enough. A week of intense activity, with never less than eight people in the house, constant parties, a race-meeting, picnics, visits to neighbouring chateaux, was followed by a night alone at home reading and listening to music:

'I can manage that – just – but I cannot be quite alone for more than two nights,' she told John Julius. 'It's against my nature, and woman's nature for that matter. I get thinking too unhappily and might do anything. Whatever you say about keeping still, and learning to be quiet and alone, I cannot. You might as well tell me to walk on my hands instead of my feet. I just have to wander around like the old Jew or the Flying Dutchman. And I do not find

it unnatural or even strange. I've had a life of love, excitement, endeavour, success for fifty years. I can't live another one completely.'

Fortunately there were many friends who were happy to cater for her
needs. Evelyn Waugh proved notably loyal. In April, 1955, he spent
two long evenings reading aloud his new novel *Officers and Gentlemen*. Diana appreciated the effort, but, surprisingly, not the book
itself, finding it 'as true as life and war and equally boring'. There
were too many incomprehensible military titles, too little story, no
memorable character except 'the man with the thunderbox, who
died', too many delicate nuances and under-currents which no reader
could hope to perceive without Waugh's constant asides to help them.
It was something that Mrs Stitch played a role – 'not bad and acting
exactly as I would in the end' – but she could not redeem a failure. 'I
fear it cannot be a seller, and he does need money to feed the hungry
seven.' Waugh was on his best behaviour, acting with loving solici-
tude and only making mischief when the Duc de Brissac cross-
examined him on the intricacies of English prosody. With satisfaction
Waugh gave him all the wrong answers.

Randolph Churchill was another regular visitor, in particular
favour with Diana because he was doing stalwart work raising money
for Duff's memorial. 'Twice of an evening he danced a *pas seul*,
bouncing with the lightness of a pingpong ball, his dropsical body
gyrating and elevated by neat little stockinged feet. Then he'd hurl
himself pancake flat on to a sofa, and breathe like a grampus's death
rattle.' On Sunday night, like every other summer guest in 1955 and
1956, he was led across the park to find the great chateau 'fading and
waking under modulating lights' while spectral voices pealed out its
history: the death of Vatel, the building of the gardens by Le Nôtre.
The hounds in full cry passed by out of human sight. Diana was
entranced by this miraculous entertainment: '"Son et Lumière," they
call this great advance in pageants.'

The Harveys had now been replaced in Paris by the Jebbs, a change
which worked immeasurably to Diana's advantage. From being a
distrusted adversary she found herself transformed to honoured
friend: constantly invited to the Embassy; consulted on the finer
points of social etiquette; Chantilly a regular port-of-call for ambassadorial guests in need of amusement. There were, indeed, so many
people pouring through the doors that it was easy not to notice how
few of them were French. Such as did come tended to have Anglo-
Saxon connections; conversation was almost always in English; talk
more likely to turn to the rival merits of Gaitskell and Macmillan than

the prospects for Mendès France; to Graham Greene's new novel than the thoughts of Jean-Paul Sartre or the feelings of Françoise Sagan. *La bande* had dispersed: dead or disaffected or too busy to come often to Chantilly. Even with Louise de Vilmorin the relationship had grown cool. When, after a long separation, Diana arranged to spend two nights at Verrières, Louise forgot and muttered excuses about hard work and a man coming to make a recording. 'I said nothing,' Diana wrote, 'but found myself harbouring bitterness, so went to bed.'

More and more her interests seemed to be centred on England; Chantilly no more than a redoubt where life could be carried on until the time came for a retreat to the homeland. One obvious way by which this might have been brought about was by remarriage. Lady Waverley wanted her to marry R. A. Butler, which Diana interpreted as a sure sign that she had her eye on him for herself. 'When I say "Perish the thought" she will ask me why not, which puts me in the devil of a spot as my reasons, she would think, should apply to her. How could I, at my age, when I have had the *best*? Now she wants me to marry Heathcoat Amory, which shows she is out to fish in new waters.'

But though she had no intention of remarrying, she was far from abandoning the battle to maintain her beauty. In 1958 she went into the London Clinic for a face-lift. Strict secrecy was observed, even John Julius was at first told she was having a tooth dealt with. The amount of morphia the Clinic offered proved wholly inadequate and Diana had to persuade them that she was a former addict who needed double the normal dose. When she came to she found herself swathed in a blood-crusted iron helmet. The doctor assured her that she would have a nice surprise when the bandages came off. 'I don't like that,' she noted darkly. '*Les bonnes surprises* often work out as *mauvaises plaisanteries*.' In the event she was modestly relieved by what she found. 'The gobble-gobble has gone leaving a pure curve, but the stitches round the swollen ears stick out like porpentine's quills and my neck is a Turner sunset.' She passed her convalescence reading Anthony Powell's latest novel which, with a bold stab at accuracy, she called '*At Aunt Mabel's*'. She liked it greatly but it filled her with disquiet: 'Quite a bit of Evelyn Waugh, a dash of Proust, and the purpose – description of the slow decay of top people due to social revolution – a grim subject to me, excruciatingly funny for those who are not of noble class.'

There were few signs of the top people's decay at Buckingham Palace where Diana went for the state visit of General de Gaulle. The evening held all the splendour and pageantry that she adored; the only sadness coming from the sight of 'the man that was – poor wrecked Winston' hobbling off alone to the throne-room where dinner was to be served. Diana went with him and sat at his side till the other guests arrived. 'He seemed to know me – "my dear" covers all-comers – but I can't be sure. It was painful, painful; his emaciated and feeble leg looks loose in its garter which is sewn on.' At dinner she sat between the French Ambassador and the Lord Chamberlain and a blast of icy air from the service door behind her blew her hair all over her cheeks. 'Can we do anything about the draught?' asked the Ambassador, whose wife had a temperature of 101°. 'Can we do any-thing about the draught?' Diana asked the Lord Chamberlain. 'Can we do anything about the draught?' the Lord Chamberlain asked a major domo behind him. 'Can we do anything about the draught?' the major domo asked some junior lackey. 'Nothing whatever,' came the firm reply, which was passed back down the line to the resigned Ambassador. The food was equally unworthy of the occasion: unin-spired nursery broth with bits in it was followed by 'le saumon Balmoral-republican' which turned out to be none-too-tasty rissoles and finally by 'Glace Croix de Lorraine'. 'The crucifix, laid flat on a lordly dish and dripping with cream and custard shocked me too much to scoop an arm off it, so I don't know if it was just plain vanilla.'

The fireworks, however, left no room for criticism. Diana pro-duced a blue ticket and was told first that she must go upstairs, then that she should head to the left and finally that the corridor to the right was her proper route. After groping her way down an endless passage which she thought must have taken her almost to Consti-tution Hill, she was ejected on to a balcony, to be blinded by the blaze of fireworks. Only when her eyes adjusted to the darkness did she realise that just in front of one side she had the Queen in all her glory and on the other the portly President himself – 'The *Tour Eiffel enceinte de la France* and merry as a medlar.' As soon as the fire-works were over she fled the Palace to drive to a party given by the Hofmannsthals. Her car was slow in coming and so she sat with the coachmen, gorgeous in scarlet and gold coats, black and gold top hats and eighteenth-century golden-headed malacca canes with which to poke the ladies' trains into carriage doors. She enjoyed this half hour as much as any of the evening. 'They told me where they lived and *coulisse* tit-bits. Every few minutes they called my car again, nothing doing. "'E's gone for a pint"; "'E's found a bird." "You don't know Mr Presley, he's not like that. I don't believe your tannoy works." "Tannoy always works. 'E's gone to the Blue Man."'

Visits to England always involved the seeing of friends and in-

numerable parties. A grandly formal ball at Blenheim or Wilton
would be followed by a dance given by Laurence Olivier at Terence
Rattigan's country house for Marilyn Monroe and Arthur Miller.
'Marilyn Monroe charmed everyone with her pretty face and *mal
pendue derrière – mal pendue* yet featured by having so thin a layer of
material that every fold and muscle and contraction of its cleft could
be studied. She danced in ecstasy and exclusively with her husband.'
Then might come a picnic given by Ann Rothermere on the crumbling terraces of the Crystal Palace: vodka and prawns, chicken and
white wine among the great drifts of willow herb, the urns, the fountains, a suburban Angkor where lichen and ivy reigned triumphant
over Victorian balustrades and Paxton's heroic bust. It was a fantasy
world of beautiful people in beautiful places, and she saw just enough
of it to convince her that she wanted more and could only be happy
when home again for ever.

Home was not only balls and picnics. In July 1957 she revisited
Mells, the house in which she had once been so happy, to find an aged
and saddened Katharine Asquith nursing a dying Ronald Knox. Mrs
Asquith had told Diana about his appearance, but no warning had
prepared her properly for 'this spectre of skin and bone, swollen with
wind and dropsy. The beautiful skull face was as vivid a yellow as the
phosphorous red one sees in advertisements, and in this startling
colour eyes yellower still and fearfully living. I can't wipe the picture
out. I long to forget it. Poor, poor old thing.' Diana was not obsessed
by death, it occupied her thoughts very little, whether her own death
or that of other people. But the spectacle of suffering was something
else; she rejected and would flee from it. It had taken her days of
distress to persuade herself to Mells and was to take many more weeks
to banish the awful vision from her mind. Ronald Knox's was the last
death-bed she was to visit; the thought that the one death-bed she
could not escape must be her own was more a relief than a cause of
fear.

Long before Duff died Diana had played with the idea of writing
her memoirs. 'I was always determined not to, and rather despised
those who did'; but then she read Maurice Baring's *Puppet Show of
Memory* and was struck both by the pleasure it gave her and the ease
with which it seemed to be written. 'It would be an interest and an
absorption – delving into the past I shall forget the future,' she wrote,
while still wrapped in the gloom that followed her eviction from the
Embassy. Then Duff had begun work on his own autobiography, *Old*

Men Forget; Diana recaptured her pleasure in life; the delights of authorship dwindled, the pains seemed more apparent. It was not until 1955 that the idea was revived. Rupert Hart-Davis, Duff's nephew and a publisher of great distinction, read the letters which she had written to Conrad Russell from South East Asia and Algiers and urged her to write a book about her life. 'They are absolutely wonderful,' he wrote, 'so vivid, amusing, original, witty and *you*. You are a natural writer, with your own style which could not be anyone else's.' The book would be fun to write, a delight to read and, never low in Diana's list of priorities, might make a lot of money.

Reading the first volume of Osbert Sitwell's quintet, Diana had said to Conrad Russell: 'There is a lack of inhibition and of humour in autobiography. It's awful cheek!' Now that she came to the point she found herself neither humourless nor inhibited. She had kept almost every letter written to her, her childhood memories were rich and vivid, the book poured out like a river in flood, bearing with it the bric-à-brac of a lifetime's occupations. Her approach to evidence was cavalier – letters were ruthlessly truncated or amalgamated, words and dates changed, recipients muddled – but though her attitude to detail might make the historian wince, the whole was truthful. Diana in her autobiography presented as honest a portrait of the writer as it was within her powers to give: nothing extenuated, little held back; aware throughout of the extraordinary luck that had given her position and beauty, never falsely immodest about the contribution her own efforts had made to her success; frank, funny and in its essentials remarkably exact.

When she read the first 10,000 words she was appalled. How could anyone be asked to read this shapeless mish-mash? Evelyn Waugh had gallantly volunteered to act as editor-cum-ghost-writer. Diana declined the offer: 'He has better stuff of his own and does not have the time or the pocket, besides it would make me much too nervous.' Now she almost wished she had accepted. She compared notes with Charlie Chaplin, who was also at work on his memoirs, to find that all he could think of was the number of words he had written each day. He did not even seem to know what point in his life he had reached. 'I suppose it's planchette again, only dictated planchette, and maybe for that reason v. good, for if Charlie stops to think his genius stops simultaneously. He has no art left, poor clown, except for breeding children and loving his darling wife.'

She turned for help to her Roman friend, Jenny Crosse. She would pour out her unrevised memories on paper; Jenny would transform them into grammatical and lucid prose, disentangle her knotted ramblings, impose order on chaos. When Mrs Crosse had finished the first chapter, Diana found that the end product was no more pleasing to her than the original, 'I found myself so tenacious of my tripe that I hated the tampering'. She sent the original and the revised version to Rupert Hart-Davis, who was delighted by the first and dismayed by the second. A few specimens of Mrs Crosse's work survive in the final text. 'Geneva,' wrote Diana, 'is the place for any girl who wants confidence in her sex-appeal bucked up a bit.' 'Geneva,' amended Jenny Crosse, 'is certainly the place for a lady who needs her confidence in her desirability bolstering up.' Rupert Hart-Davis was having none of this. He told Diana that she must write her own book and that editorial interference should be confined to the correction of spelling and the addition of the odd comma here and there. 'My editor insists on making a proper monkey out of me,' Diana told Jenny apologetically. 'I shall call it *The Old Visiters*, thereby taking the comparison with Daisy Ashford out of the reader's mouth.'

What to put in and what to omit was the problem that worried her most. What about love-letters? Was it common to include them? 'Stuff them with love-letters,' advised Waugh firmly. 'You've never been one for ghastly good taste, have you? It's the bastard in you – Edmund and Edgar constantly at strife.' Apprehensively Diana obeyed, and awaited a barrage of hostile criticism. She had no need to worry. *The Rainbow Comes and Goes* was published in 1958 to an almost ecstatic reception. It is fair to say that most of the critics in the grander papers were personal friends, but their names still make up a roll-call of the literary establishment. 'Brilliantly fresh and vivid and charming,' wrote David Cecil; it captivated Raymond Mortimer 'both as a picture of a vanished world and as a revelation of a character'; Harold Nicolson said that it was 'one of the most genuine self-portraits I have ever encountered'; Evelyn Waugh called it 'poetic, idiosyncratic, poignant, funny, unflagging, scintillating, simple, stylish'. The *Sunday Times* paid the then massive sum of £6000 for serial rights, 11,800 copies were sold by the time of publication, 30,000 by 1959, bringing her, for sales of the Hart-Davis edition alone, £12,535. Hatchards had a signing session which produced most gratifying sales, though Evelyn Waugh, who put in an appearance 'tight and very jolly', claimed that eighty per cent of the sales were made to resident shop-girls rather than customers. By any standards the publication had been a resounding success.

The Rainbow Comes and Goes took its title from Wordsworth's 'Intimations of Immortality': 'The rainbow comes and goes, and lovely is the rose'. For her next volume, taking her from the end of the First World War to the outbreak of the Second, she chose the ending of the noblest of all the stanzas of that great poem:

'At length the Man perceives it die away
And fade into the light of common day.'

The Light of Common Day did indeed show some decline from the fantastical fairyland of Diana's childhood memories. It was far more dependent on letters to and from Duff and, in the later parts of the book, Conrad Russell; instead of re-working them into a narrative she allowed them to speak for themselves. 'Less of a book and more of a scrapbook,' complained Cyril Connolly. 'I wish she would try to build up serious portraits of her friends instead of leaving it all to their letters.' On the whole the tone of the reviews was friendly enough, but Diana, predisposed to believe that her work was drivel, heard it as a chorus of abuse. 'Darling, I'm awfully sorry for you,' she wailed to Rupert Hart-Davis, who replied contentedly that sales were well up on the previous volume.

She embarked on her third volume with nauseated apprehension. Her zest had gone, her nerve had gone, only drudgery remained. 'Quite lost and incapable as a drunk in a gutter,' she described herself to Hart-Davis. 'I must have got those two books written in a trance.' Dutifully she ploughed her way through the Second World War, depending ever more heavily on the diary-letters which she had written Conrad Russell and on his replies. Vivid, exuberant, original in phrase and outlook, her letters were in fact works of art of a high order, but she became less and less inclined to do more than string them together with a tenuous commentary. By the time she had reached 1944 she was near despair. Then inspiration struck:

> 'My eyes can't see my own book,' she told her publisher, 'its dimensions, its balance, its throttling tedium or original naiveté. All I can see is a slough of despond. I am working in the dark like a black mole, unconscious of what I am throwing up and miserable. Suddenly a winged thought! Why not end the volume with Algiers? I am sure it will be long enough and I have a phantom fourth volume that John Julius can do after my death. This way the French section will be postponed until historically and socially it will be respectively more interesting and less expurgated. The author can deal touchingly with my death and romantically with Duff's... All those beastly people will forgive me if I am dead. The author can pile on the *"amie de la France"* which I have never been. They can make a glamorous Chantilly sequence, which I cannot. And then my *pompe funèbre*.'

The winged thought was swiftly brought to the ground. Rupert Hart-Davis pointed out that a chapter on the French Embassy was a crucial part of her story; John Julius was notably unenthusiastic about the proposal that he should take on the fag-end of his mother's life. Reluctantly she gritted her teeth and set to work on the last chapter herself.

For a title she once more looked to the 'Intimations of Immortality'. *Trumpets from the Steep* might not seem to have any very obvious relevance to the story, but it sounded splendid and struck a vaguely valedictory note. Sentimentality and self-pity could easily have become the keynotes of this account of fading beauty and grandeur slipping away for ever, but Diana was never one to indulge herself in such feebleness. Gratitude for all she had received, a striking absence of rancour, above all a triumphant readiness to make new discoveries, to explore new fields, to live in the present and look to the future, mark the end of her story as forthrightly as they had the beginning. 'This is one of the most perfectly realised autobiographies of our time,' wrote Margaret Lane, and certainly few autobiographies can have caught more authentically the personality of the author.

Her job was done, and though she was heartily grateful to have it behind her, it left a larger gap than she had expected. Once again the pattern of her life required examination. While the books were being written and the profits rolling in, she had been determined to remain in France and save her income from what seemed to her the unacceptable depredations of the Inland Revenue. Now she was ready to return to England. It was just as well, for the Institut de France, which administered Chantilly and all its outlying chateaux, had been growing increasingly restive. Their first sighting shot had been fired in November, 1956, when the Board of Directors wrote to say that, as her lease was almost at an end, they had decided to dispose of the house and would like her to be out within six months. The letter was signed by M. Fossier, the administrator of the Domaine de Chantilly. Diana appealed to higher authority but got nowhere. 'I must start fighting it, I suppose. The stinking, sodden Connétable offers as an excuse that "*M Fossier ne vous aime pas*". His next suggestion was that the rent was too low. They've put it up twice in nine years and they've only got to give me the chance of accepting the increase or getting out.' Paul Louis Weiller was called into action, and hired a lawyer to defend Diana's interests, but whether she could hold out for the three years she needed to finish her book seemed very doubtful.

The press got wind of the battle. Sam White, the perpetually well-informed correspondent of the *Evening Standard*, telephoned to ask if it were true that she was to be evicted.

'What, Mr White, will you never learn? You've never got a word out of me. Why should I feed your paper?'

'Well, Lady Diana, the *Evening Standard* is always very good to you.'

'Wrong, Mr White! They've twice said I was having a face-lift and they print my age in brackets whenever they print my name.'

'You're so amusing, Lady Diana.'

'Of course if you paid me, Mr White, that would be another matter and more interesting. They pay *you*, don't they? What will they pay me?'

'Oh, you're so amusing, Lady Diana.'

'Good-bye, Mr White.'

But Sam White had the last laugh when he procured from the Domaine de Chantilly details of the still modest rent that Diana was required to pay and put the information in his column.

Figaro took up the story. It announced that the veteran Algerian nationalist Messali Hadj was to have St Firmin placed at his disposal. 'As a matter of fact this château is at the moment being rented by a distinguished English lady. The Institut, however, formally contests her right to sublet.' Diana had sailed decidedly close to the wind by sub-letting St Firmin for several months at a time while she was on her travels or writing her autobiography in Rome; it was at the most, however, no more than a technical breach of the terms of her lease and would have been discreetly ignored if it had not formed part of the Institut's campaign to evict her. Other causes of friction abounded. Hugh Gaitskell, then Leader of the Opposition, was caught climbing out of the park at 7.30 a.m. after taking a morning ramble from St Firmin and feeling a sudden urge for a cup of coffee in the village. A few days later Nancy Mitford and some other friends were found trespassing by the Duc de Broglie himself, head of the Institut de France, who 'sent them spinning home with his rage'. In 1960 came a polite letter from Henri, eldest son of the Comte de Paris, to say that he understood she was leaving the chateau and that he was greatly looking forward to living there himself. When exactly did she expect to move?

By now the last volume of her autobiography was published, the bulk of the income safely banked, she was ready to retreat. All that remained was to decide where she should go. England certainly. London certainly; she could not afford houses in both London and the country, she would never be short of friends whom she could visit all over Britain, a base in the capital was indispensable. The more elegant areas in the centre were far beyond her purse. John Julius and Anne had recently leased a house in so-called Little Venice, a picturesque area on the canals beyond Paddington. Diana cast her eyes in that direction. Anne incautiously held forth on the delights of Clapham, an area as far south of the Thames as Little Venice was north. Diana interpreted this as meaning that she was to be exiled far from her family.

'I can't conceal that it is a body-blow to me,' wrote Diana in distress. 'I was forewarned from the day you both talked of the pleasures of Clapham, for I saw what must happen. I had looked forward too long to the end of loneliness, a double house or two flats with dressing-gown access... I expect when I collect myself I shall realise it's all to the good. I shouldn't write you this and I was determined not to and put off writing, and now I feel if I bottle up my sadness it will cork, so this is really an anti-corking letter.'

This *cri de coeur* had immediate effect. A house was discovered in Warwick Avenue – 'the Red Light District' as Evelyn Waugh described it – not with 'dressing-gown access' but only a few hundred yards from the Norwichs' house in Blomfield Road. It was not ideal but it had a garden, a big drawing-room, a large and tranquil bedroom in which Diana could conduct the greater part of her activities, enough room for the most cherished books, pictures and ornaments. It would do well enough for what she had satisfied herself would be her few declining years.

The idea of leaving Chantilly caused her little distress, the physical process of so doing almost broke her nerve. 'My mind reels with what has to be done,' she told Katharine Asquith. 'Change of residence is as hard as reversing gravity.' There were problems with the British customs, problems with the tax authorities, problems with the Institut. What was to be taken and what left behind was the most painful problem of all. Duff's library preoccupied her particularly. Somehow it must be broken up – 'no space in the Space Age' – but which books should go to Warwick Avenue, which to John Julius, which to the Embassy? Her friends poured out from Paris to help her with the work of demolition. On the last day Diana urged her assistants to pick every flower in sight and leave the garden a green desolation. It was a reflection of her mood.

And so the gates closed for the last time on the ravaged garden, the empty rooms already possessed by the peculiar squalor and bleakness that afflicts a house deserted by its owner. She had lived there for fifteen years, some of them among the happiest of her life, some the most miserable. A link with Duff was severed, but she knew she would feel close to Duff wherever she was, no less in London than Chantilly. What distressed her was not what she was leaving behind but what lay ahead. She was almost seventy years old. At Chantilly she had been in touch with her younger self, there was a thread of continuity which linked her to middle age. Now the thread was cut, she was beginning life again as an old lady. Bleakly she visualized an existence of increasing decrepitude; fading faculties; pain; worst terror of all, senility. Her infinite capacity for expecting the worst led her into a welter of anticipatory gloom. All was for the worst in the worst of possible worlds; all that remained was to sit it out until released by the merciful quietus of the grave.

FIFTEEN

Old Age

Twenty years later, now aged eighty-eight, the quietus of the grave has still been denied her. It has come as a surprise to nobody except herself that the intervening years have not been ones of sombre inactivity, but varied, energetic, enjoyable. There are many ways of growing old gracefully but almost all of them involve some degree of resignation, an acceptance of the fact that age imposes limitations, that incapacity must curb enterprise however actively the spirit may desire the contrary. Diana is not one for resignation. She will not go gentle into that good night, but will fight every inch of the way. She fears the decay of beauty, the loss of health, hearing, sight; but most of all she fears that she might no longer feel. The anaesthetic of old age, to many people a merciful mitigation of suffering, is to her intolerable. If she must suffer, she will do so in full consciousness; if she must sink it will be with all flags flying. Inevitably there are things that she cannot do, tasks beyond her powers, but only the total incapacity of her body is accepted as an excuse. So long as she remains alive there will be no failure of her resolution.

It would have been wholly uncharacteristic of Diana if she had not found the first few months of her new life in London intolerably painful. John Julius and Anne were so preoccupied with each other and their pursuits that she felt they had little time for her. Artemis now went to the Lycée Français, which she adored 'and which has in a twinkling scotched her love for me – now it's "O, you and your Greeks and your Round Table, Noona!".' Jason, her grandson, had but to see her on his threshold to set up a yell to waken the dead. 'So horrible has it been,' she told Susan Mary Patten, 'that I feel past recovery. No pangs for Chantilly, or rather no wanting it back, but I miss the beauty desperately and the sort of shape life had.' And yet she knew herself well enough to realise that her woe was exaggerated, and even to introduce some element of self-parody into her words. Martha Gellhorn understood her well when she wrote about this time: 'The first suggestion of change fills you with horror, whereupon in no time you adore the new place and life. Oh, Diana, what if really you have a golden and blessed nature? And are happy as a sandboy always? Surely, unless you are lying in your teeth, the sum total of your life is 99.9% life-loving and therefore happiness?'

Partly to combat her depression, partly from her fear of missing something good, mainly because she enjoyed it, she was soon leading a social life by normal standards impossibly hectic. Three October nights, picked more or less at random, illustrate the pattern of her existence. On the first she was dragged – protesting, she maintained, though the protests can hardly have been vociferous – to a night club called the Ad Lib where she spent 'two really monstrous hours not hearing a word, not having a seat to myself, and not, on account of total darkness, seeing the Mods and Rockers dancing like Holy Rollers, nor yet the Beatles who go there nightly to relax'. Next night was a dinner for Charlie Chaplin. Diana sat next to one of Britain's most eminent literary figures, who pinched her knee black and blue and demanded a kiss. 'Worse was to come. He seized my hand as the Commendatore seized Don Giovanni's and started to drag it to you know where. I was purple in the face, not so much with the shame as with the strain of writhing away. When the battle looked all but lost he was called on to make a speech, which he was far too drunk to manage. "I don't think I ever liked you, Charlie," he began, and after half a minute's inarticulate mumbles collapsed back in his seat.' The third night was dinner with Vivien Leigh and Noel Coward. After dinner they looked in on Douglas Fairbanks Junior – 'dreadfully against my will,' of course – and then Noel Coward drove her home, 'came in for a snifter and remained till 2.30 a.m. talking about his homosexuality'.

Though she grumbled about the cost, the lack of space, the inadequate cooking, she invited her friends frequently to Warwick Avenue. Cecil Beaton lunched there in November, 1963. Caroline Duff, Lady Dufferin, the Baroness Budberg, Rupert Hart-Davis and James Mossman were the other guests; Mossman, a television personality of talent, beauty and sensitivity acute to the point of self-destruction, being at that time an habitué of Diana's court. 'Rough and wroughty conversation,' Beaton recorded, 'Diana winking and joking about her old age; talk about the new President, poems of Thomas Moore recited – a treat. The food personal, original and economical; as usual melon and avocado and dill, and a fish pie.' Not only the food was economical. Vivien Leigh was in a nursing-home and Diana telephoned to ask what she would like to be sent. 'For the Lord's sake no more flowers, the place is full of them!' said Miss

Leigh's secretary. 'In which case I'll be round to grab a few for my luncheon party,' replied Diana. She rushed round, found a bath full of flowers and removed three dozen roses.

Her neighbours were a constant solace. Little Venice was a village; the inhabitants perhaps more exotic but no less parochial than those of other villages. Besides John Julius and his family there were the Lennox Berkeleys next door – 'semi-detached but wholly attached' as Diana described them. There was Diana's niece Kitty Farrell and her family; old friends from Paris, Frank and Kitty Giles; Adrian Daintry the artist; Lord Kinross the writer; Lanning Roper the gardener; a later arrival Edward Fox, the actor; Robin McDouall; the Sapiehas. Together they formed a community who used the same shops, borrowed each other's motors, visited each other's houses. They provided a framework in which Diana could feel secure and at home as had never been the case in France.

She was as little disposed as ever to let comfort or convention stand in her way. Deciding at the last minute to go to a ball at Wilton, she discovered that the houses in the vicinity were full up. Not in the least put out, she organized a caravan and asked permission to pitch camp in the park. Aged eighty-five, she wished to fly to America but the fare was too much for her. Freddie Laker had recently introduced his cut-price trips across the Atlantic, but to get on one involved queueing for several hours. Diana wrote to him, proclaiming that he was the greatest contributor to the history of travel since Magellan or perhaps Columbus and asking whether, as a frail and impoverished old lady, she might exceptionally have a seat reserved for her. A secretary replied, starting the letter 'Dear Miss Cooper', and stating firmly that she must take her chance with the rest. Neither annoyed nor distressed, Diana rose at 3.30 a.m. and set off for Victoria to join the queue for the midday plane. A friend pointed out that she was being ridiculous; even if the money was not in her bank, all she had to do was sell an ornament. 'But don't you see?' asked Diana incredulously. 'It's such an adventure.'

Saving money by fair means or foul was still one of her favourite games. Crossing from Athens to Hydra with Cecil Beaton she insisted on boarding the boat with no tickets, then seized two chairs from the lounge and installed them triumphantly on the first class deck. Stewards remonstrated. 'Bring the Captain,' trumpeted Diana. 'Squatters' rights. Possession is nine points of the law.' The purser asked to see their tickets. Diana would have none of it. 'We are first class! Look at my credentials. I'm too old to move.' Cecil Beaton made as if to flee and was promptly rebuked for his cravenness. As they left the boat, he waited nervously for the police to arrive. But

Diana reassured him: 'Well, we got away with that one!' Even worse was her habit of imposing economy on her friends. Ann Fleming, visiting Paris and longing to stay at the Ritz, was bullied into camping in the deserted house of Paul Louis Weiller, without heating, without hot water, and with a furiously resentful concierge denying her any nourishment.

No year went by without a month or two of travel, sometimes more. For several years she went every September to stay with Noel Coward in Switzerland, taking particular pleasure in the public swimming pool in Montreux. On her first visit she gazed enraptured at the glare of colour – electric-blue water, orange marigolds, blood-red roses, shocking-pink begonias. 'Oh I do love it so,' she said to her companion, Peter Coats. 'It's so pretty and so gay and not overburdened with taste.' Later she took to spending part of the summer at the Hofmannsthals' house in Austria. She went to Portugal with Iris Tree; to the West Indies several times; on safari to Kenya and Tanzania; to Nigeria to visit the Heads. In Kano she fell into the town sewer, bruised her leg painfully and removed much of the skin, tottered to her feet malodorous and bleeding, sharply instructed her fellow-travellers to stop fussing and resumed her tour of the bazaar. In Moscow she became so indignant when dinner had not arrived by 10 p.m. that, liberally primed with vodka, she invaded the kitchen and performed a Russian dance and songs taught her nearly fifty years before by Chaliapin. 'All the kitchen joined in, I was the whizz of the scullions, they all kissed me, but I don't think the dishes were hastened.' She revelled in every new experience, yet there was always a suspicion of dismay behind the pleasure. At the end of a blissful holiday in Kenya with John Julius, Anne and Nigel Ryan, she noted bleakly: 'I feel they've all got something to go back to and that I have not except for my little dog, though that makes up for a lot.' When only a hundred yards from home, her son had to break it to her that the dog was dead.

She scored a dazzling success in Washington, where she went in 1963. Susan Mary Patten, now married to Joe Alsop, the doyen of political columnists, organized her programme. One by one the posterns of Camelot were stormed. To dinner the first night came Robert and Edward Kennedy – 'a child with a very pretty wife'. 'Politics, politics, total interest and talk is politics, but I rather like that,' she told John Julius. 'I got on very well with the Kennedy ("identify yourself!") voice and a bombardment of questions like Max Beaverbrook. I love it, but it does land them with a saga or two.' Next day she was taken to meet Lyndon Johnson. Joe Alsop had described him as 'a frustrated force of nature' but Diana found herself unable to form any impression because of the blinding neon-light before which he sat and the inaudible mumble which came to her through the screen of the Vice-President's giant hand.

The central keep grew closer. The following day she lunched with Eunice Shriver, the President's sister, and was taken round the White House. 'She really has the wild originality of countenance and has always been in love with her brother Jack, looks like him, talks like him, but the Kennedys are all made out of the same clay – hair and teeth and tongues from the same reserves. I *loved* Eunice, so I enjoyed the very inferior plate of dog's dinner sea-food poulticed over with tomato.' They went to the Cabinet room, where the green baize was laid for a late afternoon meeting with a pad of paper in every statesman's place. Announcing she was in love with MacNamara, the Secretary of Defence, Mrs Shriver wrote a frivolous Valentine on the pad in front of his seat. Encouraged, Diana scrawled 'Love from Debo' on the President's pad; a message from his former sister-in-law, the Duchess of Devonshire, which she hoped might cause him some surprise.

At last came the day when the President came to dinner to see for himself this curious relict of a former age. Kennedy was known to have a weakness for British aristocrats but a dislike of old age; which feeling would predominate in this confrontation was anxiously debated by the Alsops. The daughter of the house was sent off to a friend, her bedroom filled with secret servicemen, a hot-line telephone installed so that the President could declare war if the mood took him, Jean the cook had her hair dyed blood-red for the occasion. The Kennedys arrived. 'Nice to see you again,' he began. 'I believe "again" is the operative word for all those in positions of patronage,' Diana told John Julius. 'He may have been right, but I don't remember ever having clapped eyes upon him.' She had, eight years before at Paul Louis Weiller's, but the meeting had hardly been a protracted one. She found him much younger than she had expected, 'less puffy than the photographs or the deforming TV makes him'.

'Dinner went as well as it was meant to. Afterwards a group round Jackie who must have, like her husband, total recall, because she'd read all my books and remembered a lot of those remarkable works. We talked about letter-writing. She said that in her whole married life she had had nine from Jack. I found Jackie much more beautiful than I had expected and a hundred times more of a personality. It is said that her near-divorce mood and his preoccupation with anything or anybody but her had turned to connubial comfort. It is said that she has the whip-hand as she cares not a

jot for what people say and might walk out of the White House any
day if so disposed. I suppose, too, vigorous animal though he is,
few other beds are possible if always he is attached by wire to "War"
or "Peace" and surrounded by tough secret servicemen.'

'What a woman!' President Kennedy said as he left the house. She
was at once invited back to the White House and fêted by all Washington. 'It was like suddenly having invited Nureyev,' said Susan Mary
Alsop, with the satisfaction of one who has scored a knock-out victory
over the other Washington hostesses.

At home she devoted much time and energy to keeping alive her
husband's memory. Diana was never one to live in the past, loathed
mawkish sentiment and the pious cliché; but the celebration of Duff
was for her a part of living, far removed from the conventional solemnities of widow's weeds and obituary addresses. She conceived the
wording of his memorial in a moment of inspiration early one
morning and wrote it on the wall of a house in a back street of Hydra.
Only when she came to look for it again did she realise that all the
houses in Hydra had white walls and all back streets looked alike. It
took two days searching to find her handiwork and then she tran-
scribed it and gave it to John Julius and Rupert Hart-Davis.

To her delight Duff's friends suggested the setting up of a fund to
endow a literary prize. Randolph Churchill was the leading spirit in
its organisation, won Diana's undying gratitude but contrived almost
to forfeit it when she met him in Monte Carlo, uproariously drunk,
having lost the list of subscribers and taken no other step. 'The dropsical brute has two secretaries and a ghost-writer,' but still got nothing
done, complained Diana bitterly; but she shamed him into action and
a handsome amount was raised. Steven Runciman's *History of the
Crusades* was favourite for the first prize, which Isaiah Berlin ruled
would 'start the thing off in a very respectable way', but in the end it
was felt a work in a single volume would be more appropriate. Alan
Moorehead was the eventual winner, for his book on Gallipoli.

Winston Churchill volunteered to present the first prize. Diana was
instructed to make sure that he limited his remarks to a few sentences
praising Moorehead and Duff himself. She lunched with him the day
of the prizegiving in his house in Hyde Park Gate which, by good
fortune, adjoined the house of Sir Roderick and Enid Jones where the
ceremony was to take place. 'The poor beloved had had his third
stroke,' Diana told John Julius. 'His face is less puffy and his beautiful

hands young, unshaking and elegant, but his mind is like love; when you think you are sure of it, it's flown, and giving up pursuit, it's back with you.' He found it impossible to grasp for more than a few moments what was expected of him. 'Do you want me to stay away?' he kept asking. Lady Churchill would patiently explain once again that he was to present the prize and make a short speech first. 'Oh, am I?' Diana then read the suggested address, broke down in tears half way through but managed at the second effort. 'Toby the budgerigar helps the long meal to be weathered – very nice and tame and sits on Winston's shoulders or one's head and talks to itself and loves him, but it's all come to that. Injurious time.'

The plan was for Churchill to shuffle through the garage between the two houses and avoid both the steep steps and the November air. Unfortunately the Jones's Rolls Royce had rusted up and refused to budge, so the old man was forced to come round by the long way. Nothing deterred, he got through his short speech fairly well; Harold Macmillan spoke too, and Alan Moorehead, 'and then it was the old war-horse saying "Ha-ha" in the battle, because warming and cleaving to his work, Winston said, "My dear, would you like me to wind up for you?" So up he got again with nothing to read from. He was for a flash the real Winston and ended with a joke about Gallipoli.' 'It was a wonderful, emotional party – perfect in every way,' Diana reported. 'I almost felt Papa was there, it was so to his taste and to his glory.'

The annual presentation of the prize, with all its complications over the selection of judges, winner and presenter, was an endless diversion to Diana. The Queen Mother presented the prize to Lawrence Durrell the second year and Princess Margaret to John Betjeman, the third. Diana for some reason was nervous about this last affair but had no cause to be. Princess Margaret looked like a 'jewelled, silky bower-bird, with a close-fitting, wild duck's preened feather hat, no hair, skin like a tea-rose, wonderfully pretty – and she made her funny, faultless speech with art and sophistication. Poor Betch was crying and too moved to find an apology for words.' Sir Roderick Jones, 'the only living man shorter than the Princess,' insisted on winding up with an interminable speech about the Empire, punctuated by whispers from his wife – half-proud, half-explanatory – of 'You know, he's eighty-one!' He caused some offence to the Chairman of the Judges by referring to him as Sir Horace Bowra, an exploit matched the following year by the immensely aged Canon Andrew Young who remarked that Duff would always remain illustrious for his slim volume *Operation Handbrake*. The worst gaffe at a prizegiving came, however, from Diana herself some years later. Robert Lowell, who was to present the prize, suffered a serious nervous breakdown and was taken to a mental home. A substitute was arranged. Then at the last moment John Julius was told that Lowell had discharged himself and was on the way to the ceremony. At all costs he must be kept away from any kind of alcohol. John Julius rushed to the spot, to find Lowell, on his third glass of champagne and talking to Diana. 'Darling,' said Diana brightly. 'I've just been telling this gentleman how the principal speaker has lost his marbles and been carted off to a loony-bin!'

Her life in Warwick Avenue was sometimes more eventful than even she desired. 'There are more burglars than occupiers in this dusky district, who laugh at locksmiths,' she wrote apprehensively as she was moving in. They struck first in 1966, when Iris Tree was staying in the house. Masked men broke in and tied up the two women. Diana watched with resignation as jewels and furs, including Paul Louis Weiller's precious 'coat of shame', were bundled into suit-cases, but protested when they came to the box containing love-letters. Fortunately the burglars proved to have little interest in such irrelevancies. 'Why should this happen to me?' she enquired histrioni-cally. 'I've done no harm and I'm charitable!' Then the absurdity of her words struck her, and in spite of fear and discomfort she laughed aloud.

'I wasn't all that frightened at the time,' she told Katharine Asquith, 'but I got a reaction of fear ten days later. I listen now for the bell to ring and for those muffled feet and featureless faces to return for what they didn't take.' The worst affront came when she left the house to resume her interrupted evening and found that her car had been stolen too. She still managed to get to Covent Garden for the last act. 'Sorry, but I was rather tied up,' she remarked as she entered the box, a line which she had been long awaiting an opportunity to use. To Evelyn Waugh it was the loss of dignity which seemed most hor-rifying – a point of view which would have surprised Diana if she had heard of it. 'There should be a Praetorian Guard of Pansies,' Waugh told Nancy Mitford, 'to keep a standing 24 piquet on all these widows . . .' Nancy Mitford unsympathetically suggested that Diana had organized the burglary herself because the coat of shame was growing shabby and needed replacement from the insurance money. Paul Louis Weiller himself reacted more generously. '*Achète-toi un nouveau manteau chez Balmain,*' he telegraphed next day.

Some months later the muffled feet returned. This time Daphne Wakefield, still loyally helping out on the secretarial side, was in the house upstairs. She heard Diana say haughtily: 'If only you would consult your colleagues you would know that this was not worth while.' A few moments later came a cry of pain: 'Oh, God, I've got a lump there. Don't do that, you're hurting me!' Mrs Wakefield threw herself into the fray and got coshed for her pains. The burglars ransacked the house and, worst of all, took the ring which Duff had given Diana for their engagement and which had somehow been missed in the previous raid. When Daphne Wakefield recovered, she was horrified to hear of this loss. 'It's only a possession. What does it matter?' said Diana calmly.

In both cases the police were friendly but ineffective. They were less friendly in 1968 when they invaded the house in search of drugs. Diana was delighted. 'Never did I enjoy myself more since youth's diversions.' She talked endlessly to the press, questions were asked in parliament and there were even two half-hour debates on the adjournment. Nothing was found and the reason for the police suspicions was never fully explained. 'Who cares anyway if a very old lady drugs or not?' asked Diana plaintively.

Daphne Wakefield had had troubles more painful than a mere coshing. Some years before her daughter had been taken ill with polio and Diana put up the money to send her to a private hospital. She died before she even got there and Diana then insisted that the money be spent on a holiday to help the Wakefields recover from the shock. When Mrs Wakefield returned, still crushed by her loss, Diana rallied her with a firm: 'Well now, Daphne, you've got to take pride in fortitude. The first thing to do is to have another baby.' She did, and Diana was godmother. It sometimes seemed to Diana as she grew older her main purpose in life was to comfort the survivors when her friends and relations died. 'You are the most wonderful friend,' Ann Fleming told her. 'No wonder there is always a queue of Kitty, Judy etc on your doorstep, all loving you, all with problems and relying on your courage, fabulous vitality, unselfishness and common sense.'

One of the most painful features of old age is the gradual extinction of one's friends, and the greater the talent for friendship, the longer grows the list of losses. Evelyn Waugh she saw for the last time shortly before he died. 'He has lost all *joie de vivre*, eats nothing, drinks a fair amount and thinks a journey to London a labour of Hercules. I attribute it to sleeping-pills, parendahyl in massive quantities, etc. O dear, O dear, it haunts me. I'm so very fond of the little monster!' Iris Tree, whom she had helped financially and succoured for twenty years; Raimund von Hofmannsthal, 'the dearest and goodest of men and the most generous and compassionate'; his wife and her niece Elizabeth Paget and her sister Caroline; Louise de Vilmorin; Churchill; Noel Coward; Katharine Asquith; Cecil Beaton – even to start to compile a list is to marvel at the number and variety of people who counted Diana among their dearest friends. And yet, though each new death pained her, in taking Duff death had already done its worst. She no longer had it in her to suffer deeply except over the tiny group of people who were everything to her. Michael Astor – soon sadly to be one of the losses himself – thought her at the age of eighty a little like 'Queen Elizabeth in her later years: clever, hard, fine and formidable. Underneath the façade there is something cold and lonely.' The coldness was there, but it was the chill of something long extinguished. A candle had burnt out. When a friend died she had always tended to put them out of her mind, to cut her losses. Now the loss itself seemed inconsiderable. She wrote sombrely to Bridget McEwen when her husband died that she had no words of comfort. 'It can never again be what it was. Years don't help all that much. One's own death is less fearful, that's all ... nothing is any good when the love of one's life is gone.'

Yet she never ceased to make new friends, seek new experiences. At dinner she was almost as likely to find herself between Mick Jagger and Andy Warhol as Harold Macmillan and the Apostolic Delegate; in both cases she would be amused, intrigued, insatiably curious about what was going on and what her neighbours were thinking and doing. Nigel Ryan, forty years her junior, became one of her closest friends, 'the last attachment' as she half self-mockingly described him. Four times he had sat next to her at dinner and she had asked him who he was. The fifth time he refused to tell her, 'I've told you too often'. The sixth time she turned to him again: 'Now, who are *you*?' 'Martin Bormann,' said Ryan. She never forgot him again. Aged eighty-six she took up with Sir Robert Mayer, then about to celebrate his hundredth birthday, and was delighted when the *Daily Mail* announced their imminent engagement. A near contemporary had been jeering at her for spending so much time with somebody as young as Nigel Ryan. Now she herself was being squired everywhere by a man of thirty odd, while Diana's name was coupled with someone by far her senior. 'My dear,' Diana wrote to her sweetly, 'when you are my age you will realise that what you need is the maturer man.'

Her dog was almost as great a solace to her as any friend. Writhing, twitching neurotically, as much an insect as an animal, 'Doggie' – and later Doggie II and Doggie III – was a chihuahua, charmless to most of those who knew it but to Diana possessed of supernatural love-liness. Lurking in her sleeve, wrapped loosely in a shawl, it went everywhere with her; to Covent Garden, to Buckingham Palace, the more inaccessible the venue the more determined Diana was that it should not be left behind. Usually it behaved, when it did not Diana quickly repaired the damage. In a smart Soho restaurant Doggie

escaped and defecated lavishly at the feet of a prosperous business
man. Ugly scenes threatened but Diana rose to the occasion and
within a few moments the bemused but enchanted business man was
agreeing that really what was needed in the restaurant was a few more
dogs; it was ridiculous of the head waiter to try to keep them out. In
the innermost fastness of her bedroom, Doggie and the television
helped to keep loneliness at bay, providing a soothing background of
rustles, yaps and conversation, a convincing simulacrum of company
when company was absent.

There was anyway a retinue of courtiers ready to be summoned if
she felt in need of support. She used them as ruthlessly as she had
always used her friends, though no more ruthlessly than she used
herself when her friends had need of her. Violet Wyndham was one of
the most faithful members of the inner circle. Diana would go to great
lengths to help her, sacrificing a precious last afternoon with Nigel
Ryan before he left for New York because she had long before promised to spend it with Mrs Wyndham. But she would also treat her
friend with singular roughness. Driving her from Covent Garden one
afternoon, the brakes failed and she bounced off a stationary lorry
and ended up half way down some area steps. Diana was unhurt,
Violet Wyndham in mild shock. Diana rapidly calculated that, if Mrs
Wyndham were taken home in an ambulance, it would still be possible to get to her next appointment on time. An ambulance arrived.
'But I'm quite all right,' protested Mrs Wyndham. 'Of course you're
not,' said Diana, pushing her in. Then she discovered that the ambulance would not take a patient home, but only to the hospital. Violet
Wyndham would have to be escorted there and would need visiting.
Diana flung open the ambulance door and told her friend that plans
were changed. Mrs Wyndham, by this time cosy on her bunk and
rather enjoying the fuss, complained weakly that she needed hospital
attention. 'Of course you're all right!' said Diana, pulling her out and
looking round for a taxi.

A prosecution followed for dangerous driving. As soon as the
magistrate ingratiatingly said 'Do sit down, Lady Diana,' she
reckoned she was in with a chance. Her defence was that the brake
had suddenly failed. The prosecution counsel demonstrated at length
why this was difficult to accept. At the end of his address Diana leant
forward and said quaveringly: 'I'm afraid I did not hear a word of
what you said.' He restated his case. 'I'm afraid you really must speak
up. I'm an old lady, you know.' The third time the prosecution
sounded altogether less compelling. 'Was the brake hanging down
before you started?' he wanted to know. 'I'm afraid I very rarely look
under my car,' replied Diana. By this time the prosecution was estab-

lished as a brutal bully and Diana as his frail old victim. She was acquitted.

Some time later she ran into a large lorry on the Brighton road, her only defence being that she had not seen it. Remembering her earlier triumph she was anxious to appear in court and give witness in her own defence, but her solicitor, appalled at the thought of this blind old lady groping her way to the witness box and probably ending up on the magistrate's bench instead, insisted that she remain at home. He got her off with a fine: to her own vast relief and the dismay of anyone likely to encounter her during her progresses at the wheel. 'It's like driving a swallow,' she exclaimed after her first trial of a Mini – a comment which said as much about her technique as about the car itself. Somehow she always survived unscathed, in terms of life and limb unscathing too, though she tested the nerves of her grandson when she taught him how to drive. Aged eighty-six Diana drove herself to the north of Scotland and back again, an exploit which she threatened to repeat.

Parking in London was a problem, but she relished the challenge of devising notes that would soften the heart of the traffic warden. 'Dearest Warden,' she wrote one afternoon when entertaining Artemis. 'Have pity. Am taking sad child to cinemar.' 'Dearest Warden,' read another note. 'Front tooth broken off; look like 81-year-old pirate, so at dentist 19a. Very old – very lame – no metres.' The last message of all had about it the ring of incipient triumph. 'Dear Warden. Please try and be forgiving. I am 81 years old, *very* lame and in total despair. Never a metre! Back at 2.15. Waiting for promised Disabled Driver disc from County Hall.' Benevolent authority provided the disc, and from then on she could park with impunity on spots even more outrageous than those she had used before.

Though she rarely allowed it to interfere with her driving, let alone her social life, infirmities came thick and fast as she moved on into the eighties. 'I've broken a rib by coughing and am clothed in inertia'; 'I have broken my hands and cannot write'; her knee was drained of fluid for the second time in two months and rendered her temporarily a total cripple; 'my thigh muscle has withered as it did in childhood. On my other side I've a lump of great pain in my wrist. Test match bowlers get it.' Frail bones snapped with increasing ease, slipping when falling downstairs, stumbling over a stone when carrying Doggie and crashing full on her face rather than dropping the dog and using her hands to protect herself. Twice her nose was broken; the indignity of her appearance offending her more than the pain. Pain was something she had learned to live with and subdue. Once she broke a bone when her regular doctor was away and was visited by his keen, young stand-in.

'I don't want you!' said Diana brusquely. 'I want a pusher.'

'But Lady Diana,' protested the doctor, not keen on prescribing morphia or heroin or whatever it was his patient had in mind, 'all you need is something to relieve your pain. Have you ever tried alcohol?'

'Idiot!' snapped Diana. 'Don't you know I'm an alcoholic?'

She never was an alcoholic but she would take drink to quell pain, nerves or melancholy. Always she used a modicum of restraint in her indulgence. Once in the West Indies she was taken to dinner with Claudette Colbert, who had long wanted to meet this legendary figure. Her conversation made little sense and at one point she laid her face on the warm plate and seemed to pass out. *'Elle s'endort?'* enquired Miss Colbert above the recumbent figure. 'Certainly not,' said Diana, rallying with dignity. 'I never sleep at meals.'

'No money left,' she wrote to Katharine Asquith, 'weak at the knees, dragged painted face, dim eyes that veil many devastations, mustn't groan.' She had met George Brown at dinner the previous night, drunk as the lord he was shortly to become, who said when he was told her name: 'It *can't* be!' '"It can be," I replied. "I tell you it *can't* be." He was then shuffled off by someone and never will I know if he meant, "Well done, keep it up!" or "That it should come to this!"'

Her sight was a constant problem, particularly when driving. She had always found difficulty in recognizing her closest friends, indeed her reputation when young for insolent hauteur stemmed largely from her unavailing struggles to focus on whoever it was who was addressing her. Now she found it still more difficult, exacerbated by nerves when she knew that much was expected of her. Nigel Ryan was detailed to escort her to Buckingham Palace. Diana swept past the queue on the stairs, announcing that her leg would not let her stand, and rushed to a sofa in the corner. Nigel was told that it was his duty to warn her who was approaching. Since he knew few people there he was doubtful how helpful he would be, but said that he would do his best. A woman in white came over and said 'Good evening, Diana. We meet tomorrow, I think.' Diana's hand tightened convulsively, a sure sign she needed help. Luckily Ryan could oblige; the woman in white was the Queen Mother.

She did still worse at the concert at the Festival Hall in honour of Sir Robert Mayer's hundredth birthday. There was a reception afterwards and Diana, looking neither to left nor right in fear of not recognising someone she ought to know, was wandering towards the bar. She got into conversation with a friendly little woman who apparently knew her well. Only when she recognized the magnificent diamonds did she realise that she was talking to the Queen. Belatedly she sketched out an arthritic curtsey and blurted out: 'Ma'am, O ma'am. I'm sorry, ma'am. I didn't recognise you without your crown!' 'It was so much Sir Robert's evening that I decided to leave it behind,' concluded the Queen sweetly.

Sense of smell gone; sense of taste gone; eyesight impaired; hearing faltering; far from sans everything yet near enough to recognise the threat: Diana can face it all. What she *cannot* face is the terror of senility, the crumbling of the mind that is so much more dreadful than the body's slow disintegration. In 1979 she flew to Strasbourg to help Paul Louis Weiller entertain the Queen Mother. She arrived at her hotel in mid-morning, felt tired and rather ill and lay down to have a short rest. After, as it seemed, a few moments, she woke, dressed in her best Marks and Spencer frock and large straw hat and set off for luncheon. She found the other guests absurdly over-dressed: did they imagine that they must wear long dresses in the middle of the day just because the Queen Mother was a fellow-guest? Looking out of the window she remarked how curiously dark it was. 'Not really, for 8 p.m.,' replied her neighbour. She had arrived, not late for luncheon, but in good time for dinner. 'If I can do that, I can do anything,' she concluded. She made a joke of it, elaborated it into one of her sagas, dined out on it for months; but there was real fear too. If she can do that, she can do anything.

Death she positively looks forward to; dying is another matter. To cease upon the midnight with no pain is an enticing prospect, but to cough your lungs out at five o'clock in the morning seems altogether less desirable. The arthritic C.B. Cochran had been scalded to death in his bath. Next door his wife heard his cries and thought affectionately what a boy Cocky was, singing in his bath at the age of seventy-nine. The image haunts Diana; it plagues her every time she has a bath. She is ready to die, but she wants to pick her own way.

To pick her own time, too. If offered the most easeful death at midnight, her answer would be: 'Thank you very much but would you please make it next Tuesday.' She is still too concerned with life to welcome quick extinction. There is always a book she wants to finish; a friend to talk to; a party to attend, a play or opera to visit; John Julius is coming round for a drink; Artemis is expected back from America the day after tomorrow. Once, ill and dejected, she retreated to bed. Her grand-daughter went up to see how she was. 'Artemis,' she croaked weakly, 'I think I'm going to die.' 'Oh, really,' answered

Artemis brightly. 'When?' Deciding it was hardly worth dying if that was the only reaction she aroused, Diana got out of bed and came down to dinner. Besides, there was a programme on television she did not want to miss. Tomorrow would be soon enough to contemplate the end.

Some would have pleaded for extra time to make their peace with God. Diana has no conviction of an after-life, no certainty that she will be on her way to see Duff again. Death will mean a cessation of pain; if it is also a beginning that will be a delightful bonus, but the prospect is not to be counted on. Thoughts of eternity preoccupy her not at all. She is wistfully envious of those with stronger faith, but no more believes that she can emulate them than that she can dance like Nureyev or sing like Chaliapin. She prays every night, but it is a childhood habit, never dropped for long but of little greater significance than brushing her teeth or turning on the light. Its principal value, indeed, is that of a soporific; sleep usually supervenes before she has completed her incantations. The framework of her prayers was taught her by Evelyn Waugh. ACTS is the magic word: A for Adoration; C for Contrition; T for Thanksgiving; S for Supplication:

'A for Adoration. I can't manage that at all. You need a lot of faith and I just haven't been born with it. I *have* tried, but I've failed. *I'm sorry, God, if you wanted me to adore you, you should have made me differently.*

'C for Contrition. That's a wash-out too. Hilaire Belloc said the obstacle in my race to heaven was lack of remorse. I pray to God in my under-five way to give me remorse, but he never has. It's not that I haven't committed sins. I've committed thousands, scarlet as anything – not that I think adultery really counts. But I don't feel in the least sorry about any of them. *I'm sorry, God, but it's your fault again. I'm sorry I can't feel sorry.*

T for Thankfulness. This is where I really begin to score. It's too easy. I can open the gates of thanksgiving for a start for the three people who most affected my life. *Thank you, God, for my mother, for Duff and for John Julius. Thank you for all those I have loved and who have loved me.* Raymond, Conrad, I don't mention them by name, of course; it would be too hurtful if someone got left out. I know how lucky I have been in life and how much I have been given which other people haven't had. *Thank you, God, for giving me so much.* He might have made a job of it while he was about it and let me off my depressions, but mustn't grumble. *Thank you for my friends.* I've been so lucky in my friends.

S for Supplication. Of course for all and every one, the sincerest of all. First of all for John Julius; it goes on and on like an insurance policy. *Protect, O protect him from crashes and hi-jacking and bombs and kidnapping and violence of all kinds.* There's a bit about the grandchildren and the rest of the family but it really concentrates on John Julius. Every time he goes on the motorway it's two days of dread, two days to recover and come out in nervous spots. It's dreadful to be so cowardly. Then there's a prayer for the dead, singularly ill-formed, and a short prayer for Duff himself. I pray a little for myself. *Take all my other senses if you must, O God; cripple me and deafen me; but please spare me what's left of my sight. And please don't let me have a stroke and become a vegetable.*

'You see how pathetically simple it is. In church I can't pray at all. I think that's really all there is to it. O no, there's one more thing, if I'm still awake by then. *Please, God, dear God, grant me an easy death and let it be quite soon.*'

Note on Sources

The most valuable manuscript source has been Lady Diana Cooper's own letters. The recipients have tended to preserve these and it has therefore been relatively easy to secure correspondence covering almost all her life. The three most substantial collections are those to her husband, her son and Conrad Russell. Her letters to members of her immediate family, her father and mother, her two sisters, Lady Violet Benson (formerly Lady Elcho) and the Marchioness of Anglesey, and her brother, the ninth Duke of Rutland, are also of particular interest. Other useful groups of letters are those written to Susan Mary Alsop, Raymond and Katharine Asquith, Maurice Baring, Sir Cecil Beaton, Lord Beaverbrook, Hilaire Belloc, Thomas Bouch, June Churchill, Lady Juliet Duff, Sir Rupert Hart-Davis, Edward Horner, Dr Rudolph Kommer, Patrick Leigh Fermor, Charles Lister, Lady McEwen, Venetia Montagu, Alan and Viola Parsons, Patrick Shaw-Stewart, Lord Vernon and Evelyn Waugh. Lady Diana kept almost every letter she received, and the other half of most of these correspondences is therefore also available.

Duff Cooper kept a diary for most of his life and this has yielded much valuable information. So also has his correspondence with many of those listed above. Letters exchanged between other members of the family, now preserved at Plas Newydd, are a useful source of material.

To list all those to whom I have spoken about Diana Cooper would be a pointless task. All those who have made significant contributions should be found in the Acknowledgments at the beginning of this book.

It would be equally inappropriate to list all the printed sources I have consulted. A few works can, however, be picked out for their especial importance. Pre-eminent are Lady Diana's own three volumes of autobiography: *The Rainbow Comes and Goes* (1958), *The Light of Common Day* (1959) and *Trumpets from the Steep* (1960); and Duff Cooper's autobiography *Old Men Forget* (1953). Others that should be mentioned are: Susan Mary Alsop *To Mariette from Paris* (1975); Lady Cynthia Asquith *Diaries 1915–1918* (1968); Cecil

Beaton *The Wandering Years, The Years Between, The Happy Years, The Strenuous Years, The Restless Years* (1961–1976); *Chips: The Diaries of Sir Henry Channon* ed. Robert Rhodes James (1967); Daphne Fielding *Mercury Presides* (1954); Rupert Hart-Davis *The Arms of Time* (1979); *Raimund von Hofmannsthal A Rosenkavalier* (1975) privately printed in Hamburg; John Jolliffe *Raymond Asquith: Life and Letters* (1980); Nicholas Mosley *Julian Grenfell* (1976); Viola Tree *Castles in the Air* (1926); Evelyn Waugh *Diaries* ed. Michael Davie (1976) and *Letters* ed. Mark Amory (1980).

Index

323